African Americans
in Global Affairs

African Americans in Global Affairs

CONTEMPORARY PERSPECTIVES

EDITED BY
Michael L. Clemons

Northeastern University Press
BOSTON

Published by University Press of New England
HANOVER AND LONDON

Northeastern University Press
Published by University Press of New England
One Court Street, Lebanon NH 03766
www.upne.com
© 2010 Northeastern University
All rights reserved
Manufactured in the United States of America
Designed by Kaelin Chappell Broaddus
Typeset in Minion Pro by Integrated Publishing Solutions

University Press of New England is a member of the Green Press Initiative.
The paper used in this book meets their minimum requirement for recycled paper.

For permission to reproduce any of the material in this book, contact Permissions,
University Press of New England, One Court Street, Lebanon NH 03766;
or visit www.upne.com

Library of Congress Cataloging-in-Publication Data
African Americans and global affairs: process, power and impact /
edited by Michael L. Clemons Northeastern University Press.
    p. cm.
Includes bibliographical references and index.
ISBN 978-1-55553-719-7 (cloth : alk. paper) — ISBN 978-1-55553-722-7 (pbk. : alk. paper)
1. African Americans—Politics and government. 2. African American politicians.
3. African American legislators. 4. Political participation 5. World politics.
6. International relations. 7. United States—Politics and government. 8. United States—
Foreign relations. I. Clemons, Michael L.
E185.615.A5927   2010
323.1196'073—dc22   2009035925
5 4 3 2 1

Dedicated to everyone worldwide
who has ever struggled for foreign policy justice

CONTENTS

ACKNOWLEDGMENTS

This book reflects my ongoing struggle to understand the nature and meaning of African American participation in global affairs. This work raises at least as many questions as it addresses. The chapters herein point to the growing dimensions and increasing complexity of the international arena and black people's relationship to it, as well as the need to extend the scholarly imagination.

First, hearty thanks are extended to everyone who gave me the optimism, strength, support, and humor to bring this project to fruition. I am especially grateful to the contributors, some of whom are relatively new to the small scholarly cohort in the field, while some are prolific veterans such as Charles P. Henry, Minion K. C. Morrison, Ronald W. Walters, and Hanes Walton, Jr. These individuals are among the pioneers of research focused on black participation throughout the African Diaspora. I am extremely gratified that Ronald Walters stepped up to the plate to write the introduction to this volume. In his provocatively classic style, Walters provides timely and critical insights of appropriate analytic rigor, which lend focus, content, and range to our overarching treatment of the contemporary process, power, and impact of black global participation.

Special thanks are in order for everyone at the University Press of New England (UPNE) who was in any way involved in the production of this book, including Elizabeth Brash, Lori Miller, and Lys Weiss. In particular, I would like to express my gratitude to Ellen Wicklum, with whom I initially came into contact at UPNE, for her encouraging support and the vision to take on this project. When she departed UPNE, I was fortunate that Phyllis Deutsch, the press's editor-in-chief, was able to assume the project and usher it forward with alacrity.

Moreover, I would like to express my sincere appreciation to the numerous known and anonymous peer reviewers of the chapters who offered valuable suggestions for improvement at various stages. I especially appreciate the critical reviews provided by Vernon Johnson of Western Washington University and Karin Stanford of California State University, Northridge. Their close reading of the text prompted a number of useful changes, which strengthened the book.

Through it all, I have been privileged to have some wonderful colleagues and friends at Old Dominion University in Norfolk, Virginia, and around the country who have read chapters, shared sources, and suggested important revisions. I especially thank the Department of Political Science and Geography and the College of Arts and Letters for their support.

Finally, without the patience and support of my wonderful wife Sharon, and my daughters Miisha, Nyasha, and Nia, this book likely would never have been completed.

PROLOGUE

This volume crystallizes the notion that African Americans have long been cognizant of the racial, cultural, ideological, and political nexus of domestic and international politics. It shows that black participation in foreign affairs and foreign policy has achieved mixed results with a ray of optimism. Presented herein is a unique and timely collection of essays that focus on the contemporary issues, problems, and practices associated with the varied nature of African American global participation. The quality of black participation in world affairs and in U.S. foreign policymaking is due to the group's unique historical experience. Much credit is owed to the struggle for civil rights since it led to the breakdown of the institutional pillars of white supremacy, which forbade black social participation. The movement resulted in some fundamental social advancements, notably, passage of the Civil Rights Act of 1964 and the Voting Rights Act of 1965; the latter aimed squarely at obliterating remaining legal barriers to the right of black citizens to vote. However, as Carol Anderson pointed out, "The 'prize' they sought was not civil rights, it was human rights." It is ironic, therefore, that the National Association for the Advancement of Colored People (NAACP), under attack by southern anticommunists, had to shift focus to a more limited civil rights platform—one that was less subject to a Cold War–based ideological and political assault. Thus, this contraction led to the evolution of a rights- and material-based struggle at the domestic level, emphasizing the acquisition of political and economic civil rights.

The assassination of Rev. Martin Luther King, Jr. in 1968 brought the civil rights movement virtually to a halt. The result was the retardation of the movement's evolution to a struggle of global import more broadly focused on human rights. As some of the authors in this volume suggest, political and social development throughout the African Diaspora, and particularly in Africa, was detrimentally impacted by the decline of the civil rights movement. Although the subsequent era of black power became a model for radical social change through the world, the harsh exercise of U.S. state police power hastily facilitated the movement's demise in the domestic arena.

The relevance of foreign affairs and foreign policymaking for the standing of African Americans at home and abroad is shown by their active and creative involvement in the world political arena. In a compelling essay that expands on some of the contemporary themes presented in this book, Ronald W. Walters in chapter 1 argues that a black interest in foreign affairs does indeed exist and that it is salient. He maintains that black participation in foreign affairs and foreign policy matters for several reasons: African Americans and their organizations played path-breaking roles; their participation has worked as a monitor of democracy in foreign affairs; and their participation has been a struggle for justice through the opposition to U.S. foreign policy. Walters highlights the decline in black interest in foreign affairs and assesses the probability of a shift toward racial foreign policy justice in light of the election of Barack Obama to the American presidency.

Chapter 2 presents a conceptualization of the foreign affairs participation of African Americans, and applies this framework to investigate the Congressional Black Caucus and TransAfrica Forum. It identifies the formal and informal dimensions of black global participation, and investigates the effect of the issues, domestic environment, global climate, and the strategies and tactics employed to gain insight into the motivations, means, and results of these two groups' efforts to influence foreign affairs and U.S. foreign policymaking.

Ronald Williams II in chapter 3 examines the general role and impact of African American political organizations on Africa. He chronicles some of the ways in which African Americans, through political organizations and domestic and transnational social movement activities, have connected themselves with the politics of continental Africa. African Americans' engagement with African affairs evolved extensively from the first reverberations of Pan-Africanism in the late eighteenth and early nineteenth centuries.

In chapter 4, William G. Jones provides a meticulous account of the behavior of members of Congress in foreign policymaking related to the Africa Growth and Opportunity Act (AGOA). In particular, he investigates race and business interests as competing, conflicting, and consolidating influences. Jones concludes that African Americans have called AGOA's value into question and that the legislation has been detrimental to apparel workers in the United States and in Africa.

Indeed, a hallmark of politics in the United States has been the emergence of the race variable in a variety of venues including Congress, and the presence of race in the confirmation process of appointed foreign policy officials is no exception. Thus, Josephine A. V. Allen, Alvin Tillery, Jr. and Hanes Walton, Jr. in chapter 5 shed light on the role and function of race in the Senate confirmation hearings for the first two African American secretaries of state. Specifically of interest is whether race directly and indirectly influenced the Senate's confirmation of Colin Powell and Condoleezza Rice. The study's results suggest that although the race factor was present in several manifestations in the confirmation process, it did not play a decisive role in the deliberations of the Committee on Foreign Relations.

One of the salient patterns of black participation in foreign affairs and foreign policy has been the tendency toward foreign policy dissent. In chapter 6, I investigate Colin Powell's tenure as head of the U.S. State Department. The actions and policies advanced by Powell are considered against the backdrop of the bureaucratic actor model and the foreign policy dissenter framework. This chapter shows that although Powell was a bureaucrat, he frequently was the lone voice of dissent, although a weak one in the conservative excesses of the Bush administration. Powell's experience suggests the need for research to gain a better understanding of the constraints, limits, and effects of formal or institutional involvement in foreign affairs and policymaking.

With Madeleine Albright's appointment to head the Department of State, the proverbial glass ceiling in foreign affairs was finally shattered on behalf of all women. To be sure, Condoleezza Rice's appointment punctuated not only the gender implications of Albright's historic role, but also the racial implications of Powell's historic appointment. In chapter 7, Supad Ghose and I assess the backgrounds, worldviews, and rise to power of these two women. Of particular interest is how Albright and Rice overcame gender, ethnic, and racial barriers, as well as how the factors functioned to condition their agendas and policies during their respective terms as secretary of state. We conclude that these women are far more likely to be viewed in history as transcendent figures of race, ethnicity, and gender than as advocates for their respective racial and ethnic groups, which does not bode well for the future of identity politics in the global arena.

In chapter 8, Charles Henry persuasively makes the case that following the rise of a strong black voice in foreign affairs, the evaporation of a black progressive voice in American politics has contributed to the contemporary decline of political Pan-Africanism. He laments the absence of progressive black voices in events such as those in Rwanda and Darfur, and points out that these situations raise concerns about Pan-African solidarity and the African American commitment to human rights. In the end, he asserts that what is needed is a "new self-critical Pan-Africanism" that analyzes the class nature of state power and takes into consideration the perspective of the masses instead of their domination by the elite.

It would be interesting to test whether a "self-critical Pan-Africanism" would lend itself to cohesion, if not unanimity, among people of African descent throughout the Diaspora regarding the issue of reparations. The matter of reparations for the descendants of former slaves in the United States persists as an issue in the twenty-first century, and it has even assumed global dimensions. Ife Williams, in chapter 9, provides a painstaking examination of the role of African Americans in the African Descendants Caucus at the 2001 World Conference Against Racism (WCAR), in advancing the declaration of the transatlantic slave trade and slavery as crimes against humanity. The achievement of this goal was pivotal in that it would establish the legal foundation for the compensation of enslaved African descendants. Member states were able to condemn the slave trade and slavery; however, a core agreement among participants on reparations could not be achieved. Williams maintains that reparations will continue to be an issue in the future due to the fundamental need for acknowledgment and disclosure, and their effect on the psychological and emotional well-being of descendants.

In chapter 10, Minion K. C. Morrison provides a detailed update and context for the Afro-Descendant Legislators, who had their organizational meeting in 2003. The goal was to develop an inclusive organization that would bring together all of the elected legislators of African descent in the Americas and the Caribbean. In chronicling this development, Morrison finds a number of important intersections in their agendas, as well as some factors that weaken the potential for participation and influence by the organization.

According to Sekou M. Franklin in chapter 11, African American and black Venezuelan alliances, which he refers to as "transnational contention," constitute dissident political behavior because such activities conflict with the norms and rules of the American foreign policy establishment. To analyze the efficacy of "contentious black transnationalism," Franklin offers a theoretical framework and discusses three forms of black transnational contention present in relations between black Americans and black Venezuelans. Franklin concludes that transnational contention allowed African American activists and elected officials to build programmatic bridges between their constituents and Venezuelans.

A concise examination of black interests in Chinese communism during the Cold War, in light of the work of socialist black power theoretician

James Boggs, is the subject of chapter 12, by Robeson T. P. Frazier. Frazier argues that vast parallels exist between Mao Tse Tung's philosophical writings on revolution, social relationships, politics, and political engagement and Boggs's effort to frame the black power movement conceptually with the Chinese communist revolution. He concludes that the engagement of black internationalists with Chinese communism and Maoism is an example of the significance of non-Western societies to the development of black political activism and theoretical analysis.

The epilogue looks toward the future of African American participation in foreign affairs and foreign policy, by focusing on Barack Obama's rise to the office of president of the United States. In weighing the salience of this historic development, we consider multiculturalism's role and the implications of Obama's use of the deracialization strategy for a new international engagement whereby foreign policy justice consistent with the interests of black Americans and progressive societal forces is a major objective.

Collectively, the chapters of this book establish the need, direction, and parameters for scholarly research dealing with black global participation. This work is a useful resource for students and teachers of foreign policy, international affairs, American and African American politics, and Africana studies. Clearly, however, the subject is one of ever-changing complexity as multiculturalism evolves, both in practice and as an ideology, in the United States and internationally. Moreover, the increasing complexity of the subject of black participation in global affairs will undoubtedly affect the direction and parameters for such studies in the future.

African Americans
in Global Affairs

ONE

Racial Justice in Foreign Affairs
Ronald W. Walters

Black Interests and Ideology

This book is an ambitious undertaking in updating and reconceptualizing so much of African American interests in international politics and foreign policy, but it initially begs at least two essential questions: what is the character of black interest in foreign affairs, and why does it matter? The manner in which blacks came into U.S. citizenship, the dynamics of their original and evolving American identity, the continuing ties with Africa and other peoples of African descent, and the prospects of a Pan-African relationship have worked to order their interests in international affairs. These interests have been ordered in two fundamental directions: maintaining direct ties with peoples of African descent outside of the United States, and participating in policy formation to enhance the human value of those relations between African peoples and all citizens of the United States.

An essential problem was that the condition of slavery placed blacks at the bottom of American society, and racism kept them there. This shaped blacks' interests in both domestic and foreign affairs as rehabilitative projects to construct positive relations between Africans and peoples of African descent, and between the nations and continents that contain such peoples. Thus, the counterpoise to this has caused blacks to construct the same paradigm of justice seeking in foreign affairs as in the domestic arena. I suggested this concept in an article, "The U.S. War on Terrorism and Foreign Policy Justice," where I first used the term *foreign policy justice* "in order to point out that analysts have not considered sufficiently the moral content or the racial interests of a policy in their determination of which party to a dispute should be advantaged. With the result that the handling of foreign policy by those in power often shielded moral content by striking a neutralist or defensive interpretation of policy, the existence of unequal power and unequal loss posed a substantial question of the justice in the resolution of the problem."[1]

African Americans always have had strong incentives to seek justice because we have often been the community that was debilitated as a result of the decisions to make war instead of peace. Julianne Malveaux has discussed the concept of a "shared status," where the decision to deploy resources for one reason affects another.[2]

Martin Luther King, Jr., is widely remembered for this idea, contained in his famous Riverside speech on the Vietnam War, when he noted that bombs dropped in Vietnam were blowing up in Harlem and Watts. This is still true, since an analysis by Joseph Stieglitz found that the cost of the war in Iraq as of 2007 had soared to an estimated $1 trillion to $3 trillion, a sum that the Hillary Clinton campaign said could provide health care to all 47 million of those without it, provide quality prekindergarten for every American child, solve the affordable housing crisis, make college affordable for all, and provide tax relief to millions of middle-class Americans.[3] John Broder of the *New York Times* notes that war spending could have also developed renewable energy resources, funded a nationwide public works program, paid for a long-term fix in Social Security, and fixed the loophole in the Medicare drug benefit. This view is also supported by the American people, 67 percent of whom responded in a NewYorkTimes/CBS news poll that the war had contributed "a lot" to American economic problems.[4] The point here is that African Americans are disproportionally deprived of the resources that could have been provided by spending for domestic causes rather than for war.

But the decision to go to war is made doubly erroneous and costly because the decision to deploy those resources, especially in times of war, not only affects American citizens and soldiers, but also creates a future cause of retribution for those whom U.S. munitions kill or harm as a result of that deployment. This shows that the search for a subjective sense of justice in international relations is universal, as seen in the recent history of the Middle East.

A *New York Times* reporter, in a story about how young people are drawn to the more conservative versions of Islam, interviewed Muhammad Fawaz, a Jordan University education student. Fawaz stated that he wanted to study in the United States, but was unable to find the right connections, which he called "wasta" and which students generally referred to sarcastically as "Vitamin W." Apparently, wasta modulated many kinds of opportunities from which he and many of his associates were excluded, which provided him an explanation for joining the Islamic Movement: "I joined the Islamic movement because this movement will achieve for me some kind of justice and will offer me opportunities through which I can discover myself and be part of the society I live in."[5] Thus, it should be no surprise that the long relations between the United States and Jordan in the official sector have created a civil route to privilege that will be opposed by the growing Islamic fundamentalist movement among the youth there, as it has in other parts of the Middle East.

Therefore, the progressive perception that evolves about the need felt by blacks to pursue justice in foreign affairs is at first a matter of Afrocentrism in its African Diasporic context, but since it also takes into consideration those who are often the international targets of American policy, it has fostered a Third World perspective that prevents black interests from being conceived on the basis of a tightly constructed American nationalism.

In fact, in its view of the universality of justice it emanates from many of the universalistic principles of human rights that led to the development of the United Nations. But in its domestic origins, the perspective of African Americans in foreign affairs is contained in the social linkages of events that begins with the domestic status of blacks and the degree to which they share justice with others on an equitable basis, which guides their response to foreign crises as either furthering this interest or harming it. This has been the basis of their strong and consistent opposition to U.S. involvement in most wars: the inequality in the shared status of blacks with others in society produces a disproportionate sacrifice on the part of the black community in terms of the participation of its members and the resources taken from the nation that might have gone to that community. But the targets of U.S. wars since World War II have been Third World peoples whose condition reflects the same forces of social, political, and economic oppression, resulting in unequal status with the rest of the world. The inequality in this shared status thus creates the evaluation that American policy is unjust, but the response by blacks to this has often been to conform to the American direction in any case, influenced by the fact that their conformity has become a badge of loyal citizenship. More than that, it has become a method of legitimizing citizenship and therefore, using that conformity to achieve other social goals naturally and generally available to others. Thus, there is and has consistently been tension in the black community between the competing goals of foreign policy justice and achieving full citizenship.

Why Does It Matter?

This is a question that has heretofore only been addressed in piecemeal fashion. But black interests and activities in foreign affairs matter to African Americans—first, because of the manner in which they entered the

United States as slaves from the continent of Africa, a fact that has defined a category of interests in maintaining ties to Africa by establishing direct relations between the two communities, even as both have confronted the massive challenges of the subjection of their peoples over various historical periods. Second, when the fog of the American Civil War cleared and blacks were pronounced as citizens of the United States, they began to participate as elected officials and as diplomats in helping to implement public policy of their nation, but that role would often place them in a contradictory relationship to effect a progressive relationship between their country and other African and Caribbean states.

Nevertheless, African American participation in foreign affairs and foreign policy has mattered to the nation for other important reasons, such as the seminal role of black individuals and organizations, American racism perceived as a barometer of democracy in international affairs, the justice of black opposition to U.S. foreign policy, and the globalization of America's present and future. These factors will be elaborated below, in brief, emphasizing and expanding on some of the themes presented in this work. Then, I will address in historical sequence two other subjects: why black participation in foreign policy appeared to decline after 1980; and what the future holds in terms of continuities and change of foreign policy influence, especially as the political regime of Barack Obama unfolds.

Rationalizing the Importance of Black Participation in Foreign Affairs

OPPOSITION TO U.S. FOREIGN POLICY

By opposing the historical forces of slavery and colonialism that had kept much of the peoples of the globe in a condition of servitude to the advanced industrial countries of European heritage, African American leaders and activists often forged ties with progressives in other countries. Such opposition often positioned American blacks against their own government because of its ties with such European powers and therefore, its participation as an associate in their enterprises. Therefore, as movements arose in both Europe and the United States against these historical forces, American blacks were often found in opposition to the prevailing policies. As Michael Clemons has said:

> It might indeed be the case that history has rendered African Americans more likely than other racial groups to formulate and/or evolve foreign affairs interpretations and positions that are antithetical to the stance maintained by the American foreign policy establishment. Both

formal and informal foreign affairs actors of African descent, therefore, may be more prone to behave in a manner inconsistent with official governmental policy.[6]

The very presence of people who descended from Africa and who were subordinated by people who were descended from Europe, the masters of the slave trade and eventually colonialism, would create a natural contradiction that would be manifest in nonofficial circles where African Americans expressed their foreign affairs interests. This is shown by Elliott Skinner's description of the opposition of the black AME church establishment and other organizations and intellectuals to U.S. support for Belgian imperialism in the Congo in the 1890s after the infamous Berlin Conference that divided up Africa into spheres of European colonial interests.[7] However, Brenda Gayle Plummer says:

> Afro-Americans rarely benefitted from a harmony of interests with the U.S. government. Indeed, black perspectives on U.S. diplomacy often began with basic disagreements about the national interests, and consequently involved struggles over symbolic legitimacy as well as conflicts over specific directives. Here, debate touched the sensitive core values of society itself. The problem of racism lies at the heart of black dissent. The continued salience of race and the intractability of racism in the United States limit the usefulness of ethnicity alone for understanding black American engagements with foreign policy.[8]

She goes on to describe an early example of this in the conflict over the Italian-Ethiopian war of 1936. When the Roosevelt administration attempted to foster measures such as an embargo on critical materials that would limit Italian military actions against Ethiopia and met opposition to these moderate steps from politicians, African Americans attempted to move Roosevelt to action, but to no avail. However, while activists in New York City, professors at Howard University, and others led a drive to bring Emperor Haile Selassie to the United States at the moment he was overthrown by the Italians in 1936, others sought to organize a military contingent to go to Ethiopia to fight the Italians.[9]

The progressive character of the burgeoning internationalism of African Americans in this period is persuasively captured by Robin Kelly, in a discussion of the organization of the Lincoln Brigade that went to Spain to fight fascism in 1936. He notes that their unique background and experiences suggest that their decision to go to Spain "was motivated largely by a political outlook that combined black nationalism and Pan-Africanism with a commitment to the Communists' vision of internationalism. Like the American Jewish brigadists whose cultural and national identities constituted a central element of their radical politics, ethnic nationalism and internationalism were not mutually exclusive."[10] He explains that many who went to Spain had wanted to go to Ethiopia and therefore, their presence there constituted a proxy war against the Italians. In any case, the attribution Kelly makes, that the source of the progressive internationalism of blacks who fought in the Lincoln Brigade was the communists, requires some caution, given the wide contacts of black leaders who understood the connection between black suppression in the United States and its roots of support among European powers. These sentiments were voiced, not only in the Universal Races Conference of 1911, but in the Pan-African Conferences sponsored by Du Bois.

In fact, in the 1920s Marcus Garvey would have been virtually alone as a leader whose internationalist conception was based almost solely on the relationship between and among peoples of African descent—which was the source of his international strength. This strength was seen in the expansion of the movement overseas to the Caribbean nations, Latin America, and Africa. Garvey preached a strong message of Pan-Africanism, dignity and unity among peoples of African descent; his anticolonial position conflicted with the interests of colonial governments and between them and their black populations who accepted Garvey's message. Rupert Lewis shows that between 1904 and 1914, when the United States built the Panama Canal, the zone felt the influence of the Garvey movement among the black population, and the message of pride was often the motivating factor in worker strikes.[11] But his message had also touched workers to strike in the United Fruit Company there.

In Liberia, Garvey also confronted a colonial power, even though it was run by the black Americo-Liberians, who thwarted his designs to initiate a rehabilitation project in that country. Garvey's drive in 1920 was also opposed by the American-based Firestone Rubber Company, which had just secured a lease of land in perpetuity for its rubber interests. But the concerns of American, British, and French governments was with the widespread thrust of Garvey's influence in other places on the continent, such as the oil-rich Nigeria, Congo, and South Africa. Lewis says that "around 1920 the UNIA [United Negro Improvement Association] had eight branches in South Africa, three in Sierra Leone, two in the Gold Coast, two in Liberia, two in South West Africa, and one in Nigeria."[12] This expanse was significant enough for Garvey to call his own International Convention of the Negro Peoples of the World in 1920 and again in 1922.

However, Tony Martin concludes that in the 1920s Garvey's movement was considered dangerous to American interests and became a primary target of the American foreign affairs surveillance activities in the attempt by U.S. officials to limit Garvey's influence. He cites a series of reports in the 1920s that reveal American interest and concern for Garvey's overseas activities, reflected in Garvey's own sense that "20 percent of my employees were United States Secret Service."[13] By this time, Martin says, J. Edgar Hoover, who would become the nemesis of Martin Luther King, Jr., began an extensive campaign against Marcus Garvey: "United States surveillance against Garvey's activities abroad was as diligently pursued as surveillance at home. American consular agents and 'confidential sources' from Sweden to Liberia, from Canada to Trinidad, kept a close watch on Garvey, his organization and its ramifications in their areas."[14]

Thus, the threat that Garvey's ideology and movement presented to the global interests of the United States and its colonial partners had to be removed, such that by February 1925, he was imprisoned by the U.S. government on charges of mail fraud.

THE INTERNATIONAL CONTRIBUTION OF BLACK LEADERS

When African Americans became government officials in the foreign policy establishment, they exercised opposition to what they considered regressive American policies, but their position meant that they also had to become midwives of policies their government demanded should be carried out. This often created a conflict between the progressive intentions of such officials and their official roles.

The first African American representative in foreign affairs appointed by a president was Ebenezer Bassett, appointed in 1869 to the post of ambassador to Haiti by President Ulysses S. Grant (1869–77). Earlier, however, William Alexander Leidesdorff was appointed U.S. vice consul in Yerba Buena, Mexico (known today as San Francisco), in 1845 by Thomas O. Larkin, U.S. consul at Monterey, New Mexico. Horace Dawson, director of Howard University's Ralph Bunche International Center, made the discovery concerning Leidesdorff through references stating that Leidesdorff was considered to be "dark in appearance" owing to his mixed ancestry.[15]

However, far more interesting is the fact that Bassett was the initial example of the post–Civil War political spoils system, which saw the Republican party leadership reward black leaders by assigning them to Haiti as the place where a string of black ministers resident and consuls general (U.S. representatives were not called ambassadors until 1893) were posted. While the list begins with Bassett, it also includes John Mercer Langston

(April 16, 1869–June 30, 1885), George Washington Williams (appointed but never assumed his post), John E. W. Thompson (May 7, 1885–October 17, 1889), Frederick Douglass (June 26, 1889–July 1891), John S. Durham (September 3, 1891–November 7, 1893), Henry M. Smythe (September 15, 1893–March 9, 1897), and William F. Powell (June 17, 1897–November 30, 1905). The history of these postings was also confirmation of the racial sensitivity of both Republicans and the blacks sent there, confident that they would seek to serve admirably because racial integrity was leverage for Republicans and a cause for the black representatives serving and securing the interests of the United States and African descendants in Haiti as well.

A record of this exists in the career and writings of Frederick Douglass, a leader of the Republican party and the most venerable black leader of the nineteenth century, who recommended Bassett's appointment. But when Douglass himself was appointed minister to Haiti, he felt at the time that there was resistance to the appointment of blacks by some politicians but mostly by the press, feeling that his dark skin color made him "not rightly colored for the place" and that he lacked diplomatic experience. They preferred a white man, but Douglass not only felt that he was "matched well with the color of Haiti" but that the Haitians would be "shockingly inconsistent" to reject someone of their own color.[16] Indeed, charges of incompetence did erupt when the United States attempted to secure a naval station in the bay of the Mole St. Nicholas in Haiti and when the negotiations between Rear-Admiral Gherardi, stationed there, and the Haitian government fell through. Douglass was accused of not having set the stage for the transaction in his first year, even though he was unaware of this objective. In any case, his perspective is pertinent to the importance of race for these early initiates in the U.S. diplomatic service. He said:

> Prejudice sets all logic at defiance! It takes no account of reason or consistency. One of the duties of minister in a foreign land is to cultivate good social as well as civil relations with the people and governments to which he is sent. Would an American white man, imbued with our national sentiments, be more likely than an American colored man to cultivate such relations? Or would he play the hypocrite and pretend to love negroes in Haiti when he is known to hate negroes in the United States,—aye, so bitterly that he hates to see them occupy even the comparatively humble position of Consul-General to Haiti? Would not the contempt and disgust of Haiti repel such a sham?[17]

He goes on to suggest that even if a white man could gain something more than a black representative from Haiti by virtue of his alleged superiority, he should not do so because the relative power of the United States would signal an exploitative relative relationship—in other words, that the core of the relationship would be unjust.

No doubt, such feeling continued to follow the career of blacks in the foreign service, as the initial appointment by President Grant of blacks to Haiti and Santo Domingo, was followed by twenty others from 1897 to 1909, expanding to Liberia, but also to Latin America. Benjamin R. Justesen describes, in a fascinating but brief expose, how the first decade of the twentieth century "found African-Americans performing consular duties at more than a dozen foreign posts, both in independent nations like Brazil, France, Honduras, Nicaragua, Paraguay, Russia and Venezuela, and in a number of European colonies in Africa and the Caribbean, including the Danish and French West Indies, Jamaica, Madagascar, Senegal and Sierra Leone. In all, at least 20 black consuls served during the Republican administrations of William McKinley and Theodore Roosevelt between 1897 and 1909, with eight of them remaining abroad for a decade or more."[18] This began the expansion of black diplomatic personnel into many areas of the world, but their stories are strangely muted as a part of American diplomatic history, even though Justesen says that several of them contributed significantly to the larger picture of American experiences with other nations. James Weldon Johnson, for example, wrote an interesting account of his experiences as an American consul in the Latin American countries of Nicaragua and Venezuela at a time when their histories were fraught with the instability of military rule.[19] Johnson, trapped in Latin America and unable to persuade Secretary of State William Jennings Bryan to keep his promise to move him to a more desirable post, felt that he was "up against politics and race prejudice" and wrote his resignation letter in late 1913.[20]

Outside of government service, several African American individuals were prominent as international actors. Here, I will discuss briefly W.E.B. Du Bois, Paul Robeson, Marcus Garvey, and El Hajj Malik El Shabazz (Malcolm X) as examples of leaders who were significant in their international exploits and for this reason incurred government attention to and concern over their activities. W. E. B. Du Bois became active in international movements abroad. One of his first international conferences was the Pan-African conference held in London in 1900 and organized by Trinidadian lawyer, H. Sylvester Williams. Du Bois was not the prime focus of attention at this meeting that attracted other prominent African Americans. The second international conference, the Universal Races Conference held in London in July 1911, was actually suggested by Du Bois, according to a scholar of

Pan Africanism, Immanuel Geiss. Geiss considered the primary basis of Du Bois's progressive thinking "naive" in his belief that an aesthetic bond of spirituality would grow among participants that could lead to world peace.[21] Beyond his interests and activities in Pan-Africanism, throughout his lifetime Du Bois maintained his interests in world peace, and by the time of a 1949 International Conference for World Peace he was well known abroad for his role. In fact, Shirley Graham Du Bois writes that when Du Bois opened the conference, there was such cheering that he was said to have remarked that "it appears they know who I am."[22] Du Bois was known internationally as a progressive, to which Shirley Graham Du Bois provides eyewitness testimony concerning some attendees at the 1949 Paris Peace Conference who said of Du Bois: "That's a prof who's been around for a long time, a black man who talks back. Let's listen to him."[23]

The beginning of black mass interests in foreign affairs was shaped during World War I and its aftermath by the interests of African Americans in the condition of their relatives, friends, and Diasporic cousins, and the disposition of their lands. But the war was important as the first in which blacks were united on the side of the country against a foreign aggressor. Formerly, they had been divided, as on the side of the British or the Americans in the Revolutionary War and the War of 1812, or for the North or the South during the Civil War. It was at first known by blacks as the "white man's civil war," but also the first war when so many eventually wore the uniform of their country participating in a foreign adventure. The interest of blacks was so strong with respect to the condition of black soldiers and the disposition of African territories that the NAACP sent an emissary to the Paris Peace Conference. W. E. B. Du Bois, as the organization's representative, devised a Pan-African conference as the modality by which he would seek to assess the condition both of the colonial peoples and of the territories involved in the defeat of Germany. Without entering into a detailed rendition of this project, which expanded to four other meetings after 1919, the theme of these meetings was important in crafting a relatively common set of issues by peoples of African descent with regard to international affairs.

Du Bois shared his passion for peace with Paul Robeson, who had partnered with Du Bois, as board members and leaders of the Council on African Affairs, to lead the first black American lobby on Africa, founded in the late 1930s. Like Du Bois, Robeson was passionate about these issues and well known internationally as a singer, but his political posture as a progressive on these issues was equally unrelenting.

For both of these men, the issue of domestic and global justice was defined as the fight against racism in America and the achievement of peace in the world that would dampen the fires of imperialism and colonialism. This volume offers a new look at the importance of China in the twenty-first century international relations with Africa, but for Du Bois and Robeson, alliances with countries such as China and Russia in the first half of the twentieth century were a manifestation of cultivating relations between peoples and a state on the basis of their pledge to construct non-racist societies.[24] In other words, Du Bois and Robeson harbored similar views that such countries represented progressive models of international relations on the basis of their stated pursuit of justice for all their citizens. In 1944, under the auspices of the Council on African Affairs, Robeson made a speech in which he began by noting the similarity of China and Africa as future continental powers, then went on to expose why he supported the Chinese communists, saying that he opposed the "click [clique]" supporting Generalissimo Chiang Kai-shek, against the pro-Nazi communists whose "sole aim is the attainment of national unity, freedom from fascist aggression, and the development of democratic institutions which will provide for the participation of all parties and sections of the people in the war against the enemy and in the post-war development of their country."[25] Similarly, he spelled out his views about the Soviet Union in a speech, "The Negro People and the Soviet Union," in New York in November 1949, in a hypothetical answer to the question that some black had asked him, "Yes, I know Paul, . . . but what has Russia ever done for us Negroes?" He said:

> the Soviet Union's very existence, its example before the world of abolishing all discrimination based on color or nationality, its fight in every arena of world conflict for genuine democracy and for peace, this has given us Negroes the change of achieving our complete liberation within our own time, within this generation. For where, indeed, would the Negro people's struggle for freedom be today, if world imperialism had not been critically wounded and its forces weakened throughout the world? Where would the fight to vote in the South be today if this new balance of power in the world did not exist?[26]

These alliances and sentiments would eventually bring both men great difficulties in the Cold War period. Both were targeted by the House Un-American Activities Committee in the wake of the McCarthy period that investigated communist linkages among activists, intellectuals, and entertainers, and were forced to testify with respect to the funding and activities of the Council on African Affairs. Robeson was eventually prevented from travel by the confiscation of his passport and confined to the United States. Du Bois adopted membership in the Communist party in the early 1960s and became a citizen of Ghana. Both men were vilified by their government and by members of their racial community as well. One can see elements of that contradiction in black officials from the attempt of the first representatives to provide a more progressive U.S. presence in Haiti and Liberia to the present.

This brief review of the activities of Du Bois and Robeson shows that the strongest opposition to American policy has come from individuals and organizations that were more independent to do so. One element of this opposition was Malcolm X, another historic individual who dissented from the general cast of American policy in Africa, as an outgrowth of his fierce opposition to American racism. On a trip to Africa in 1964, he challenged Africans to oppose American racism and U.S. policies, a line that was clearly not well received by American officials in countries where he stopped, such as Kenya. Once there, U.S. Ambassador William Attwood considered him a troublemaker and alerted Kenyans and other posts in Africa as to Malcolm's presence and intentions.[27] At one of his first stops in Ghana, he pointed out, in a talk at the University of Ghana, the hypocrisy of Africans charging Portugal and South Africa with racism "while our black people are being bitten by dogs and beaten with clubs."[28] Malcolm X was already known to Africans as someone who was truthful and straightforward about the condition of people of African descent and therefore, he became the first African American to be invited to speak at the assembly of the newly formed Organization of African Unity. On that occasion, he said, in part, "My purpose here is to remind the African heads of state that there are 22 million of us in America who are also of African descent, and to remind them also that we are the victims of America's colonialism or American imperialism, and that our problem is not an American problem, it's a human problem. It's not a Negro problem, it's a problem of humanity. It's not a problem of Civil Rights, but a problem of human rights."[29] He felt that there was a bond among the white nations of Europe and America that rendered the official national distinctions of little difference when it came to the treatment of people of African descent. Arriving from Accra, Ghana, in May 1964, he noticed that Nigeria was full of Americans and that "the same whites, who spit in the faces of blacks in America and sic their police dogs upon us to keep us from 'integrating' with them, are seen throughout Africa, bowing, grinning and smiling in an effort to 'integrate' with Africans . . . they want to 'integrate' into Africa's wealth and beauty. That is ironical."[30] He went on to suggest that Nigerians were strongly concerned with African Americans, but that the U.S. Information Agency promoted the myth that there was no basis for a progressive unity between them and African Americans, since the latter were experiencing such progress in their country.[31] Thus, Malcolm X connected with Africans, helping to cement what would be a more intense Pan-African period in the United States a few years after his death in February 1965.

In 1969 Rep. Charles Diggs, Jr., of Michigan was elected to the post of chair of the African Affairs Subcommittee of the House Foreign Affairs Committee. In that role, he used his committee to conduct hearings on the role of many American corporations in South Africa, despite the racist policies of that country's white minority regime. However, appointed to the U.S. delegation to the United Nations in October 1971, he walked out of the U.N. session and resigned his membership in the U.S. delegation that December because of his opposition to his government's refusal to stop receiving chrome from South Africa's ally, the equally racist white-minority Rhodesian government, in opposition to U.N. resolutions. He could do so because of his independent base in the House as a leading black legislator and leading member of the Democratic party. Somewhat later, the newly formed Congressional Black Caucus sued the U.S. government for violating American trade policy in its acceptance of Rhodesian chrome. Diggs's aggressive pursuit of a progressive Africa policy at a time of rising politics, however, made him a target that eventually cost him politically, as he was indicted in October 1978 by Republican federal prosecutors in the Justice Department in a kickback scheme involving his staff salaries and mail fraud. He was censured by the House in the summer of 1979, resigned from Congress in 1980, and served fourteen months in prison.

AMERICAN RACISM IN THE COLD WAR

American racism emerged as an issue on the world stage in the post–World War II era, and Paul Robeson was correct that it complicated the Cold War competition between the United States and the Soviet Union. The end of World War II created a structure of international organizations that promptly provided an avenue through which black intellectuals could describe the domestic atmosphere in which the United States entered the Cold War. U.S. officials were unprepared for the country's racial history to be exhumed by the Soviets and used as a basis to challenge America's democratic pretensions.

Shortly after the United Nations was established, W. E. B. Du Bois and some of his colleagues drafted a petition known as "An Appeal To The World" that chronicled the history of American racism, and asked that the record be released to the member states and that it be assessed by duly appointed bodies of the new organization, such as the Division of Human Rights. This division was the logical place, since it was working on the Universal Declaration of Human Rights that was released in December 1948, and after much delay, the Du Bois "Appeal" was finally released by the division in January 1948 after a three-month delay in its presentation to the institution.[32] This saga of obfuscation of the document by the U.S. State Department, the NAACP, and U.S. allies in the United Nations is somewhat outside of the scope of this work, but it deserves serious attention because of the difficulty it exhibits when black organizations and individuals have had to work through institutions of American foreign policy, presenting issues and views that were at odds with those who dominated those institutions.

To be sure, the seeds of the decolonization movement were found in World War II, when the ties of European countries to their colonial possessions were weakened by the depletion of their resources and by the contradiction of fighting a war against Nazi fascism and racism only to be the image of it themselves. The independence of Ghana in 1957, the first state below the Sahara to become independent, occurred in the midst of the Montgomery Bus Boycott that ignited the ground game of the American civil rights movement. And although representatives of that movement were in Ghana to celebrate its independence and maintained ties with the burgeoning African independence movement, African Americans fully dedicated to this cause would not arise until the end of the 1960s and early 1970s.

Several organizations, such as the African Liberation Support Committee and later TransAfrica, sprang up in the late 1960s and early 1970s as manifestations of the Pan-African movement, which was an outgrowth of the black nationalist movement, but these organizations were addressed to the direct support of African independence movements rather than to change in American policy. Peniel Joseph describes the massive 1972 demonstration at the State Department opposing American policies toward Africa and cites Rep. Charles Diggs as saying in his speech on that occasion that "no longer will the movement stop at the water's edge."[33] In any case, demonstrations were held to protest aspects of U.S. policy, such as America's close association with South Africa, but it was up to TransAfrica to successfully challenge the policy of constructive engagement, set in place by President Richard Nixon and maintained by Presidents Jimmy Carter and Ronald Reagan.

This volume adequately describes the activities of TransAfrica Forum, a successor to TransAfrica, Inc., founded in 1977 as a lobby organization to influence American policy on Africa and the Caribbean. It is little known, however, that when TransAfrica was established, one of its first significant acts was not to support an African country, but to oppose it. Sergeant Samuel Doe of Liberia came into power in 1980 as the result of a coup that eliminated the regime of William Tolbert, Jr., and the 133-year reign of the Americo-Liberians.[34] Shortly after Ronald Reagan became president in 1981, his administration immediately increased economic assistance to the Doe government, because of its maintenance of U.S. strategic installations there, rising from $46 million to over $400 million by 1985. However, Doe's regime grew more corrupt and held executions of his potential claimants to power, posing a moral challenge to TransAfrica. It decided to oppose the Doe regime and its American support rather than legitimize its rapacious rule of murder and mayhem. Nevertheless, it was a necessary step in building the integrity of the organization later as a leader in the anti-apartheid movement.

The opposition to Doe presented a confusing paradigm for many, since TransAfrica came into existence as an organization to support African states, but the leadership reasoned that they could not pursue a progressive Africa policy with clean hands if support for various regimes did not contain humane standards.[35] Using moral standards as a basis of political action often complicated alliances among Pan-Africanists in the United States and between them and continental Africans who supported various factions of the existing independence movements and African governments in power.

For several years, both TransAfrica, Inc., and TransAfrica Forum existed side by side, one with a mission to influence U.S. policy and the other to cultivate African American cultural relations with Africa and the Caribbean. However, it was TransAfrica, Inc., that led the anti-apartheid protest movement of the mid-1980s, which opposed Ronald Reagan's policy of constructive engagement and led to a cessation of U.S. trade relations with the South African government. Rep. William Gray of the Congressional Black Caucus led the organization in its opposition to the Reagan policy by crafting and sponsoring the Anti-Apartheid Act, which passed in 1986 and effected a policy of no new economic relations between the United States and South Africa.[36]

A legacy of the continuing opposition to American policy ironically surfaced in South Africa, during the preparation for and implementation of the United Nations Conference in Durban in opposition to racism, xenophobia, and political intolerance. That meeting, discussed in this volume, was also a profound example of the differences in U.S. policy with respect to issues such as reparations and the Palestinian/Israeli conflict. The official U.S. delegation withdrew from the conference on orders of the sitting secretary of state, Colin Powell, whose legacy as an African American was superseded by his responsibility for the dominant view of the national interest. The U.S. government, through Powell, was concerned about the potential damage to the image of Israel this meeting could present, even though American Jews were heavily represented in the nongovernmental organization delegation to the conference.[37] As Ife Williams suggests, there was much prior deliberation in a series of meetings over the context of the conference and whether its leadership would allow African slavery to be declared a crime against humanity and whether Zionism would be allowed to be equated with racism. Failing to receive what he considered adequate assurances, Powell withdrew the U.S. delegation with the following statement:

> Today, I have instructed our representative at the World Conference Against Racism to return home. I have taken this decision with regret, because of the importance of the international fight against racism and the contribution that the Conference could have made to it. But, following discussions today by our team in Durban and others who are working for a successful Conference, I am convinced that will not be possible. I know that you do not combat racism by conferences that produce declarations containing hateful language, some of which is a throwback to the days of "Zionism equals racism," or supports the idea that we have made too much of the Holocaust; or suggests that apartheid exists in Israel; or that singles out only one country in the world—Israel—for censure and abuse.[38]

By this act, Powell also privileged the position of Israel and the Jewish community in the United States over the historic damage that racism had done to the black community, Native Americans, Hispanics, Asians, and other nonwhite groups. Rev. Jesse Jackson, Sr., head of the Rainbow/PUSH civil rights organization, immediately condemned the withdrawal and suggested that it was also done to avoid dealing with other sensitive subjects, such as reparations. In addition, well-known entertainer Harry Belafonte referred to Colin Powell as a "sellout to the Black race" in response to this and other perceptions that Powell did not represent the interests of the African American community.[39]

Thomas Borstelmann suggests that pressure from the exposition of American racism influenced U.S. foreign policy from the Truman administration to that of George H. W. Bush.[40] In fact, American racial conditions are still a subject of international concern, as seen in a 2007 report of the Committee of the International Convention on Civil and Political Rights, a 1976 treaty based on the Universal Declaration of Human Rights. The United States ratified the treaty in 1992 with such substantial reservations that, according to the Convention, "the United States is a signatory in name only." In any case, a recommendation was made to the U.S. response to the damage done by Hurricane Katrina:

> In the aftermath of the Hurricane Katrina, the State party (US) should increase its efforts to ensure that the rights of the poor, and in particular African-Americans, are fully taken into consideration in the reconstruction plans with regard to access to housing, education and health care. The Committee wishes to be informed about the results of the inquiries into the alleged failure to evacuate prisoners at the Parrish prison, as well as the allegations that New Orleans residents were not permitted by law enforcement officials to cross the Greater New Orleans Bridge to Gretna, Louisiana.[41]

The U.S. response amounted to a reassuring reply that it was committed to "helping all victims and particularly those who are in the greatest need," saying that the Department of Housing and Urban Development had been tasked to initiate the "operation home sweet home" program as a concentrated project to expose housing discrimination in areas recovering from the hurricane.

The Decline in Black Interest in Foreign Affairs

There is a natural historical sequence between the preceding discussion and what follows that is concerned with the period of the most dynamic opposition by blacks to U.S. foreign policy and their justice-seeking activities, whether in their direct relations with the African Diaspora, or as seeking to influence U.S. policy, and how after the 1980s such activities begin to diminish, and little attention has been given to the causes of this demise.

Charles P. Henry argues persuasively in this volume that the decline in the interest of African Americans in foreign policy is accounted for by the parallel decline in the progressive ethic, characterized by the former intense movement of the 1960s and 1970s devoted to the furtherance of the ideology of Pan-Africanism and the activities related to it.[42] That is a logical assertion in light of the emergence of the conservative political culture on the American scene that contested and defeated the progressive era, but it also helps to underline factors that may account for the decline. However, let me suggest a few other factors that might be considered: the end of the liberation period, the rise of black state leadership, the devaluation of the intellectual legacy of direct action and revolutionary change, and the impact of globalization on Pan-Africanism.

THE END OF THE AFRICAN LIBERATION PERIOD

The end of the colonial period and the attendant liberation movements in several countries appeared to create the impression that the coming of African governments would create the normal channels of both domestic governance and international statecraft through which the needs of the people would be met. In fact, the end of this period of activity more often than not placed the new governments in the hands of global banks, foreign government, and international financial institutions, which structured their prospects for development into a global capitalist context and instantly made them debtors to the system. The difficulty of finding a place in this new order by complying with the terms of these institutions for cash, while devolving Western political institutions and dealing with ancient African ethno-political systems, defined a pace and complexity of change that was generally overwhelming and tortuously slow.

Pan-African activists did not anticipate that the struggle for socioeconomic viability on the part of the African masses would be even more difficult than their liberation from the yoke of colonialism, given the centuries of misuse of African economies and the criminal lack of preparation of the people to enter into the economies of the twentieth and twenty-first centuries.

Consequently, what we see in each case is the decline of organizations in the United States that constituted the movement for the support of Pan-African practices in Africa and the Caribbean, and the decline of movements in those areas of the world that were seeking independence from European colonial states. The remnant of this process that lasted into the 1980s was South African apartheid and the drama of the anti-apartheid movement.

THE RISE OF BLACK STATE LEADERSHIP IN THE DIASPORA

The entry of black Americans into a new era of participation in electoral politics promoted an emphasis on the presence and participation of people of African descent in official corridors of power. In Africa, the state system was created that resulted in thirteen independent states by 1963, over thirty by the end of the 1960s, and fifty-four today. The emergence of heads of state and their administrations created an imbalance in the status among peoples in the African Diaspora, where some people were represented by state leaders, and other African descendants in the Diaspora within white-dominant societies were represented by members of a different history and culture. With respect to the latter case, it can be suggested that the interests of African descendants were conceived to be secondary, and that generally independent governments provided the strongest representation for continental Africans, except where the leaders of some African states appeared to represent their own individual interests to the detriment of their people.

Likewise, with the end of the civil rights movement in the United States, many of those who formerly worked in southern towns and cities decamped into northern urban areas rather than stay in the South after significant battles to achieve important national legislation had been won. In fact, as a consequence of the Civil Rights Act and Voting Rights Act in particular, they took up these new instruments of electoral politics to become part of the administration of public policy.

African Americans made considerable strides in achieving positions of prominence, both in national politics and in the foreign policy establishment. In 1965 fewer than 400 elected officials were in place; this number has grown to over 9,000 by the early twenty-first century. This growth has enabled Rep. James Clyburn of South Carolina to become the third highest ranking member in the House of Representatives as Democratic party whip, and Rep. Donald Payne of New Jersey, to become the chair of the House Subcommittee on African Affairs. This study analyzes the work of the first two African Americans to become secretary of state, General Colin Powell and Condoleezza Rice. However, growth in the foreign policy establishment has also included Susan Rice as the National Security Council staff director for Africa in the Clinton administration and Jendayi Frazer as the Africa director in the National Security Council in the first administration of George W. Bush. Both Rice and Frazier became assistant secretary of state for African affairs, and Rice is the U.S. ambassador to the United Nations in the Obama administration.

The number of African Americans in the foreign service of the United States has increased, but much more slowly than for other officials. The number of blacks in the foreign service has always been low, largely because of the "continuing problems of marginalization, limited advancement opportunities and other injustices and indignities."[43] African Americans constituted 5.4 percent of foreign service officers in 1985; twenty years later, they made up only 6.5 percent of the 6,500 total officers on duty.[44] The reason for this may not be only that suggested by Susan Rice: that the foreign service is lacking in diversity because African Americans are naturally drawn to the unfinished business of domestic issues.[45] It may also be that increasingly, the foreign affairs institutions do not guarantee that one's career can be constructed around an interest in the African Diaspora, because the mobility of diplomats meets the needs of their administration, and also the direction of American policies is often not regarded as enlightened.

Against this background of the growth of black officials, the organizations and individuals who had the most to do with creating the grassroots atmosphere (involving publicizing U.S. policies that supported African subjugation and opposing them through various means) that enabled the public to know, and thus support, progressive policies toward Africa and the Caribbean were devalued. The contradiction emerged that activists who supported independence movements could provide leaders of the new states with few governing resources, such that the new officials of these states needed to collaborate with the powerful leaders of those countries which were their former adversaries. The end result was that the inequality in status and the movement of official leaders toward their counterparts in the developed industrial states prevented the achievement of the goals of Pan-Africanism.

A symptom of this contradiction was discovered after the African National Congress took charge of South Africa in 1995 and Nelson Mandela made his first visit to the United States. The official proceedings were marked by the presence of U.S. government officials, while those who had led the movement for South African black majority independence in the United States were sidelined. As one of the authors of this volume discusses, African financial resources were most often expended by African states on white consultants, business leaders, and heads of nongovernmental organizations as an alternative to blacks who had come into official leadership positions in business or government or who began to possess considerable unofficial political influence. Thus, the new posture of governance often broke the linkage among Africans fighting their own subjugation by the colonial process and their allies and supporters in the African Diaspora.

HISTORY OF THE REVOLUTIONARY MOVEMENT DEVALUED

The liberation movement of the 1960s and 1970s produced a rich literature that both described and analyzed the motives and activities of the anti-colonial movement and as such posted a most severe intellectual critique of the oppression of African descendents on the African continent, Europe, the Caribbean, and Latin America. This intellectual contribution to the history of struggle, however, has been severed from the "normal" body of work that informs students and the lay public of the aims of oppressed people to achieve truly democratic societies and material equality. Apparently such studies constitute dangerous thought to be exiled in the archives of history rather than referred to as something that exists for mass consumption, especially as activities of Third World people become a more dynamic aspect of the global system. Today, little of that literature is referred to by intellectuals seeking to understand issues such as the origin and maintenance of poverty and disease and social disorganization, the motivation of Third World peoples to seek liberation, and their capacities to resist subordination. In fact, the institutionalization of the movements of that era has been sanitized to comport with the perspective that presents a comfortable companion with the continued existence of racism, the spears and sharp edges of the anticolonial, anti-racist messages being shorn off or excluded altogether. The suppression of the voices of black revolutionaries, Pan-Africanists, and their allies in the white progressive community and abroad meant that their views could not be given legitimate public voice in the debates over whether to have war or peace in the Middle East.

With respect to the concept of foreign policy justice, I suggested, for example, that if President George W. Bush's advisors truly understood the capacities of the indigenous people of Iraq to resist the attempt to colonize them, they might not have made such disastrous miscalculations. This means they either had not read, or had not privileged in their thinking the lessons of Vietnam, described by Bernard Fall in such works as *Hell in a Very Small Place* (1967), *The Vietnam Reader* (1965), or *Vietnam Witness* (1963). By the same token, they could not have read *Tell No Lies, Claim No Easy Victories* (1965) by Amilcar Cabral, who led the movement to overthrow the Portuguese in Guinea Bissau and Cape Verde on the west coast of Africa, and perhaps they did not see *The Battle of Algiers* (1966), a film that showed the ingenuity of those who fought to liberate Algeria from the French, or Frantz Fanon's *The Wretched of the Earth* (1961), which presents a classic understanding of the way in which colonialism and racism formed a unique commitment among oppressed people to seek their freedom.

The severance of this intellectual history from the public discourse by the careerism of the new professoriate, by intellectual elites, or by the managers of media vehicles that present public debates over policy has been one reason why power relations are misunderstood, and why direct action tactics are deprecated as "old" tactics of struggle and the "new" forms of incorporation are favored that offer less complicated routes to upward mobility within the social system. Being publicly opposed to racial oppression, for example, advocating for divestment from South Africa, or joining the many demonstrations to achieve the Anti-apartheid Act of 1986 did not often ensure status within American academic or economic institutions, and very often was a recipe for exclusion from status roles in society.

While episodic works have been written on the more radical aspects of the domestic black movement in the United States, only recently has there been a series of works on black power, exemplified by Peniel Joseph's *Waiting 'Til the Midnight Hour*, that connects these movements to the support structure that existed to oppose what were perceived as harmful U.S. policies and promote humane policies toward Africa and the African Diaspora.[46]

THE FORCE OF GLOBALIZATION

In the process of a wide-ranging assessment of the condition of Pan-African activities in various parts of the world, I argued in *Pan Africanism in the African Diaspora* that the theory of Pan-Africanism was elaborated along dimensions of the global system where Africa served as the central point and where those African communities in various other parts of the world—within states—attempted to express and achieve unity.[47] However, I felt that this unity was envisioned as a necessity for the strengthening of their cultural legacy and identity and thus for the future development that would occur mutually in both Africa and the African communities in the Diaspora through various concrete interactions. Indeed, I envisioned Diaspora communities as central to the maintenance of the concept of Pan-Africanism. "Attention to the obligation to improve one's immediate community is a necessary precondition to effective Pan Africanism because it is there that the resources are developed for strategies directed to both aspects of African survival. In theoretical terms, it is the 'national question' that is primary and that affects the way in which Pan African relations evolve among peoples and states in the Diaspora."[48] I agree with Charles Henry that the theory and practice of Pan-Africanism has waned in this part of the Diaspora both because of the decline in the social movement that strengthened it in the 1960s and 1970s and because the cultural integrity of the "black community" in the United States that was at the base of the Diaspora concept has been under attack by conservative political culture.

The subject of "globalization and survival in the black Diaspora" is, in fact, the subject and title of an edited work by Charles Green that examines such factors as the relevance of the knowledge-based cultural transformation of African descendants to their employment prospects, and the decline of low-wage, low-skilled labor, connecting these to the regressive policies of the G-7 and the relative lack of rapid progress in Africa and its Diaspora.[49] His view and that of his coauthors is that globalization has had and is having a deleterious effect on urban communities, and insofar as that is where so many peoples of African descent reside and to which they are continually attracted, the factors associated with globalization are having a disproportionate effect on them. My view supports this conclusion in that, by extension, if the urban base of the black community is threatened by globalization, then black communities in the African Diaspora are less likely to be able to achieve the unity that is at the base of the theory and practice of Pan-Africanism. The sense of stress redirects the energies of the people to their own survival, and the disorganization of the social structure through the lack of economic investment, gentrification, crime and the attendant mass incarceration, and other factors displaces the population and weakens the social structure.

In this sense, there are many challenges presented by globalization that have compounded problems experienced by most states in the African Diaspora, as exemplified by the global economic crisis that began in 2008. The interrelated financial institutions that had managed the economics of globalization were all affected by the slowdown in economic activity, the mass unemployment, and the loss of financial resources, all of which affects African peoples who exists at the bottom of society either in developed states of Europe and America or within the African continent itself. Africa will be unable to utilize the human and financial resources of those in the African Diaspora and will emerge from the global economic crisis more dependent upon the advanced industrial states.[50] Indeed, they will emerge more dependent in any case because the resources from these very states will be diverted to their own survival as well.

Conclusion: Foreign Policy Justice in a Changing Nation

SUMMARIZING THE IMPEDIMENT TO JUSTICE ISSUE

Racism within the foreign policy establishment is linked ultimately to differences in the conceptualization of the national interests. What we mean very often by "racism" is that foreign policy leaders privilege their history and culture and, as a white dominant racial group in America, their derivative associations with the European nations of their civilization and the interests they share. Those interests are often not only counter, but detrimental to the conceptualization of foreign policy justice by African Americans. Thus, the extent to which there is an "American foreign policy" that is not conflicted revolves around those issues about which there are no strong racial or domestic considerations on either side of the racial divide. The American foreign policy that is conflicted remains so because of the contradictions in the domestic arena that have to do with the socieconomic inequality linked to the disproportionate cost and benefits of certain foreign policies, even when they are not directed toward areas of strong racial or ethnic interests.

This summary of the problem reveals the interests and motivations that allow the dominant leaders in foreign policymaking institutions to perform in ways that exclude the interests of African Americans, such that those interests have become targets of change over time. However, the irony is that many African Americans who have had the highest esteem and high-level posts have not overtly pursued the end to racism in foreign policymaking. They follow instead, perhaps, a silent theory that by their presence and excellence in performance of their duties, they advance the prospects of racial equality. That is, of course, a plausible theory and type of behavior, but it is also a most conservative approach to the pursuit of justice in foreign policymaking, with respect to either the role of African Americans in the process of decisionmaking, or the advancement of the progressive thrust of American policy where various issues are concerned.

BLACK OFFICIALS' RESPONSE TO BLACK ISSUES

This, I believe, to a large extent characterizes the careers of the first African American secretaries of state, Colin Powell and Condoleezza Rice, and the meaning of the term "indeterminacy of the racial variable," as used by Josephine Allen, Alvin Tillery, Jr., and Hanes Walton, Jr., in their chapter in this volume. They define the term as the degree to which one is able to determine whether or not race has been acknowledged by the two individuals of African descent who have occupied the top of the state hierarchy of decisionmaking in American foreign policy. The hope of many, of course, was that they would exert the type of administration of foreign policy that elevates African American interests to a reasonable balance with others. However, one finds that their loyalty to the regime that appointed them was a powerful limitation on their range of behavior. The real issue here is that Colin Powell and Condoleezza Rice are of the African American community in terms of identity, but politically the representative function they perform has been fundamentally antithetical to the dominant interests represented in that community.

This phenomenon might be suggested as a general problem with the appointment of blacks to high posts in various administrations. After a survey of several administrations, Robert Smith found that the attitudes and behavior of black appointees in the political system expressed far greater fidelity to the institutional mores and processes than to their function as representatives of the community of which they were a part.[51] What we conclude is that they are not "free agents" to exercise the choice to privilege certain interests. The result, then, is that whether blacks in foreign policymaking institutions would pursue justice depends upon, first, the political situation with respect to the range of flexibility they experience, then their ideological orientation, and perhaps the extent to which the national interests were related to Africa and the Caribbean or some other part of the world.

The racial politics of foreign policy institutions is one of the reasons why linkages were sought by private black organizations to alternative pathways of foreign affairs participation in such international organizations as the United Nations. Several black nongovernmental organizations (NGOs) are accredited to the U.N. system where they have a voice in international affairs. More recently blacks have participated in a variety of international organizations, such as UNESCO, as researchers involved in the investigation of African slavery and as special "roving ambassadors," such as famous actors Harry Belafonte, Danny Glover, and others. Black church organizations are affiliated with the World Council of Churches and their officials often occupy staff positions in that organization at its headquarters in Geneva, Switzerland. The International Labor Organization has been a vehicle for contacts between black labor in the United States and their counterpart organizations in Africa, the Caribbean, and Latin America. And blacks have served as staff lawyers on the World Court and other institutions of the U.N. system and its affiliated organizations.

THE BARACK OBAMA ADMINISTRATION

In the postelection stage of the Barack Obama administration several trends begin to be evident: his presence as a most important international resource for the American image; the promise of change of U.S. foreign policies, beginning with the war in Iraq; and perhaps the strengthening of American relations with African and Caribbean states. The symbols of this promise are his Kenyan heritage, which has set up expectations that he should be both sensitive to and desirous of change in America's approach to Africa, as well as the extremely positive global reception that accompanied his election.

Immediately, Obama's election success was used to explain the extent to which America began as an imperfect democracy and why achieving a more perfect democracy would take a substantial period of time. For example, discussing U.S. policy with regard to Turkey, a State Department official noted: "We know from our own experience that the job of building Democracy is never done. Political ideologies must adjust to broader societal change. It took our country nearly a century to abolish slavery, and only now, 145 years later, has an African American emerged as a top Presidential candidate."[52] Then, in a daily press briefing, the State Department spokesman referred to the evolving democracy in Iraq and the tendency of Secretary Rice to talk about its slow evolution: "Secretary Rice is fond of talking about the evolution of our own democracy which is taking a couple of centuries to get to the point where we are now. We have a black American that has been elected president of the United States. That's quite a journey."[53] So, it is becoming clear that the election of Barack Obama will be used both to support dominant group interests of American policy and to justify American progress in the field of race relations.

Most important, there is the issue of strengthening relations with African Diaspora states, and one must begin here with the legacy of President George W. Bush. To be fair, the legacy of Bush in Africa was considerably more positive than that of the Clinton administration, largely because of the dominance of Congress by conservative politics. Thus, in that era, the African Growth and Opportunity Act (AGOA) was initiated, as the creation of the consensus between Democrats who wanted something for Africa and Republicans who were willing only to support legislation that would favor a capitalist model of development, as indicated by the strong support of this legislation by the then Speaker of the House, Newt Gingrich. As suggested elsewhere in this volume by William Jones, AGOA provoked serious division between members of the Congressional Black Caucus, who sought to achieve the best possible outcome for Africa, and others who supported it as the only approach possible to financially support African development.

The Bush administration continued to build AGOA and promoted glowing reports of its success. For example, Deputy Secretary of State John Negroponte said in 2008 that the level of exports from African countries under the act had reached $50 billion since its enactment in 2001. However, he failed to say that approximately 80 percent of that amount was accounted for by increases in the oil trade and that this increase was also responsible for the negative politics that made the United States tread lightly on critical issues, such as the fair distribution of Nigerian oil profits, the linkage of Sudanese oil to the Darfur crisis, and other issues.[54] Nevertheless, one must consider that the racial variable was of the determinacy of Secretaries Rice,

Powell, or both, in the motivation of the Bush administration to push support for African issues beyond the boundaries of the previous Democratic and Republican administrations alike.

Beyond AGOA, John Negroponte's address to the Congressional Black Caucus annual Legislative Conference emphasized several achievements of the Bush administration:

- Quadrupling economic assistance to Africa in the largest expansion since the Marshall Plan
- Compacts with ten African nations in the Millennium Challenge Account, amounting to 4.3 billion
- Launching the Malaria Initiative in 2005, which had reached 25 million people, causing a decline in malaria in some parts of the continent
- Contributing to the fight against hunger $5.5 billion for FY 2008 and 2009, a substantial part of which went to Africa.[55]

Comparatively speaking, however, progress on the political front has been far less effective, and many of these issues, as suggested above, will become subjects of the Obama agenda.

The Obama administration faces a formidable set of crises on both the domestic and international fronts: the war in Iraq, a potential nuclear Iran, increasing military actions in Afghanistan, stabilization of Pakistan as a partner while insulating it from a major problem with India, rebuilding of relations with Europe, and the Israeli/Palestinian conflict that erupted into a military confrontation just two weeks before Obama's inauguration. In that context, the priority of issues that derive from African Diaspora interests remains to be established and maintained. A reasonable expectation for both building and sustaining an African-oriented agenda is to develop a new definition of U.S. "strategic interests" that includes tending to issues that have the power to destabilize countries, such as HIV/AIDS, hunger, environment/climate change, energy, and others that are part of the global systemic agenda.

In any case, it is uncertain to what extent the Obama administration will pursue—or be permitted to pursue—interests of the African American community as part of the national interest that will achieve foreign policy justice for peoples of the African Diaspora. In part, it depends upon the space afforded by the heavy weight of global crises that he inherited from the previous administration and the strength of his determination to do so. But it most probably will depend upon the degree of commitment among African Americans themselves to mobilize those interests.

NOTES

1. Julianne Malveaux and Reginna A. Green, eds., *The Paradox of Loyalty: An African American Response to the War on Terrorism* (Chicago: Third World Press, 2002), 233.
2. Ibid, 185–97.
3. See Joseph Stieglitz and Linda Bilmes, *The Three Trillion Dollar War* (New York: W. W. Norton, 2008). Also Manning Marable, "Economics of War: From King to Obama," Hudson Valley Press Online, http://www.hvpress.net/news/166/ARTICLE/6061/2008-12-24.html. Joel Berg, author of *All You Can Eat: How Hungry Is America?* says that three months of war spending could eradicate hunger in America. http://www.nydailynews.com/ny_local/2008/12/03/2008-12-03_us_must_invest_in_endi... OP Ed.
4. John M. Broder, "Views on Money for Iraq War, and What Else Could Be Done with It," http://www.nytimes.com/2008.04/14/us/politics/14warcost.html?_r=1&fta=y&page want...
5. Mona El-Naggar, "Jordan's Generation Faithful, in Their Own Words," *New York Times*, December 23, 2008. http://www.nytimes.com2008/12/23/world/middleest/24voices.htm.?_r=1&pagewanted...
6. See chapter 6.
7. Elliott P. Skinner, *African Americans and U.S. Policy toward Africa, 1850–1924* (Washington, D.C.: Howard University Press, 1992), 215–45.
8. Brenda Gayle Plummer, *Rising Wind: Black Americans and U.S. Foreign Affairs, 1935–1960* (Chapel Hill: University of North Carolina Press, 1986) , 10–11.
9. Ibid., 51–81.
10. Robin D. G. Kelly, *Race Rebels: Culture, Politics, and the Black Working Class* (New York: Free Press, 1996), 124.
11. Rupert Lewis, *Marcus Garvey: Anti-Colonial Champion* (London: Karia Press, 1987), 115.
12. Ibid., 167.
13. Tony N. Martin, *Race First: The Ideological and Organizational Struggles of Marcus Garvey and the Universal Negro Improvement Association* (Westport, Conn.: Greenwood Press, 1976), 177.
14. Ibid., 179.
15. Horace Dawson, Jr., "First African American Diplomat," *Foreign Service Journal* (January 1993): 42.
16. Frederick Douglass, "Life and Times," in *Autobiographies* (New York: Library of America, 1994), 1023.
17. Ibid., 1028.
18. Benjamin R. Justesen, "African-American Consuls Abroad, 1897–1909," *Foreign Service Journal* (September 2004): 72–76.
19. See James Weldon Johnson, *Along This Way: The Autobiography of James Weldon Johnson* (New York: Viking Penguin, 1961), 227–93.
20. Ibid., 293.
21. Immanuel Geiss, *The Pan African Movement* (New York: Africana Publishing, 1974), 217.

22. Shirley Graham Du Bois, *His Day Is Marching On: A Memoir of W. E. B. Du Bois* (New York: J. B. Lippincott, 1971), 109.

23. Ibid.

24. See Marc S. Gallicchio, *The African American Encounter with Japan and China: Black Internationalism in Asia, 1895–1945* (Chapel Hill: University of North Carolina Press, 2000).

25. Philip S. Foner, ed., *Paul Robeson Speaks: Writings, Speeches, Interviews, 1918–1974* (New York: Brunner/Mazel Publishers, 1978), 156.

26. Ibid., 240.

27. William Attwood, *The Reds and the Blacks: A Personal Adventure* (New York: Harper and Row, 1967), 188.

28. William Strickland and Cheryll Y. Greene, ed., *Malcolm X: Make It Plain* (New York: Viking Press, 1994), 156.

29. Orlando Bagwell, *Malcolm X: Make It Plain,* documentary film (1994).

30. George Breitman, ed., *Malcolm X Speaks* (New York: Grove Press, 1965), 62.

31. Ibid.

32. David Levering Lewis, *W. E. B. Du Bois: The Fight for Equality and the American Century, 1919–1963* (New York: Henry Holt, 2000), 529–34.

33. Peniel E. Joseph, *Waiting 'Til The Midnight Hour: A Narrative History of Black Power in America* (New York: Henry Holt, 2006), 285.

34. Lawyers Committee for Human Rights, *Liberia: A Promise Betrayed: A Report on Human Rights* (New York: Lawyers Committee for Human Rights, 1986), 11–25.

35. The writer was a board member of TransAfrica at this time.

36. The writer was senior staff member in Rep. Gray's office.

37. The writer was a delegate to the conference.

38. Issued by the State Department spokesman, State Department, Washington, D.C., September 3, 2001.

39. "Belafonte Slams Colin Powell as a Race Sellout," www.Reuters.com, October 14, 2002.

40. Thomas Borstelmann, *The Cold War and the Color Line: American Race Relations in the Global Arena* (Cambridge, Mass.: Harvard University Press, 2000).

41. "U.S. Follow-up Report on Implementation of ICCPR," paragraph 26, United States Responses to Selected Recommendations of the Human Rights Committee, U.S. Department of State, October 10, 2007, Washington, D.C. http://www.state.gov/s/I/2007/112673.htm.

42. Charles P. Henry,U.S. this volume, chap. 8.

43. "A More Representative Foreign Service," U.S. Diplomacy, Association for Diplomatic Advancement and Training. http://www.usdiplomacy.org/history/service/representative.php.

44. Ibid.

45. Remarks, "Dangerously Lacking in Diversity," Conference on Campus Progress, Washington, D.C., December 14, 2005. http://www.campusprogress.org/toos/691/dangerously-lacking-in-di.

46. Joseph, *Waiting 'Til The Midnight Hour,* 277–95.

47. Ronald Walters, *Pan Africanism in the African Diaspora* (Detroit: Wayne State University Press, 1993).

48. Ibid., 338.

49. Charles Green, ed., *Globalization and Survival in the Black Diaspora: The New Urban Challenge* (Albany: State University of New York Press, 1997).

50. There was agreement with this view, expressed by Assistant Secretary of State Frazer in a discussion sponsored by the Africa Unity Caucus on January 8, 2009. U.S. State Department, Washington, D.C.

51. Robert Smith, *We Have No Leaders: African Americans in the Post–Civil Rights Era* (Albany: SUNY Press, 1996), 139.

52. Remarks, Matt Byrza, "Invigorating the U.S.–Turkey Strategic Partnership," Turgot Ozal Memorial Lecture, Washington Institute for Near East Policy, Washington, D.C., June 24, 2008.

53. Daily press briefing, Sean McCormick, Department of State, Washington, D.C., November 17, 2008.

54. John Negroponte, Deputy Secretary of State, "Remarks at the Foreign Affairs Brain Trust on Africa," Congressional Black Caucus Legislative Conference, Washington, D.C., September 26, 2008.

55. Ibid.

PART I

African American Foreign Affairs Participation

NATURE AND DYNAMICS

ZZ	SINGLE Fr	S

Customer:
deborah young

American Politics and the African American Quest for Universal Freedom (6th Edition)

Hanes Walton, Robert C. Smith

W2-N060-95

O5-DQX-029

No CD

Used - Good

9780205079919

Picker Notes:
M _____ 2 _____
WT _____ 2 _____
CC _____

44285889

[Amazon] betterworldbooks_: 105-2003719-2617032

1 Item

1041390723

Friday Singles REG SHLV

Ship. Created: 5/12/2016 9:08:00 AM
Date Ordered: 5/12/2016 7:51:00 AM

TWO

Conceptualizing the Foreign Affairs Participation of African Americans

STRATEGIES AND EFFECTS OF
THE CONGRESSIONAL BLACK CAUCUS
AND TRANSAFRICA

Michael L. Clemons

The general exclusion of African Americans from the formal arena of foreign policymaking has historically been a prominent reflection of the significance of race in global politics. It was not until the end of World War II that government officials and those in pursuit of elected office finally took seriously the implications of the domestic race problem in the United States for foreign policymaking. Prior to that time, the lack of presence of people of color, especially those of African descent, was of little concern to a government that maintained diplomatic relations with countries responsible for the subjugation of the nonwhite peoples of the world (Lincoln, 1970; Isaacs, 1970).

Some social analysts and citizens have begun to question whether and how the recent emergence of African Americans and people of color on the institutional scene will affect the substance and direction of, and global response to, American foreign policymaking. Of course, black Americans, even before the opportunity for institutional roles, were involved in foreign affairs activity. Interestingly, the rise of African Americans to prominent institutional roles within the foreign policy establishment starkly contrasts with the muting of race, ethnicity, and culture as important analytical constructs in international and domestic politics, and consequently is sidelined in favor of a complementary multicultural perspective. In other words, multiculturalism's amorphous effect on perceptions of race, ethnicity, and culture has led to the minimization of these key variables in a way that

33

undercuts the objective of fully extending democracy to all racial and ethnic groups. Indeed, as generally articulated, multiculturalism as a concept obscures or even ignores racial and ethnic differentiation. Its usage and evolved meaning precludes objective measurement of social progress to alleviate racial and ethnic inequality, and therefore, imposes on the extension of democracy and social equity. Multiculturalism as a concept also potentially precludes the opportunity of the nation to parlay its tremendous ethnic diversity in the global arena to achieve desired foreign policy objectives and outcomes.

Despite the willingness of black people to engage the global arena on their own behalf as deprived citizens and on behalf of the United States as official representatives, there have frequently been points of tension and challenge with the formulation of foreign relations and policies. Indicative of individual and group connectedness in a global community, these tensions and challenges suggest the need for a more inclusive approach to foreign policymaking, one that is genuinely concerned with fairness, equity, and justice. Largely, the twentieth-century independence movements of African, Latin American, and Asian states were instrumental in prompting the need for inclusiveness in foreign policymaking. As countries in these areas of the world have enhanced their global economic importance, and in particular their economic salience in relation to the United States, policymakers have gradually begun to acknowledge the potential benefits associated with inclusiveness. The turn of the millennium brought with it the conclusion of the Cold War, and it simultaneously converged with the global democratization movement to initiate the alteration of the contours of global politics (Yaffe, 1994; Morris, 1992). Developments such as these, combined with a state's economic advancement in an era increasingly based on the application of soft power, heighten the need to ameliorate racial discord and incorporate people of color into the foreign policy process. These developments also lay bare the notion that the quality of domestic social relations partially affects a state's foreign relations, and they demand a conceptual framework of African American participation in foreign affairs that takes into account their unique background and experiences at the domestic level and globally.

This chapter presents a conceptual approach to African American participation in foreign affairs. We apply this approach to two of the premier sources of African American foreign affairs organizations—the Congressional Black Caucus (CBC) and TransAfrica Forum—with the aim of assessing their influence in foreign policymaking. Although models are inherently limited, they should depict reality with as much precision as possible. Lave and March (1975) suggested the following general guidelines for model building: (1) focus on process; (2) identify the implications of the model; and (3) find generality. Conceptual frameworks built on these criteria are likely to provide robust descriptive and explanatory power, and these qualities have been considered in the framework's design. The largely descriptive and atheoretical nature of scholarly research on black participation in U.S. foreign policymaking and foreign affairs suggests the profound importance of a conceptual approach that helps order, discover, and investigate the empirical dimensions of black global behavior. Increased interest in world affairs among African Americans, due partially to enhanced global communications networks, a calculated boldness on the part of black policymakers to include global affairs in their political agendas, and gains made by the subgroup in the executive and legislative branches underscore the need for such an approach. It is unequivocal that these developments portend better opportunities than ever before for black global participation and influence.

However, recent gains (including the posts of secretary of state and national security advisor) in institutional representation appear circumspect relative to embracing African American global views and interests. In fairness, a variety of factors and conditions likely help explain this situation. Still, recent developments in the institutional arena show that African Americans as a group remain on the periphery of foreign policy decision-making. More time and a concentrated effort are needed to challenge the forces that operate to sustain these dynamics.

Linking Race and Foreign Affairs

Isaacs (1970) astutely observed that the element of race "cannot be separately assigned or portioned out between our internal and external affairs . . . the role of the United States as a world power will be determined by the nature and quality of American society" (33). It is unfortunate, however, that U.S. foreign relations is perceived by many worldwide as tainted due to the persistence of racism and associated socioeconomic deprivation at the domestic level (Morris, 1972; Derryck, 1992). To the detriment of the United States and its image abroad, policymakers have not yet been able to alleviate inequities in income, infant mortality, incarceration, educational achievement, and home ownership, to name a few of the areas where inequities have been persistent along racial lines. Further, domestic racism, reinforced by the long and conspicuous absence of African Americans and other nonwhites from high-level positions in the U.S. foreign policy establishment, reified the pervasive view abroad of American hypocrisy, held by both Western and non-Western states. Consequently, to the disadvantage of the United States in the critical era of globalization, the development of authentic trust and partnerships between the United States and progressive nation-states has been stifled, if not prevented. As Brenda Gayle Plummer (2003) has explained, "Racism undermined U.S. global leadership and strained its relations with countries that had a stake in achieving global racial equality" (7). Hence, over time, because of the dominance of a homogeneous approach to foreign policymaking, the nation's capacity to challenge its adversaries and to strengthen its relations with allies has weakened.

Contemporary events illustrate the link between race and foreign policy. An example is the American public's reaction to Nelson Mandela's tour of the United States in June 1990. The outpouring of support and jubilation for Mandela's release from prison and his long commitment to the black freedom struggle in South Africa helped to propel him to that state's co-presidency. Another example is the Rodney King police brutality case that concluded with the acquittal of four white police officers and extensive conflict among blacks, whites, law enforcement officials, and the judicial system. Beyond mass media coverage, the international impact of this case also stemmed from charges made by Kenya, Zaire, and Malawi that the United States was hypocritical in its apparent stance on human rights and that the country had failed with respect to fully integrating people of African descent into the foreign policymaking process (Robinson, 1992).

Current Research

The literature on African Americans in foreign affairs is a small but relatively diverse body of material. It consists largely of qualitative research with limited studies of an empirical nature. Despite the strength of variation it reveals, the research literature glaringly reflects the dearth of attention paid by scholars in the disciplines of political science, international studies, and Africana studies to the formulation of a systematic approach that sheds light on the quality, nature, and effects of black global participation (Plummer and Culverson, 1987). However, the extant research does provide a logical source to unearth the essential analytic components needed for a conceptual lens that can potentially lead to a general theory of African American participation in foreign affairs and foreign policymaking. University of Michigan political scientist Hanes Walton, Jr. (1985), once noted that "few words by political behavioralists on international politics have ever included, in any fashion, black groups and individuals as forces and actors" (269). Although the state and quality of the body of knowledge is evolving gradually and the interest of African Americans in foreign affairs continues to grow, as a subgroup they essentially remain marginalized, such that their actual and potential role in foreign policymaking in reality is hindered. The situation is especially troubling, as contemporary qualitative societal changes, including the crystallization of identity politics in America, demand increased attention to the actions of individuals and the interest groups they represent in order to understand the nature of their foreign affairs participation and how this participation has affected foreign affairs and foreign policy outcomes.

The behavioral movement in international politics concentrates largely on the study of nation-states and the decisionmakers associated with them. A three-tiered analytic approach encompassing international political behavior at the system, state, and individual levels is the basis for much of this research (Holsti, 1988; Rourke, 1993). Specifically, the dilemma of the individual versus the nation-state as the appropriate level of analysis (Walton, 1985) and the concentration on the system level at the expense of the consideration of individuals are revealed in the literature (Yaffe, 1994). Holsti (1988) reasons, however, that "we can attempt to explain the behavior of states by reference not just to the external environment (the system), but primarily to the domestic conditions that affect policy" (14). Domestic conditions have been and continue to be salient to black global participation, and this is demonstrated by research analyzing the connection between domestic conditions and international behavior.

A few important studies have been conducted recently that focus on the relationship between domestic race relations and global conflict. Principally, the broad issue addressed in this work is whether domestic racial inequality influences the international behavior of nation-states. Although refuted by more recent studies (see Henderson and Tucker, 2001; and Tusicisny, 2004), Samuel Huntington's "Clash of Civilizations?" in which he posits that global conflicts in the post–Cold War era will increasingly stem from cultural divisions (ethnic and religious) among humankind rather than from ideological and economic sources, has helped prompt this emerging body of research. For example, Caprioli and Trumbore (2003) demonstrate that the level of racial (ethnic) discrimination in a country has two important effects: it increases the chances that a state will be the first to respond in an international conflict with violence, and that violence will be intensely applied in an international conflict. Building on this research, Knoll (2008) investigated the link between domestic racial inequality and international violence and found that "domestic levels of political discrimination begin to exert a belligerent international effect only as the size of the minority population on the receiving end of that discrimination increases as well" (11).

While the power to shape foreign policy is vested in positions of formal authority, individual citizens can play significant roles (Rosenau, 1990; Rourke, 1993; Stanford, 1995). "Citizen diplomacy" is an example of an individual-level approach to participation in global politics. This approach involves the advancement of "diplomatic efforts of private citizens in the international arena for the purposes of achieving a specific objective or accomplishing constituency goals" (Stanford, 1995, 19). Moreover, interest or pressure groups have the *potential* to influence foreign policymaking. However, since they do not exercise any formal authority in the policy formation process, their impact is highly circumscribed unless they can convince key government officials and the public (at home and abroad) of the appropriateness of their policy viewpoints. In the effort to achieve constituent goals, interest groups mobilize moral criticism and present timely and significant information to Congress and the public (Cohen, 1959). However, the difficulty of understanding interest group participation is compounded by the fact that it is extremely difficult to demonstrate that such groups "have an overriding interest in an issue apart from that of the nation as a whole" (Jensen, 1982, 137–38).

Several factors help to account for how interest groups are situated in the foreign policymaking process: behavioral attributes; organizational characteristics; the structure of the decisionmaking system; relationships among interest groups and other actors in the international political environment; and the policy issue (Trice, 1976). The internal characteristics of interest groups, including membership, interests served, age, budget, formal structure, and leadership play a vital role in their overall effectiveness (Key, 1961; Truman, 1971; Cohen, 1957, 1959).

A number of key variables affect interest group influence, including constituency goals, the timing of group actions, and the strategies and techniques employed. Authoritative governmental decisions resulting from "compromise, coalition, competition, and confusion among government officials" and others, including interest groups, illuminate the relevance of these variables (Allison, 1999, 439). However, interest group pressure does not necessarily yield influence (Bard, 1988). Analytically speaking, there is the inherent problem of showing that an interest group's actions lead to policy outcomes.

Technological innovations in computers, satellite communications, and transportation have had the unanticipated effect of increasing a sense of collectivism and promoting transnationalism among international racial and cultural groups. There is no doubt that technology and the abridgment of the barriers of time and distance have fostered a heightened awareness of global interdependence. More than two decades ago, one scholar acknowledged that the world is now in an "age of international politics of ethnicity," marked by the decline of distance as an impediment to national and transnational cultural groups (Said, 1977). In this context, nation-states potentially concede to technological innovation as the principal arbiter for the expression of group interests in the global arena.

However, it seems that scholars have yet to heed Said's warning about the need for greater treatment and application of the "ethnic operatives" of international politics. This pattern in the research literature runs against the grain of tradition in a field that emphasizes the categorization of various kinds of operatives. For example, Gabriel Almond (1962) identifies four categories of foreign policy influencers: political elites, bureaucratic elites, communication elites, and interest elites. Similarly, Miller (1983) classifies participants as political and bureaucratic elites that include the incumbents of various diplomatic posts and members of the diplomatic corps, U.N. representatives, high-ranking military personnel, and state department personnel. Walton (2008) partitions black foreign policy participation into two groups: managers and influencers. Like managers, influencers from within the black community have traditionally been interest elites, but without the legitimacy accorded by holding an official position.

With respect to race-based and ethnic-based interest elites, at least two factors contribute to their success. First, regardless of veracity, convincing the establishment that they represent a large segment of the respective group is important to their success. The perception that a leader represents the bulk of a given subgroup can influence the seriousness with which citizens, policymakers, adversaries, and friends recognize them as players in the process. In addition, the extent to which an organization and its leadership are regarded as "issue experts" is important in assessing potential impact on foreign affairs and policymaking (Miller, 1983). As issue experts, the interest elite is in a position allowing them both access and potential soft-power influence in policymaking.

According to Skinner (1992), African American international strategy manifests itself through both formal and symbolic structures. Formal or institutional-based structures include the government and government-related foreign policy posts to which African Americans are elected or appointed. The Du Boisian notion of dualism has led some analysts to point out that a "double consciousness" potentially shapes and affects the group's efforts in foreign affairs. This may have important implications for how formal structures operate. For example, the notion of double consciousness implies the ability to see matters from the vantage point of the domestic majority as well as that of foreigners (Skinner, 1992). Applying similar logic, Walters (1981) concludes that the disadvantaged position of black Americans as a group in comparison to whites cultivated a Third World orientation toward international politics. While dualism can afford enhanced objectivity and sensitivity in the analysis of global problems and the development of solutions to these problems, it has yet to affect tactically the conduct of U.S. foreign policy.

In contrast to formal structures, symbolic structures, according Skinner (1992), include educational, emigrationist, religious, and other social functions. The organization of the international Pan-African conference and congresses, and movements focused on transcendent issues of concern to people of African descent, are poignant examples of symbolic structures. Interest group mobilization at the international level benefits from symbolic structures since these can facilitate international propaganda and consequently affect interstate relations. In this way, symbolic structures can exert a substantive impact (Skinner, 1992).

In summary, although the scholarly literature on black participation in foreign affairs lacks the cohesion afforded by a unified approach or theory, some of the pertinent conceptual parameters are already elaborated. In the following section, I draw from the extant literature to construct a conceptual approach to African American participation in foreign affairs and foreign policymaking.

Configuring African American Foreign Affairs Participation

The conceptual framework seeks to provide a comprehensive, issue-centered approach to understanding the motivations, purposes, nature, function, and results of African American foreign affairs and foreign policy participation. Predicated on research and theory generated in the fields of foreign policy, international relations, and African American politics, the need for an inclusive conceptual approach to African American global participation cannot be overstated. According to Mack H. Jones (1971), "comprehensiveness is especially important when one wishes to study the politics of a people who are either on the periphery or outside the formal political structures, because traditional or more formalistic schemes of analysis—usually in-group oriented—may leave out much that is important" (10). The utility of the framework is in its capacity to identify important concepts and questions leading to the generation of data to support descriptions and explanations about the nature of participation. J. K. Holsti (1988) observed that "only when facts and events are fitted against some framework of concepts can they be seen essentially as illustrations of general and recurring processes in international politics" (12).

QUESTIONS AND ASSUMPTIONS

African American participation in foreign affairs functions as a dependent variable influenced by several factors, including issues, the domestic environment, and the global climate. These elements combine with the effects of race, ethnicity, and culture to yield appropriate opportunities for participation. At the same time, African American participation operates as an independent variable in relation to U.S. foreign policymaking and foreign affairs more generally. The effects of such participation, however, are uneven depending upon the conditioning of that participation, the issues, domestic environment, and the global climate, and how these variables combine with each other. An underlying assumption is that the particularity of the experience of African Americans—contrary to pluralism and other major theories widely employed by social science researchers—is fundamental in determining the quality, nature, and results of participation. Also taken into account is that the pursuit of black interests has frequently been accompanied by unique domestic and international political and social circumstances that affect the overall configuration and possibly the results of participation.

It is my contention that a framework can be constructed based on existing research and theory, and that black participation and influence can be viewed within the broader evolving context of American politics. Figure 2.1 depicts the configuration of African American participation in foreign affairs. The domestic environment, global climate, and the issues shape African American foreign policy participation and influence capacity in foreign affairs. These factors are conditioned by the interplay with societal racial, ethnic, and cultural factors. Participation is affected by the synthesis and separate interaction of the domestic environment, global climate, and issues. Hence, strong and variable patterns are revealed in the foreign affairs participation of people of African descent in the United States, as illustrated by their involvement in both the institutional or formal arena *and* the noninstitutional or informal dimension.

FIGURE 2.1

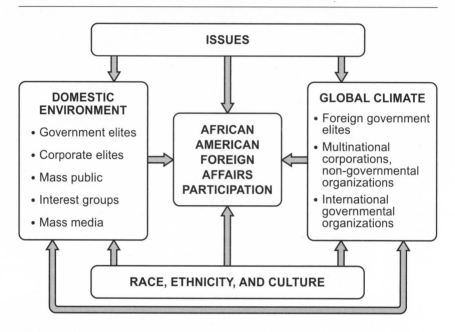

Race, Ethnicity, and Culture

The exclusion of people of African descent from the American political process historically has been a prerequisite for white domination in the domestic sphere and in the foreign affairs domain. Access to the foreign policymaking arena, of course, has varied from group to group and not been guaranteed; indeed, some groups have had more access than others (Ray, 1990; Bard, 1988). These results help to distinguish the case of African Americans, who were once subject to the conditions of slavery and second-class citizenship based on skin color. In the contemporary period, the effects of these conditions have lingered and are apparent in the socio-economic differences between blacks and whites that structure individual and group capacity to engage the political process.

Issues

The application of race, ethnicity, and culture as a basis for domination and exploitation has given rise to a complex approach geared toward influencing American foreign affairs and policies on an *issue basis*. The approach can be described as *issue-centered* since its analytic point of departure is a relevant foreign affairs issue or set of issues identified by African Americans and their leaders. Action motivated to influence policy is directed in light of issues (see figure 2.1) and it further takes into account a process "based on configurations—political, institutional, bureaucratic, etc.—that change with overall shifts in relations in society" (Plummer, 1989, 67).

Domestic Environment

While the decline of bipolarity did not necessarily signal the demise of realism as the predominant paradigm in international relations, the need to refocus attention on nonsystemic factors is at least more pronounced in the post–Cold War period (Yaffe, 1994). One nonsystemic factor is *Innenpolitik*, or the domestic environment (Zakaria, 1992). This dimension is central to a broad theory of African American participation in foreign affairs. The domestic environment interacts with the global climate and the issues to exert an important influence on the configuration of global African American participation. Issues can affect the behavior of principal actors as well as that of the interest group.

The political, social, and economic conditions prevalent at a given point in time characterize the domestic environment. Principal actors in the domestic environment include government elites, corporate elites, mass media, interest groups, and the mass public (Trice, 1976). The effect of the domestic environment on black participation in foreign affairs can be labeled supportive, neutral, or nonsupportive. Characterized largely by the behavior of the principal actors, the domestic environment is supportive when positions and actions that publicly endorse or uphold a given policy stance are articulated. A neutral or nonsupportive domestic environment occurs when these entities are unable or unwilling to publicly take action to uphold a policy position, or when they decide to take positions and actions publicly that are contrary to those of the interest group. Hence, the domestic environment has frequently been significant in bringing about differential material results among citizens. With respect to interest group activity, differential results have frequently been derived from the domestic environment for African Americans and non–African American interest groups and elites. The discrepancy reiterates Jones's (1971) suggestion that a conceptual framework focused on African Americans "should begin by searching for those factors which are unique to the black political experience, for this is the information which will facilitate our understanding of blacks in the American political system" (8). At the issue level, race frequently emerges to help govern system response and black interest group interaction with the domestic environment in the pursuit of defined foreign policy objectives.

The domestic environment partially conditions the pursuit of African American foreign policy initiatives. An extreme case in point is the transatlantic slave trade that marked the initial injection of race into American foreign policy (Walton, 1985). The legally mandated subordinate social position of slaves and freed men and women generally prevented their political participation. During the eras of slavery and Jim Crow, patterns of white power and nonwhite powerlessness characterized social relations between blacks and whites nationwide, and the pattern was even starker among southern states of the Old Confederacy.

In the contemporary era, an increasing number of blacks have emerged as important actors in the foreign policymaking realm, including Condoleezza Rice, Colin Powell, Jesse Jackson, and Randall Robinson. While the channel of participation principally utilized may be an indicator of the nature of the policies pursued, there can be and have been instances (such as the anti-apartheid movement) where black formal and informal participation operated in tandem to alter U.S. foreign policy. Regardless of the convergence of objectives, it is clear that the mode or channel of participation has important implications for the strategies and tactics employed for foreign policy objectives. When there is convergence of objectives, the obvious result is a broader and more systematic means to influence the process.

Global Climate

The global climate, which takes into account the major global issues of the day, is another important determinant of African American participation. Three basic categories of global actors tend to dominate the disposition of the global climate: (1) foreign government elites; (2) multinational nongovernmental actors; and (3) international governmental organizations (IGOs) (Trice, 1976). Issues and events that attract worldwide attention and command the involvement of the United States and the United Nations can influence the global climate and consequently the behavior of global actors. Prevailing political, social, and economic conditions also substantially shape the global climate, and can have an enormous effect on the quality, nature, and influence of black global participation. In the same way that the effect of the domestic environment on black participation in foreign affairs can be characterized as supportive, neutral, or nonsupportive, we can gauge the effect of the global climate on participation by the degree to which it is supportive of identified policy objectives. The effect of the global climate on black participation in foreign affairs can be characterized as supportive, neutral, or nonsupportive. Foreign government elites, multinational nongovernmental actors, and IGOS facilitate a supportive global climate when they take positions and actions publicly that endorse or uphold a given policy stance. A neutral or nonsupportive global climate prevails when global entities are unable or unwilling to publicly take action to uphold a policy position, or when they decide to take positions and actions publicly that are contrary to those of the interest group. Hence, the global climate, similar to the domestic environment, has frequently been significant in bringing about differential material results among nation-states and their citizens. For example, nonwhite nation-states are typically impoverished and are more likely to experience political and economic instability associated with the legacies of colonialism and imperialism. Dichotomies of inequity such as this have reified the global theme of the "haves versus the have-nots," and have sensitized the world to the effects of race, culture, and ethnicity on global material outcomes and perceptions of issues relative to the national interests.

African American participation in foreign affairs can be broadly conceptualized in terms of the formal and informal channels through which interest group foreign policy initiatives are advanced. Participation consists of the roles assumed and the actions taken by individuals and groups because of these roles to achieve specified policy results. (See figure 2.2.) Race, ethnicity, and culture at the domestic and global levels can exert considerable influence on the configuration, dynamics, and results of foreign affairs participation.

The formal participation channel includes official posts within the foreign policy establishment geared toward formulating, executing, and enforcing U.S. foreign policy. Allison (1994) noted that "positions define what players may and must do" (145). Key positions and categories include the presidency; the secretaries of state, defense, and treasury; joint chiefs of staff chairman; national security advisor; the intelligence community; and bureaucratic positions, such as state department career officers and U.S. Foreign Service officers. (See figure 2.2.) In 1960 there were only 30 black state department career officers; by 1990 the number had grown to almost 280 (Robinson, 1992). Barack Obama's ascendancy to the U.S. presidency, while both substantive and symbolic, reflects the continuing and evolving nature of black participation in foreign affairs and foreign policymaking.

Informal participation includes activities performed beyond, but not necessarily independent of, the formal institutional framework. Leaders of

FIGURE 2.2

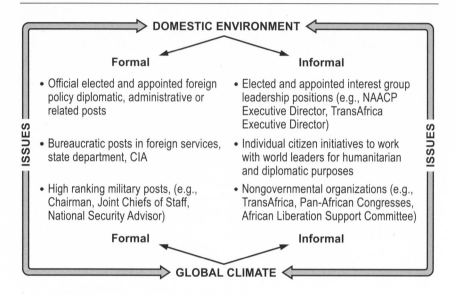

interest groups and nongovernmental organizations, as well as individual citizens, carry out externally channeled activities to influence official policy outcomes. (See figure 2.2.) Over time, social and political conditions have fostered informal participation as the predominant strategy, thus suggesting a greater likelihood that the foreign policy goals of interest groups would be divergent from those of the foreign policy establishment.

In contrast to formal participation, the informal participation channel lends itself to greater functional flexibility and fewer constraints. Andrew Young's resignation in 1979 from the post of U.N. representative following a meeting he had with the U.N. representative of the Palestinian Liberation Organization (PLO) provides an insightful example. Young's actions as an institutional actor were clearly inconsistent with the prevailing policy of the Carter administration. Although Young was not the first administration official to dialogue with PLO representatives, he became the administration's "fall guy" as it attempted to shore up Carter's political support in the Jewish community (Rubenstein, 1982, 98–99; DeRoche, 2003). Although in his memoirs Carter insisted that Young's resignation was due to his equivocation about the meeting (DeRoche, 2003, 114), still it was Young's deviation from official policy that provided the rationale for his forced resignation. Interestingly, the Southern Christian Leadership Conference (SCLC) and People United to Save Humanity (PUSH) subsequently carried out a number of missions in the Middle East that for a short time obviated the dialectic of black America's support for Israel and its support for the Palestinian cause (Walters, 1981). Indeed, the publicity and political fallout surrounding the Young affair might have sparked the apparent increase in interest group activity. This is significant because unlike their formal counterparts, informal actors do not necessarily seek to avoid confrontation with the foreign policy establishment. Formal actors are more likely than informal ones to seek to avoid conflict with the foreign policy establishment, and when they do choose to operate from a position of deviance, it can have a penetrating effect on the public tenor of foreign policymaking and implementation.

Strategies and Tactics

The effective pursuit of foreign affairs objectives by an interest group necessitates careful application of strategies and tactics, which vary with the channel of participation. For example, informal actors are more likely than formal actors to use direct action strategies and tactics. As seen in figure 2.3, the strategies and tactics of informal participation include citizen diplomacy (Stanford, 1995) and the application of direct action, including marches, demonstrations, and protests. The Pan-African Congresses, African Liberation Day marches and rallies, and other international assemblies hastened the decline of colonialism, imperialism, and the South African apartheid regime by applying such tactics and strategies. TransAfrica, Inc., routinely organized and promoted demonstrations and marches at the South African embassy to influence foreign policy and the decisions of policymakers abroad to apply pressure through divestiture and other means. To a degree, however, the ability to influence foreign affairs is a function of the size of the constituency that interest group leaders are perceived to represent (Miller, 1983). Expressed mission and relative interest group "importance" as perceived by the foreign policy establishment are key criteria for assessing the potential significance of a group's global affairs activity (Trice, 1976).

In this context, perceptions are crucial. Perceptions at the global level, influenced partially by the issue in question, also affect *whether* African Americans participate and *how*. For example, global and domestic perceptions unsympathetic to a group's interests enhance the likelihood that such interests will not be pursued *beyond* the informal channel. In contrast, formal participation strategies may be employed when an issue has acquired international attention and consensus among foreign government elites, multinational nongovernmental actors, and IGOs. Interestingly, the application of informal strategies and tactics was a prerequisite to the generation of broad mainstream support against South African apartheid. That nonwhites in the foreign policy field typically accept the president's consideration of the political orientation of the potential envoy and the host state helps illustrate the problem of global and domestic perceptions in the pursuit of foreign policy objectives (Skinner, 1992).

Black participation in foreign affairs and foreign policymaking entails the utilization of informal mechanisms to conduct relations with foreign leaders and nations to gain influential public support at the domestic and global levels. Such approaches can lead to the establishment of official policy although the lack of a balanced approach (utilizing formal and informal channels) might suggest the group's marginalization within the formal process and simultaneously the aversion of black Americans to prevailing policy.

The strategies and tactics employed by formal participants to achieve "national" goals and objectives include the full range of options derived from formal authority associated with the position. Generally, formal participants seek to maximize support for their foreign policy objectives by exercising four options: persuasion, bargaining, compromise, and coercion (Art and Jervis, 1992). The exercise of one option over the other has important implications for the specific strategies and tactics used to influence policy outcomes. Depending upon the integration of formal actors within the foreign policy establishment, strategies can range from diplomacy to appropriately measured state-sponsored military action.

Coalitions and alliances are potentially another important strategy for both formally and informally based foreign affairs participation. Potential coalition partners can be found at the domestic and global levels. They may be established among governmental leaders, the leaders of interest groups, and multinational nongovernmental organizations (such as international labor organizations and corporations). A coalition-based strategy that "would not be the purblind allegiances of the past, but calculated, if sometimes transient, alliances built around concrete goals" (Plummer 1989, 79) may well prove to be a cornerstone of African American global politics.

Policy Orientation

The strategies and tactics employed by African Americans in foreign affairs correspond with the policy orientation of the interest group actors in question. This view assumes that the African American community consists of a range of heterogeneous groups rather than being a single homogeneous

FIGURE 2.3

POLICY ORIENTATION CHARACTERISTICS

Formal	Informal
• Consistent with national policy	• Conflicts frequently with national policy
• Amenable to compromise within the existing framework	• Emphasizes greater inclusion of groups/ideas
• Geared toward incremental change	• Geared toward incremental or radical change

CORRESPONDING STRATEGIES AND TACTICS

Formal	Informal
• Pursuit of national political office and application of power	• Direct action, e.g., protest politics, marches, demonstrations, conventions
• Lobbying foreign policy official	• Citizen diplomacy
• Direct contact abroad	• Direct contact abroad
• Media utilization and propaganda	• Media utilization and propaganda
• Join coalitions	• Join coalitions

group. Two broad policy orientations flow from the channels of participation (see figure 2.3). First, individuals and organizations that operate within the formal realm tend to pursue foreign affairs goals consistent with national policy. These agencies are cognizant of the institutional and structural limitations circumscribing their role. The pattern of goal-directed activity they exhibit is indicative of a policy orientation that is open to compromise in the conduct of foreign affairs and foreign policymaking. There is acceptance of the notion that policy formation evolves in concert with the predominant mainstream view and that change will occur in an incremental fashion. Furthermore, the pattern of goal-directed activity of informal actors is indicative of the policy orientation of interest groups. In contrast to formal actors, informal actors are more likely to pursue goals that conflict with mainstream foreign affairs objectives. They value democracy and consequently, place a premium on an inclusive foreign policymaking process. The policy option interests of informal actors can range in nature from incremental to revolutionary.

Below we examine the global engagement of two premier contemporary agencies of black global participation: TransAfrica, Inc., an informal or noninstitutional mechanism for participation that emerged in the 1980s, and Congressional Black Caucus (CBC), one of the formal or institutional foreign affairs mechanisms through which African Americans have participated since 1971. Utilizing the conceptual approach already outlined, we first analyze and discuss the factors affecting foreign affairs participation on selected foreign affairs issues. This is followed by a general assessment of the influence of black participation on the foreign policy.

TransAfrica Forum: Informal Channel of Participation

Randall Robinson, the first president of TransAfrica Forum, founded the organization in 1981 to address issues present throughout the African Diaspora. The organization emerged in response to the continuing social, economic, and political struggles of people of African descent worldwide. TransAfrica seeks to improve democracy, human rights, and economic development through advocacy of U.S. policies pertaining primarily to Africa and the Caribbean. Self-described as a black global justice organization TransAfrica Forum partnered with the now defunct TransAfrica, Inc., which widely promoted itself as the "African American Lobby for Africa and the Caribbean." The slogan of the Forum, derived from the Fifth Pan-African Congress, is "We believe the success of Afro-Americans is bound up with the emancipation of all African peoples and also other dependent peoples and laboring classes everywhere."

Outlined in TransAfrica Forum's statement of mission are four main principles. First, that there is an important historic link among African Americans and African peoples on the continent of Africa and throughout the Diaspora. Second, that African Americans should not be concerned with Africans only, but rather with all of the oppressed peoples in the world. Third, that there is a social and economic divide in the United States and in the world. Fourth, that the Forum should participate in shaping U.S. foreign policy and public opinion through activism, scholarly research, and awareness.

Effects of the Domestic Environment and Global Climate

TransAfrica's establishment in 1981 coincided with the resurgence of conservative ideology in the United States under the leadership of Ronald Reagan, a development indicative of the general tenor of the domestic environment. Over time, domestic government elites, corporate elites, mass media, interest groups, and the mass public combined to contribute to a supportive global climate by taking positions and actions that publicly endorsed TransAfrica's policy positions. A supportive domestic environment has been an essential component of TransAfrica's influence capacity in foreign affairs.

Along with the domestic environment, the global climate helped to propel the participation of TransAfrica in foreign affairs. The 1980s witnessed the continuation of the protracted struggle to eradicate the vestiges of colonialism and European domination. Victorious political movements in Angola and Mozambique were among the culminating events in this regard, and they generated much optimism about the future of the continent of Africa.

TransAfrica Forum has had an important influence in Africa and throughout the African Diaspora. Research, activism, and education have been the main strategies implemented by TransAfrica Forum to achieve the goal of improving economic, political, and social conditions in Africa and the Caribbean. These strategies encompass both informal and institutional interest group politics. TransAfrica's tactics have involved protests, boycotts, sit-ins, and picketing, as well as coalition building and formal styles of political influence. South Africa, Haiti, and Rhodesia are among the countries that benefited from TransAfrica's avid support for the people of the African Diaspora.

The organization's use of conventional lobbying is exemplified by its attempt in the 1990s to help broker a new democratic government for Nigeria. While TransAfrica's president made use of conventional policy-influencing methods, many African American leaders were incensed with the ongoing policy and politics of Nigeria. Robinson successfully arranged meetings with two influential Nigerians in Washington, D.C. During the meetings, they discussed ways to replace Nigeria's military-controlled government with a democratic government. Robinson achieved excellent rapport with one individual at the meetings. This particular person, when alone with Robinson, offered Robinson up to $1 million dollars. Initially Robinson agreed, acknowledging that TransAfrica Forum was actually in dire need of money. In the end, however, the funds came at a huge cost for Robinson. Funds were to come directly from the Nigerian government in exchange for Robinson's silence on Nigeria.

When Robinson initiated conventional and fair diplomacy to bring about change in Nigeria, he experienced backlash (Robinson, 1998, 225–26). Not only was he offered a bribe from a Nigerian whom he had once believed was on his side, the Nigerian government attacked Robinson and

TransAfrica through the American media. Over one hundred "demonstrators" protested outside Robinson's apartment in 1995. It was determined later that the demonstrators were actually paid mercenaries who earned $300 daily for participating in such protests. Similar protests had occurred outside the headquarters of TransAfrica, but never outside Robinson's home. The media heavily covered the demonstration at Robinson's residence. Newspaper reports made malicious and slanderous attacks on Robinson and the TransAfrica Forum. The newspaper articles were signed by poor organizations in Nigeria that clearly could not have funded these articles alone. In the end, the Nigerian government fell short of stifling the debate about Nigerian democratization. Officials calculated, therefore, that the next best option would be to attack Robinson by paying protesters, small Nigerian companies, and the U.S. media (Robinson, 1998, 231–32).

Bringing Down South African Apartheid

Although lobbying has been a cornerstone strategy, TransAfrica Forum has employed other nontraditional approaches. Using the methods of protest politics employed in the civil rights movement in the United States, TransAfrica Forum played a key role in shutting down the South African apartheid system. As illustrated below, the case of South Africa demonstrates the cooperative participation of black institutional and noninstitutional actors to achieve the eradication of apartheid. Both timing and issue potency helped to propel this dual-channel participation strategy.

BOYCOTTS AND SIT-INS

On November 21, 1984, Robinson staged a sit-in at the office of South African Ambassador Bernardus G. Fourie. The sit-in took place on an impromptu basis, as the initial plan was for a meeting between the ambassador and several anti-apartheid advocates, including Robinson, Eleanor Holmes Norton, and Walter Fauntroy. TransAfrica Forum's organization of protesters outside the embassy to augment the meeting created mass media frenzy. Eleanor Holmes Norton even went as far as addressing the press, while Robinson and Fauntroy remained in the ambassador's office. She revealed the demands of TransAfrica concerning South Africa and stated that her colleagues would not leave the office of the ambassador until their demands were met. Robinson presented the demands behind closed doors to Ambassador Fourie, while Holmes Norton addressed the public (Robinson, 1998, 151–52).

TransAfrica's demands comprised two elements, both of which concerned South Africa's apartheid government. The first demand was that all of South Africa's political prisoners be freed. Nelson Mandela, Govan Mbeki, and Walter Sisulu were among the most recognizable names of the prisoners. The second demand was that apartheid be immediately abolished. TransAfrica understood the complexity of its job and that it would not be a simple task to rid South Africa of apartheid. A segment of the demands even included a timetable for ending apartheid. Ambassador Fourie rejected these demands, and it was not long before he demanded that Robinson and Fauntroy leave his office. They refused and were arrested. The initial meeting, demands, protests, and arrests were all broadcast nationally and internationally by the media (Robinson, 1998, 154–55).

The dramatic protest outside the embassy provided the "fuel to the fire" that eventually led to congressional legislation discouraging apartheid in South Africa. TransAfrica Forum created furor in the national and international community through protests that served essentially to educate the public about apartheid and to apply political pressure on lawmakers to make change. The actions of TransAfrica eventually led to the creation of the Comprehensive Anti-Apartheid Act of 1986. This legislation passed both houses of Congress but fell to veto by President Reagan. The act overcame two presidential vetoes and became law in 1986 (Robinson, 1998, 160–62).

Seeking Justice for Haitian Political Refugees

The Haitian refugee dilemma is another issue of protracted concern to Americans of African descent, and like the case of South Africa, it illustrates how and why African Americans participate in foreign affairs and demonstrates the possible outcome of participation. In 1994, Randall Robinson initiated a hunger strike to protest U.S. policy toward Haiti. Many Haitians were fleeing from the military (FRAPH), which took over the country and victimized thousands of civilians. Haitians had one of two choices in order to escape from the FRAPH. They could hide within the interior of the country or they could flee the country by water. Haitians who endured and made it to the U.S. coast were returned to Haiti, in accordance with policy. This policy enraged many African Americans, especially Randall Robinson, to the point where he began a hunger strike.

Robinson initiated the strike with the intention of creating immediate political change. Members of the CBC who supported him through civil disobedience complemented his informal participation. Every Friday night, a candlelight vigil was scheduled. Robinson received much attention from the media, yet the publicity generated by his actions needed to reach the government in order to bring about a change in policy. On April 30, 1994, Robinson received a letter from Morton Halperin requesting a visit. Halperin was a specialist who assisted President Clinton on issues of national security. As Robinson worked with the executive branch of the government, the CBC fought vigorously in Congress. Ronald Dellums introduced a comprehensive bill on Haitian refugees known as the Dellums Bill. The "Dellums bill was the 'centerpiece' of a 'new and decisive offensive' for Haitian democracy launched by the CBC's Task Force on Haiti" (Opitz, 1999, 258).

Generating an outbreak of media attention, Robinson was rushed to the hospital on the twenty-fourth day of the hunger strike. The following day, a very ill Robinson was featured in *USA Today* (Robinson, 1998, 206). Two days after Robinson was admitted to the hospital, President Clinton ended the automatic repatriation of Haitians. Tactically, the hunger strike was an extreme form of protest that apparently was influential for TransAfrica and the Haitian people (McCarthy, 1994, 10).

BUILDING TRANSNATIONAL COALITIONS

An important thrust of TransAfrica has been the formation of transnational coalitions among the peoples of the African Diaspora. Its 2004 annual report highlighted Haiti, Afro-Latino solidarity, and Pan-African institution building as major programmatic focus areas. In addition to fighting for the rights of Haitian refugees, TransAfrica seeks to build solidarity between black and brown people internationally, and to help establish organizations to enhance development and progress in Africa. Further evidence of TransAfrica's efforts in this regard is revealed by the establishment of the "One Standard Coalition" initiative that endeavored to build the base of support among other activists for Haiti. Based in Washington, D.C., the coalition included activists from many organizations and major U.S. cities. The group actively engaged the media, constituents' organizations, and lawmakers on the main issues concerning Haitian refugees. One Standard Coalition ably advanced a campaign with several main goals explicitly concerning the fair treatment of Haitian refugees. Chief among these goals was the safe and legal treatment of Haitian refugees according to the DHS Security Detention Standards. A second goal was that Haitians be treated fairly when it comes to acquiring a lawyer and receiving assistance to fill out all the legal paperwork necessary for asylum. In addition, the coalition sought to overturn the policy forbidding Haitian refugees release with bond. Because the coalition worked so vigorously to help Haitian refugees it encountered resistance from the Bush administration.

In 2004 TransAfrica sought to build "Afro-Latino solidarity" while partners with Venezuela. In that year, a delegation from the TransAfrica Forum traveled to Venezuela to broaden communication and deepen the Afro-Venezuelan partnership. The actual visit encompassed three main goals. The first was to make Martin Luther King's birthday an international celebration. The second goal was to discuss racism in Latin America with the government and Afro-Venezuelan representatives. Finally, the delegation wanted to gain more insight about the Hugo Chavez movement in Bolivia. Overall, the trip was productive in terms of education and dialogue, notwithstanding the anti-Chavez attacks from some of the Venezuelan media.

Institution building in Africa has been a dominant issue on the agenda of the TransAfrica Forum, especially concerning education and trade. In 2004, the Southern Africa Trade Union Leadership Academy (SATULA) was established with assistance from the American Center for International Labor Solidarity and the Southern African Trade Union Coordinating Committee. The purpose of SATULA was to enable countries in Southern Africa to organize and promote their own educational programs. It sought to integrate the educational curriculum and economic system across country borders. TransAfrica Forum member Harry Belafonte engaged the African Union (AU) to discuss specific ways that the Western Hemisphere could help Africa. His efforts helped open the lines of communication between TransAfrica and the AU to focus on ways to generate economic and trade benefits for Africa.

In summary, TransAfrica was formed to aid the African Diaspora, and this continues to be the organization's major concern. TransAfrica has employed a variety of techniques to alert the public about issues within the Africa Diaspora in an attempt to affect foreign policy decisionmaking. These techniques have proven helpful because they heighten awareness and issue saliency, inform the public, and encourage legislative action. Perhaps more important, the success of TransAfrica Forum in influencing legislation concerning South Africa, Nigeria, and Haiti over the past thirty years can be accounted for by the organization's skillful application of direct-action strategies and tactics. In addition, a complementary domestic environment and a facilitative global climate strengthened TransAfrica's capacity for influencing foreign policy. Still, more than a decade after the dramatic hunger strike of Randall Robinson, the fair and legitimate treatment of Haitian refugees remains a huge concern. Political, economic, and social problems on the African continent also abound. TransAfrica's experiences and the persistence of the problems outlined here clearly suggest the necessity of trade policies that seek to eliminate the great dependency of much of Africa on the developed world. This is necessary for the continent's fate and the economic vitality of people of African descent worldwide.

Congressional Black Caucus: A Formal Participation Mechanism

Established in 1971 initially as the Democratic Select Committee, the Congressional Black Caucus (CBC) was formed by thirteen initial members as a separate entity from the U.S. Congress to represent African American constituents. Consisting of elected representatives to the national legislature, the CBC reflects the formal channel of black participation in foreign affairs and foreign policy. The organization battles for justice and equality for African Americans in the United States and abroad. Achieving equality and justice for the African Diaspora is a top concern of the CBC. Human and civil rights issues at the domestic and global levels are its focus (Hammond, Mulhollan, and Stevens, 1999, 583).

As a separate entity that operates as a "caucus" in the national legislature, the CBC functions outside of the rules of Congress. Although it is not under the formal jurisdiction of Congress, the Caucus has as its main goal to influence U.S. legislation. To this end, the CBC seeks a unified position by functioning as a voting bloc. Historically, the CBC has voted uniformly on roll-call issues. It has proven to have strong voting cohesiveness in most issue areas (Pinney and Serra, 1999, 602).

Since its members are elected government officials, the CBC can introduce and pass legislation with members and allies in the House in specific leadership positions and with large numbers. When the CBC was formed, many of the founding members, all of whom were Democrats, lacked both seniority and power. Charles Diggs, the first chair of the CBC, chaired the House Subcommittee on Africa. The Caucus relied on him to deal with legislation concerning Africa. In the late 1970s, the domestic environment continued to change favorably, and increasing numbers of African Americans were elected to Congress. This development strengthened the Caucus's hand, allowing it to push for favorable legislation concerning Africa. For example, in 1989 William H. Gray, a member of the CBC, assumed the post of majority whip. By 1991, CBC membership had doubled from thirteen to twenty-six members, providing the critical mass to enhance its influence in Congress. Given that CBC members are also members of the Democratic party, their ability to attain leadership positions in the House of Representatives is greatly constrained by whether the Democrats hold the majority in both houses of Congress (Schraeder, 1991, 397–98).

Strategies and Tactics

The strategies and tactics employed by the CBC straddle the formal and informal arenas. In addition to the formal power of the CBC as an organization and as a collective of individuals, each with an independent vote, it uses coalition building, protests, and other forms of nonconfrontational politics to influence foreign policy outcomes. In addition to exercising any formal power ascribed to them as individual members of Congress, the organization's members have found the drastic forms of protest that were utilized during the civil rights movement to be effective for the CBC.

BOYCOTTS AND SIT-INS

As was the case for TransAfrica, dramatic forms of protest have proven to be tactically important to the work of the CBC. In 1971, Rep. Charles Diggs requested that President Nixon meet with the members of the CBC to discuss issues relevant to African Americans. Nixon denied this request, causing the CBC to implement a protest strategy in response to the rebuff. The entire membership of the CBC boycotted the president's State of the Union Address. This boycott led to a meeting between President Nixon and the CBC. Members of the CBC brought to the table a list of sixty-one recommendations. In the realm of foreign policy, the list included: a large reduction in the money allocated for defense; a substantial increase in money geared toward Africa; sanctions against South Africa due to apartheid; and an increase in opportunities for African American leaders in foreign policy. Although the boycott was "extreme" in light of the institutional role of CBC members, it was successful in obtaining the meeting with Nixon (Copson, 2003, 9).

COALITIONAL POLITICS

In the early 1980s, the Congressional Black Caucus formed coalitions with African American organizations to weld a firm and united stance on South African apartheid. Randall Robinson of TransAfrica, along with several civil rights activists, made a bold statement when they occupied the South African ambassador's office. They were there to push for the release of political prisoners in South Africa. This action eventually escalated and led to the arrest of the activists. CBC members, including Charles Hayes and Ronald Dellums, protested outside the South African Embassy for the next several days. They also were arrested for their protest activity, which brought further attention to the controversial issue of apartheid. These demonstrations initiated the Free South Africa Movement (FSAM) (Copson, 2003, 11).

In 1994, the CBC again revealed its dissent from American foreign policy by engaging in protests and demonstrations. At that time, members of the CBC were dissatisfied with the Clinton administration policy toward Haitian refugees. Congressional representatives Kweisi Mfume, Donald Payne, and Joseph Kennedy formed a human chain outside the White House to protest during a conference on Africa. Not only were the congressional members protesting Clinton's policy concerning Haiti, they also were publicly expressing support for Robinson's hunger strike. Many members of the CBC were frustrated, too, by the lack of support for genocide victims in Rwanda. One outcome of the protest was a promise by the Clinton administration that the CBC would receive detailed briefings about the matters discussed during the conference (McCarthy, 1998, 11).

Utilization of Institutional Power

The utilization of the traditional formal mechanisms and associated institutional power by African Americans to effect progressive change in the foreign affairs arena has largely been limited as a function of the number and types of positions they have occupied in the foreign policy establishment, the hub of which resides in the U.S. State Department. The CBC employs formal institutional approaches to foreign policy, including conducting special hearings, writing letters in their official capacity, introducing legislation, and supporting passage or rejection of legislation by the governing body.

Rep. Charles Diggs, who in the early 1970s used his position as a subcommittee chair to publicize the conditions in Africa, illustrates the use of the special hearing to influence foreign policymaking. Diggs attributed his expertise in Africa and foreign policy to his numerous trips to the continent, and over time he gained considerable respect from his colleagues and the public for his expertise. During this period, Africa was beginning to recoup from colonial reign and domination. Diggs sought to engage Americans on the subject of Africa and persuade them to support the continent's efforts for recovery. "Policy toward Africa for the Seventies" was the title of the longest set of hearings conducted. These hearings began in 1970 and concluded in 1973. In addition to these, Diggs chaired many other hearings that covered an array of topics, including the Sahel drought during the 1970s (Copson, 2003, 12).

Personal letters written in their official capacity and addressed to high-ranking officials provided another means for affecting U.S. foreign policy. In one instance, the Caucus as a whole devised a letter to the commerce secretary in the fall of 1982 concerning the exportation and licensing of shock batons. The action was stimulated by the CBC finding that South Africa was not entitled to license such devices. The letter suggested that South Africa should no longer have access to the shock devices. Buttressing this action were suggestions from the CBC to Clinton in the form of formal letters (Copson, 2003, 14).

The Congressional Black Caucus comes together to generate and support legislation dealing with relevant foreign policy. During the late 1970s, the CBC made sanctions on Rhodesia a high priority. The group pushed for sanctions through the repeal of the Byrd amendment because of the "white rule" in Rhodesia. Essentially, the amendment required that funds generated from duties on imports deemed unfairly priced or subsidized be distributed to the injured U.S. companies. The Byrd amendment facilitated circumvention of sanctions imposed on Rhodesia by allowing the importation of various metals. As part of the Carter administration's strategy to improve relations with African leaders, in March 1977 the Byrd amendment was successfully repealed. The strong congressional action was a reflection of the political support among interest groups throughout the United States (Masters, 2000, 24). The CBC had helped spearhead much of this support.

In addition, sanctions on South Africa were attained through the CBC and the House Africa Subcommittee (Copson, 2003, 22). Beginning in 1981, CBC member Rep. William Gray introduced legislation demanding economic sanctions on South Africa. Legislation imposing sanctions did not pass the House until 1985, and failed to pass the Senate. The Anti-Apartheid Act of 1985, introduced by Gray, included many harsh economic sanctions, such as measures to prevent South Africa from obtaining new investments. Finally, in 1986 sanctions were imposed upon South Africa by the United States, in large part through the strong support of the CBC (Copson, 2003, 26).

The case of Somalia also demonstrates the CBC's application of an institutional approach. In this instance, widespread famine and war in Somalia encouraged the CBC to take legislative action. The CBC was responsible for the House approval of resolutions concerning Somalia that were introduced by members of the CBC. Members of the CBC, along with fellow congressional members, voted for an amendment concerning the Defense Department authorization. The amendment gave Congress more power over U.S. military support in Somalia (Copson, 2003, 32).

The CBC and the United Nations

The Congressional Black Caucus and the United Nations share similar goals on the issue of the development of Africa. The organizations have worked together to promote the needs of the continent. From January 1997 to January 2007, Kofi Annan, a native of Ghana, led the United Nations as secretary-general. His position allowed him to encourage development in Africa. Annan traveled to Washington, D.C., in September 2005, where he attended the Congressional Black Caucus's thirty-fifth Annual Legislative Conference.

At the CBC conference, Annan reported on the progress made in Africa. He addressed some of the accomplishments as well as current goals the groups shared in improving Africa. Among these accomplishments, he noted that the United Nations and CBC had achieved the decolonization of Africa and they had played important roles in the independence of some African countries. In addition, Annan pointed out that apartheid, racism, and other forms of discrimination had always been chief concerns for the U.N. and the CBC. He acknowledged that both groups had played a major role in installing and ensuring democracy in newly freed countries. Racism is still a huge problem for Africa, and it has evolved to become an increasingly complex phenomenon across regions and states, as well as within states. Indeed, democracy requires long-term attention, and in a racialized context, its extension and maintenance is a poignant challenge.

Annan also reported the achievements of the "In Larger Freedom" summit directly to the CBC conference. He confessed that he did not achieve everything he expected from world leaders at the summit. However, some monumental steps did take place. For example, increased international support was achieved for the U.N. Millennium goals, and in addition, financial assistance was acquired through developmental programs, Third World debt relief, and Third World health assistance. Annan encouraged the CBC to continue to support fair trade with Africa. Specific pledges went to the Democracy Fund in excess of $40 million. He specifically thanked members of the CBC for their support in ending U.S. farm subsidies, which prevent African commodities from penetrating U.S. markets, and for backing U.N. peacekeeping missions in Congress. U.N. peacekeeping usually provides well-paid jobs for people in Third World countries, and often these individuals come from African countries. U.N. peacekeepers have played vital roles when sent to the continent of Africa. Annan concluded his speech at the CBC conference by asking the organization to continue to support the U.N. and Africa through positive encouragement.

Conclusion

The purpose of this chapter has been to present a conceptual framework of African American participation in foreign affairs at the issue level. Based on extant research and theory, the approach sheds light on the patterns and processes of black global participation and U.S. foreign policymaking. The framework was applied to investigate aspects of the foreign affairs behavior of two prominent, contemporary African American groups engaged in global affairs: TransAfrica Forum and the Congressional Black Caucus. Results indicate that TransAfrica and the CBC, as entities operating on behalf of African Americans and other progressive segments of the U.S. population, have experienced measurable success in their efforts to influence global affairs and foreign policy. The effective application of strategy and tactics is revealed with regard to the eradication of South African apartheid and the repatriation of Haitians fleeing from political repression. Instrumental to the success experienced by these groups is the application of formal strategies, including conducting legislative hearings and engaging in coalition building, and informal strategies, including boycotts, sit-ins, and other legitimate passive-resistance tactics, such as the hunger strike used by Robinson to bring attention to the injustice of Haitian repatriation.

Interestingly, the use of strategies and tactics by TransAfrica and the CBC has not been circumscribed based on policy orientation. Although individuals and organizations operating in the institutional or formal realm tend to pursue foreign affairs goals consistent with national policy and are cognizant of the institutional and structural limitations circumscribing their role, there is no restriction imposed on this basis when it comes to the use of strategies and tactics. As the foregoing analysis demonstrates, consistent with TransAfrica, the CBC employed the strategies of protest politics coupled with the institutional tools at its disposal. Further efforts should be undertaken to retool and systematically apply the framework to investigate the participation of African Americans and interest group behavior in U.S. foreign policymaking.

Although African Americans remain on the periphery of U.S. foreign policymaking, there have been some advances. Much remains to be done, however, to fully incorporate the group in the international affairs of the nation. At the heart of such incorporation will rest an empathetic yet ambitious national leadership and bureaucracy capable of integrating the divergent experiences of American citizens in weighing foreign policy judgments and actions. Moreover, there must be acknowledgment and treatment of the erosion of international stature due in part to the ambiguous treatment of race, ethnicity, and culture domestically and the eventual complicity of the United States in the persistence of colonialism and imperialism. The quality of incorporation suggested here implies a newfound sensitivity and willingness to affirmatively respond to global matters of significance to African Americans and people throughout the African Diaspora.

Finally, U.S. foreign policymakers should be concerned about the image of the nation projected to the world. This matter is of particular import since nation-states are increasingly allowing domestic social relations to dictate foreign relations. The reality is that in the twenty-first century nonwhite nations are more active on the global scene, particularly in world and regional bodies such as the United Nations, the African Union, and other nongovernmental organizations. Movement toward the substantive incorporation of African Americans into the foreign policymaking process of the nation is one means of demonstrating that the United States is not the hypocrite it has come to be regarded as in many areas of the world. Such measures over the long run will enhance the ability of Americans to remain at the forefront of international leadership.

REFERENCES

Allison, Graham T. 1999. "Conceptual Models and the Cuban Missile Crisis." In *American Foreign Policy: Theoretical Essays,* ed. G. John Ikenberry. New York: Longman.

Almond, Gabriel T. 1962. *The American People and Foreign Policy.* New York: Praeger.

Art, Robert J., and Robert Jervis, eds. 1992. *International Politics: Enduring Concepts and Contemporary Issues.* New York: HarperCollins.

Bard, Mitchell. 1988. "The Influence of Ethnic Interest Groups on American Middle East Policy." In *The Domestic Sources of Foreign Policy: Insights and Interpretations,* ed. Charles Kegley and Eugene Wittkopf. New York: St. Martin's Press.

Caprioli, Mary, and Peter F. Trumbore. 2003. "Ethnic Discrimination and Interstate Violence: Testing the International Impact of Domestic Behavior." *Journal of Peace Research* 40, no. 1: 5–23.

Clark, John F. 1998. "The Clinton Administration and Africa: White House Involvement and the Foreign Affairs Bureaucracies." *Journal of Opinion* 26, no. 2: 8–13.

Cohen, B. C. 1957. *The Political Process and Foreign Policy: The Making of the Japanese Peace Settlement.* Princeton: Princeton University Press.

———. 1959. *The Influence of Nongovernmental Groups on Foreign Policy-Making.* Boston: World Peace Foundation.

Copson, Raymond W. 2003. *The Congressional Black Caucus and Foreign Policy (1971–2002).* Hauppauge, N.Y.: Novinka Books.

"Danny Glover Donates $1 Million to TransAfrica Forum's Capital Campaign." *Jet,* May 10, 1999, 37. Located at http://find.galegroup.com/.

DeRoche, Andrew. 2003. *Andrew Young: Civil Rights Ambassador.* Lanham, Md.: Rowman and Littlefield Publishing Group.

Derryck, Vivian L. 1992. "Premises, Promises and Paradoxes: U.S. Policy toward the Black World." *TransAfrica Forum* 9, no. 2: 11–24.

D'Innocenzio, Anne. 1990. "Reebok Grant to Help Form Africa, Carib Institute." *Footwear News* 46, no.13, 47.

Halperin, Morton H., and Arnold Kanter. 1992. "The Bureaucratic Perspective." In Art and Jervis 1992.

Hammond, Susan W., Daniel P. Mulhollan, and Arthur G. Stevens. 1999. "Informal Congressional Caucuses and Agenda Setting." *Western Political Quarterly* 38, no. 4: 584–605.

Henderson, Errol A., and Richard Tucker. 2001. "Clear and Present Strangers: The Clash of Civilizations and International Conflict." *International Studies Quarterly* 45, no. 2: 317–38.

Holsti, K. J. 1988. *International Politics: A Framework for Analysis*. Englewood Cliffs, N.J.: Prentice Hall.

Huntington, Samuel P. 1993. "The Clash of Civilizations?" *Foreign Affairs* 72, no. 3: 22–49.

Isaacs, Harold R. 1970. "Race and Color in World Affairs." In *Racial Influences in American Foreign Policy*, ed. George W. Shepherd. New York: Knopf.

Jensen, Lloyd. 1982. *Explaining Foreign Policy*. Englewood Cliffs, N.J.: Prentice-Hall.

Jones, Mack H. 1971. "A Frame of Reference for Black Politics." In *Black Political Life in the United States*, ed. Lenneal Henderson, Jr. San Francisco: Chandler.

Key, V. O. 1961. *Public Opinion and American Democracy*. New York: Knopf.

Knoll, Benjamin R. 2008. "Reexamining the Effects of Race and Ethnicity on International Conflict." Paper presented at the Great Plains Political Science Conference, Cedar Falls, Iowa, September 27.

Lave, Charles A. and James G. March. 1993. *An Introduction to Models in the Social Sciences*. Lanham, Md. University Press of America.

Leanne, Shelly. 1998. "The Clinton Administration and Africa: Perspective of the Congressional Black Caucus and TransAfrica." *Journal of Opinion* 26, no. 2: 17–22.

Lincoln, C. Eric. 1970. "The Race Problem and International Relations." In *Racial Influences on American Foreign Policy*, ed. George W. Shepherd. New York: Basic Books.

Lusane, Clarence. 2006. *Colin Powell and Condoleezza Rice: Foreign Policy and the New American Century*. Westport, Conn.: Praeger.

Masters, Paul E. 2000. "Carter and the Rhodesian Problem." *International Social Science Review* 75, nos. 3–4: 23–33.

McCarthy, Colman. 1994. 27 May. "Classic 27-Day Hunger Strike Convinces Clinton." *National Catholic Reporter* 30, no. 30: 10.

Miller, Jake. 1983. *The Black Presence in American Foreign Affairs*. New York: University Press of America.

Morris, Milton. 1972. "Black Americans and the Foreign Policy Process: The Case of Africa." *Western Political Quarterly* 25, no. 3: 454–59.

———. 1992. November. "Blacks and the New World Order." *Focus* 20, nos. 10–11: 3.

Opitz, Gotz-Dietrich. 1999. *Haitian Refugees Forced to Return: Transnationalism and State Politics, 1991–1994*. Berlin: LIT Verlag.

Pinney, Neil, and George Serra. 1999. "The Congressional Black Caucus and Vote Cohesion: Placing the Caucus within House Voting Patterns." *Political Research Quarterly* 52, no. 3: 583–608.

Plummer, Brenda Gayle. 1989. "Evolution of the Black Foreign Policy Constituency." *TransAfrica Forum* 6 (Spring–Summer): 67–81.

Plummer, Brenda Gayle, ed. 2003. *Window on Freedom*. Chapel Hill: University of North Carolina Press.

Plummer, Brenda Gayle, and Donald R. Culverson. 1987. "Black Americans and Foreign Affairs: A Reassessment." *Sage Race Relations Abstracts* 12, no. 1: 21–27.

Ray, James Lee. 1990. *Global Politics*. 4th ed. Boston: Houghton Mifflin.

Robinson, Randall. 1992. "Building a Democratic Peace." *TransAfrica Forum* 9, no. 2: 39–46.

———. 1998. *Defending the Spirit: A Black Life in America*. New York: First Plume Printing.

Rosenau, James. 1990. *Turbulence in World Politics: A Theory of Change and Continuity*. Princeton: Princeton University Press.

Rourke, John T. 1993. *International Politics on the World Stage*. 4th ed. Guilford, Conn.: Dushkin Publishing Group.

Rubenstein, W. D. 1982. *The Left, the Right and the Jews*. Ann Arbor: University of Michigan Press.

Said, Abdul Aziz. 1977. "A Redefinition of National Interest, Ethnic Consciousness, and U.S. Foreign Policy." In *Ethnicity and U.S. Foreign Policy*, ed. Abdul Aziz Said. New York: Praeger.

Schraeder, Peter J. 1991. "Speaking with Many Voices: Continuity and Change in U.S. Africa Policies." *Journal of Modern African Studies* 29, no. 3: 373–412.

Skinner, Elliot P. 1992. *African Americans and U.S. Policy toward Africa, 1850–1924: In Defense of Black Nationality*. Washington, D.C.: Howard University Press.

Stanford, Karin L. 1995. "Citizen Diplomacy and Jesse Jackson: A Case Study for Influencing U.S. Foreign Policy toward Southern Africa." *Western Journal of Black Studies* 19, no. 1: 19–29.

TransAfrica Forum Annual Report 2004. Located at transafricaforum.org.

Trice, Robert H. 1976. *Interest Groups and the Foreign Policy Process: U.S. Policy in the Middle East*. Beverly Hills, Calif.: Sage Publications.

Truman, David B. 1971. *The Governmental Process: Political Interests and Public Opinion*. New York: Knopf.

Tusicisny, Andrej. 2004. "Civilizational Conflicts: More Frequent, Longer, and Bloodier?" *Journal of Peace Research* 41, no. 4: 485–98.

United Nations, Congressional Black Caucus Share Commitment to Africa's Rights. September 26, 2005. Located at http://www.unis.unvienna.org/unis/pressrels/2005/sgsm10123.html.

Volman, Daniel P. 1998. "The Clinton Administration and Africa: Role of Congress and the Africa Subcommittees." *Journal of Opinion* 26, no.2: 14–16.

Walton, Hanes, Jr. 1985. *Invisible Politics*. Albany: State University of New York Press.

Yaffe, Michael D. 1994. "Realism in Retreat? The New World Order and the Return of the Individual to International Relations Studies." *Perspectives on Political Science* 23, no. 2: 79–88.

Zakaria, Fareed. 1992. "Realism and Domestic Politics: A Review Essay." *International Security* 17 (Summer): 177–98.

THREE

From Anticolonialism to Anti-Apartheid

AFRICAN AMERICAN POLITICAL
ORGANIZATIONS AND AFRICAN
LIBERATION, 1957–93

Ronald Williams II

African Americans have always had an interest in Africa. This awareness can be traced back to the arrival of the first slave ships in the New World in the early seventeenth century. Considering the migratory conditions of this culturally and geographically displaced population, it is no surprise that this group would feel some attraction to their ancestral homeland. By the nineteenth century African Americans, both enslaved and free, became more than merely interested in Africa. They possessed more than a longing for their ancestral homeland. As the social status of African Americans rose after the abolition of slavery, so, too, did their ability to participate in the political and economic struggles of the African Diaspora. As they became more aware of the conditions of African people throughout the world, they realized that their struggles against the various manifestations of American racism were inextricably linked to the experiences of their oppressed brethren the world over. This understanding of a common experience of oppression and diasporic longing was the basis upon which nationalist sentiments and movements emerged.[1] However, this notion of a diasporic nationalism became complicated by the varying ideological approaches of dominant African American protest organizations and movements throughout the twentieth century. Nevertheless, the transnational social realizations served as the basis of the emerging sense of obligation that African Americans felt to aid in the struggles of African people throughout the Diaspora.[2] By the late nineteenth century African American interest in Africa and the African Diaspora was evolving into Pan-Africanism—a transnational movement focused on the liberation of African people all over the world from the forces of European colonial domination. In marrying the often-conflicting ideologies of integration, nationalism, and socialism/ Marxism, a cadre of African American intellectuals and political figures were immensely involved in the liberationist efforts on the domestic front, while remaining committed to a Pan-African vision. They, to varying measures, understood the struggles of African Americans as linked to the struggles of oppressed Africans and African descendants all over the world. This understanding of a common struggle and fate thrust African Americans into African affairs in particular and international affairs in general.

This chapter chronicles the sundry ways that African Americans, through their work with political organizations and domestic and transnational social movement activities, connected themselves with the politics of continental Africa.[3] Specifically examining the years between 1957 and 1993, this chapter explores the rising social position of African Americans and the changing political dynamics in the then new and soon-to-be independent nation-states of continental Africa. It points to some of the major ideological conflicts in the efforts of well-known African American intellectuals and political organizations to connect with the political affairs and liberation struggles of the various parts of continental Africa during the same time period. By examining the work of these organizations and their respective leaderships, this chapter illustrates how ideological conflicts during this period were prevalent among African American leaders in domestic freedom struggles and in what was understood as a global African freedom struggle. Focusing on the advances of the civil rights movement and the black power movement,this chapter shows how African American political organizations differed over the role that African Americans should play in the global African freedom struggle.

The efforts of African Americans to influence U.S. foreign policy toward Africa in the 1970s and 1980s, particularly policy toward South Africa, illustrate the crystallization of various approaches to African American politics both domestically and internationally. This chapter attends to the often-overlooked contributions of radical-minded organizations and individuals to the advancement of the global African freedom struggle. In its totality, this chapter traces African American involvement in foreign affairs from the first ruminations of Pan-Africanism in the nineteenth century to the late twentieth-century and early twenty-first-century work of organizations and individuals to directly influence U.S. foreign policy in both official and unofficial capacities.

The central assertion that foregrounds the analysis offered in this chapter is that as the social position of African Americans began to change, the ideological conflicts operating among African Americans became increasingly pronounced, particularly on issues related to global African Diaspora freedom struggles. However, the integration of African Americans into the American political and social arrangement also functioned to alter, and in some ways limit, the approach that most African American intellectuals and political figures pursued in their efforts to influence the U.S. government on issues understood to be important to African Americans, particularly those related to Africa, Latin America, and the Caribbean.

Anticolonialism Abroad and Civil Rights and Black Power at Home: African American Political Pan-Africanism Comes of Age

The independence of Ghana in 1957 marked a major turning point in what was understood by many as a global African freedom struggle. This event marked the beginning of the end of European colonization of Africa, a condition that had lasted for nearly three-quarters of a century. Because Ghana's independence (and that of the numerous nation-states that won their freedom struggles shortly thereafter) coincided with the civil rights movement under way in the United States, many African Americans began to reconceptualize the African continent and their relationship to it. In particular, the excitement surrounding Ghana's independence caused many well-known African American intellectuals and political figures to reconsider the relationship between the wars they waged on behalf of African Americans and the freedom struggles under way on the African continent. As Meriwether (2002) points out, Ghanaian independence harmonized "the dual paths of universalist integrationism and racialist nationalism" and repositioned Africa as a place from which African Americans could heighten their self-concepts and formulate their authentic diasporic identities.[4] However, Ghanaian independence, as a marker of progress in what was then a decades-old movement for a more liberated Africa, must be situated within the overall trajectory of the movement for global Pan-Africanism. The beginning of the end of colonial rule in Africa was facilitated by the transnational efforts of African Americans dating back to the emergence of Pan-African sensibilities in the late nineteenth century. Ghana's independence was part and parcel of the vision of Pan-Africanism that had matured from a sentiment into a movement during the first half of the twentieth century.

Ruminations of Pan-Africanism on the part of African Americans date back to the nineteenth-century work of noted African American nationalists Henry Highland Garnet and Alexander Crummell. It evolved into a transnational program decades later through the efforts of Trinidadian attorney Henry Sylvester Williams, who is known for having coined the term and for helping to organize the first Pan-African conference in 1900. However, it was W.E.B. Du Bois who stewarded Pan-Africanism's transformation from a nineteenth-century idea into a full-fledged transnational movement in the early twentieth century. Du Bois's involvement is representative of the centrality of African Americans to the first four Pan-African Congresses that were organized under his leadership. These congresses embraced the overarching goal of uniting Africa and African descendants all over the world. Although they evolved over time, the objectives of the Pan-African Congresses remained consistent with the vision that Williams had articulated almost twenty years before: to bring down the European colonial powers' domination over the people and governments of continental Africa. This vision would remain consistent in the succeeding meetings of the Pan-African Congress, and progress would be made toward it over the next thirty-plus years. The Pan-African Congress would meet five times between 1919 and 1945, and again in 1974 and 1994, each time with varying levels of participation, effectiveness, and opposition.[5] However, the Fifth Pan-African Congress remains noted for its particular success. Owing a great deal to its evolution from a movement of bourgeois intellectuals into a united effort of "intellectuals, workers, and farmers in the struggle against colonialism,"[6] the Fifth Pan-African Congress created the space for many like-minded people to unite around the cause of liberating the peoples of the various societies of continental Africa from the oppressive forces of European colonization. Du Bois's vision of Pan-Africanism, for which he had labored for nearly four decades, was by 1945 becoming a reality.

During the twenty-nine-year period between the Fifth and Sixth Congresses (1945 and 1974), several key events occurred that altered both the political and economic situation throughout the African world and the relationships between African Americans and continental Africans. Significantly, some forty African countries won their battles for independence from their European colonial powers, including Ghana, which gained its independence from Great Britain in 1957. This was a particular advance for Pan-Africanism, as Kwame Nkrumah, who had been intimately involved with Du Bois and the work of the Pan-African Congresses, was the first head of state of the newly independent Ghana, serving first as its prime minister and later as president. Three years later, in 1960, affectionately heralded as the "Year of Africa," some twelve states gained independence from France and five others received their independence from Belgium and the United Kingdom. By 1963 eight additional states had received their independence, including Sierra Leone, Algeria, Uganda, and Rwanda. Nineteen sixty-three was also the year that Du Bois, on the eve of the famous March on Washington, died in Accra, Ghana, at ninety-five years of age. The combination of Du Bois's death, the presence of free African states, and the rise of a black power politics in the United States, the Caribbean, and Canada that embraced a general concern for the welfare of Africa and the African Diaspora created the opportunity for the resurgence of the Pan-African Congress movement, which had not met since its meeting in Manchester in 1945.[7] However, it would be 1974 before the Sixth Pan-African Congress actually convened. By this time, Nkrumah, too, had died, leaving Kenya's Jomo Kenyatta and Guinea's Sekou Touré as the last remaining of the original leadership of the Pan-African Federation and the Pan-African Congress Movement.[8]

Convened in Dar Es Salaam, Tanzania, in 1974, the Sixth Pan-African Congress was the first to take place in continental Africa. Present at this meeting were representatives from all parts of the African Diaspora, including the United States, the Caribbean, Europe, South America, and, of course, the newly independent nation-states of Africa. By now, political leaders from the various nation-states of continental Africa were able to fully participate—some as duly elected heads of state—in a movement that had begun nearly three-quarters of a century earlier. Although formal European colonial rule of Africa was a thing of the past, the Congress's leadership recognized that a legacy of colonialism still remained. Thus, the group recognized the need to continuously fight against politics and programs of segregation and discrimination predicated on racism. Different from previous congresses, the Sixth Congress marked the beginning of revolutionary Pan-Africanism.[9] This form of Pan-Africanism is deemed revolutionary in that the Congress's leadership recognized the need to take revolutionary measures to ensure that the movement did not become coopted by the colonial powers that it had fought so earnestly to defeat.[10] Therefore, this Congress took important stances against the exploitative capitalist states of the world. It recognized the inherent ills of North Atlantic capitalism and worked to organize around a program that focused on the collective unfettering from the legacies of colonialism in continental Africa and the programs of legalized segregation and discrimination in the United States and other parts of the African Diaspora. The Sixth Pan-African Congress furthered the notion of a collective/global African world freedom struggle. Extending this notion of African people's responsibility for each other to the populations of Africans residing outside the continent, the

General Declaration of the Sixth Pan-African Congress acknowledged the inseparability of the successes and failures of black peoples in other corners of the globe.[11]

The leadership of the Sixth Pan-African Congress also underscored the spirit of a collective struggle. Tanzanian president Mwalimu Julius Nyerere and Sekou Touré delivered the opening remarks at the Sixth Pan-African Congress. A long-time anticolonial activist and a key player in previous Pan-African Congresses, Touré was elected president of the Sixth Congress. The remarks of these two leaders revealed the changing character of Pan-Africanism. They both paid homage to many of the now-deceased intellectuals who had stewarded the cause of Pan-Africanism for the greater part of the twentieth century, paying special recognition to the centrality of Du Bois to this movement. These men made it clear that the Sixth Congress was part and parcel of a refocused Pan-Africanism. Centrally, they made the point that racialism was still prevalent and increasingly institutionalized in Africa and throughout the world. It is in light of this that the leadership and participants at the Sixth Pan-African Congress saw their work as still relevant.[12] In this spirit the Congress focused its energies on embarking on revolutionary measures in the fight against the forces of colonialism and other forms of race-based segregation, discrimination, and oppression.

Although the Sixth Pan-African Congress embodied the collective spirit of its predecessors, efforts to organize Africans and African descendants around a program of collective liberation were not without their share of conundrums. There were clear rifts in these efforts. As African nation-states gained their independence from the European states, increasing emphasis was placed on the significance of North Atlantic capitalism as a force that limited the opportunities for continental and diasporic Africans—particularly those from Europe and the United States—to be truly aligned in a collective Third World class struggle. The founding of organizations such as the Organization of African Unity (OAU) and the earlier founding of the All-African People's Organization are illustrative of this sentiment. Both organizations allowed representation from other parts of the African Diaspora, but restricted full participation to representatives from the nation-states of continental Africa.

Let us return briefly to our earlier discussion of Du Bois. It was his work with the Pan-African Congress movement, coupled with the fractures in what he hoped would persist to be a global African freedom struggle, which raises some important considerations about the role that African Americans have played in transnational freedom struggles. For much of the first half of the twentieth century, Du Bois was the leading African American intellectual working to coordinate international cooperation around the cause of decolonization. When considered in relation to other social movements with transnational aspirations, the Pan-African Congress movement is by far the longest lasting and most effective, and has had the farthest reaching impact. Thus, Du Bois remains foundational in the overall trajectory of African American involvement in international affairs. Through his work with the Pan-African Congress movement, Du Bois transformed African American interest in Africa into more than merely an affinity for an ancestral homeland. His work turned this fondness for Africa into a program of mass collective action. However, the founding of exclusive organizations such as the OAU and the increased emphasis placed on attacking the ills of North Atlantic capitalism by the Sixth Pan-African Congress reveal marked conflicts around the ideological effectiveness of nationalism as it had been theretofore understood. Some African Americans embraced the notion of a collective identity and global struggle. Yet some African leaders believed otherwise. In short, there was, and is, no consistency on the part of African Americans or continental Africans about the idea of a collective struggle and destiny, even though leaders of all groups came together for the Sixth Pan-African Congress and espoused such ideals.

In this light, some African American intellectuals, including Du Bois, began to rethink nationalism as the ideology most appropriate for the realization of African American and African world liberation.[13] His particular evolution is representative of the numerous other African American intellectuals and political figures who began to reconsider their ideological footing and move away from nationalism as it had previously been understood. A chief example of this phenomenon is the life and work of Malcolm X. In the domestic sphere, Malcolm represented an alternative to the integrationist strategy dominating the civil rights movement in an almost hegemonic way. He was ever critical of the dominant civil rights establishment for its belief that black liberation could be achieved through integration of existing institutions and apparatuses. One of his major qualms concerning the movement was that its leadership fell far short of calling America to consciousness on the prevailing ideology of race and racism.[14] Significantly, Malcolm saw that "behind the façade of racial equality, African Americans were frozen at the bottom of the political, economic, and social pyramid, even though the structure of legal segregation and discrimination was being dismantled."[15]

Malcolm's creation of the Organization of Afro-American Unity (OAAU), remains one of the pointed manifestations of his ideological evolution. Owing to his heightened awareness (through extensive international travel) of the conditions of oppressed people throughout the world, Malcolm, in the last few years of his life, became a Pan-African internationalist.[16] It was from this ideology that the OAAU was born. Similar to earlier Pan-Africanists, Malcolm regarded the African American as unquestionably African and believed that the domestic and international conditions were linked to each other. However, different from other nationalist understandings of the relationship between African Americans and continental Africans, Malcolm did not look to Africa as a place for the African American's glorious return home. Another difference was that Malcolm posed vehement challenges to American capitalism, which he saw as a major impediment to the true realization of African and African American liberation.[17] His two sojourns in Africa and the Middle East acquainted him with the efforts of African leaders to create socialist societies. Through the OAAU, Malcolm sought to connect with the leadership of the newly independent African states in his efforts to locate economic and political ideologies alternative to capitalism.[18]

Founded in 1964—eight months before Malcolm's assassination—the OAAU was the first effort in the 1960s to mobilize African Americans around a Pan-African nationalist program. The OAAU's preeminence as a 1960s Pan-African nationalist organization is particularly notable in light of the dominant integrationist dogma of the civil rights movement. A product of Malcolm's commitment to internationalizing the African American freedom struggle, the OAAU represented his efforts to reframe the international African freedom struggle as more than a project of civil rights, instead arguing that it was a human rights endeavor.[19] In conceiving the OAAU, Malcolm modeled the organization after its continental Africa counterpart, the OAU.[20] With the OAU as its archetype, the objectives of the OAAU were articulated in its basic unity program, announced at its founding rally in 1964. Most notably, these objectives and principles held that the OAAU was a collective effort of African Americans and was patterned after the OAU in both letter and spirit.[21] However, different from the OAU, the OAAU committed itself to the nationalist project of unification of all Africans and African descendants, particularly those in the Americas. The ambitions of the OAAU included a belief in the United Nations and in the U.S. Constitution as a document that, if followed, could allow the state to adequately meet the needs of all its citizens. Its principles held that the founding documents of the United States and the United Nations, "if put into practice, represent the essence of mankind's intentions."[22] Reflecting its desire to serve as a unifying force among African Americans, the OAAU wanted all African Americans and their organizations to amalgamate under its program as a means to the end of elevating African Americans to full citizenship in the United States and to achieving the liberation of the continental Africans. This is not to suggest that African Americans were previously oblivious or not committed to African liberation during the latter part of the civil rights movement. However, Malcolm's popularity as a notable ideological alternative in the movement contributed immensely to the maintenance of African issues in the consciousness of African Americans.

The Pan-African internationalism upon which the OAAU was founded undoubtedly lasted beyond Malcolm X's lifetime. Through the OAAU, Malcolm reconnected African Americans with one of the original objectives of Pan-Africanism, which emphasized the mobilization of African descendants worldwide in support of the liberation of Africa from colonialism. The reasserted notion of a collective fate of Africans and African descendants throughout the world influenced the principles of numerous African American political organizations that emerged in the late 1960s and beyond. Most notably, the OAAU became associated with other far-left radical African American organizations in the 1960s and gave birth to the similar groups that emerged in the 1970s. This is owed, in part, to Malcolm X's significance as a radical black nationalist. Through his work with the Nation of Islam and after his departure, Malcolm served as an icon for African American radicals, many of whom wanted to participate in the domestic and international freedom struggles but recognized the major shortcomings of the dominant civil rights movement organizations. These radical sentiments framed the black power movement that both overlapped with and followed the civil rights movement.

Malcolm's insistence on a mental return to Africa added further depth to the relationship between African Americans and Africa, and uncontrovertibly gave rise to African American cultural nationalism.[23] Indicative of a resurgent radicalism among African Americans, cultural nationalists were closely associated with African American radical organizations. This radicalism was part and parcel of the sentiment of some African Americans seeking an alternative to the nonviolent direct-action strategy of the SCLC and the legal-action approach of the NAACP that dominated the civil rights movement. Ideologically, Malcolm's radicalism and openness to taking up arms in defense of African American civil and human rights provided a much needed option for African American leaders and laypeople desirous of an alternative to the dominant civil rights establishment. Many of the eminent radical organizations emerged from the local-level activism of African Americans who had previously work to advance African American causes through local chapters of the NAACP. On local levels, African Americans faced acute resistance in their efforts to radicalize chapters of the NAACP. Examples include noted civil rights leader Robert F. Williams, who was ousted from his position as president of the Monroe, Louisiana, chapter of the NAACP over disagreements with the national leadership of the organization. Similar to the leadership of the NAACP (and the SCLC), Williams was a supporter of, and advocate for, integration. However, different from those leaders, Williams believed in the use of armed self-defense to achieve it.[24] These unresolved inter- and intra-organizational conflicts ushered in the establishment of organizations such as the Revolutionary Action Movement, of which Williams served as international chairman. Consistent with this tradition were the Black Panther Party and certain factions of the Student Nonviolent Coordinating Committee (SNCC).[25]

However, Malcolm's influence on African American radicals was not limited to their domestic activities. Malcolm also served as an ideological influence on the internationalist efforts of many of his contemporaries, including Williams, who, like noted cultural nationalist Amiri Baraka and other African American radicals, persisted in efforts to take the African American freedom struggle to the international community. Although Malcolm is noted as the first African American of national prominence to travel to the African continent since Ghana's independence in 1957, many others followed in his footsteps.[26] For example, Williams's international efforts were advanced through his activities with the Revolutionary Action Movement (RAM). As well, Williams took the African American freedom struggle abroad through his travels to North Vietnam and different parts of continental Africa. Fervently opposed to the U.S. position on the Vietnam War, Williams forged relationships with like-minded international leaders and worked to mobilize African American soldiers stationed in Vietnam in opposition to the war.[27]

Baraka, too, worked to advance transnational efforts in support of Africans and African descendants worldwide. His efforts crystallized with the establishment of the Congress of African People (CAP). Like RAM, CAP was a response to the marginalization of nationalist and radical sentiments present among African Americans. Still, it represented an effort to raise and maintain the consciousness of African affairs in the psyches of African Americans. Consistent with the sentiments of Williams and RAM, Baraka had long been dissatisfied with the exclusion of African American radicals from the political milieu and insisted that African Americans develop ideological alternatives in order to liberate themselves from the effects of domestic and international racism.[28] In his estimation, this new political ideology needed to embrace the greater African world as part of a collective struggle of Africans worldwide. He understood the African American situation as closely related to the challenges facing Africans on the continent and throughout the world, even though formal colonialism had ended. Like the experience of colonized Africans, Baraka believed that African Americans' collective experience had been one of "internal colonialism," a brand of oppression that he and others recognized as different from subjugation because of class and race alone.[29]

The Congress of African People represented an effort to mobilize African Americans and other African descendants around a program of *black self-determination.*[30] The initial meetings of the Congress brought together a cross-section of representatives from the African American nationalist, integrationist, and radical political camps. The Congress of African People was also significant because it, as Woodard (1999) observes, "signaled an important early step in the formation of a national Black political community."[31] Moreover, CAP maintained an authentic Pan-African focus and worked to foster relationships among African Americans, Africans, African descendants, and the Third World. Consistent with the ideology of cultural nationalism, these efforts led to the organization of African Liberation Day and the establishment of the African Liberation Support Committee. Significantly, CAP was committed to programs and projects focused on advancing the situations of Africans, African descendants, and other oppressed peoples both domestically and internationally.

The efforts of Malcolm X and the OAAU, Williams and RAM, and Baraka and CAP (and there were others) represented the radical wing of the civil rights movement—a coterie of African American intellectuals and political leaders whose contributions have been too often marginalized. Certainly, these sentiments ushered in the radical activities of the black power organizations of the 1970s. However, African American radicalism did not emerge as a result of the ideological conflicts of the civil rights movement alone. Hints of African American radicalism were evident in the activities of earlier movement organizations, including the African Blood Brotherhood and the Council on African Affairs (CAA), and among notable African American personalities such as Du Bois, Richard Wright, C. L. R. James, Paul Robeson, and Max Yergan.[32] One of the challenges that faced these radical organizations was the accusation of communist influence. In both radical and liberal organizations in the 1940s and beyond African Americans were constantly dealing with surveillance of their activities and continued investigation by the Federal Bureau of Investigation (FBI) and the Central Intelligence Agency (CIA).[33]

Tracing African American radicalism back to organizations like the Council on African Affairs illustrates part of the trajectory of African American engagement with Africa through political organizations that have worked to influence U.S. and U.N. policy toward Africa. Founded by Paul Robeson and Max Yergan, the CAA was one of the significant ways that African Americans engaged in the anticolonial, anti-imperialist cause in Africa in the interwar years and in the early years between the Fifth and Sixth Pan-African Congresses. In addition to advocating decolonization of Africa, the CAA became an important force among African Americans concerned about the conditions of blacks in South Africa. Although South Africa was counted—along with Egypt, Liberia, and Ethiopia—in the number of free African states in the 1940s,[34] a plethora of issues prevailed in South Africa that were reminiscent of a colonial condition. These included famine, racism, and oppressive working conditions for South Africa's laboring classes. As Von Eschen (1997) points out, this organization proved instrumental in organizing around the working conditions of South Africa's mineworkers. As well, the CAA, through public rallies and protests, focused its efforts on a campaign for famine relief in South Africa.[35] However, the CAA's work became increasingly important with the election of Daniel Malan as South Africa's prime minister in 1948. As leader of the Nationalist Party and a proponent of Afrikaner nationalism, Malan in his first two years in office advanced a legislative agenda that imposed the system of apartheid rule, which was consistent with the platform on which he and his party were elected. The state of race relations in South Africa was particularly problematic because it was far out of step with the direction of many of other nation-states. Insightfully, Meriwether (2002) points out the relative backwardness of South Africa's state of race relations that was cemented with "Malan's victory [which] highlighted the reality that while most of the world was moving away from policies of racial discrimination and segregation, White South Africans were tightening their grip."[36]

The imposition of apartheid rule in South Africa (a system that outlasted colonial rule on the continent) was understood as one of colonialism's legacies. Consequently, South Africa prevailed as a priority on the policy agendas of radical African American political organizations. This included the CAA and the various organizations that followed it. Despite organizational problems that led to a stalemate in CAA activities in the early 1940s, South Africa served as a cause around which the CAA leadership could collectively mobilize. However, interest in the affairs of South Africa on the part of the African American masses was minimal at first. This began to change with the Campaign of Defiance of Unjust Laws, initiated by black South Africans in protest over apartheid rule. The Defiance Campaign provided a means through which cross-sections of African Americans could join in protest with black South Africans. This became a means through which African Americans could protest their own social conditions in America and those of their counterparts in South Africa at the same time.

Although African American consciousness of the South Africa situation increased with the emergence of the Defiance Campaign, concerted efforts by prominent African American political organizations remained limited. Different from the CAA, organizations like the NAACP proved reluctant to involve themselves in the politics of South Africa.[37] Despite being the African American organization best suited to pressure the U.S. government on international policy questions, the NAACP held fast to its focus on domestic issues.[38] However, because of the growing concern among rank-and-file African Americans about the South Africa situation, the NAACP was thrust into foreign policy debates. At its 1952 convention, with pressure from its leadership and membership, the NAACP board of directors adopted wholesale resolutions on the South Africa situation. These actions by the NAACP reflected the growing awareness among African Americans of the need to influence the U.S. foreign policy agenda toward South Africa. Significantly, African Americans saw that the United States had been strategically passive in dealing with the state of race relations in South Africa, the Congo, and Rhodesia. This was evidenced by a foreign policy agenda that focused largely on forging alliances with South Africa in the name of anticommunism and ignoring race relations.[39] Not only did the U.S. government strategically ignore race relations in South Africa, but it was also involved in activities that demonstrated its support for South Africa's apartheid regime. This is evidenced by the allegations of CIA involvement in the 1962 arrest of Nelson Mandela that led to his twenty-seven-year prison sentence.[40] The foreign policy debates were not limited to South Africa, however. The Congolese political crisis of the 1960s was another issue of concern to African Americans, and it showcased the racist and imperialist foreign policies of the United States.[41] Moreover, U.S. involvement in the Congolese crisis was furthered by the politics of the CIA, which was involved in the coup d'état leading to the ouster and assassination of Congolese prime minister Patrice Lumumba shortly after his election in 1960 and the subsequent appointment of Joseph Mobutu as dictator.[42]

Opportunities for African Americans to effectively influence U.S. foreign policy toward Africa were still limited throughout the 1960s. Not surprisingly, white racist groups had considerably greater access and influence in their efforts to weigh in on the U.S. foreign policy debates regarding Africa. Conversely, black organizations were largely prevented from entering these conversations on foreign policy toward Africa.[43] This situation was complicated by the scarce representation of African Americans in either House of Congress, which was appropriately understood as one of the most effective avenues to shape U.S. foreign policy.[44] This lack of representation was one of many factors that prevented African Americans from having an effective voice in U.S. foreign policy debates. Thus, organizations dominant in the civil rights movement and the black power movement committed their resources to fighting the effects of domestic racism, which had impeded, among many other things, African American political participation.

The work of civil rights and black power organizations facilitated the passage of legislation that protected the civil and human rights been previously denied to African Americans. The combined efforts of these organizations, particularly those that outlasted the civil rights movement, advanced African American access to the democratic process to include the ability to exercise the franchise. As well, these organizations did the work necessary to ensure that African Americans were able not only to vote in elections, but also to participate fully in the nominating process—in particular for the Democratic party.[45] The successes of the civil rights movement are owed to the combined efforts of both its integrationist-minded and nationalist-minded coteries. The same is true for the anti-apartheid movement in the 1960s, 1970s, and beyond. In addition to the prominent integrationist organizations of the civil rights movement, the successful movement to end U.S. passive sanctioning of South Africa's racist social policies also involved the work of the radical African American political organizations of the 1960s and the black power organizations of the 1970s.[46] These groups not only concerned themselves with the conditions of South Africa's black citizens, but also they were central to carrying out the objectives of the legislative victories of the civil rights movement. Despite their ideological conflicts, the cause of a free South Africa was one that most African American political organizations were able to unite around in the 1960s and beyond. The crystallization of the integrationist, nationalist, and Pan-Africanist camps—including the liberal and radical forms of each— enabled anti-apartheid to evolve into a worldwide movement, started initially by African Americans, but evolving into a cause around which people of all races and nationalities rallied.[47] The movement to end apartheid was, on the U.S. front, orchestrated by a broad coalition of sacred, secular, and political organizations. This included multiracial organizations such as Africa Policy, Africa Action, Africa Fund, and the American Committee on Africa. Descended from the Washington Office on Africa and the Council on African Affairs, these organizations focused on a broad range of issues related to Africa. In the 1970s these groups mobilized in support of the liberation of Angola, Cape Verde, Guinea-Bissau, Mozambique, Namibia, and Zimbabwe, as these were countries whose freedom struggles received scant attention.[48] Nevertheless, the anti-apartheid movement was central to these groups' activities in the 1970s and 1980s. During this period, African American political leaders undertook new measures to address the U.S. role in African problems. The primary organization involved in this effort was the Congressional Black Caucus (CBC). Established in 1971, the CBC and its members served as the foundation for the formal involvement of African Americans in U.S. foreign policy. The CBC gave birth to Trans-Africa, the institutionalized African American foreign policy lobby that would advocate issues related to Africa and the Caribbean. Owing to the timeliness of the issue, anti-apartheid was the foreign policy issue that served as the impetus for this organization's founding.

TransAfrica, the Congressional Black Caucus, and the Rise of the African American Foreign Policy Lobby

On the Friday after Thanksgiving in 1984—just two days after being arrested for a sit-in at the South African Embassy in Washington, D.C., Randall Robinson, Walter Fauntroy, Mary Frances Berry, and Eleanor Holmes Norton appeared before the press to officially announce the establishment of the Free South Africa Movement (FSAM).[49] The objective of this organization "would be the passage of comprehensive economic sanctions against South Africa."[50] Robinson, Fauntroy, Berry, and Norton were the first of over three thousand people arrested between 1984 and 1985 at South Africa's Washington, D.C., embassy alone, sparking a national protest resulting in arrests at South African embassies and consulates across the nation. Less than two years later, the U.S. House of Representatives overrode a presidential veto and passed into law the Comprehensive Anti-Apartheid Act of 1986. Concerning the congressional action, Robinson wrote, "We had won. We had turned the course of the most powerful country on earth. Democracy in South Africa, something I had pursued for nearly twenty years but thought I would never live to see was within sight."[51] Eight years later, in 1994, South African apartheid had ended and former political prisoner

Nelson Mandela was elected president of the African National Congress. Although apartheid's legacies remain present in South Africa, the political rule of oppression through separation formally ended in 1990, and African American activism unquestionably contributed to this.

TransAfrica emerged in a historical moment that was ripe for influencing U.S. foreign policy toward South Africa. By the 1970s there were more African Americans elected to state, local, and federal offices than ever before. This included a marked increase in African American representation in the U.S. Congress.[52] This body, which had traditionally been a hindrance to the advancement of African American interests both domestic and transnational, now had a sizable number of African American members poised to call national attention to issues affecting African Americans and Africans abroad. From this increase in African American representation in Congress emerged the Congressional Black Caucus (CBC). During the early 1970s the CBC established itself as a visible, permanent, and influential force in national political affairs. This first decade also enabled African American congressional representatives to stabilize their electoral bases in their respective districts, while solidifying their footing on issues pertaining to African Americans. Also during this time period, African American members of Congress, through the CBC, worked diligently to ensure that issues pertaining to Africa—in particular to South Africa—continued to be pushed in the U.S. government's legislative and executive branches. The success of the anti-apartheid movement in the United States, as well as the continued presence of African issues on the legislative agenda and conscience of the U.S. Congress, is owed in great part to the women and men of the CBC.[53]

TransAfrica came into being as the product of CBC's efforts to pressure the U.S. government to take more active policy positions on South Africa. Aware of the influence of the U.S. government and American corporations on the politics and economics of South Africa, and the African continent as a whole, the CBC recognized its ability to pressure the state to make substantive policy changes. Members of the Caucus were aware of the U.S. government's passive endorsement of the oppression and disenfranchisement of South Africa's black populations for almost three decades. With this in mind, the Caucus convened its Black Leadership Conference on Africa in 1976, bringing together a cross-section of representatives from prominent African American political and social organizations. From this meeting, the CBC devised its African American Manifesto on South Africa and established a task force to develop a formal organization that would provide a venue for African Americans to place external pressures on the

U.S. government on issues related to the Caribbean and continental Africa.[54] It was in pursuit of the foregoing objective that TransAfrica was born.

The African American front for the anti-apartheid movement, Trans-Africa remains a force in organizing prominent African Americans around issues related to Africa and the African Diaspora. Through the anti-apartheid movement and the foreign policy campaigns that preceded it, TransAfrica solidified itself as an avenue through which African Americans have continued to engage in activist work on behalf of Africans around the world. The group continues to coordinate African American foreign policy efforts toward Africa, the Caribbean, and Latin America, through protest activities, policy briefs, and position papers.

Discourses about TransAfrica present another opportunity to reconsider the ways that the efforts of individuals and organizations active during the civil rights and black power movements created the space for the involvement of African Americans in foreign affairs through the U.S. foreign policy process. Although organizations such as TransAfrica and the CBC are able to participate in the U.S. foreign policy process in more institutionalized ways than ever before, these activities represent the crystallization of various approaches to African American politics in domestic and international spheres. While these ideological foundations have historically been in conflict with one another, the work of TransAfrica and the CBC in U.S. foreign policy discourses is the product of the various ideological camps operating in African American domestic and international politics.

TransAfrica takes its mission from the general declaration of the Fifth Pan-African Congress, embracing the notion of a connection between the conditions of African Americans and those of other Africans and African descendents. Considered in tandem, its mission and its activities speak to a combination of ideologies of Pan-Africanism, integration, and nationalism. It is Pan-African in the sense that its objectives remain consistent with earlier organizations, including the Pan-African Congress movement and the Council on African Affairs. Its advocacy through the U.S. foreign policy process (a result of access to institutions from which African Americans had been long excluded) reveals its apparent integrationist character. Still, the notion of a connection between African American success and the success of African peoples everywhere, while clearly a Pan-African sentiment, in many ways speaks to the presence of nationalist sensibilities as well. By embracing the Fifth Pan-African Congress's declaration of support for the world's laboring and dependent classes, TransAfrica also reveals strands of marxist thought, engaging in critiques of capitalism and class stratification. Historically, TransAfrica reflected some of the characteristics of the Pan-African Congress movement as it had evolved by its fifth meeting at Manchester in 1945. By combining the efforts of celebrities and intellectuals with mass participation, TransAfrica initially presented itself as a mass-action social movement organization. Thus it reflected the Fifth Pan-African Congress's progress in expanding its own circle of participation to include both intellectuals and laypeople.

African American Political Organizations and Africa in the Postapartheid Era

By the early 1990s, victory had been achieved in South Africa. The anti-apartheid movement was over, and in the republic's first general election since the fall of apartheid rule, Nelson Mandela was elected president of the African National Congress. Throughout apartheid's existence in South Africa, African Americans played a key role in the movement that resulted in universal suffrage for all citizens of South Africa. Partnering with other multiracial organizations in the United States and abroad, TransAfrica and the Congressional Black Caucus served as the African American front on South Africa at the height of the anti-apartheid movement. They effectively forced the United States to respond to apartheid in a way it had previously resisted. The now-famous protests at the South African embassies in 1984 and 1985 had achieved their objectives. Not only did the U.S. Congress pass the Comprehensive Anti-Apartheid Act of 1986, but by the early 1990s the ultimate objective of eliminating apartheid in South Africa had been achieved.

The fall of apartheid in South Africa marked a turning point among African Americans and African American political organizations that had been committed to the struggle to realize the democratization of South Africa. What had been the contemporary rallying cry for these organizations was no longer such. Thus, the early 1990s marked a watershed for Pan-Africanism as well. African American and multiracial organizations that had become institutionalized during the anti-apartheid movement faced the daunting task of determining what causes they would focus on next. Just as Ghana's independence in 1957 caused African Americans to reconsider their relationship with Africa, so too did the end of South African apartheid. As this analysis has shown, African Americans have, in a very evolved way, shown an understanding that they play an important role in advocating on behalf of Africa and the countries of the African Diaspora.

African American engagement with African affairs has evolved extensively from the first rumblings of Pan-Africanism in the late eighteenth and early nineteenth centuries. Once understood as a mere affinity or longing for an ancestral homeland, African American interest in Africa has developed into involvement and influence. For nearly a century, African Americans have inserted themselves into political discourses on Africa. They have engaged in these discourses notwithstanding tensions that surfaced in the face of continental African nationalism. Progressive and somewhat oppositional organizations such as TransAfrica and the Congressional Black Caucus, raise important questions about the marrying of ideological approaches to African American politics that have been historically understood to be conflicting. Both organizations have advocated and legislated issues related to Africa domestically and internationally in ways not previously possible. Certainly, this represents Pan-Africanism's ideological continuity. However, African American advocacy on behalf of Africa and all of its diasporic centers disrupts the traditionally triangular debates over nationalism, integration, and radicalism as the most effective liberation strategy. These debates have long prevailed in African American politics, both domestically and internationally. In many ways, the evolution of African Americans into more active players in international affairs represents an amalgamation of these various ideological camps. Organizations like TransAfrica and the Congressional Black Caucus exist in consequence of the successful integration of African Americans into the American political and social arrangement. Still, their work on behalf of Africa and the African Diaspora is rooted in notions of Pan-Africanism, an ideology born of sentiments of African American nationalism.

However, the elevation of African Americans into prominent roles in the U.S. diplomatic corps must also be considered in these discourses. From Ralph Bunche's work with the U.S. Department of State and the United Nations in the mid-twentieth century, to Andrew Young's 1977 selection as U.S ambassador to the United Nations, to the appointments of Colin Powell and Condoleezza Rice as secretary of state in 2001 and 2005, respectively, African American diplomats—from both of the dominant American political parties—add another dimension to the ideological approaches and objectives of the involvement of African Americans in international affairs, particularly those concerning Africa and the various nation-states of the African Diaspora. Certainly the appointments of Powell and Rice as secretary of state by Republican administrations also complicate notions of solidarity among African Americans in debates about U.S. foreign policy toward Africa. The election of Barack Obama to the

American presidency adds yet another dimension to an already complicated subject. The appointments of Secretaries Powell and Rice, and the election of President Obama necessitate reconsideration of the role of African Americans in international affairs through organizations like TransAfrica. If these organizations were founded to ensure that African Americans had some form of organized voice on issues and questions of U.S. foreign policy, how do they change now that there is an African American presence in the upper echelon of the U.S. diplomatic corps? Thus, the task remains of developing a theoretical or ideological approach to describe these contemporary African American transnational activities.

Today the involvement of African Americans in international affairs, particularly concerning Africa and the various centers of the African Diaspora, necessitates further conversation on class dynamics and the ability of African American politicians and intellectuals to actually stand in solidarity with struggling and oppressed classes. That the primary African American voices in U.S. foreign policy are members of Congress, secretaries of state, and now a U.S. president raises questions about the dominance of a certain class group in these activities. Thus, we must question the ways in which class and political interests may impose limitations on these transnational actors. This conundrum creates an opportunity to further analyze the civil rights movement for its success at elevating the social status of middle-class and elite African Americans, while being less than fully responsive to the political, social, and economic needs of working-class and poor African Americans. African American engagement with the politics of Africa—whether through legislation, official and citizen diplomacy, lobbying efforts, or civil disobedience—also raises questions about the degree to which African Americans are really connected to Africans and other African descendants throughout the world. As Africa has become increasingly distant for African Americans, is it accurate to assume a connection between these geographically separate groups other than that which has been historically embraced because of like phenotype? African American involvement in international affairs as advocated by the Du Boisian brand of Pan-Africanism unquestionably contributed immensely to the eradication of colonialism in continental Africa. Surely, the work of TransAfrica under the leadership of Randall Robinson represents the continuity of this. After all, the fall of apartheid in South Africa was scarcely an issue of international concern before the women and men involved in TransAfrica made it so. But now that these victories have been achieved, does this brand of Pan-Africanism (that is, Pan-Africanism through the protest tradition) have any relevance or effectiveness? Now that African Americans have achieved the proverbial goal of having an African American elected to the U.S. presidency, is the only way to effectively express concern about the conditions of Africans and other African descendants through official channels sanctioned by the U.S. government? Surely it would be a false assumption that an African American secretary of state, member of Congress, or president—by the mere fact of being African American—will somehow situate the interests of the nation-states of Africa and the African Diaspora at a place higher than what are understood as "national interests." Thus, international advocacy work of organizations like TransAfrica and the Congressional Black Caucus, as well as the work of countless known and unknown Americans to hold their government responsible for advancing a foreign policy agenda that considers the preservation of the human rights needs of the peoples of continental Africa and the African Diaspora, remains relevant.

NOTES

1. See Essien-Udom, 1971, 6.
2. Historian Wilson J. Moses (1996) would associate these sentiments with what he calls "Classical Black Nationalism," which he associates with African Americans' desire to create an independent nation-state that separates them from the culturally, socially, and politically oppressive conditions they endured in the United States.
3. I am indebted to Ula Taylor, Charles P. Henry, Robert Allen, Kim Voss, Shantina Jackson, Dmitri Seals, Lorenzo Morris, and Jonathan Fenderson for their insightful feedback on previous versions of this chapter.
4. See Meriwether, 2002, 151.
5. George Padmore provides a thorough description of the history of Pan-Africanism and the first five Pan-African Congresses. See Padmore, 1956. Also see Mathurin, 1976.
6. Padmore, 1956, 171.
7. See Rodney, 1974, 38–47. Also see Hill and Claude, 2008, 50–60; and Austin, "All 2007, 516–39.
8. It was also during the period between the Fifth and Sixth Pan-African Congresses that Nkrumah organized two conferences focused on uniting Africa. The first, the All-African People's Conference, was held in Accra in April 1958. The second was held in May 1963 in Addis Ababa. It was at the latter conference that the Organization of African Unity (OAU) was founded. See Ginwala, 2006.
9. See Touré, 1976, 15.
10. Ibid., 15.
11. "General Declaration of the Sixth Pan-African Congress," in *Resolutions and Selected Speeches from the Sixth Pan African Congress* (Dar Es Salaam: Tanzania Publishing House), 89.
12. Ibid., 6.
13. Du Bois's own ideological evolution is illustrative of the trend among some radical-minded intellectuals to gravitate toward other ideological foundations, including socialism and marxism. See Lewis, 2001. Also, see Marable, 2004.

14. See Sales, 1994, 19.
15. Ibid.
16. Ibid., 21.
17. See Malcolm X, "Speech at OAAU Homecoming Rally," in Clark, 1992, 152–53.
18. Sales, 1994, 85.
19. Ibid., 90. Also see Gallen, 1992, 79–80
20. The prevailing philosophy of the OAU was the promotion of cooperation among nation-states in continental Africa. It was particularly focused on cooperation in "economics, culture, science, and technology." Notable among the objectives and philosophy was the elimination of colonialism and all of its legacies. Pointedly, the constitution of the OAU articulated the aims of (1) the promotion of unity and solidarity among African states; (2) the eradication of colonialism; (3) the promotion of international cooperation by and through embracing the Charter of the United Nations and the organization's Universal Declaration of Human Rights. See Naldi, 1999, chap. 1.
21. See "Statement of Basic Aims and Objectives of the OAAU," in Breitman, 1967, 105–6. Also see "Excerpts from OAAU Founding Rally," Pan-African Perspective website, accessed 24 March 2008.
22. Ibid.
23. Malcolm X's influence on African American cultural nationalism is reflected in the thought of noted cultural nationalist Maulana Karenga, who cites the Pan-Africanist thought of Malcolm X as one of his influences. Malcolm's thought and work influenced the earlier thinking of Amiri Baraka who, like Karenga, cites Malcolm X as a major figure in his development as a cultural nationalist. For more on Maulana Karenga and the influence of Malcolm X on his thinking and activism, see, Brown, 2003. Also see "Interview with Maulana Karenga," conducted by the History Makers and published on November 18, 2002. Also see Woodard, 1999, 50.
24. See Tyson, 2001.
25. See Ahmad, 2007, chap. 3.
26. See Walters, 1993, 58.
27. See Tyson, 2001. Also see Ahmad, 2007.
28. Woodard, 1999, 160.
29. Ibid. Also, Robert L. Allen tends to the issue of internal colonialism and its impact in his text, *Black Awakening in Capitalist America* (Allen, 1969).
30. Woodard, 1999, 162.
31. Ibid.
32. See Cedric J. Robinson, 2000.
33. See Von Eschen, 1997.
34. It is important to note that the South African situation was not the only cause around which Africa Americans rallied in the 1930s and 1940s. While there was nearly a twenty-year gap between the meetings of the fourth and fifth Pan-African Congresses, African Americans, through the NAACP and the Council on African Affairs, were instrumental in heightening the awareness and facilitating the involvement of African Americans in the independence movement in Ethiopia. In fact, as Meriwether points out, the independence of Ethiopia in 1936 was the beginning of a time in which African Americans would come to rethink their relationship with Africa. This reconceptualization would be furthered by Ghana's independence twenty years later. See Meriwether, 2002, chap. 1.

35. Von Eschen, 1997, 65.

36. Meriwether, 2002, 90.

37. This is not to discount the degree to which the NAACP involved itself in and led efforts to pressure the United States and other governments to impose sanctions on South Africa. However, the organization was initially reluctant to involve itself in international affairs concerning the nation-states of continental Africa. This changed with the defiance campaign of 1948. Francis Njubi Nesbitt discusses the role of the NAACP in the anti-apartheid movement extensively. See Nesbitt, 2004.

38. The question of foreign policy became a major point of conflict between Du Bois (who was employed by the NAACP at the time) and the NAACP leadership. Du Bois devised programs that would have caused the NAACP to gravitate into the international policy arena. He was subsequently fired by the organization, after which time he became formally involved with the CAA. Meriwether, 2002, 101–2.

39. Ibid., 97.

40. See Minter, Hovey, and Cobb, 2008, 24.

41. Ibid.

42. Ibid.

43. Ibid.

44. During the Defiance Campaign there were only two African Americans in the U.S. Congress, a number that actually held constant from the 79th to 83rd Congresses. This number included Rep. Adam Clayton Powell, Jr., (D-New York), and Rep. William L. Dawson (D-Illinois). There were no African American members of the U.S. Senate. See Amer, 2005, table 3.

45. The work to ensure that African Americans were able to fully exercise the franchise after the adoption of the Voting Rights Act and the Civil Rights Act was extended by organizations including SNCC. Their efforts are best represented by the activities of the well-known Freedom Summer of 1964. See Payne, 2007.

46. Nesbitt describes the three ideological camps of the anti-apartheid movement as left, nationalist, and liberal. See Nesbitt, 2004, vii. Also see Ahmad, 2007.

47. Nesbitt, 2004, viii. Also see Minter, Hovey, and Cobb, 2008, 39.

48. Minter, Hovey, and Cobb, 2008, 27.

49. At the time of their arrest, Randall Robinson was executive director of TransAfrica, Eleanor Holmes Norton was professor of law at Georgetown University Law Center, Walter Fauntroy was delegate to the U.S. House of Representatives from the District of Columbia, and Mary Frances Berry was a member of the U.S. Commission on Civil Rights. See Randall Robinson, 1998.

50. Ibid.

51. Ibid., 161.

52. TransAfrica's founding in 1978 was during the 95th Congress (1977–79). At that time there were seventeen African American members of the House and none in the Senate. When the Free South Africa Movement began, following TransAfrica's first organized protest at the South African Embassy in 1984, there were a total of twenty-one African Americans seated in the 98th Congress. All of them were members of the House of Representatives.

53. Political Scientist Marguerite Ross Barnett provides a theorization of the CBC in its early stages that is particularly useful in understanding the caucus's significance and the opportunities that its existence presented to engage a wide range of issues related

to Africans and African Americans. Barnett characterizes the CBC in the first two years after its founding as being in a collective stage. This phase is characterized by the Caucus's efforts to organize its membership and solidify its place as a visible, permanent, and influential force in national political affairs. The second stage that Barnett characterizes is the ethnic stage. This period—between 1972 and 1974—was the time in which African American members of Congress were able to focus their efforts on being "just legislators" rather than on being "African American legislators." This change in focus proved instrumental in solidifying a consistent, permanent, and growing African American presence in Congress. See Barnett, 1975, 34–50.

54. See Robinson, 1979, 17.

REFERENCES

Ahmad, Muhammad. 2007. *We Will Return in the Whirlwind: Black Radical Organizations.* Evanston, Ill.: Charles W. Kerr.

Allen, Robert L. 1969. *Black Awakening in Capitalist America.* New York: Doubleday.

Amer, Mildred L. 2005. *Black Members of the United States Congress: 1870–2005.* Washington, D.C.: Congressional Research Services, Library of Congress.

Austin, David. 2007. "Roads Led to Montreal: Black Power, the Caribbean, and the Black Radical Tradition in Canada." *Journal of African American History* 92, no. 4 (Fall): 516–39.

Barnett, Marguerite. 1975. "The Congressional Black Caucus." *Proceedings from the Academy of Political Science* 32, no. 1 (Congress against the President): 34–50.

Breitman, George. 1967. *The Last Year of Malcolm X: The Evolution of a Revolutionary.* New York: Merit.

Brown, Scot Brown. 2003. *Fighting for US: Maulana Karenga, The US Organization and Black Cultural Nationalism.* New York: New York University Press.

Clark, Steve. 1992. *February 1965: The Final Speeches, Malcolm X.* New York: Pathfinder Press.

Essien-Udom, Essien Udom. 1971. *Black Nationalism: The Search for an Identity in America.* Chicago: University of Chicago Press.

Gallen, David. *Malcolm X: As They Knew Him.* New York: Carroll and Graf, 1992.

Ginwala, Frene Noshir. 2006. *Africa's Unfinished Agenda: The Legacy of Kwame Nkrumah.* Cape Coast: University of Cape Coast Press.

Hill, Sylvia, and Judy Claude. 2008. "Remembering 6PAC: Interviews with Sylvia Hill and Judy Claude, Organizers of 6PAC." *Black Scholar* 37, no. 4: 50–60.

Lewis, David Levering. 2001. *W. E. B. Du Bois: The Fight for Equality and the American Century 1919–1963.* New York: Owl Books.

Marable, Manning. 2004. *W. E. B. Du Bois: Radical Black Democrat.* Boulder: Paradigm Publishers.

Mathurin, Owen Charles. 1976. *Henry Sylvester Williams and the Origins of the Pan-African Movement, 1869–1911.* Westport, Conn.: Greenwood Press.

Meriwether, James W. 2002. *Proudly We Can Be Africans: African Americans and Africa, 1935–1961.* Chapel Hill: University of North Carolina Press.

Minter, William, Gail Hovey, and Charles Cobb, eds. 2008. *No Easy Victories: African Liberation and American Activists over a Half Century, 1950–2000.* Trenton: Africa World Press.

Moses, Wilson J., ed. 1996. *Classical Black Nationalism: From the American Revolution to Marcus Garvey.* New York: New York University Press.

Naldi, Gino J. 1999. *The Organization of African Unity: An Analysis of Its Role*, 2d ed. London: Mansell.

Nesbitt, Francis Njubi. 2004. *Race for Sanctions: African Americans against Apartheid, 1946–1994.* Bloomington: Indiana University Press.

Padmore, George. 1956. *Pan-Africanism or Communism? The Coming Struggle for Africa.* London: D. Dobson.

Payne, Charles. 2007. *I've Got the Light of Freedom: The Organizing Tradition and the Mississippi Freedom Struggle.* Berkeley: University of California Press.

Robinson, Cedric J. 2000. *Black Marxism: The Making of the Black Radical Tradition.* Chapel Hill: University of North Carolina Press.

Robinson, Randall. 1979. "Testimony before the Subcommittees on Africa and International Economic Policy and Trade." *Issue: A Journal of Opinion* 9, no. 1: 17–20.

———. 1998. *Defending the Spirit: A Black Life in America.* New York: Plume.

Rodney, Walter. 1974. "The Black Scholar Interviews: Walter Rodney." *Black Scholar* 6, no. 3 (November): 38–47.

Sales, William, Jr. 1994. *From Civil Rights to Black Liberation: Malcolm X and the Organization of Afro-American Unity.* Cambridge, Mass.: South End Press.

Shillington, Kevin. 2005. *The History of Africa*, 2d rev. ed. New York: Palgrave Macmillan.

Touré, Sekou. 1976. "Message of President Sekou Touré." In *Resolutions and Selected Speeches from the Sixth Pan African Congress.* Dar Es Salaam: Tanzania Publishing House.

Tyson, Timothy B. 2001. *Radio Free Dixie: Robert F. Williams and the Roots of Black Power.* Chapel Hill: University of North Carolina Press.

Von Eschen, Penn. 1997. *Race against Empire: Black Americans and Anticolonialism, 1927–1957.* Ithaca: Cornell University Press.

Walters, Ronald W. 1993. *Pan Africanism in the African Diaspora: An Analysis of Modern Afrocentric Political Movements.* Detroit: Wayne State University Press.

Watts, Jerry Gafio. 2001. *Amiri Baraka: The Politics of a Black Intellectual.* New York: New York University Press.

Woodard, Komozi. 1999. *A Nation within a Nation: Amiri Baraka (LeRoi Jones) and Black Power Politics.* Chapel Hill: University of North Carolina Press.

PART II

Rise to Institutional Global Power Positions

FOUR

Congress and
Africa's Constituency

THE DEVELOPMENT OF THE AFRICA
GROWTH AND OPPORTUNITY ACT
AND THE INTERSECTION OF AFRICAN
AMERICAN AND BUSINESS INTERESTS

William G. Jones

Africa's prominence as a key region in U.S. foreign policy continues. In February 2008 President George W. Bush made a trip to Africa to highlight his administration's commitment. In March 2006, the Bush administration announced the first regional military command dedicated solely to U.S. national security interests in Africa. The command was to be known as AFRICOM. The new command's purpose was to support African nations' efforts to limit the spread of radical militant Islamism and al Qaeda while increasing professionalism and capacity of Africa's military. Some foreign policy analysts see the effort as serving the dual purpose of protecting and advancing U.S. economic interests. President Barack Obama has made two trips to Africa. In June 2009, he visited Egypt to address the Muslim world and in July 2009 to deliver an address focused mainly on sub-Saharan Africa. This development comes with the background of an emerging new era in U.S. and Africa foreign policymaking. The era is post–Civil Rights, post–Southern Africa liberation, and post–Cold War. New competitors have taken the stage to challenge both European and U.S. hegemony over strategic natural and human resources in Africa. Asian powerhouses such as China, Japan, and India are more substantial competitors than in the past. European nations have focused on retrenchment of their relationship with Africa as they consider the needs of their emerging federation, the European Union (EU). African oil has grown as a key supply source for the world energy market for industrialized nations as Middle East oil has become problematic. None of these circumstances is more important than the internally generated political developments in Africa. Some African nations have experienced instability caused by dictatorship, economic stagnation, insurrections fueled by neocolonialism, and democracy movements. African nations have intensified their expressions of discontent with the current international finance systems, and others have intensified efforts to form a strong African continental federation as expressed in the African Union. Since the end of the Cold War, promoters of the World Trade Organization (WTO) have sought the region's participation, and Africa has increased its interest in fair trade. In this context the Africa Growth and Opportunity Act (AGOA) emerged.

A little over a decade earlier, in 1995, the U.S. Congress experienced a resurgent interest in Africa. In 1995 Congress voted down an amendment by Representative Hastings aimed at increasing aid to Africa by $173 million. Between 1996 and 1998, the Africa Growth and Opportunity Act began to take form as one of the most significant African policy initiatives in the post–civil rights, post–Southern African liberation, and post–Cold War era. AGOA served to support U.S. economic and trade policy toward Africa. The act was passed in Congress and was signed into law by President Clinton on May 18, 2000. This foreign policy legislation has been expanded and extended through 2015.

The development of the act embodied several dilemmas faced by African American politicians and Congress in a post–civil rights and post–Cold War era. The resurgent interest in Africa has been framed as a response to the growing influence of African American members of Congress and voters. It has been framed as a matter of business interest in expanding trade and managing markets. Also, AGOA may have been a response to rising concerns from citizens and states on the African continent over neocolonial trade regimes, super debt, seething poverty, and disease. These concerns were voiced in forums such as the WTO's Uruguay Meeting that resulted in an agreement signed in 1994. This chapter examines the behavior of members' of Congress in foreign policymaking related to the AGOA. It examines the role of race and business interest as competing, conflicting, and consolidating influences.

The theoretical framework for this study is a contemporary work centered on race, authored by Robert Smith. In *We Have No Leaders,* Smith is certain that white supremacy remains at the core of racial politics in the post–civil rights era. The influence of race in Congress and American politics is an important focus of the book. Smith extends David Easton's system model by using Harry Scoble's theory to consider various responses to stress and demands on the political system. Smith focuses on cooptation and repression as relevant system responses to the demands of the civil rights and black power movements. He carefully defines *cooptation* in terms of whether or not the values and objectives of the social movement have been effectively reflected in concrete public policy or legislative outcomes, or whether symbolic politics is the frequent response to persistent and substantive social and economic issues. One of the central questions in evaluating the AGOA is whether compromises and conditionality woven into the fabric of the legislation resulted in trade legislation that was more symbolic than substantive in its ability to address Africa's development needs. Another consideration is whether, in the end, U.S. business and neocolonial interest actually advanced over the African interest.

Although Smith focused on domestic politics, there are clearly related ideological and policy parallels reflected in domestic political rhetoric such as "work not welfare" and foreign policy political rhetoric such as "trade not aid," a phrase used in relation to the AGOA. Smith's work is a viable lens through which to view congressional behavior and the intersection between racial interests and business interests in considering the AGOA.

Modernization and dependence theories are two principal approaches that further define the points of contention and agreement on the AGOA. Members of Congress, the president, interest groups, and the public consciously and unconsciously find support for their thinking on economic development legislation such as the AGOA based in these two theoretical approaches. Interest group voices tend to be ideologically consistent with one or the other of these approaches, given their ability to build a more specific constituency by narrowing the scope of consensus. Daniel Yergin, author of *The Commanding Heights*, offers a contemporary critique on state-led approaches to development and the superiority of markets as vehicles to economic success. Yergin finds Adam Smith's description in *The Wealth of Nations* of a system based on self-interest, private property, contracts, and laissez-faire government as compelling so long as self-constraint is present. Many domestic advocates for Africa development policy and African diplomats found the AGOA's free market approach compelling as a way forward irrespective of the past.

Conceptualizing the AGOA's significance has to be placed in the context of theories that consider private markets as a necessity and Western imperialism as a significant impact on Africa's development process. Opponents questioned whether the legislation represented the extension of colonial exploitation. Africans' plight during colonialism was unnecessary for modernization, according to Walter Rodney, a noted Pan-Africanist scholar. He writes that colonialism was a retardant in Africa's development—organizing and misdirecting material, intellectual, and cultural resources toward Western development rather than the natural course of African self-development.[1] Advances toward globalization, structural adjustment, and comparative advantage as development approaches have been answered by theories centered on recolonization[2] and neocolonialism. Kwame Nkrumah, African scholar and nationalist political leader, argued for a theoretical effort to find consistency between theories of modernization, development, and the traditional "African personality."[3] He considered several factors necessary to this course. These factors included the requirement for comprehensive socialized modes of production, large-scale human and investment capital, and cohesive socialist planning.[4] Most important to development was the creation of a unified continental government capable of defending African sovereignty and promoting economic self-reliance. Nkrumah saw a system of neocolonialism as the major impediment to development. Nkrumah's political philosophy often finds less than coherent application in contemporary scholarship, yet the perspective it brings to the Africa policy discourse and the positions of interest groups, legislators, and theorists is fundamental to understanding business interests and the interests of Africa and African Americans.

Black politics has explored features of neocolonialism as a domestic form in relation to African American communities and the larger sociopolitical system. Lorenzo Morris states that "while substantial progress may have been made, it often serves to distort and disguise the scarcely altered continuity of the legal and political structure for dealing with racial problems."[5] The essence of Robert Smith's work in *We Have No Leaders* and other similar works leads to the conclusion that African Americans find themselves in a policymaking dilemma similar to that described by neocolonialism's theorists. AGOA represents the convergence of a variety of domestic interests, mainly business and racial, dressed in the cloth of foreign policymaking. These theories assist in providing an explanation of the congressional behavior concerning this important piece of legislation.

Role of Congressional Committees and Interest Groups in Foreign Policymaking

This literature review looks at aspects of the congressional role in foreign policymaking. It considers, more specifically, the foreign policymaking process, including the role of African American legislators and interest groups as they relate to Africa foreign policymaking efforts. It looks at the congressional role in Africa foreign policymaking and strategies used in legislative policy development, including the operation of committees. Committees are a key place where congressional leadership is exercised and where interest groups attempt to exert influence. This chapter also examines partisanship and the role of interest groups in relation to their influence in the Africa foreign policymaking process.

Even with the increasing role of individual leadership, committees are still often the instruments in which partisanship, ideological struggle, and interest group pressures are set. *Committees in Congress* by Christopher Deering and Steven Smith reviews the major theories of the function and importance of congressional committees. Deering and Smith examine several theoretical approaches to committees. They include the distributive theory, where interest groups and personal interests are an important determinant; party-dominated, where party leadership is determinant; and, chamber-dominant, where the House of Representative and the Senate have institutional interests, including the need for information and expertise in competition for leadership.

Committees play an important role in the exercise of influence, and the passage of the AGOA was no exception. Committees were the stage where a great deal of action occurred around the act. Considering the AGOA, the Appropriations Committee leadership had its most frequent interaction with authorization committees responsible for foreign policy. James McCormick considers the different strengths and activity levels between the Senate Foreign Relations Committee and the House Foreign Affairs Committee.[6] Sen. Jesse Helms had an impact when he was minority leader. Helms's leadership in the Foreign Relations Committee was important in the course of the AGOA legislative process. Former chairman Richard Lugar (R) provided balanced leadership. One of the most comprehensive works on the role of foreign policymaking related to committees is by James Lindsay. Whereas James McCormick seems to withhold an evaluation of Congress's role, Lindsay clearly believes Congress's role in foreign policy is constructive and relevant. Lindsay disputes several conceptualizations of congressional foreign policy behavior and frames them as fallacies. The "Electoral Fallacy" is that Congress is not a slave to electoral politics, rather it acts conscientiously. The "Technocratic Fallacy" is that Congress does not use public hearings and the media merely to showboat or focus irrelevant technicalities; rather, it constructively uses hearings to gather needed information and needs media attention to focus public attention on issues important to the national interest. Finally, the "Adversarial Fallacy" is that overall congressional-executive relations are more cooperative than conflictual.[7]

In *Congress and the Politics of U.S. Foreign Policy*, Lindsay states that eight congressional committees are important in foreign policymaking. Four of the most prominent committees that deal with trade and tariffs are the Senate Foreign Relations Committee, House Foreign Affairs Committee, House Ways and Means Committee, and Senate Finance Committee. The other committees are involved with various aspects of foreign policymaking and trade in a less direct way. In the past, the Senate Foreign Relations Committee and House Foreign Affairs Committee have lost power and often failed in their ability to pass congressional robust foreign aid bills and authorize new programs. Foreign policy decisionmaking has become more influenced by the increasing number of party caucuses focused on addressing economic interests and special interest concerns.

In the development of the AGOA, both business-based and African American–based group interests played key roles. Corporations involved with Africa were active influences as they have been with other trade agreements. African Americans were important supporters and opponents. Interest groups may not always be important players in foreign policymaking, but in the case of the AGOA they were very active players.

David Truman's *The Governmental Process* considers that interest groups are innumerable but not pervasive in society and politics. Interest groups have the power to define the political agenda, but they have their limits established by the general public. These interests, in their formal organizations, act on the policy process at a number of key points in the policymaking process. The strategies and tactics of these organizations are often based on their size and capabilities.

Interest groups achieve influence through the acquisition and strategic transmission of information that legislators need to make good public policy and get reelected. Interest groups' approaches are often public relations campaigns, grassroots efforts, or Washington lobbying or, at times, all three. Resources at a group's disposal are key to determining what strategies and tactics to use. Coalitions can help broaden groups' reach, especially on the floor and across branches of government.

African American participation in the AGOA was prominent. The character of African American participation was an important development in the post–civil rights and post–Cold War eras. While African Americans have a long history of participation in foreign policy, up to the 1970s it was predominantly as outsiders with little consistency. Hanes Walton documents the emerging maturation of African Americans in foreign policymaking. Walton focuses on the era immediately before and after the Ralph Bunche era. He highlights the contributions of Ralph Bunche, Andrew

Young, Goler Teal Butcher, and other insiders.[8] While concentrating on the effectiveness of the insiders, Walton also acknowledges and documents the importance of interest groups, such as TransAfrica lobby and the "Free South Africa Movement." TransAfrica played a major role as an opponent of the fundamentally conservative policy approach embedded in key elements of the AGOA.[9]

Race is a factor in foreign policymaking among legislators, interest groups, and the general public. In the past, African Americans have principally seen their role as an important voice for humanitarian causes, altruism, democracy, and opposition to white supremacy and imperialism. The AGOA provided new opportunities for Congress and interest groups to establish the character of American democracy and foreign policy.

AGOA and Congressional Parties Trade Places: New Balance of Power and Interests Emerge

In 1994 two monumental changes occurred that affected the context for the AGOA's legislative development. Republicans won a majority in both the House of Representatives and the Senate. The former states of the Confederacy were key to the conservative triumph in the House of Representatives.[10] The new Congress seated 231 Republicans and 203 Democrats in the House, and 53 Republicans and 47 Democrats in the Senate. At the same time, William Jefferson Clinton won the presidency, which elevated a southern Democrat to the post of chief executive and chief diplomat for the first time in twelve years. President Clinton received an overwhelming majority of the African American vote. A declared centrist, he employed camouflage and cover along with conciliatory and cajoling rhetoric to continue the swing to the right. A conservative political milieu limited the possibilities for substantive progressive policies and promoted symbolic political gestures.

The Congressional Black Caucus (CBC) found itself embattled in a struggle to push forth an agenda representing not only a racial minority but also an ideological minority. African American members of Congress were almost exclusively concentrated in the Democratic party. The few African Americans who held committee chairmanships lost them under the Republican majority. African Americans also lost some seats on key congressional committees under the new House leadership of Speaker Newt Gingrich.[11] In addition to lost congressional committee chairs and committee clout, the new House leadership reduced committee staff, and numerous African American staff members lost their positions. The Congress had been successfully realigned to a conservative ideological focus led by a Republican party that had a base of strong commercial interests and conservative theocratic interests that financed and supported the conservative thinktanks and political organizations. The government was divided between a conservative Congress and a centrist president. African American members of Congress held on to their seats at the table but had lost access to the kitchen and other rooms in the house. This situation left little choice for African Americans in deciding what would be on the political menu in Washington.

From NAFTA and GATT to the AGOA

With little fanfare, the Uruguay Agreements Act passed Congress in 1994 with a simple majority in both the House and Senate. In the House of Representatives, 65 percent of Democrats voted in favor of the General Agreement on Tariffs and Trade (GATT) Uruguay Round, proceeding to agreements, and 68 percent of Republicans voted in favor of the act. Debate on the agreements included vigorous discussion.

Prominent African American members of Congress opposed the Uruguay Agreements as they did the application of "fast track" to the agreements. They expressed concern about the impact on job loss and negative consequences for Africa and the Caribbean economies. Kwesi Mfume's remarks to the House encapsulated the views of many African American legislators:

> Unfortunately, the legislation will result in a continuation of the old expression "the rich get richer and the poor get poorer." This is true on both the domestic and international levels. . . . The largest job losses are expected to occur in the apparel, fabricated metal products, and furniture industries. Estimates vary from a total loss of 30,000 jobs to as many as 912,000 jobs in the manufacturing sector. . . . I do not believe that it is reasonable to expect a person who has been living in inner city Baltimore for most of their adult lives to move to rural Nebraska for a job that may not even exist. . . .And nowhere in the legislation before us is there a remedy. . . . NAFTA gave one nation— Mexico—a distinct edge . . . most of the industrialized signatories to the Uruguay Round agree that most sub-Saharan African nations will suffer as a result of the Uruguay Round.[12]

The comments by Detroit, Michigan–area Rep. John Conyers echoed the speech by Kwesi Mfume. Conyers, like Mfume, represented a district where the future of families greatly depended on the stability of America's urban industrial base as their staircase to the middle class as generations of white American families had before them. Conyers also expressed reservations about the impact of the trade agreements on countries in Africa and the Caribbean.[13]

The AGOA's legislative journey began with Congress passing the Uruguay Round Agreements Act, Public Law 103–465 (URAA). The URAA required the president to submit annual reports to Congress outlining the U.S. comprehensive trade and development policy for Africa. The responsibility of producing the reports and delivering each report to Congress was coordinated in the White House by the United States Trade Representative (USTR). This position was created by the Congress to assist the presidency in managing the growing complexity of international trade relations and was designed to serve as a trade negotiator, ombudsman, and lightning rod for politically difficult international trade relations and their domestic repercussions. The USTR presented the Africa trade reports to the Ways and Means Committee's Subcommittee on Trade.

In Congress, the House Ways and Means Committee exercises significant authority over the life of legislation. The committee gave the AGOA its principal sponsors during its course through the House of Representatives. Rep. Phillip M. Crane (R-Ill.) was a prominent member of the committee and an early sponsor of the AGOA. Rep. Charles B. Rangel (D-N.Y.), a leading Democrat and senior African American member of Congress, was a prominent sponsor of the AGOA. Also, Rep. James McDermott (D-Wash.) was a key early sponsor of the AGOA. House Speaker Gingrich appointed Rep. Bill Archer of Texas to chair the Ways and Means Committee, while Rep. Crane chaired the Trade Subcommittee. The Ways and Means Committee would serve as the venue for many of the public hearings for the AGOA and related trade policies. According to Rep. McDermott, initial work on Africa Growth and Opportunity Act was advanced by a bipartisan team composed of Reps. Crane, McDermott, and Rangel.[14]

The Ways and Means Committee's Subcommittee on Trade held a public hearing to review a wide range of trade initiatives in March 1997. The hearings reviewed the direction of trade policy initiatives in Asia, Latin America, and Africa. The principal testimony for the Clinton administration was given by Charlene Barshefsky, USTR. Her testimony reviewed current initiatives and mentioned the need to engage Africa, given its rich natural resources, and the need for the United States to participate in encouraging the Africa movement toward the transforming magic of the market and trade. At the public hearing, a number of members of the Subcommittee on Trade raised domestic issues related to foreign trade. Some committee members used the opportunity to assert the need for trade initiatives to be sensitive to the impact on jobs standards and environmental standards in order to ensure that competition between domestic and foreign employment was fair. The USTR and business witnesses stated that trade meant new jobs and a stronger economy. Much of the hearing reflected on the virtues and problems of the North American Free Trade Agreement (NAFTA).

Two weeks before the vote on the URAA, the House of Representatives considered NAFTA. The NAFTA was similar in some respects to the AGOA in that it was intended to address U.S. trade relations with a region. It would clearly have an impact on specific U.S. domestic industries and jobs, and would affect domestic commercial legal regimes in participating nations. The AGOA was referred to as the NAFTA for Africa. Congress passed NAFTA by 234 yeas to 200 nays. In contrast to their voting on the URAA, the majority of Democrats voted against NAFTA.. However, the measure passed with a coalition of "free trade" Democrats (102, or 40 percent) and a majority of Republicans (132, or 75 percent) voting for NAFTA.. The passage of NAFTA was a feather in the cap for President Clinton. At their convenience, the new Republican majority would reward Clinton's center-right leadership consistent with the conservative agenda; otherwise he found his leadership in a quagmire.

NAFTA received a favorable vote, as did the URAA, even where labor interest and interest expressed by representatives of predominantly African American congressional districts opposed the legislation. Members of the CBC voted in greater proportion against the NAFTA than did the Democrats and Republicans. African American representatives voted 26 out of 35 (74 percent) against NAFTA. Majority-minority district representatives voted 18 out of 24 (75 percent) against NAFTA.

The March 1997 trade hearing reflected the conflicting interests and influences that members of Congress serve. Competing interests are particularly difficult for African American representatives where party loyalty, racial interest, and business interests are entangled. Finding the appropriate emphasis is problematic when party leadership roles are also a factor. Reps. McDermott, Rangel, William Jefferson (D-La.), and others questioned whether several of the underlying trade policies such as NAFTA adequately protected domestic interests involved with employment. Rangel asked if the agreement's promise to address training and education for displaced workers had been fulfilled by the administration. African Americans clearly have a large stake in employment and retraining since the types of jobs likely to be exported disproportionately were employment opportunities that African American workers and white-collar workers only recently obtained uninhibited access to during the post–civil rights era. Prior to the Ways and Means Committee markup of the bill, Rep. Rangel received a letter concerning possible job loss in districts related to AGOA from fellow CBC members Sanford Bishop, James Clyburn, Eva Clayton, Earl Hilliard, Bennie Thompson, and Melvin Watt.[15]

At the hearing, Reps. Rangel and Jefferson raised questions about trade provisions for combating illegal drugs, given the implications for low-income communities and especially African American communities heavily affected by the illegal drug trade, the criminal justice system's bias, media bias, and health issues. This illegal trade simultaneously benefited some elements of society, such as those involved in money laundering and the prison-industrial complex. While many members of Congress addressed trade issues related to employment, education, environment, and the illegal drug trade, their concerns were contradicted by their promotion of "fast track" authority for the president. Interest groups such as labor unions, Public Citizen (consumer advocacy organization), and the Sierra Club believed "fast track" legislative authority for the president without robust congressional and public scrutiny would open the door for expansion of trade agreements with few protections.

The subcommittee's hearing was heavily weighted with business representatives providing their perspective on trade initiatives. Twenty-one of the thirty-seven witnesses and submissions for the record were from businesses and business groups. Major businesses weighing in on trade included Westinghouse Electric Corporation, Salomon Brothers, Pharmaceutical Research and Manufacturers of America, the Business Roundtable, Procter and Gamble Company, and others. The steel industry was the business most reticent about the positive prospects for trade. Dumping of foreign steel and labor practices were concerns for steel manufacturers. Overwhelmingly, the business community present at the hearing supported trade liberalization in the form of bilateral agreements and multilateral agreements through the NAFTA, the World Trade Organization (WTO), and GATT. At this hearing, businesses were more focused on preserving the direction of trade policy than on expanding the policy to Africa. Reps. Rangel and Jefferson stated that while trade should be a tool for economic reform in Africa, a new policy should offer Africa the same standard of the flexible approach that was applied to China.

The next public hearing held by the Ways and Means Subcommittee on Trade dealt directly with the AGOA. The hearing featured a variety of witnesses, most of whom favored the act. Business interests were active participants along with predominantly African American groups, a few labor-oriented organizations, charitable religious-based organizations, and nonprofit organizations. Additionally, several African nations were represented at the hearing by their embassy officials; these included officials from South Africa and Ethiopia. The lead witnesses were from the executive branch. These witnesses were Charlene Barshefsky, the USTR, Jeffery Lang, deputy USTR, and George Moose, assistant secretary for African affairs from the State Department. In all, forty-seven witnesses were scheduled to appear at the hearing, and fourteen statements would be submitted from additional organizations that did not provide testimony at the hearing. This hearing would be one of the most representative public forums on the broad-ranging views on trade and aid policy toward Africa.

Unusual coalitions formed within and outside of Congress around the AGOA. Jack Kemp, former Republican representative and former secretary of the U.S. Department of Housing and Urban Development, now leader of Empower America, spoke in favor of free trade's benefit to the American consumer and Africa. Kemp used the analogy of the AGOA as being "Africa's Marshall Plan." Truman's use of the term "Marshall Plan" referred to the need to relieve poverty and avoid the seeds of oppressive regimes in the world. Speaker Newt Gingrich's presence and his remarks at the beginning of the hearing reflected a unique congressional coalition in support of the AGOA. The coalition involved African American liberal Democrats and conservative Republicans, and other free-trade Republican and Democrats. Gingrich noted that the United States had a unique interest in Africa because of its African American population and history. He acknowledged the "Africa Trade Bill" work of Democrats Rangel, Jefferson, and McDermott. McDermott is credited with placing the requirement for reporting on Africa trade policy development in the GATT legislation subsequent to the Uruguay Round Agreements.

The presence of Speaker Gingrich at the hearing signaled the importance of the Africa Trade Bill to key Republican constituencies, rather than an effort to reach out to African American voters. On many other issues of major importance to African American racial interests, the speaker had made few concessions. Gingrich, while stoking the fire of conservatism, did support the more moderate wing of the party on affirmative action in an effort to keep the party from being labeled outright racist and mean-spirited.[16] The hearings also demonstrated the possibility that passage might not be assured by unified business interests. Although large businesses supported the bill, smaller manufacturers involved with textiles were strongly opposed, as could be seen in the testimonies of the Neckwear Association of America and the Rubber and Plastic Footwear Manufacturers Association.[17] Committees in the party-dominated and ideologically dominated Congress would need the clout of the party leadership to be effective, particularly because of the narrow margin of the Republican majority.[18]

Africa was a topic in other public hearings relating to trade. U.S.–Africa trade relations were mentioned in many public hearings on trade during 1997 in the context of evaluating policy, such as NAFTA, and trade with Asian nations, such as China. Legislators and interest groups, particularly labor and small businesses, were concerned about the impact of job loss and business loss. Members of Congress posed questions and fielded cautions about expanding the trade provisions from NAFTA to other regions such as Africa.[19] These other hearings reflected the difficulty of policymaking for members of Congress in trying to strike a balance between addressing the domestic impact of "free trade policy" on working-class families and the economically disadvantaged, such as African Americans, and the need to support globalization and neocolonialism. Europe, China, and India were producing greater competition for control and access to resources. More regions were looking toward strengthening their regional markets, with a view to a self-reliance that could result in less need for American products and services. These regions were pressing forward with efforts to consolidate and expand their access to Africa's commodities and natural resources. Members of Congress supportive of the president found themselves particularly conflicted and challenged by the president's "pro–free trade" policy stands. The policies had telling impacts on many constituencies unable to find the opportunities promised by proponents of "free trade." Promised opportunities included abundant high-technology jobs, well-paying service jobs, and trade-based industry jobs. Jobs training programs were offered in the hearings as a means to soften the impact of trade-related employment dislocation. These programs would mean little or nothing to the underclass historically excluded from full access to employment opportunities in coping with social and economic challenges, such as those outlined in William Julius Wilson's *When Work Disappears*.[20]

Two other congressional committees were given jurisdiction over the AGOA by Speaker Gingrich. These were the House Banking and Financial Services Committee and the International Relations Committee's Subcommittee on Africa. The Banking and Financial Services Committee focused on generic debt-relief measures and some reforms to the International Monetary Fund. It focused less on Africa and AGOA than did the International Relations Committee. The Subcommittee on Africa of the International Relations Committee had a broad range of experience in examining problems in Africa. The subcommittee historically had been the resource for authorizations of foreign assistance bills and other bill provisions for African states. Additionally, the subcommittee's role was to examine a variety of issues and offer policy recommendations to address U.S. and Africa relations concerned with crisis situations and political developments, as well as forward policy concerns, such as democratic governance, corruption prevention, national security interest, and economic development.

The International Relations Committee was chaired by Benjamin Gilman (R-N.Y.). The Subcommittee on Africa was chaired by Edward Royce, a newly elected Republican who attained office in the 103rd Congress. A prominent advocate for Africa policy was Rep. Donald Payne of New Jersey. Payne had been a long-standing member of the subcommittee. Payne actively participated in the AGOA discussion, although the committee on the whole took a back seat to the Ways and Means Committee and its Subcommittee on Trade. In addition to Donald Payne, Georgia representative Cynthia McKinney was a member of the International Relations Committee. Over the course of the development of the trade initiative, Payne voiced concern over Africa's debt and the related support for the tragic dictatorships, such as the regime of former neocolonialist president SaSa Mobutu of the Republic of the Congo (formerly Zaire). Payne also spoke to Western countries' responsibility for debt held by some current regimes with political histories that paralleled that of Congo.[21] Further, Payne expressed interest in the fact that there was not complete unanimity in support of the proposed AGOA. At a hearing, he asked Susan Rice, assistant secretary of state for African affairs, about AGOA concerns raised by Randall Robinson of TransAfrica, Ralph Nader, founder of Public Citizen, and Rep. Jesse Jackson, Jr.[22]

Susan Rice presented the Clinton administration view that the opponents of the proposed AGOA had misunderstood the draft provisions. The provisions, according to Rice, offered something for everyone, and the conditionality incorporated in the act had broad support among African leaders. The African diplomats had expressed support for the proposed legislation at the same time as some prominent leaders in Africa, such as Nelson Mandela and Robert Mugabe, expressed reservations. Most of the reservations involved the concern that many new benefits under the act would be provided only to countries that surrendered their national economies to the worst impacts of globalization. The feared impacts included the possible destruction of industries, worker exploitation, loss of public services, ownership of national assets, and environmental degradation.

Susan Rice was a prominent administration advocate for the AGOA who initially worked in the White House on the National Security Council staff for Africa affairs. She observed that Jim McDermott and his staff lead by Michael Williams were key facilitators of the AGOA along with Reps. Rangel and Jefferson. On Charles Rangel's staff, Rosa Whitaker worked on the AGOA.[23] Rice noted that there was some reluctance about the AGOA in the office of President Clinton's first USTR, Mickey Kanton. Also, the Agency for International Development had concerns about the "trade not aid" policy approach attached to the AGOA.[24]

Hearings held by the Ways and Means Committee and the International Relations Committee on the AGOA and other related trade and foreign affairs issues provided an opportunity for both proponents and opponents of the legislation to present views on the legislation. By March 1998 the House of Representatives was ready to start debating the merits of a rule to consider the AGOA. The deliberation started with the floor discussion on a rule entitled House Resolution 383, "Providing for consideration of the bill (H.R. 1432) to authorize a new trade and investment policy for sub-Saharan Africa." The rule provided for introduction of a limited number of amendments. Only amendments incorporated in the Committee on Rules report would be heard, and no amendments to these amendments would be allowed. During the debate on the rule, Representative Moakley of the Committee on Rules declared that the rule for consideration of the AGOA was a "closed rule breaking a streak of open rules." Moakley urged members to oppose the rule, given the numerous amendments members expressed interest in offering.[25] The general debate would be limited to two hours and controlled by the chairman and ranking members of the International Relations Committee and Ways and Means Committee. With measures in place, an efficient, yet vigorous deliberation of AGOA ensued.

The deliberation of the Africa Growth and Opportunity Act in Congress both over the rule and over the act (H.R. 1432) reflects the complexity of racial and business interests in the bill. Members of Congress sought to note how the bill served or did not serve the best interest of workers, African Americans, and Africa. Few commenters raised questions regarding whether the bill adequately served the interest of large businesses. Members debated the extent of domestic economic impact of the legislation. Members of Congress were actively engaged in the deliberations among the House and congressional leadership, and African American legislators were particularly prominent in the effort to define the meanings of the bill. Several key themes emerged in the deliberations:

1. The value of trade and investment for improving the quality of life, self-sufficiency, and encouraging democracy in Africa.
2. Replacing aid with trade.
3. The bill's service to business interests at the expense of African state sovereignty and neocolonial orientation.
4. The lack of focus on labor, environmental, and Africans' social needs.
5. Parallels between AGOA and NAFTA related to possible job loss.
6. Benefits of Africa trade and investment to continued growth of the American economy.
7. The continuity of the AGOA with the American role, particularly the African American role, in the struggle for liberation from colonialism and settler colonialism in Africa.
8. Concern about whether the bill adequately addressed transshipment as a danger to siphoning-off intended benefit for African workers.
9. Recognition that some African states had already adopted market-based economies in response to IMF and other multilateral finance institutions' push for structural adjustment and the states' own experience with economic sluggishness in state-owned industries.

Reflected in the House floor debate on the legislation were the definitions of racial and business interests communicated by interest groups. The congressional dialogue on the bill reflected the aspirations and concerns voiced by interest groups. It was clear that interest groups had effectively communicated their issues to members of Congress who ably articulated their personal perspectives on the bill along with those of constituents. The bill was of latent interest to the general public. Public attention was more a creation of interest groups, members of Congress, and the White House than a deep and broadly held public policy concern. Consequently, as Gabriel Almond has indicated on such matters related to foreign policy, interest groups and the preferences of members of Congress are paramount in legislative decisionmaking.[26]

In portions of the deliberation, legislators struggled to cast the meaning of the bill related to the racial projects. Rep. Barbara Lee related the bill to the civil rights movement in saying: "Albeit some may argue and say we are not on the precipice of a Civil Rights Act today, I still take the words of Dr. Martin Luther King and say, "If not now, then when; for the first time in the history of this Nation, I do believe we have elevated the discussion of the continent of Africa, sub-Saharan Africa, 48 countries, to a level of equality and equal partnership in business."[27]

The CBC voice in the AGOA deliberation reflected almost the full range of views from conservative to liberal and from integrationist to Pan-Africanist. Rep. Jesse Jackson, Jr., offered:

> The earliest trade policy of the United States, even before the Declaration of Independence, in 1619, involved African kings and potentates selling other common Africans to shipping companies owned by whites to be sold as exploited slaves and slave masters in the new territory . . . The agricultural, shipping and plantation companies and communities served primarily as the infrastructure for American complicity in this trade policy. The question before this Congress today is who benefited then and who benefits now is really the gravamen of this debate. As we seek to establish a new trading paradigm between African nations and America, it is critically important that the new trading arrangement create a mutually beneficial partnership between black people in Africa and African Americans in the United States, which I believe will benefit all Americans.[28]

Jackson would later introduce into the House of Representative his own HOPE for Africa bill as reflecting his vision of the appropriate paradigm for U.S.–Africa trade relations. His bill would be stillborn. The CBC's absence of a unified position for or against the bill strengthened the bipartisan majority position in favor of the legislation. Opponents attempted to frame the meaning of the legislation as malicious to African and African American interests. The CBC contribution was deliberative debate, which proved valuable to proponents and opponents of the legislation.

For the CBC the point of division over the bill is most clear when the vote on Representative Maxine Waters's amendment is considered. The bill's handlers allowed for only a few amendments to be introduced. The Waters amendment was one of the few. Her amendment attempted to eliminate conditionality in the bill that "dictated African land reform from communal and national ownership to privatized ownership; placed strict limits on African government programs spending; and, eliminated African governments' sheltering private and public industries and services from foreign investments." Representative Waters articulated that the purpose of lifting the conditionality in the bill was to ensure that it was anti-exploitative of Africa's resources and its people. The Waters amendment failed to be incorporated in the AGOA. It received 81 votes of aye and 334 votes of no. The majority of the CBC, Representatives Crane, Gephardt, and others, voted for the amendment. The amendment would have principally restructured the AGOA to provide for flexibility for a variety of development approaches to be supported by extra trade, instead of purely a market approach; still, many members who voted for the amendment voted for the bill. This aspect of the CBC and majority voting behavior on the AGOA brings to the forefront the question of the extent of symbolism over substantive representation on matters of African American interest. Robert Smith notes in *We Have No Leaders* that symbolism has become a more prominent feature of post–civil rights era congressional behavior, as in the case of the Humphrey-Hawkins bill's legislative development. Humphrey-Hawkins incorporated compromises and amendments that best served business interests. In the case of the AGOA, Congress rejected amendments that might have best served the African interests of preserving trade benefits and flexible development approaches and African American working-class interests, yet maintained support of a substantial number of CBC members. Significantly, a majority of Democrats voted for the Waters amendment, although it did not pass. Conversely, a majority of Republicans voted for the final bill.

The House leadership's participation in the floor debate signified the prominence of the bill. Charles Rangel registered as both House leadership and a leader among African American legislators. Rangel, a key sponsor of the bill, argued that the bill would not result in job loss for African Americans, nor would Africans allow for transshipment that would mean less work for their citizens. He asserted that the bill advanced an American tradition of offering an alternative to European colonialism. Two of the bill's sponsors, Representatives Crane and McDermott, extolled the virtues of the democratizing influence of private investment and offered letters of support from members of the African diplomatic corps. Crane expressed the belief that the AGOA would be mutually beneficial to the growth of the private sector in America and Africa. Before closing, House Speaker Gingrich added his voice to the choir of support for the bill, cautioning against protectionism:

> This is a very important bill. It is important, first, because it says to the countries of sub-Saharan Africa that if you meet the test of the rule of law, if you meet the test of private property, if you meet the test of moving towards a market economy, the United States wants to be your trading partner . . . I have had discussions with the presidents of Uganda and Ghana, with the vice president of South Africa, all of them regard this as a significant step towards moving away from an aid-

based system towards a trade-based system and helping develop real jobs in the world market.

The bill passed out of the House March 11, 1998, with a vote of 233 votes of aye and 186 votes of no, with 12 not voting. The bill submitted to the Committee of the Whole did include from the start provisions to address certain concerns of representatives and their constituencies. It included provisions for debt relief for heavily indebted poor nations, additional aid for development and infrastructure projects, and standards intended to discourage transshipments.

The second version of the AGOA combined the bill with a Caribbean Basin Initiative and added a chief agricultural negotiator to the USTR. It passed through the House of Representative as H.R. 434. The House and Senate did add provisions for AIDS assistance to the bill; this was one of the deficiencies in the bill underlined by Rep. Barbara Lee. The Senate process was more open for amendments than the House rule, although no amendment prevailed that would have substantially changed the character of the legislation or addressed most of the opponents' reservations. The final version of the act incorporated a provision dealing with "transshipment," AIDS/HIV, and, in a limited fashion, addressed labor rights. It addressed a few opponents' issues by way of reference to existing programs that purported to adequately address these concerns or encouraged more extensive efforts to address them in the future. The bill noted support for African efforts toward regional economic integration efforts, although it offered no discernible or concrete assistance in this area of unique interest to African officials. The AGOA passed the Senate after a majority of senators agreed to the Conference Report, with a vote of 77 yeas to 19 nays. The president signed the bill into law on May 18, 2000.

Conclusion

The movement of the AGOA through the congressional legislative process involved leadership and committee work as the basic organizational structures, where the ideological orientations toward business interests and racial interests exercised authority. The AGOA attracted an unusual coalition in the Congress from both proponents and opponents. Conservatives in Congress were aligned with objectives of a business interest–oriented and pro–free trade president. Free trade and globalization were powerful as a business interest in the same form as appeared in the earlier NAFTA approval. Democratic party and Republican party free trade–oriented members of

Congress supported the legislation, while both parties' protectionists and labor supporters opposed the legislation. African American legislators supported the legislation, although with reservations. The reservations were clearly delineated by their vote in favor of Representative Waters's amendment that would have provided for the benefits without the conditions requiring absolute surrender to business interest and "globalism."

The CBC did support the legislation, although without the level of unanimity historically accompanying issues related to Africa and domestic racial issues. CBC behavior reflected parallels similar to those associated with the passage of the Humphrey-Hawkins Full Employment bill as characterized by Robert Smith. African American leadership in Congress won an important symbolic victory for Africa and African American influence in the legislative process. Considering the incremental nature of long-term policy development, CBC members who supported the AGOA may have created an unparalleled milestone in forging a new trade regime with Africa. The coalitions on both sides of the legislation were engaged in a struggle to frame AGOA's meaning as supportive of either a conservative project or a liberal pro-Africa project. Free-trade conservative, business-oriented legislators, and African Americans in the pro-AGOA coalition sought to claim the AGOA as good for business and African nations' interest. Members of the congressional coalition found a consistency with a domestic and foreign policy agenda in reducing government participation in favor of private activity and corporate interest. This consistency and parallel encapsulated the rhetorical political slogans of "work not welfare" in domestic policy and "trade not aid" in foreign policy. The AGOA's ability to form unusual associations can be seen in the Senate roll call on the bill where Senator Edward Kennedy and Senator Helms found common ground to vote against the legislation.

There are parallels in the dilemmas faced by African American leadership that focuses more vigorously on domestic issues and the African American leadership segment that focuses more vigorously on Pan-African issues. In the post–civil rights era, traditional civil rights movement leadership found consensus on political issues more difficult once legal segregation had turned to subtle forms of exploitation and suppression of robust proposals to address white supremacy, such as reparations and criminal penalty for discrimination. The post–civil rights era features a small middle class, a growing underclass, and a less-defined color line on political issues related to social justice and inequality for upper-class African Americans.

In the post–Southern Africa liberation era, Africa advocates found consensus on political issues more difficult once the white settler regimes and traditional colonialism had ended. The post–Southern Africa liberation era featured an Africa where it was more apparent that many African states could be considered neocolonial with semi-national independence and economic dependence. Africa's working class and the Diaspora found itself facing global apartheid in terms of today's international political economy—in which "undemocratic institutions systematically generate economic inequality."[29] The steps forward produced a broader set of voices, albeit more divided voices, on both the domestic and foreign policy fronts. Perspectives on the AGOA reflected business interests and African American group interests with converging and conflicting objectives. The AGOA's political value increased with the growing frustration and growing black nationalism among African Americans, as demonstrated by the "Million Man March," movement including "Million Women March" and "Million Family Movement" and their grassroots community organizing. On the African continent, the movement toward a stronger unification of African states was motivated by both historical political forces and as a response to marginalization of African interests. In July 2000 the Organization of African Unity (OAU) committed to the creation of an African Union (AU) that was intended to forge stronger political unity and greater economic development on the African continent toward gradual federation.

The AGOA could be viewed from one perspective as an extension of U.S. imperial interest in Africa based on concerns of some members of Congress and interest groups.[30] Concerns for American domestic job impacts were also present. The act might also be viewed as moving toward a new "reconciliation of foreign policy interests of the African American community and American society at large."[31]

THE CURRENT STATUS OF THE AFRICA
GROWTH AND OPPORTUNITY ACT: AN UPDATE

Congress made two subsequent modifications to the act. AGOA II and AGOA III were designed to expand and extend the act. AGOA II was made law on August 6, 2002, under the 107th Congress in H.R. 3009 and signed by President George W. Bush.[32] AGOA II clarified that apparel provisions meant that cloth that was manufactured in the United States or in eligible countries and assembled in the eligible AGOA countries could receive beneficial tariff treatment. Additionally, the modification doubled the cap for apparel made in Africa from 3 percent to 7 percent over eight years. AGOA II was a modest change to the act. AGOA III, also known as the AGOA Acceleration Act, extended the provisions of the AGOA beyond the original time frame. The tariff reduction program was extended from 2008 to 2015.

AGOA III extended the third-country fabric provision until 2007 and provided additional clarifications on the textile provisions. The legislation reinforced the congressional expectation to have African states join and comply with requirements of the World Trade Organization.

The impact and success of the AGOA remain a matter of contention. U.S. foreign policy establishment and the supporters of the AGOA maintain that the act had led to marked progress in the economic development of participant African states. The USTR has produced four of eight annual reports intended to monitor progress on AGOA implementation. The reports show an increase in trade, although much of it may be attributable to mineral commodities, such as petroleum exports to the United States. At least one year, 2002, showed a decline in exports to the United States. According to the USTR 2002 annual AGOA report:

> While imports of apparel from sub-Saharan Africa have grown 60 percent under AGOA, significantly affecting African economies, these imports still represented less than 1.6 percent of total U.S. apparel imports in 2001. Sub-Saharan Africa accounted for less than two percent of all U.S. merchandise imports in 2001. AGOA implementation is challenged by a critical lack of institutional and human resource capacity in many sub-Saharan African countries. The number of people living on less than $1 a day in the region has expanded. By nearly every socioeconomic indicator, the region continues to rank last.[33]

The 2004 annual report indicated that the total trade between the United States and Africa was $33 billion with $25.6 billion as exports from Africa to the United States. Direct investment in sub-Saharan Africa increased by 12 percent and was tallied at $9 billion for the year end of 2002. In addition, the International Trade Commission produced a second report detailing its conclusion that the impact of AGOA on the American textile industry has been negligible. A number of U.S. government departments are involved with African trade and to some degree in its implementation, training, and monitoring for AGOA. In addition to the USTR and Commerce Department, also involved are the U.S. Agency for International Development, the Agriculture Department, the Department of Energy, the State Department, African Development Bank, and others.

Groups continue to have reservations about the value of the AGOA for both Africa and African Americans. Bill Fletcher, the president of Trans-Africa (now former president), maintained the position on the AGOA originally taken when Randall Robinson was president of the organization and its principal spokesperson. TransAfrica maintains that the AGOA failed to address many pressing needs in sub-Saharan Africa, such as debt reduction, foreign aid requirements, health care needs, capital formation, and sovereignty. TransAfrica assesses the impact of the AGOA as negative because of its view that sweatshops and associated environmental problems have proliferated. The Union of Needle Trades continues to find the act detrimental to apparel workers, both in America and in Africa.[34] Africa Action and Public Citizens continue as critics of the AGOA. Africa Action believes the negative impact of other financial policies established by multilateral financial institutions such as the International Monetary Fund and the World Bank far outweighs the benefits of the AGOA. At the same time, the organization has indicated that it believes the AGOA will contribute to an 8 percent increase in African export and provide "real opportunities."[35] Members of Congress who supported the passage of the initial AGOA legislation have maintained their support throughout the subsequent modification of the legislation. Of the legislators who were critical of the AGOA, some have moderated their reservations In December 2006 President Bush signed the Africa Investment and Incentive Act of 2006 (AGOA IV), which incorporated the extension of the AGOA and its textile and apparel provisions to 2015. The United States sponsored and the government of Ghana hosted the Sixth Annual AGOA–Sub-Saharan Africa Trade and Economic Cooperation Forum in Accra, Ghana, in July 2007.[36] An eighth annual conference was held 2008 in Washington, D.C.

NOTES

1. Walter Rodney, *How Europe Underdeveloped Africa* (Washington, D.C.: Howard University Press, 1974), 27–28.

2. Daniel Tetteh Osabu-Kle, "The Politics of One-Sided Adjustment in Africa," *Journal of Black Studies* 30, no. 4. (March 2000): 532.

3. Kwame Nkrumah, *Consciencism: Philosophy and Ideology for Decolonization and Development with Particular Reference to the African Revolution* (London: Heinemann, 1966), 78–79.

4. Kwame Nkrumah, *Neo-Colonialism: The Last Stage of Imperialism* (New York: International Publishers, 1965), 11.

5. Lorenzo Morris, "The Language of Race in Public Policy," in *One-Third of a Nation*, ed. Ura Jean Oyemade Bailey and Lorenzo Morris (Washington, D.C.: Howard University Press, 2001), 33.

6. James McCormick, "Decision-making in Foreign Policy," in *The Resurgent Congress: Foreign and Defense Policy on Capitol Hill*, ed. Randall Ridley and James Lindsay (Ann Arbor: University of Michigan Press, 1993), 119.

7. James M. Lindsay, *Congress and the Politics of U.S. Foreign Policy* (Baltimore: Johns Hopkins University Press, 1994), 2–8.

8. Hanes Walton, Jr., "Foreign Policy: From Decolonization to Democracy," in *African American Power and Politics: The Political Context Variable,* ed. Walton (New York: Columbia University Press, 1997), 355–56.

9. Ronald Walters, "The African Growth and Opportunity Act: Changing Foreign Policy Priorities toward Africa in a Conservative Political Culture," in *Foreign Policy and The Black (Inter)National Interest,* ed. Charles P. Henry (New York: State University of New York Press, 2000), 21.

10. Robert E. Dewhirst, *Rites of Passage: Congress Makes Laws* (Upper Saddle River, N.J.: Prentice Hall, 1997), 6.

11. Hanes Walton, Jr., Roosevelt Green, Jr., and Ronald D. Clark, "African Americans and the Resurgent Republican Congress: Duality of Transformation," in *American Power and Politics: The Political Context Variable,* ed. Hanes Walton, Jr. (New York: Columbia University Press, 1997), 327.

12. *Congressional Record,* November 29, 1993, H11824.

13. *Congressional Record.* November 29, 1994, H11495.

14. Congress, House of Representatives, Committee on Ways and Means, Subcommittee on Trade, Hearing on U.S. Trade Policy Objectives and Initiatives, 105th Cong., 1st sess., March 18, 1997, 38.

15. Reps. Sanford Bishop, James Clyburn, Eva Clayton, Earl Hilliard, Bennie Thompson, and Melvin Watt, Letter to Rep. Charles B. Rangel, February 20, 1998 (unpublished).

16. Robert Novak, "Gingrich Explodes at Conservatives over Affirmative Action Policy," *Human Events* 51, issue 31 (August 11, 1995): 4.

17. U.S. Congress, House of Representatives, Ways and Means Committee, Subcommittee on Trade, Public Hearings on Expanding U.S. Trade with Sub-Saharan Africa, April 29, 1997, serial 105–77, pp. 267–69.

18. Christopher Deering and Steven Smith, *Committees in Congress* (Washington, D.C.: Congressional Quarterly Press, 1997), 3.

19. U.S. Congress, House of Representatives, Ways and Means Committee, Subcommittee on Trade, Public Hearings on Implementation of Fast Track Trade Authority, September 30, 1997, serial 105–65, pp. 22–25.

20. William Julius Wilson, *When Work Disappears: The World of the New Urban Poor* (New York: Vintage Books, 1997), 151–53.

21. U.S. Congress, House of Representatives, International Relations Committee, Subcommittee on Africa, Public Hearings on Africa and the World Economy, May 7, 1997, serial 105–77, pp. 267–69.

22. U.S. Congress, House of Representatives, International Relations Committee, Subcommittee on Africa, Public Hearings entitled "Preview of President Clinton's Historic visit to Africa," March 17, 1998, 31.

23. Rosa Whitaker would later be appointed sssistant United States Trade Representative (USTR) for Africa. USTR for Africa was a position proposed by Congress to ensure adequate administration of the AGOA by the presidency. After her tenure as assistant USTR, Rosa Whitaker and Michael Williams formed the Whitaker Group, a consulting firm dedicated to trade, development, and investment in Africa. Both Whitaker and Williams are African Americans who did intensive congressional work around the act.

24. Dr. Susan Rice, scholar, Brookings Institute, Foreign Policy Studies, former assistant

secretary for African affairs, U.S. Department of State, and former director of African affairs, National Security Council; interview by author (telephone), April 4, 2005.

25. U.S. House of Representatives, Committee on Rules, Report Number 105–431 Providing for Consideration of the Bill (H.R. 1432), to authorize a new trade and investment policy for sub-Saharan Africa, March 10, 1998.

26. Gabriel A. Almond, *The American People and Foreign Policy* (New York: Frederick A. Praeger, 1960), 25.

27. U.S. Congress, Congressional Record, House, African Growth and Opportunity Act, March 11, 1998, H1043.

28. Ibid.

29. Salih Booker and William Minter, "Global Apartheid," *The Nation*, July 9, 2001, 11.

30. Andrew J. Bacevich, *American Empire: The Realities and Consequences of U.S. Diplomacy* (Cambridge, Mass.: Harvard University Press, 2003), 108.

31. Hanes Walton, *African American Power and Politics* (New York: Columbia University Press, 1997), 367.

32. Trade Act of 2002, section 3108, adopted as Public Law 107–210, based on H.R. 3009.

33. United States Trade Representative, *2002 Comprehensive Report on U.S. Trade and Investment Policy toward Sub-Saharan Africa and Implementation of the African Growth and Opportunity Act: The Second of Eight Annual Reports: May 2002* (Washington, D.C., 2002), 3.

34. Bill Fletcher, Jr., "U.S. Africa Trade Relations: New Beginnings or Same Old Story?" TransAfrica Forum, electronic version of newsletter, July 2, 2003. http://www.trans africaforum.org/newsletter/news_july2_03_ustrade.html (accessed February 5, 2005). Charles Cobb, Jr., "Fight for Global Justice Is TransAfrica's Immense Task, Says Danny Glover," AllAfrica.com, reprinted in TransAfrica Forum electronic version of newsletter, http://www.transafricaforum.org/newsletter/news nov15_02.html (accessed February, 5, 2005).

35. Africa Action, "US/Africa: Trade Meeting, 1," Africa Policy E-Journal, January 14, 2003 (030114).

36. International Trade Administration, AGOA website, http://www.agoa.gov/index .html (accessed June 4, 2009).

FIVE

The Making of African American Foreign Policymakers

SENATE CONFIRMATION HEARINGS ON SECRETARIES
OF STATE COLIN POWELL AND CONDOLEEZZA RICE

Josephine A. V. Allen, Alvin Tillery, Jr.,
and Hanes Walton, Jr.

The African American experience in the New World was born before both colonial America and the United States of America, but as a product of foreign and international affairs.[1] African Americans began as part of the slave trade and long before they could speak in their own behalf. Nevertheless, their protest against and resistance to this inhumane trade would soon lead to reform movements in the metropoles that conducted it. Although it would take time for this international opposition to take root and flower, the cries and whispers and sufferings of the enslaved, their way of speaking and doing the "word," became the groundwork for influencing those nation-states whose foreign policy was built in part on the conduct of slavery.[2] And in so doing the slaves without a formal voice and an institutional mechanism to shape this type of foreign policy had set the foundation in place to become players.[3]

Long before colonial America became the United States, African American slaves and free men and women of color were speaking the words against their foreign affairs origins. The African American communities in the thirteen colonies and later the thirteen states fashioned a moral voice and set of sentiments against the fledgling nation-state foreign policy of slavery.[4] Yet, in this new nation-state, they had no presence and/or spokespersons in the Department of State to institutionalize their demands and interests. However, at the 1787 Constitutional Convention in Philadelphia, the Founders placed in Article I, which established national legislative powers in a Congress, a series of restrictions, in Section 9, which prohibited any amendments to the provisions in Article I. The first restriction in Section 9 states: "the Migration or Importation of such Persons as any of the States now existing shall think proper to admit, shall not be prohibited by the Congress prior to the Year one thousand eight hundred and eight, but a Tax or duty may be imposed on such Importation, not exceeding ten dollars for each person."[5] Once ratified, this new constitutional section prohibited Congress from passing any law that would ban the importation of slaves for twenty years, until 1808. Banning could take place after the initial twenty-year period, and the U.S. Navy was to enforce this law.[6] The question of what would happen to internal slavery would be left primarily up to the states, except in federal territories. The cries and whispers were heard, but only the international dimension would be opposed. The new nation-state had come into being without African Americans having any direct input, influence, or presence in the foreign policymaking institution or machinery. And this was not just absence at the beginning; it took nearly a century before a small reform was made: the appointment of African Americans to diplomatic posts. It then took more than another century before the first African American secretary of state was appointed. The journey to top-level African American foreign policymakers took more than two centuries in America.

Data and Methodology

Recent scholarship and research have determined that both the profession and numerous members of the political science community, with its focus on identifying causal variables, have either ignored or omitted the race variable at the epistemological and/or the political behavioral levels.[7] And this is as true of those who purport to study individuals as of those who study institutions. This chapter analyzes the race variable in one of America's major institutions, the U.S. Senate Committee on Foreign Relations, and its confirmation hearings for the two African American secretaries of state. Thus, the research hypothesis for this study concerns the role and function that the race variable played in the Senate confirmation hearings for the first two African American secretaries of state. At its Fairmont Conference in December 1980, the Republican party informed African American leaders and elites that all subsequent political appointments from this community would be made on the basis of ideology. Black conservatives, and most of the conference attendees, accepted this proposal. This meant that racial partisan loyalty would be subordinate to ideology.[8]

Hence, African Americans nominated by Republican presidents would see the race variable emerge at these hearings in terms of individual identity.

Following the relationship of this variable with the candidates, there would be the question of how southern members of the Committee on Foreign Relations would deal with the race variable. For years Senate members from this region of the country had opposed all candidates of color despite party affiliation and ideology.[9] Would they accept these candidates due to their ideology? At the same time, would Democratic members of the Committee oppose these candidates not on the basis of race but because of their conservative ideology? Would the race variable, partisanship, or ideology affect the Committee's vote and/or the full Senate confirmation vote? Besides the issue of the race variable in the political behavior of members of the Committee on Foreign Relations or in the full Senate vote, there is also the question of how this variable would affect not only regionalism but also the political behavior of the African American senator, Barack Obama, who was a member of the committee when the confirmation hearing was held for nominee Condoleezza Rice on January 18–19, 2005. Would this liberal African American Democrat support or oppose an African American conservative for secretary of state, given that his father was a native of Kenya and that he still had relatives there?

Finally, would the race variable emerge in the confirmation hearings through questions, prepared statements, and/or suggestions about policies concerning Africa and other Third World countries? Since the hearing did not call outside witnesses, would committee members react and vote on the basis of the race variable?

Overall, our research question and hypothesis seeks to find out whether the race variable, directly and/or indirectly, influenced the making of the first two African American secretaries of state. And from this case study of the two pioneering secretaries, we hope to develop a series of testable propositions that will benefit future scholars.

The data for these two case studies come from the Senate confirmation hearings on Republican nominees Gen. Colin Powell on January 17, 2001, and Condoleezza Rice on January 18–19, 2005. Our methodology is a content analysis of these hearings along with committee and Senate roll call voting records. The use of congressional hearings to explore, evaluate, and provide empirical insights into African American politics has already done much to advance knowledge of racial politics in America.[10] It is one of the few official government sources that can offer factual data on rare and unique political events involving African Americans and their relationship to the American political process and political system. Newspaper accounts of these types of political firsts in this community leave much to be desired. Therefore, data from congressional hearings offer comprehensive and systematic as well as official documentation of these rare political occurrences.[11]

In addition to these official hearings, this study uses other scholarly sources, such as monographs that cover other aspects of African American foreign policymakers from historical background and recent contextual information.[12] With these additional materials, it may be possible to situate these very recent nominees in a political context that further describes and explains how African Americans have empowered themselves and their community to help shape U.S. foreign policy.

Nature and Scope of the Senate Confirmation Hearings

The Republican party was the first political party to recognize the independence of Haiti and Liberia. President Lincoln in his annual message to Congress in December 1861 announced: "if any good reason exists why we should persevere longer in withholding our recognition of the independence and sovereignty of Haiti and Liberia, I am unable to discern it. . . . For decades Southerners had blocked the formal recognition of Haiti and Liberia." But with the withdrawal of southern states from the Union just before the Civil War, the Senate and House granted recognition and "authorized the president to appoint diplomatic representatives" to these black republics.[13] Following President Lincoln's effort, President Grant appointed Ebenezer Basset "as minister resident and consul general to Haiti" in 1869 and J. Milton Turner "as minister resident and consul general to Liberia" on 1 March 1871.[14] According to the ambassador to Burkina Faso, Elliott P. Skinner, in President Grant's appointment of Turner, "African Americans for the first time in history became official participants in the foreign policymaking process of the United States of America relating to an African State."[15] The Republicans had laid the foundation for African Americans to participate in making foreign policy. And with the appointments of Powell and Rice by President George W. Bush, this tradition was being continued, though in an uneven fashion.[16]

In point of fact, President Bush nominated both Powell and Rice and saw each of them confirmed by the U.S. Senate. Powell served as secretary of state during Bush's first term and then resigned at the end of that term. Once reelected, President Bush nominated Rice, who in his first term had served as head of the National Security Council and in the administration of his father, President George H. W. Bush, had served as advisor on Soviet politics and as a member of the National Security Council. That a conservative Republican president, in an era when the majority of African Americans belong to the Democratic party's coalition, should nominate two African Americans in succession for secretary of state makes a historic breakthrough. No Democratic president, even those where African American voters provided the balance of power, made such unique appointments. The closest that the Democrats have come is when President Carter nominated Andrew Young to the post of U.S. ambassador to the United Nations and, when he removed him, appointed another African American, Donald McHenry, to replace Young, for two back-to-back appointments.[17]

But neither Powell nor Rice at this writing has achieved what Ralph Bunche did while working at the United Nations—winning a Nobel Peace Prize.[18] Neither has risen to this level of achievement in their role as head of the U.S. foreign policymaking bureaucracy, the Department of State. However, what facilitated their rise to high office is the fact that both became Republican partisans and played the political game very well. Powell rose during the Reagan and Bush years in the White House, while Rice rose during the Bush years in the White House. And this playing of Republican partisan politics is as true today as it was during the time of J. Milton Turner.[19]

At the time of the two nominations, the Republicans controlled the Senate. However, Powell's confirmation came during the last three days of the Democratic control of the Senate. Democrat Joseph Biden of Delaware was the outgoing chairman of the Committee on Foreign Relations when the hearing on General Powell took place. Of this unusual circumstance, Senator Biden says in opening the hearing: "General, you are going to witness a little bit of a charade here today. I am technically the chairman of this Committee for another 2 days or whatever. But I have no illusions who the real chairman is.... So, with the permission of the real chairman, Senator Helms, who I will turn the gavel over to after the opening statements ..."[20] He continued: "then Senator Helms and I will make our opening statements and then we will turn to you, General, for your opening statements and then we will get to questioning."[21] The confirmation hearing for General Powell went so well that it was finished in the first day. However, long before that day ended, Chairman Biden relinquished his chairmanship position, turning it over to Republican senator Jesse Helms. Here is how the transfer of power took place, two days before the Republican takeover was scheduled: "Senator Biden. Now I not only turn to the Senator from North Carolina for his opening statement, I literally and figuratively turn over the gavel and end my very brief tenure as chairman of the Foreign Relations Committee.... Well, Chairman Helms, if I cannot be chairman and I have to have a Republican, I am delighted it is you."[22] At this point, Senator Helms responded, "Amen." From this point on, Senator Helms chaired the Committee on Foreign Relations and the confirmation hearing for General Powell.

Thus, with Senator Biden stepping down, the Republicans had nine members of the committee, as did the Democrats. However, at the Rice hearings,[23] Sen. Richard Lugar of Indiana had the chairmanship, and the Republicans had ten members to the Democratic party's eight. Among those eight was the new African American senator, Barack Obama.[24] This committee hearing for Rice was the first in which an African American senator served on the Committee on Foreign Relations and participated in the making of an African American secretary of state. Thus, Senator Obama would have another opportunity to vote for this nominee when her confirmation came up on the Senate floor.

Moreover, Senator Obama, whose father hailed from Kenya, would have a chance to question nominee Rice about U.S. foreign policy toward Africa as well as her thinking about the Iraq war because when that war was launched, on the basis of there being weapons of mass destruction (WMD) in Iraq, she was head of the National Security Council and supported that war.[25] This was both a rare reality and a unique situation because Senator Obama had opposed the war from the outset.

Finally, there is the matter of a southern senator of the old school, Jesse Helms, who came from the southern tradition of racial conservatism. Not only was he chairing the Committee on Foreign Relations, but also in both the 1990 and 1996 Senate elections his Democratic opponent was the former African American mayor of Charlotte, North Carolina, Harvey Gantt. And in the 1990 election, Senator Helms played the "race card" to defeat challenger Gantt. Senator Helms did not apologize for playing the "race card."[26]

Senator Helms had exhibited similar antiblack behavior in 1983 when he launched a filibuster against the passage of the Martin Luther King, Jr., Holiday bill. Sen. Robert Dole was the Senate majority leader, and he asked the Reagan White House to call Senator Helms off or the Republican majority would vote for "cloture" in order to stop Helms, thereby embarrassing the White House. After much political maneuvering behind the scenes, the King bill passed the Senate and President Reagan signed it into law over strenuous objections from Senator Helms.[27] Thus, the Rice confirmation hearing offered this senator of the old school a chance to once again voice his longstanding opposition to African Americans in politics and in public policy.

Overall, these two nominees' confirmation hearings took place in a political and public context that would allow the race variable to become a factor in influencing and shaping senatorial behavior as to whether or not these candidates would be confirmed. And all of this political maneuvering took place as the Republican party claimed that it wanted to reach out and bring more racial minorities into its electoral coalition.

Racial Identity and the Senate Confirmation Hearings

In searching for the impact and influence of the race variable , one must ask how the candidates saw it in relation to the Republican party's ideological requirement of conservatism. In General Powell's opening statement, he made these remarks: "I have to pause in my admiration of Jefferson during this week of celebration of the life of Dr. Martin Luther King, Jr., and reflect on how Dr. King helped to answer Jefferson's prayers for black Americans whose forbears at that time were considered to be property, slaves, even in Jefferson's own custody."[28] He continued:

> I am before you today as Jefferson's admiring successor, thankful for all the sacrifices that were made by Dr. King and so many others to make Jefferson's dream possible for people like me, a dream that I hope will continue to inspire my fellow Americans and inspire people around the world because there is still so much that needs to be done here at home and around the world to bring that universal Jeffersonian dream to the whole world.[29]

General Powell returned to this issue of racial identity just before he ended his opening statement. In the last two paragraphs, before the final one in which he once again praised the first secretary of state, Thomas Jefferson, he remarked:

> I am honored to be following in the footsteps of Thomas Jefferson and in the footsteps of George C. Marshall, two giants. I am in their footsteps. I can never be in their shadow, but I will try to do my very, very best. I am proud to be the first African-American to be Secretary of State of the United States. But I am very, very honored to be the first African-American Secretary of State designate and Secretary of State, if you so confirm my appointment, honored to be following in the footsteps of Secretary Albright who did such a terrific job as the first woman Secretary. I think it shows to the world our model and over a period of time, from our beginning, if you believe in the values that we

espouse, you can see things as miraculous as me sitting before you to receive your approval.[30]

Unlike his initial remarks, these last two paragraphs are not found in General Powell's prepared statement for the official record. Whether missing or not, Powell's comments and remarks show that he embraced his racial identity instead of his ideological identity, and placed this before the committee before their vote to confirm him.

We turn now to the opening statement of Condoleezza Rice, to see if her remarks and comments addressed the matter of racial and ideology identity. In her opening statement, Rice said:

> Four years ago, Secretary Powell addressed this Committee for the same purpose that I do now. Then, as now, it was the same week that America celebrates the life and legacy of Dr. Martin Luther King. It is a time to reflect on the legacy of that great man, on the sacrifices he made on the courage of the people he led, and on the progress our nation has made in the decades since. I, personally, am indebted to those who fought and sacrificed in the civil-rights movement so that I could be here today.
>
> For me, this is a time to remember other heroes, as well. I grew up in Birmingham, Alabama—the old Birmingham, of "Bull" Connor and church bombings and voter intimidation, the Birmingham where Dr. King was thrown in jail for demonstrating without a permit. Yet there was another Birmingham, the city where my parents, John and Angelina Rice, and their friends built a thriving community in the midst of terrible segregation. It would have been so easy for them to give in to despair and to send that message of hopelessness to their children, but they refused to allow the limits and injustices of their time to limit our horizons. My friends and I were raised to believe that we could do or become anything; that the only limits to our aspirations came from within. We were taught not to listen to those who said, "No, you can't."[31]

Immediately after making these remarks and comments about her racial identity, and then individualizing the civil rights movement in Birmingham and giving praise to her parents, Rice immediately went on to include her ideological identity:

> The story of Birmingham's parents and teachers and children is a story of the triumph of universal values over adversity, and those values, a belief in democracy and liberty, and the dignity of every life and the

rights of every individual, unite Americans of all backgrounds, all faiths, and all colors. They provide us a common cause and a rallying point in difficult times, and they are a source of hope to men and women across the globe who cherish freedom and work to advance freedom's cause. And in these extraordinary times, it is the duty of all of us—legislators and diplomats and civil servants and citizens—to uphold and advance the values that are core to our identity and that have lifted millions around the world.[32]

In these comments, Rice never mentioned "equality" or "inclusion," two of the values that King and the civil rights movement in Birmingham fought for. Nor does she mention the "Letter From a Birmingham Jail," which came to symbolize that moment in time, or the 1964 Civil Rights Bill, which was directly linked to the protests in Birmingham.[33] Cleverly, she leaves out that neither she nor her parents participated in any of the demonstrations in this city. Yet, by leaving out the concern of the King-led mass demonstrations for equality, she could tie that movement to liberty and through it to conservatism and individualism. The mention of King and the racial context does not link it to her values and beliefs nor to the values and beliefs of the civil rights movement. Since they were co-joined, one must ask why.

These opening remarks on racial and ideological identity are in sharp contrast to those of Secretary Powell. In addition, all of Rice's remarks show up in her prepared statements except for the following statement, which was left out. In her prepared statement she said: "And if I am confirmed, I will be especially honored to succeed a man I so admire—my friend and mentor, Colin Powell." This remark preceded her opening comments on racial identity. Rice made sure that in her opening remarks and prepared statement, her racial identity was carefully linked to her ideological identity. This is not true with General Powell's opening statement and prepared remarks. This is not to say that his values and beliefs were not there, for they were, but they were not juxtaposed in the same manner.

Race, the Southern Chair, and the Senate Confirmation Hearings: Sen. Jesse Helms

If the race variable could come from the candidates themselves at the confirmation hearings, we have noted that it could also evolve from members of the Committee on Foreign Relations, particularly southern members and, in this case, the southerner who chaired the committee. Analyzing the opening statement and prepared remarks of Chairman Helms, one finds the following comments:

> Now, in choosing you, General Powell, President-elect Bush hit a home run. One of my earliest memories of you was during the Reagan administration when I had the pleasure of attending a briefing at which you were the central witness in the cabinet room down at the White House. You were splendid in uniform. You were erect and you had your easel and you knew what you were talking about. Well, I was sitting to the right of the President, and we had a habit of passing notes to each other. So, I reached for one of the memo pads in front of me and I scribbled a two-word question to President Reagan: "Joint Chiefs?" I slid it over to the President. He looked at it and grinned and wrote something and moved it back to me. On there, he said: "Chairman."[34]
>
> Now, I've got that piece of paper somewhere in my files for Posterity. What I am saying is that Ronald Reagan admired you as do I. I think you know that. I can imagine no better qualified person to serve as the first U.S. Secretary of State in the 21st century. We welcome you, sir and look forward to your testimony.[35]

The evidence from Helms's opening statement and prepared remarks is that Senator Helms did not oppose General Powell because of his race, nor did he ever raise in any negative way the issue of the race of the appointee. The ideology of the presidents that nominated General Powell were enough for Senator Helms to let ideology in this instance trump race. Further reading of all of Senator Helms's comments, remarks, statements, and questions in the hearings shows them to be devoid of concerns about the race of the candidate. The senator studiously avoided any connection between his past behavior and this hearing. The closest he ever came to his past was in his welcoming of General Powell to the hearing, when he suggested that "now, you may have noticed it in the newspapers, a small item last week, that I visited with the members of the American Enterprise Institute (AEI)—a conservative and right wing think tank in Washington, D.C.—this past Thursday. . . . Suffice it to say, my purpose in visiting with the AEI was to lay out some of the vital issues which this Committee and the Congress will confront in the months ahead, issues which I hope that we will work to address together in the coming year."[36]

Seemingly, the point here is that these conservatives, the Senator and the institute, will instruct the secretary-to-be in the years ahead. None of the other southerners on the committee, Senators Bill Nelson of Florida,

Frist of Tennessee, and Allen of Virginia, had the background and relationship to race that Senator Helms had.

Southern senators on the Committee of Foreign Relations that held the confirmation hearing for Rice included Senators Nelson of Florida, Allen of Virginia, and Martinez of Florida. They lacked the background and history of race that Senator Helms had, and they did not raise the race matter at this confirmation hearing. Nor did it matter this time that the chairman, Senator Lugar, was not a southerner but hailed from Indiana. He, like Helms, avoided the issue and concerns of race. Hence, the southern preoccupation with race did not surface in either of these two confirmation hearings.

Race and the Committee on Foreign Relations Members at the Confirmation Hearings

Once and only once during the entire hearing on Powell did the issue of race surface. Senator Sarbanes raised the issue to General Powell about his concerns and interests in human rights issues, as well as the interest and concerns of President-elect Bush. Here is General Powell's response:

> I will never forget the day when Foreign Minister Shevardnadze (Soviet Union) was lecturing us back across the table in Saint Catherine's Hall and I was on George Shultz's right and a good friend of all of ours, Ambassador Rozanne Ridgeway, was on his left. Shevardnadze was going on about "how you treat your blacks and your women," and then he looked up from his notes, he looked at Roz and then he looked at me and he said: "Oh, never mind; next point."[37]

Powell continued:

> So by our example, by our example of what is achievable, you can show to the rest of the world a model. . . . We have military . . . political . . . economic . . . strength, but the greatest strength we have is the strength of our example, to show to the rest of the world what a nation as diverse as ours, drawn in from all over the world, what we can do because we respect the rights of individuals, and where we have not done that in the past we are going to improve ourselves in the future.[38]

General Powell here raises the race issue and uses it effectively and poignantly to show his interest and concern with the worldwide issue of human rights. Thus, besides this indirect question by Senator Sarbanes and the direct response of General Powell, no other committee member raised the race issue with General Powell.

Rice, in her hearing, did not respond to any question by a senator where she specifically used a racial example like General Powell, even when senators—like Allen and Feinstein—introduced racial matters. They were the only two members at Rice's confirmation hearing who raised racial matters. The lone African American senator, Obama, did not raise any racial matters with her. In her introductory remarks, Senator Feinstein said, "She returned to the White House, as the first African American woman to serve as National Security Advisor, in January 2001." She continued: "As a young girl, Condi stood at the gates of 1600 Pennsylvania Avenue with her father, telling him that, quote, 'Daddy, I'm barred out of there now because of the color of my skin, but one day I'll be in that house,' end quote. She's delivered on that promise. Now she is the President's choice to be our country's next Secretary of State."[39]

Like Senator Feinstein, Senator Allen in his remarks brought in the race issue. He said at the hearing:

> And I do think that when you talk about your life story and bring up Birmingham, I would encourage some of my colleagues, there's a civil-rights pilgrimage every year. . . . This year, Senator Corzine on the Democrat side, me on the Republican side, will be heading a delegation there for the 40th anniversary of the Voting Rights Act. And it goes—you go to Birmingham, that church that was bombed that I know that you are a member of, as well as Montgomery and Selma. And I found it a very moving, profoundly impacting, and very meaningful event for me.[40]

Later, in the business meeting of the Committee on Foreign Relations, when the committee was deciding to vote, Senator Allen once again raised the race matter. He said: "But through it all Dr. Rice has never gone off stride. She's the embodiment of the modern day American dream for all people who have an equal opportunity to compete and succeed regardless of their gender, their race, or their religion. That is the meritocracy we have in this country."[41]

All of these complimentary remarks to and about Rice as to how she did not let her racial situation hinder her from making endless achievements, even where they were erroneous, did not lead to any corrections on her part or any comments and reflections about how these achievements were useful for U.S. foreign policy initiatives. And in the end, neither did these glowing remarks engage her to indicate that the racial barriers in Alabama and elsewhere did have a broad-based inhibiting effect on others of her race in the state and nation, and that it required national legislation to remove these obstacles. Not everyone could attain such accomplishments on personal initiative.

After these racial references by Senators Feinstein and Allen, no similar comments were made by other members of the Committee on Foreign Relations or by Rice herself.

Race, Sen. Barack Obama, and the Senate
Confirmation Hearing for Condoleezza Rice

As we explore how the race variable might have entered the confirmation hearings on the two recent and back-to-back African American secretaries of state, we need to explore how an African American senator who served on the Committee on Foreign Relations might have engaged the variable. Only one African American was in the Senate when Rice came up for confirmation. It was the newly elected senator from Illinois, who had won in an open-seat race in 2004, Barack Obama. Here is how he raised the race issue in his comments during the hearing on Rice:

> Dr. Rice, it's wonderful to see you here, and I've been very impressed, obviously, with your mastery of the issues. Since it's the day after King's birthday, obviously 20 to 30 years ago it's unlikely that I'd be sitting here asking you questions. And so, I think that's a testimony to how far we've come, despite how far we still have to go. And I think everybody, rightly, is extraordinarily impressed with your credentials and your experience in this field.[42]

Clearly, the senator in his opening statement is indicating how important the race variable is at this moment in time and in the confirmation hearings. But Rice never acknowledges this or responds in any way to this matter. She instead answers his questions that follow these comments. Senator Obama's statement is not only complimentary, but also suggestive in terms of the future, particularly when the senator says that the nation has a long way to go on the race issue.

However, Senator Obama does not follow up on his opening remarks on the race issue. He tells the nominee that he is interested in getting her reaction to three matters: the issues of nuclear proliferation, nuclear entrepreneurship, and the Proliferation Security Initiative.[43] Later, he raises questions with her about the war in Iraq. In none of his queries does he raise a question that has always been a top concern with African American diplomats and ambassadors: how to get more of them in this category and more of them in the Foreign Service. Numerous committee members raised questions with Powell about getting more black Foreign Service Officers (FSO); no one, including Senator Obama, raised this issue with Rice. And she never took a moment to comment on this high-priority item for former African American diplomats. Thus, the opening by the lone African American member on the committee simply went nowhere. The race variable, though raised by that member, was not pursued by him, by other members, or by the nominee herself.

Race, the Senate Confirmation Hearings, and African and Haitian Policy

One last way that the race variable could come into play in the confirmation hearings before the committee vote is in the area of current and future foreign policies of the nation. This started immediately with General Powell and continued through the Rice hearings. In his opening prepared statement, General Powell had this to say about Africa: "Mr. Chairman, as we continue to look at our various responsibilities, I would just like to touch on a region of the world that perhaps we do not spend enough time thinking about, or talking about. I want to talk about Africa for just a few moments."[44] He continued: "Mr. Chairman, as we continue to look at our responsibilities across the Atlantic, we need to maintain our outreach to Africa—and with more substance."[45] Senator Feingold questioned him about President Bush's commitment to this area, because the president-elect in an interview "on the *News Hour with Jim Lehrer*" had said that "while Africa may be important, it doesn't fit into the national strategic interests, as far as I can see them."[46] Senator Feingold felt that General Powell's concerns with a potential new African policy might be misplaced if not misguided. General Powell responded:

> I think the President-elect was just touching on some of his top priorities and the things that sort of press in on you from day to day. But in my conversations with him, I know that he believes that there really is no region in the world that can be ignored. Priorities may come up and down, but I am quite confident that he will be interested in Africa, he will be interested in some of the conflicts that exist on that continent that need to be resolved. I know we have talked about the problems of HIV/AIDS and the devastation that that is wreaking across the southern part of the continent. So, I am confident that he will be engaged and he will see it as a priority. I would not have started out my transition by first having briefings from the African Bureau and, in the comments I made subsequently, if I was not confident that I was representing and speaking for the President-elect.[47]

General Powell noted two things in this confirmation hearing. First, he let it be known that U.S. foreign policy toward Africa was one of his top public policy priorities and that the State Department under his leadership would reach out to work with African nation-states. Second, he offered his personal guarantee that the president-elect would be interested also. Given that the president-elect had indicated that this continent would be a low priority during his administration, General Powell did not declare that the president-elect would support his interest but only suggested that events and crises on the continent would possibly bring about a change in the president-elect's position.

Rice, in her opening statement, also remarked on Africa: "from the Philippines to Colombia to the nations of Africa, we are strengthening counterterrorism cooperation with nations that have a will to fight terror but need help with the means. We're spending billions to fight AIDS and tuberculosis and malaria among other diseases, to alleviate suffering for millions, and help end public-health crises."[48] After this remark, she offered another: "In much of Africa and Latin America, we face the twin challenges of helping to bolster democratic change while alleviating poverty and hopelessness. We will work with reformers in those regions who are committed to increasing opportunity for their peoples, and we will insist that leaders who are elected democratically have an obligation to govern democratically."[49]

Rice's prepared statement had these same remarks about Africa. They are quite different from those of General Powell. Rice speaks of Africa only in relationship to America's foreign policy of fighting counterterrorism and establishing democratic governments around the world. Next, she indicates what the United States has done and is doing for the crises on the African continent. However, she never singles out Africa as a focus; it is always discussed in conjunction with other nation-states or global regions. Thus, Africa is not a top priority for her as it was with General Powell from the outset.

During the questioning of Rice, the matter of U.S. foreign policy with respect to Africa came up only twice. The first time it only involved the matter of Islam in North Africa and East Africa, and she indicated that a moderate brand of Islam was winning out over any type of radical Islam.[50] The second question arose from Senator Feingold: "I'd like you to explain how the President's emergency plan for AIDS relief will help build infrastructural capacity in Africa, particularly in the area of training healthcare practitioners, especially community health workers and discouraging the medical brain-drain."[51] He states further: "I found one of the most heart-breaking . . . conversations in Botswana with the president of that country, President Mogae, who was acknowledging that they had a 40 percent AIDS rate, and that they were trying to deal with it, but whenever they'd get some local healthcare workers trained, they were poached by American health-care entities or European healthcare entities, and they couldn't keep the very people that were trying to deal with this situation."[52]

Rice answered: "I hadn't thought much of the—about the problem of well-trained healthcare workers being siphoned off, but we'll go back and give that some thought." But she did say that "the Ugandans . . . have a very effective system of delivery," in terms of providing healthcare in fight-ing AIDS.[53] But this is the extent of her remarks about Africa during her questioning. At no point during the two days of the confirmation hearings did she try to state that a briefing on Africa, like that of General Powell, was her first action. Nor does she say anything about the president's policy toward Africa in his second term. Neither does she volunteer any informa-tion, as General Powell did, about where Africa stands in terms of her priorities. In her hearings, Africa comes into view indirectly, primarily when the AIDS crisis surfaced. The lone exception is when she gave addi-tional answers for the record.

Moving from U.S. policy toward Africa to U.S. policy toward Haiti, we can once again probe for the race variable. Beginning with General Powell, we find that while he discussed concerns in the Western Hemisphere and Mexico, he did not make any remarks about Haiti. During the questioning period, Senator Dodd raised the following concern: "on Haiti . . . you played a very critical role, along with President Carter and Senator Nunn, back a number of years ago to start Haiti down a road toward democracy. I commend you for your courage and your willingness to join in that par-ticular effort."[54]

To this concern, General Powell responded: "I think we have to engage with President Aristide. It seems that our goals remain what they were some 10 or 12 years ago, how to get that democracy and that economy started and how to keep the Haitian people at home and not on the seas heading toward Florida. That is where we came in."[55] This was the only time the issue came up during the questioning, but it did resurface in ad-ditional written questions submitted to General Powell for the record. Sen-ator Helms wanted to know about U.S. policy toward "the regime of Jean Bertrand Aristide." General Powell told him:

> I believe we must engage the Government of Haiti in order to advance
> and protect our national interest there and in the region. We intend to

hold President-elect Aristide to his December commitment to former President Clinton to rectify serious problems with elections, drug trafficking, the security and judicial systems, human rights, illegal migration and other key bilateral issues. We will also encourage the Government of Haiti to halt political intimidation and violence.[56]

To Senator Helms's question about protecting political opposition, General Powell wrote: "you can be sure that the Bush administration will press President-elect Aristide to fulfill his December 27 commitment to install a broad-based government that includes technocrats and members of the opposition."[57] General Powell is indicating that his policy toward Haiti will be one of ensuring that that nation meets its responsibilities to the United States. There are no new initiatives and his policy will be one of enforcement. Haiti has to improve its internal institutions and political structures. This policy is quite different from his African policy.

In the confirmation hearings for Rice, questions about Haiti did come up. Senator Bill Nelson asked her about the country, since he represented Florida, where the refugees were landing. Rice responded: "unfortunately, Haiti seems to be a place where natural and man-made disasters have come together in a really terrible way for the Haitian people. They do have a new chance now. They have a transitional government that is trying to arrange elections in the fall."[58] She added: "the best course with Haiti is to work with them to take full advantage of the Caribbean Basin Initiative, to work with them on job creation through some of the programs that we have out of our economic support fund for Haiti . . . I understand fully the concerns about Haiti, both from a humanitarian point of view and also from a stability point of view."[59] She concluded: "we probably dodged a bullet, in the earlier days, with the ability to get Aristide out peacefully, because he had lost the ability to control that country, to govern authoritatively in that country."[60]

During the additional questions for the record, Senator Nelson, who had queried her on Haiti during the hearings, raised five additional questions. In responding to a question about the U.N. peacekeeping forces in Haiti, Rice stated that the United States was supporting the U.N. Stabilization Force in Haiti with both manpower and $6 million in funds. As to the U.S. role in peacekeeping, she indicated that this was a U.N. operation. And to a question about recent storms and flooding, the nominee replied, "We have signed contracts for rehabilitation of irrigation systems, hillside stabilization, road repair, and other infrastructure projects. Over 5,000 Haitians are employed by USAID's Office of Foreign Disaster Assistance in a clean-up program."[61]

Next came the question about the goal of U.S. policy toward Haiti. The answer was that "our goals in Haiti are to give the Haitian people the tools they need to create a democratic government, stable institutions and a viable economy."[62] And finally, there was a question about the HERO act that was designed to create jobs in Haiti. The nominee responded: "while the Senate passed the HERO legislation in the last Congress, the House took no action and the administration has not taken a position on the HERO legislation. If confirmed, I want to work with the Congress to fashion legislation that will find the right balance between job growth in Haiti and maintaining jobs here at home."[63]

From Rice's numerous answers on Haiti, seemingly her interest would be primarily like that of her predecessor, Secretary Powell—the enforcement of policies and programs already on the books. The tasks and responsibilities would rest upon Haiti and its new government. Thus, there is little difference between the two African American secretaries of state on the nation's public policies toward Haiti.

When U.S. policies toward Africa and Haiti are taken collectively, Powell and Rice diverged on the former and converged on the latter. The race variable seemed to have affected Powell much more than Rice, particularly in terms of concern, interest, and initiatives for Africa. When asked for the record what were her top five foreign policy priorities, Rice did not refer to Africa until the very last sentence in her written response. Here she wrote: "in Europe, in Asia, in Africa, the Americas, and the broader Middle East, we seek to mobilize and lead the efforts of all free nations, while maintaining strategic relationships with other global powers, all in the interest of strengthening a balance of power that favors freedom."[64] Once again, she mentions Africa only in a collection of continents and global regions. It does not stand alone, but always with others as one of the group. Its problems are not treated as unique and requiring different types of policy initiatives and formulations. Race, when seen from the public policy perspective, seems to have shaped Powell's outlook but not that of Rice.

Race and the Votes for and against Confirmation in the Committee on Foreign Relations and on the Senate Floor

General Powell's confirmation hearing did not include a business meeting like the one for Rice. Moreover, neither hearing provides a roll call vote from the full Senate. Did the race variable appear in the committee and full Senate votes? At the Committee on Foreign Relations' voice vote on Rice, the result was 15 votes in favor and 2 negative votes (table 5.1).

TABLE 5.1
Senate Foreign Relations Committee's Vote on Rice Confirmation

SENATOR	STATE	PARTY	VOTE
Lugar (chair)	Indiana	Republican	Yes
Biden	Delaware	Democrat	Yes
Hagel	Nebraska	Republican	Yes
Allen	Virginia	Republican	Yes
Coleman	Minnesota	Republican	Yes
Voinovich	Ohio	Republican	Yes
Alexander	Tennessee	Republican	Yes
Murkowski	Alaska	Republican	Yes
Martinez	Florida	Republican	Yes
Sununu	New Hampshire	Republican	Yes
Sarbanes	Maryland	Democrat	Yes
Dodd	Connecticut	Democrat	Yes
Kerry	Massachusetts	Democrat	No
Feingold	Wisconsin	Democrat	Yes
Boxer	California	Democrat	No
Nelson	Florida	Democrat	Yes
Obama	Illinois	Democrat	Yes

Senators Barbara Boxer and John Kerry, both Democrats, were the two votes against Rice. Senator Kerry stated that he opposed the nomination because "Dr. Rice is one of the principal architects, implementers, and defenders of a series of administration policies and choices that in my judgment have not made our country as secure as we ought to be in the aftermath of 9–11."[65]

Senator Boxer indicated that the nominee showed a lack of candor during her nine hours of questioning. Therefore, Senator Boxer concluded:

> I hope if nothing else Dr. Rice now gets the difference between her role as the National Security Advisor where she wasn't in any way responsible to come before Congress, but went to the American people and sold a war, and continued to repeat things that were not so. And her role now where she is responsible to the American people as well as to the President, and to the American people through us. And so I just hope we have better times ahead and I will not be able to support this nomination even though I know I'm in a—quite a minority. Thank you.[66]

Although these two Democrats voted against Rice, the lone African American Senator joined with the other five Democrats and voted for confirmation. Overall, five Democrats and ten Republicans voted for her con-

TABLE 5.2
Senators Who Voted against Rice's Confirmation in the Body-of-the-Whole

SENATOR	STATE	PARTY
Boxer	California	Democrat
Byrd	West Virginia	Democrat
Kennedy	Massachusetts	Democrat
Kerry	Massachusetts	Democrat
Levin	Michigan	Democrat
Jeffords	Vermont	Independent
Reed	Rhode Island	Democrat
Dayton	Minnesota	Democrat
Akaka	Hawaii	Democrat
Bayh	Indiana	Democrat
Lautenberg	New Jersey	Democrat
Harkin	Iowa	Democrat
Durbin	Illinois	Democrat

firmation, nearly 90 percent of the Committee on Foreign Relations. The race variable did not enter into the voting behavior on the committee. And with this vote, the nomination was passed on to the Senate floor.

The historical record demonstrates that there was far more opposition to Rice's confirmation in the body-of-the-whole than there was in the Committee on Foreign Relations. Indeed, thirteen members of the Senate cast votes against Rice's confirmation (see table 5.2). The partisan breakdown of the nay voters shows that all of Rice's opponents, with the exception of Senator Jeffords of Vermont, who caucused with the Democratic party, were Democrats.

Summary and Conclusions

Evidence from our content analysis of the Senate confirmation hearings for the two pioneering African American secretaries of state reveals that the race variable surfaced in several different ways in the confirmation process. However, it did not become decisive in the Committee on Foreign Relations deliberative and voting processes. Both Democratic and Republican senators discussed it and applauded each of the nominees for overcoming their racial background. But the voting went strictly along party lines. Two of the Democrats defected, but the rest of the Democrats voted together. The lone African American senator voted with the majority of his party. Hence, in the final analysis, the outcome of the committee vote was neither partisan nor racial.

However, while the race variable may not have been a committee factor, it was indeed an individual factor. General Powell made it a primary element in his drive to attain and achieve this position, and pointed to his nomination as a credit to his race. Rice made it an individual factor in discussing how she overcame the limitations and burden of race. She achieved her goals despite its presence and power in the system. She saw her nomination as a credit to her own talents, skills, and the drive of her mother and father. In her view, she symbolized individual success in the face of adversity.

General Powell clearly noted that the race variable would be reflected in how he would both manage and carry out foreign policies in the State Department. In addition, he let the committee know that he would launch new initiatives and policies where they could help people of color. Despite the president-elect making Africa a low-priority agenda item, his nominee had it at the top of his agenda. Such was not the case with Rice. This continent never surfaced as a top agenda item. And her proposals about it stayed within the realm of America's national interest and not in the mode of humanitarian needs and concerns.

African American political scientist Clarence Lusane's pioneering book on Powell and Rice did not address or analyze the data from the confirmation hearings on these two nominees. He concluded: "neither Powell nor Rice, unlike many black Republicans who focus on domestic issues, deny or distance themselves from their racial identity or the country's racial past. In fairly sophisticated ways, they have linked their race and racial experiences to their political roles."[67] However, had he probed these hearings, he would have seen many differences between the ways in which Powell used his racial identity in the confirmation process as he addressed the nation's political elites, movers and shakers, and what Rice did when she confronted them. It was an important clue to their political behavior in office, which he sought to explain.

Both of these pioneering African American secretaries of state had exemplary resumes with a great deal of experience, making them highly qualified for this cabinet-level position. Thus, the question of qualifications was a moot issue from the start, and this made the race variable easier to investigate. These two case studies might in the end be so exceptional that they do not give a full-fledged and balanced perspective on the race variable in this arena.

The development of additional, similar case studies will make possible a more balanced perspective on the race variable. This can occur when hearings for nominees of color for secretary of state or similar high-level cabinet positions are analyzed. The hearings surrounding the confirmations of Andrew Young, Donald McHenry, and Susan Rice for the position of U.S. ambassador to the United Nations await similar exploration. The current work has laid the groundwork for much-needed extended analyses.

Keeping in mind the relevance of this research, some associated propositions also may be explored: First, race will be viewed as a critical factor among senators of color who are members of the Senate Foreign Relations Committee; among senators who represent constituencies in the southern United States; among members of the Senate generally; and among Senators who are Republicans. Second, ideology will be viewed as a critical factor among senators who are members of the Senate Foreign Relations Committee when considering the confirmation of nominees for high-level positions in foreign affairs; among members of the Senate generally; among senators of color; among senators who are Democrats; and among those who are Republicans. Third, gender will be viewed as a critical factor among Senators who are members of the Senate Foreign Relations Committee when considering the confirmation of nominees for high-level positions in foreign affairs and among senators generally.

Southern chairs of the Senate Foreign Relations Committee should be considered important and should be analyzed in subsequent case studies because their presence might be an influential variable in determining the outcome of the confirmation of African American foreign policymakers. Another key testable proposition to emerge from these two cases is the nature of U.S. foreign policy toward African and Caribbean nations, as well as regions within Africa. Clearly, the race variable can enter via the major economic, social, and political issues affecting these countries and geographic regions, given the history of the United States in its policies toward nations in the global South versus those in the global North. Future case studies must also focus upon this factor.

Exploring these propositions in the context of Senate confirmation hearings over a larger number of cases in an extended time period will lend greater credibility to the conclusions drawn from the case studies presented in this work.

NOTES

1. Walton, Jr., Stevenson, and Rosser, Sr., 2007, 1–3, 23–38. See also Walton, Jr., 1985, 269–87.
2. Walton, Jr., 1969, 277–80. See also Ward, 1969.
3. Miller, 1978.

4. Tillery, Jr. 2007, 45–68. See also Walton, Jr., Clark, Rosser, and Stevenson, 1983, 80–92.

5. O'Connor and Sabato, 2008, 297.

6. Du Bois, 1896.

7. Walton, Jr., and Smith, 2007, 24–37.

8. Institute for Contemporary Studies, 1981. See also Tate and Randolph, 2002.

9. Caro, 2001.

10. See Walton, Jr., et al., 1993, 629–46.

11. See Hamilton and Hamilton, 1997. This work makes outstanding use of congressional hearings from the New Deal.

12. Walton, Jr., Rosser, Sr., and Stevenson, 2002; Plummer, 1996; Krenn, 1999; and Von Eschen, 1996.

13. Quoted in Walton, Jr., and Smith, 2008, 272–73.

14. Skinner, 1992, 69.

15. Ibid.

16. Lusane, 2006.

17. Walton, Jr., and Smith, 2008, 241.

18. Walton, Jr., 1997, 354–56. See also Walton, Jr., 2004, 147–58.

19. Walton, Rosser, and Stevenson, 2002, 11–14.

20. U.S. Senate, Committee on Foreign Relations, 2001, 1.

21. Ibid.

22. Ibid., 12.

23. For a look at the American presidents who have appointed African American women to diplomatic posts, see Walton, Jr., 1995.

24. U.S. Senate, Committee on Foreign Relations, 2005, ii.

25. Obama, 2007; Obama, 2006; and Mendell, 2007.

26. Prysby, 1996, 29–46; and Wilson, 1993, 176–93.

27. Walton, Jr., 1997b, 24.

28. U.S. Senate, Committee on Foreign Relations, 2001, 15.

29. Ibid.

30. Ibid., 27.

31. U.S. Senate, Committee on Foreign Relations, 2005, 12.

32. Ibid.

33. Walton, Jr., 1971. See also King, Jr., 1958.

34. U.S. Senate, Committee on Foreign Relations, 2001, 13.

35. Ibid.

36. Ibid.

37. Ibid., 57.

38. Ibid.

39. U.S. Senate, Committee on Foreign Relations, 2005, 10.

40. Ibid., 47.

41. Ibid., 200.

42. Ibid., 46.

43. Ibid., 86–87.

44. U.S. Senate, Committee on Foreign Relations, 2001, 24.

45. Ibid., 33.

46. Ibid., 44.
47. Ibid., 45.
48. U.S. Senate, Committee on Foreign Relations, 2005, 14.
49. Ibid.
50. Ibid., 177.
51. Ibid., 178.
52. Ibid.
53. Ibid.
54. U.S. Senate, Committee on Foreign Relations, 2001, 66.
55. Ibid.
56. Ibid., 108.
57. Ibid.
58. U.S. Senate, Committee on Foreign Affairs, 2005, 78.
59. Ibid., 79.
60. Ibid.
61. Ibid., 268.
62. Ibid.
63. Ibid., 269.
64. Ibid., 257.
65. Ibid., 200.
66. Ibid., 199.
67. Lusane, 2006, 196.

REFERENCES

Caro, Robert. 2001. *Master of the Senate: The Lyndon Baines Johnson Years.* New York: Knopf.

DuBois, W. E. B. 1896. *The Suppression of the African Slave Trade of the United States of America, 1638–1870.* Cambridge, Mass.: Harvard Historical Studies.

Hamilton, Donna Cooper, and Charles V. Hamilton. 1997. *The Dual Agenda: The African American Struggle for Civil and Economic Equality.* New York: Columbia University Press.

Institute for Contemporary Studies. 1981. *The Fairmont Papers: Black Alternative Conference.* San Francisco: Institute for Contemporary Studies.

King, Martin Luther, Jr. 1958. *Stride toward Freedom.* New York: Harper and Row.

Krenn, Michael. 1999. *Black Diplomacy: African Americans and the State Department 1945–1969.* New York: M. E. Sharpe.

Lusane, Clarence. 2006. *Colin Powell and Condoleezza Rice: Foreign Policy, Race and the New American Century.* Westport, Conn.: Praeger.

Mendell, David. 2007. *Obama: From Promise to Power.* New York: HarperCollins.

Miller, Amistad Jake. 1978. *The Black Presence in American Foreign Affairs.* Washington, D.C.: University Press of America.

O'Connor, Karen, and Larry Sabato. 2008. *American Government.* New York: Longman.

Obama, Barack. 2006. *The Audacity of Hope: Thoughts on Reclaiming the American Dream.* New York: Crown.

Obama, Barack. 2007. *Dreams from My Father: A Study of Race and Inheritance.* New York: Random House.

Plummer, Brenda Gayle. 1996. *Rising Wind: Black Americans and U.S. Foreign Affairs, 1935–1960*. Chapel Hill: University of North Carolina Press.

Prysby, Charles. 1996. "The 1990 U.S. Senate Election in North Carolina." In *Race, Politics, and Governance in the United States,* ed. Huey Perry. Gainesville: University Press of Florida, 29–46.

Skinner, Elliott. 1992. *African Americans and U.S. Policy toward Africa 1850–1924: In Defense of Black Nationality.* Washington, D.C.: Howard University Press.

Tate, Gayle, and Lewis Randolph, eds. 2002. *Dimensions of Black Conservatism in the United States.* New York: Palgrave.

Tillery, Alvin B., Jr. 2007. "G. Mennen 'Soapy' Williams and the American Negro Leadership Conference on Africa: Rethinking the Origins of Multiculturalism in U.S. Foreign Policy." In *The African Foreign Policy of Secretary of State Henry Kissinger,* ed. Walton, Stevenson, and Rosser, 45–68. `

U.S. Senate, Committee on Foreign Relations. 2001. Hearing before the Committee on Foreign Relations, Nomination of Colin L. Powell to Be Secretary of State. 107th Cong., 1st sess., January 17, 2001. Washington, D.C.: U.S. Government Printing Office.

U.S. Senate, Committee on Foreign Relations. 2005. Hearings before the Committee on Foreign Relations, Nomination of Dr. Condoleezza Rice to Be Secretary of State. 109th Cong., 1st sess., January 18 and 19, 2005. Washington, D.C.: U.S. Government Printing Office.

Von Eschen, Penny. 1996. *Race against Empire: Black Americans and Anticolonialism, 1937–1957.* Ithaca: Cornell University Press.

Walton, Hanes, Jr. 1971. *The Political Philosophy of Martin Luther King, Jr.* New York: Greenwood Publishers.

Walton, Hanes, Jr. 1985/1969. *Invisible Politics: Black Political Behavior.* Albany: State University of New York Press. Originally published 1969.

Walton, Hanes, Jr. 1995. *Black Women at the United Nations: The Politics, a Theoretical Model and the Documents.* Borgo Press.

Walton, Hanes, Jr. 1997a. "African American Foreign Policy: From Decolonization to Democracy." In Hanes Walton, Jr., *African American Power and Politics: The Political Context Variable.* New York: Columbia University Press, 354–56.

Walton, Hanes, Jr. 1997b. *African American Power and Politics: The Political Context Variable.* New York: Columbia University Press.

Walton, Hanes, Jr. 2004. "The Political Science Educational Philosophy of Ralph Bunche: Theory and Practice." *Journal of Negro Education* 73 (Spring 2004): 147–58.

Walton, Hanes, Jr., Ronald Clark, James Bernard Rosser, and Robert Louis Stevenson. 1983. "Henry Highland Garnet Revisited via His Diplomatic Correspondence: The Correction of Misconceptions and Errors." *Journal of Negro History* 68 (Winter): 80–92.

Walton, Hanes, Jr., James Bernard Rosser, Sr., and Robert Louis Stevenson, eds. 2002. *Liberian Politics: The Portrait by African American Diplomat J. Milton Turner.* Lanham, Md.: Lexington Books.

Walton, Hanes, Jr., and Robert C. Smith. 2007. "The Race Variable and the American Political Science Association's *State of the Discipline* Reports and Books, 1907–2002." in *African American Perspectives on Political Science,* ed. Wilbur C. Rich. Philadelphia: Temple University Press, 24–37.

Walton, Hanes, Jr., and Robert Smith. 2008. *American Politics and the African American Quest for Universal Freedom,* 4th ed. New York: Longman.

Walton, Hanes, Jr., Robert Louis Stevenson, and James Bernard Rosser, Sr., eds. 2007. *The African Foreign Policy of Secretary of State Henry Kissinger: A Documentary Analysis.* Lanham, Md.: Lexington Books, 1–3, 23–38.

Walton, Hanes, Jr., et al. 1993. "The Congressional Hearing on National Freedom Day: An African American Holiday." *Southeastern Political Review* 21 (Summer): 629–46.

Ward, W. E. 1969. *The Royal Navy and the Slavers.* New York: Pantheon.

Wilson, Zaphon. 1993. "Gantt versus Helms: Deracialization Confronts Southern Traditionalism." In *Dilemmas of Black Politics: Issues of Leadership and Strategy,* ed. Georgia Persons. New York: HarperCollins, 176–93.

SIX

Colin L. Powell and the Iraq War

BUREAUCRATIC ACTOR AND
FOREIGN POLICY DISSENTER

Michael L. Clemons

Although race, ethnicity, and culture have been substantial motivating forces in the arena of U.S. foreign policymaking, only recently have African Americans penetrated the upper echelon of the foreign policy establishment. The harsh reality of African American exclusion from institutional participation is a reflection of the racial double standard that guided U.S. foreign policy for many years. The observation made by James A. Moss almost forty years ago continues to hold: "Our foreign policy posture is alarmingly colored by the racial complexion of the countries with which we are involved. We do, indeed, have a bipartisan and racial and ethnic foreign policy; one which operates positively toward countries most similar to us—predominantly white, and another which operates negatively for countries whose inhabitants are predominantly non-white" (Moss, 1970, 80). This perception abroad has been compounded by a lack of diversity among State Department personnel, a trend that has reinforced the view that U.S. foreign policy is racially biased.

It is somewhat ironic in the face of recent developments that the long tradition of African American participation is largely overlooked by scholars. However, this may be the case for several reasons. First, in addition to the impact of racism, there has long been a disproportionate focus on the role of the state in the study of foreign policymaking. Because of this thrust, individual-level analysis and the study of nonstate actors essentially have been relegated to a position of secondary or even tertiary importance. In addition, the position of whites, the dominant group, all too often has become the expression of "the national interest." Elucidating this point, Charles Henry asserts: "Foreign policy debates often obscure the fact that states are political entities while nations represent a cultural grouping. Most nation-states reflect the domination of and expansion of the national interest. This is true of the United States as it is of developing societies" (Henry, 2000, 11). However, even in a democratic context this can lead to a lack of capacity for inclusion in foreign policymaking and ineffective consideration of the effects of racial, ethnic, and cultural variation on the accomplishment of objectives and goals.

Further, Johnson (2007) astutely observes, "African-Americans have rarely benefited from a melding of interest with the U.S. government due to racial inequality. The African-American perspective regarding American foreign policy begins on an uneven playing field because of the nation's interest and struggle over the legitimacy of American democracy" (49). Although cloaked in the values and motives of nationalism and patriotism, the failure to evolve a paradigm that takes into account factors of race, ethnicity, and culture, domestically and internationally, is a continuation of the denial of the global linkages of U.S. citizens and the perpetuation of a xenophobic foreign policy marked by ethnocentrism.

The study of foreign policymaking and international politics reinforces the perspective that African Americans are disengaged as a group by neglecting racial and cultural variables and negating their significance at the domestic and international levels. However, with the rise of African Americans to high-profile, institutional foreign policymaking posts, it is critical that these dimensions be addressed to understand the possible effects of diversity on foreign affairs and the achievement of foreign policy goals and objectives.

On November 12, 2004, Colin L. Powell announced to the world his decision to resign from the office of secretary of state—a position he occupied during the first term of the administration of President George W. Bush. Powell's resignation, which reflected the solidification of the administration's policy in regard to Iraq, drew myriad reactions. This conclusion, potentially damaging to Powell's legacy, gave rise to the pervasive opinion held by insiders and laypersons alike that he had been asked to resign, in part because many of his views tended to conflict with White House policy. Major news sources filed reports indicating Powell's interest in continuing as secretary. For example, CNN reported that "for months Powell said he served at the pleasure of the president, suggesting he might stay if asked." However, the president opted not to make such a request, and neither was Powell asked to leave. Why did Powell's illustrious career end with a thud rather than the kind of thunder that could have potentially catapulted him to a place among the historically revered, and if he so desired, to the zenith of U.S. domestic and global power—the office of the president of the United States?

Purpose and Hypothesis

This chapter focuses on Colin L. Powell's tenure as head of the U.S. Department of State. By focusing on the Powell experience, we explore whether and how the actions and policies advanced by Powell and other African Americans who occupy high-profile foreign policymaking roles are affected because of their position relative to the president's elite inner circle. The possible effects of elitism, class, and ideology in bureaucracy are considered, along with race.

Specifically, this research delves into whether Secretary Powell operated principally in a way consistent with the *bureaucratic actor model* or the *foreign policy dissenter framework* in the execution of his responsibilities as secretary of state from 2000 to 2004. It is hypothesized that despite his extraordinary military career and long association with key foreign policy establishment players, Powell, as secretary of state exhibited a contrasting tendency (relative to those in the inner circle with whom he worked) toward foreign policy dissent. He did so often in conflict even with his own efforts to operationalize a genuine bureaucratic approach to managing the Department of State.

Utilizing the bureaucratic model and the foreign policy dissenter framework, this research assesses the productivity and impact of Secretary Powell's tenure during the first term of George W. Bush's presidential administration. Powell's rise to power as the first African American secretary of state in U.S. history is of particular interest, as is the eventual erosion of his power, and the consequent loss of his effectiveness within an increasingly micromanaged, highly secretive, and bureaucratized White House. An underlying question is whether Powell's dissent led to his eventual relative isolation in the Bush cabinet and his resignation from the position of secretary of state.

Context of U.S. Foreign Policymaking: Race, Ethnicity, and Culture

This research is based in part on the fact that Powell was the first person of African descent in the history of the United States to rise to the high-profile position of secretary of state. For much of U.S. history, people of African descent were categorically excluded from formal participation in American politics. Although Powell was able to break down the barriers to institutional access, he would find himself constrained not only by the domestic political environment and the global operational context, but also by an intertwined bureaucratic framework that increasingly was reproduced along with the actors within to ensure implementation of the administration's policies in Iraq and in the Middle East. In the end, Powell would find himself in the proverbial crosshairs of the U.S. foreign policy establishment as reconfigured by Bush and his inner circle, rather than at its helm.

It is only in recent years that racial hurdles in institutional foreign affairs positions have been overcome beyond diplomatic appointments and legislative incumbency. Although domestic discrimination virtually preoccupied African Americans, the group made its collective voice heard nationally and around the world. An important subtext is whether African Americans are more likely than whites to experience the limitations and constraints imposed by governmental structure and the culture and dynamics of relationships among bureaucratic actors. With the exception of Barack Obama, who was elected president of the United States in 2008, no other African American has acquired the establishment-level support Powell was able to galvanize (Miller, 2000, 32).

To place into perspective Powell's circumstances as head of the Department of State, factors at the aggregate level that potentially influence the quality, capacity, and results of high-profile African American foreign policy participation are considered. Chief among these variables are the domestic environment and the global climate. In broad terms, they shape behavior singly and in combination with racial, ethnic, and cultural factors.

Race relations have had a long and arduous evolution in the history of the United States. In the eighteenth-century American slave trade and the nineteenth-century colonial enslavement of Africans by European imperialists, the mold was set for the post–civil rights era relationship between African Americans and Africans, and U.S. foreign policy toward Africa (Adekeye, 2004). Concurrent with developments abroad, African Americans faced domestic policies that undermined their inclusion at the institutional level and that generally promulgated white supremacy not only as ideology, but also as a basis for public policy.

The development of the Jim Crow system following centuries of institutionalized slavery demonstrated the persistence of those who believed that the inferiority of people of African descent justified their subordination. The Jim Crow system legalized racial segregation and discrimination. De facto segregation operated on a parallel basis with de jure segregation. Not until the civil rights movement of the 1950s and 1960s did the racial caste system began to undergo deterioration, allowing it to be supplanted by a system that would promote universal equality. However, by the time de jure segregation and blatant racism declined, symbolic racism had emerged in their place. Symbolic racism, according to Henry and Sears (2002), occurs in both abstract and ideological terms. Symbolic racism is indicative of the moral code held by whites about how society should be organized. Accordingly, instrumental beliefs are relegated to a back burner, and rather than focus on black people as individuals, they are dealt with at the group level (Henry and Sears, 2002).

At the individual level, the bureaucratic model seeks to provide a lens that views foreign policy as the outcome of a bargaining process structured by bureaucratic resources and interests. The rise of African Americans to high-profile foreign affairs positions in the U.S. Department of State raises questions of whether and how race affects the rise to power and the exercise of institutional leadership. Since race, ethnicity, and culture are influential in the allocation of institutional access in the form of power and wealth, questions of class and elitism necessarily surface. A feature of African American global participation is that the foreign affairs behavior of blacks has been circumscribed by the exigencies of racism and the widely held belief that members of this racial group are uninterested, and/or do not have the time for "lofty matters" that only tangentially affect the immediate quality of life. History may make it likely that African Americans, more than other racial groups, will assume foreign affairs interpretations and positions that are antithetical to the stance maintained by the U.S. foreign policy establishment.

Following a brief examination of Colin Powell's rise to power, an overview and discussion of the bureaucratic actor model and the foreign policy dissent framework is presented. Powell's experiences as secretary of state during George W. Bush's initial term (in the aftermath of the terrorist attacks of September 11, 2001, and the Iraqi invasion) are weighed against these theories to ascertain the consistency of his decisions and policy actions with foreign policy dissent exhibited over time by African Americans within and outside the foreign policy establishment. Also considered is whether the bureaucratic actor and the foreign policy dissenter frameworks are mutually exclusive characterizations of African American global behavior or rather compatible and potentially mutually reinforcing.

Powell's Rise to Power

Individual background characteristics and life experiences can provide important insight into the choices and decisions made by those who occupy leadership positions and make public policy. In this section, Powell's background is briefly examined to shed light on life experiences that may have influenced his behavior, decisions, policy positions, leadership approach, and management style during his tenure as secretary of state.

Born to Jamaican immigrants in Harlem, New York City, in 1937, Colin Luther Powell shattered the glass ceiling long imposed on African American participation in U.S. foreign policymaking. He forged a critical new path for the incorporation and growth of black participation in the institutional affairs of government. A product of the public schools in the South Bronx, Powell graduated from Morris High School, and he later studied geology and graduated with a bachelor's degree from the City College of New York. Following his second tour of duty in Vietnam, he enrolled in George Washington University where he earned an MBA degree (Powell, 1995).

Powell realized that he was destined for the military when he joined the Reserve Officer Training Corps (ROTC) while in college. His dedication led to an appointment as commander of his unit's precision drill team, and in 1958 he graduated at the top of his class with the rank of cadet colonel, the highest rank in the ROTC. Upon graduation, Powell was commissioned second lieutenant. Between 1958 and 1989 he catapulted through a variety of command and staff positions, and eventually achieved the rank of general. At the relatively youthful age of forty-nine, while retaining his army commission as a lieutenant general, Powell became President Ronald Reagan's national security advisor. He served in this capacity from 1987 to 1989 (Powell, 1995).

At the conclusion of his tenure in 1989 with the National Security Council, George H. W. Bush (also referred to as Bush I) promoted Powell to the rank of four-star general. He thus shared the distinction enjoyed by Dwight D. Eisenhower and Alexander Haig as the only post-World War II generals to achieve four stars in the absence of experience as division commander. During the term of Bush I, Powell served as commander-in-chief (CINC) of the U.S. Army's Forces Command. In this capacity, he oversaw the entirety of Army, Army Reserve, and National Guard units in the continental United States, Alaska, Hawaii, and Puerto Rico (Powell, 1995).

Following a brief stint as CINC, Powell was appointed chairman of the Joint Chiefs of Staff. Powell served in this capacity, the highest military position in the Department of Defense, from October 1, 1989, to September 30, 1993. The invasion of Panama in 1989 to topple the regime of Manuel Noriega and the invasion of Panama and Operation Desert Storm in 1991 were among the twenty-eight crises he oversaw during his tenure as chairman (Powell, 1995).

In the 2000 U.S. presidential race, Powell, serving as a key foreign policy advisor, campaigned for Texas governor George W. Bush. Because of his support of the campaign and of the Republican Party, President Bush rewarded him with the appointment of secretary of state. Clearly highly qualified for the post in terms of knowledge, skills, and experience Powell became the first African American to hold the highest rank in the U.S. foreign policy bureaucracy. Rather strikingly, however, within the markedly conservative Bush administration, Powell, by many measures, was a moderate. Still, a key asset was his extraordinarily high popularity with the American public. His popularity stemmed partially from his personification of the American Dream. Powell, the son of Jamaican immigrants, demonstrated that with hard work and dedication, anyone could be a success. His status as a genuine war hero and his success as a military leader weighed heavily in the public's support of Powell's elevation through the ranks of high-profile foreign policymaking.

In the section that follows, the bureaucratic model and the foreign policy dissenter framework are presented. These approaches are employed to describe and assess the nature, quality, and consequences of Powell's vision and positions for U.S. foreign policy in Iraq while secretary of state. This overview is followed by an analysis and discussion of Powell's experience in light of each of these conceptual frameworks to shed light on the nature of his behavior while serving as secretary.

Bureaucratic Politics Model

The domestic environment within which U.S. foreign policy unfolds frequently conditions the quality, nature, and implementation of such decisions. For example, domestic conditions and social relations can affect the timing of new foreign policy developments. The Republic of South Africa represents a case in point. As a system, apartheid began to fray and ultimately deteriorate concurrent with the implementation of legal remedies to secure the acquisition of political and social rights for black people in the United States. As the foreign affairs bureaucratic structure underwent some alteration because of the domestic environment, the trajectory of U.S. foreign policy in South Africa too was altered. As this example illustrates, the domestic environment and its attendant dynamics have important implications for bureaucratic actors.

The bureaucratic politics model, also known as the bureaucratic perspective, rests on several important assumptions. First, it assumes that different governmental institutions can stifle the behavior of bureaucrats with divergent institutional interests and preferences. This means that the be-havior of the bureaucratic player is potentially restrained. It suggests that the behavior of the bureaucratic player is predictable based on his or her organizational role. The second assumption is that players see the stakes involved in any given situation according to their own interests. Consensus building, compromise, bargaining, and negotiation are mechanisms for decisionmaking.

The bureaucratic politics model also assumes that foreign policy is the outcome of a bargaining process structured by bureaucratic resources and interests. In reference to the consensus building, bargaining, and compromise the connection between foreign policymaking and domestic conditions and social relations becomes salient. Since the bureaucratic model sees foreign policy as the result of bargaining, which to a considerable degree is determined by the allocation and distribution of power (including that stemming from interests) and resources, bureaucracy operates in effect to shape the application of these mechanisms. Depending upon its output, bureaucracy is subject to readjustment and fine-tuning to achieve policy objectives that are consistent with defined state interests.

The power of the bureaucratic politics model is in its penetrating and enduring insight that "foreign policy is often more the product of a dysfunctional decision making process than of a rational assessment of various objectives." In contrast to the rational actor model (cast by Graham Allison as a "monolithic process" reflective of the "unitary behavior" of the state, which is much like that of an individual), "bureaucratic organizational politics . . . resulted from the interaction of individual bureaucrats playing political games to advance their own and their organizational interests" (Smith, 1990, 110). Foreign policy is equated with national policy, thus, foreign policy objectives should be national objectives. Nevertheless, very often, in pursuit of foreign policy objectives bureaucratic fissures resulting from individual and organizational interests and biases that are part of the context of bureaucratic decisionmaking deflect rationality. This results from the interaction between aspects of the domestic environment (corporate elites, mass elites, mass media, government elites, and interest groups) and the foreign policy bureaucracy.

In turn, the international environment impinges on bureaucratic dynamics—that is, relationships of power between bureaucratic actors. The bureaucratic perspective, "implies (1) that change in the international environment is only one of several stimuli to which participants in the foreign policy process are responding (possibly among the weakest and least important) and (2) that events involving the actions of two or more nations can best be explained and predicted in terms of the actions of two or more national bureaucracies whose actions affect the domestic interests and objectives of the other bureaucracies involved" (Halperin and Kanter, 1992, 397). Conceptually, the bureaucratic model situates the president and foreign policy officials at the "helm" of the bureaucratic enterprise. Rather than the president and key foreign policy leaders exercising "objective" control leading to process decisions, the bureaucratic model holds that "the organizational politics and processes that produce decisions often color those decisions" (Ikenberry, 1999, 411).

Foreign Policy Dissenter Framework

The role of African Americans as critics of U.S. foreign policy grew out of the struggle against slavery and the intense desire of the group to gain equal rights and access to the system. In the preface to their book *American Politics and the African American Quest for Universal Freedom*, Hanes Walton, Jr., and Robert C. Smith opine that "in their attack on slavery and racial subordination, black Americans and their leaders have embraced doctrines of universal freedom and equality. In doing so they have had an important influence on the shaping of democratic constitutional government and on expanding or universalizing the idea of freedom not only for themselves but for all Americans" (Walton and Smith, 2006, xiv). Out of the conflict born of slavery and oppression in the United States, African Americans fashioned a foreign policy perspective and approach that takes into account the goal of eradicating injustice wherever it reaches on the planet. Consequently, in the informal and formal realms of global participation, the black perspective often has been an opposing or dissenting position relative to that of the foreign policy establishment.

Walton and Smith (2006) argue that in the field of foreign affairs, African Americans have been involved as foreign policy managers and foreign policy implementers. Within this intensely bureaucratic context, African Americans have been creators and innovators. Walton and Smith hasten to point out that "in their role as creators, African Americans have been critics" (263). Indeed, a brief review of foreign policy dissent in the United States shows that African Americans have participated in foreign affairs on two broad dimensions: the informal or noninstitutional and the formal or institutional realms of foreign affairs and foreign policymaking. The section below briefly discusses some specific examples of African Americans' involvement in each dimension.

Nature of Black Foreign Policy Dissent

Although African Americans are relative newcomers on the scene of American foreign policymaking, as a group they had previously established a tradition of dissent based in part on the ideal of universal freedom (Walton and Smith, 2006). Although this is far from the reality, African American foreign policy dissenters typically have been identified as informal or noninstitutional actors. However, history demonstrates an apparent tradition of dissent among those engaged from an institutional or formal vantage point within the foreign policy apparatus.

The formal and informal dichotomy of African American foreign policy participation accentuates that dissent is an American tradition. By virtue of the First Amendment to the Bill of Rights, American citizens have the constitutional guarantee of freedom of speech and expression. At the base of American democracy is the exercise of First Amendment rights that are intended to allow for the open expression and debate of social issues and freedom from prosecution by government and its agents.

The informal arena of participation consists of the plans made and the actions taken by race-based interest groups and their leaders from a vantage point that is external to the "official" foreign policy apparatus. Institutional or formal participation, in contrast, necessitates the constitutional charge to carry out the goals and objectives of U.S. foreign policy. The widely held perception that African American foreign policy dissenters are based exclusively in the noninstitutional realm may stem from the reluctance of U.S. and Western researchers to credit noninstitutional and nonstate actors as influential in the process, and the failure to formally incorporate people of color into the apparatus of U.S. foreign policy decisionmaking.

Noninstitutional (Informal) Dissent

In contrast to those who occupy institutional foreign policy positions, noninstitutional actors do not hold elected or appointed positions of power in the foreign policy establishment. Rather, these individuals usually are associated with an organizational base or identifiable group with the goal to influence U.S. foreign policy. Frequently, such goals are articulated and pursued principally through the utilization of protest politics, self-help techniques and strategies, lobbying, and the exercise of personal power. These activities have been instrumental to the capacity of African Americans to make their views known domestically and globally with the objective of influencing U.S. foreign policy outcomes. It is important to note that the democratic context within which they operate facilitates such activities.

However, the unwillingness to extend the protections of democracy and democratic participation to Africans in America did not prevent the overt expression of opposition to foreign policy, even in the era of slavery. Perhaps the earliest and most striking examples demonstrating dissent on the part of blacks were the planned and spontaneous slave rebellions that occurred in response to African enslavement in the Americas. In his documentary work, *American Negro Slave Revolts*, Herbert Aptheker points out that the fear of slave rebellions harbored by many white southerners was associated with the belief that if the slave trade ceased slave rebellions would no longer be a threat (Aptheker, 1974). George Mason, James Madison, and Thomas Jefferson, even before the Revolution, came to believe, like Anthony Benezet, an influential Quaker leader, that "this fear may be carried too far, for it is certainly yet more dangerous to withhold from the generality of people the knowledge of danger they will be in, thro' a continued importation of Negro Slaves" (Benezet, cited in Herbert Aptheker, 1974, 40–41). Enslaved Africans, as suggested by the evidence, were aware of the effects of insurrection, including its potential for helping to bring about an end to the importation of slaves and the institution of slavery itself.

Patterns of social exclusion persist in the post-civil rights period, and during the Jim Crow and civil rights eras noninstitutional actors seeking to influence foreign policymaking frequently resorted to some combination of unconventional strategies and tactics (including protest politics, self-help techniques and strategies, lobbying, and the exercise of personal power) to bring about desired policy results. Ironically, the residual effects of exclusionary politics helped fabricate and set into motion the application of extra-systemic or noninstitutional approaches to social change, including those used in the arena of foreign policymaking. More often than not, as illustrated by the case of South Africa, African Americans have articulated and advanced a "balanced approach," employing institutional and noninstitutional approaches to achieve policies consistent with expressed group interests.

It is interesting that African Americans have such a long and rich tradition of dissent when in fact the group has demonstrably been one of the major supporters of U.S. foreign policy. The support given to U.S. foreign policy by African Americans is fairly well documented, and a good deal of that documentation focuses on their contributions to the armed services. In a fundamental sense, dissent is an American tradition indicative of patriotism and citizens' interest in the well-being of the nation. However, little attention has been given to African Americans' dissent from U.S. foreign policy despite the numerous examples throughout history demonstrating such dissent.

Frederick Douglass provides a case in point. Demonstrative of the idea of universal freedom, Frederick Douglass, in 1848, strongly condemned the United States for its policy of aggression against Mexico. This condemnation amounted to an anti-imperialist, anticolonialist stance, in an era when colonialism and imperialism widely and overtly were believed to be the appropriate course of action for European states and for the United States as an emerging world power. In his July 4, 1852 speech, "What to the Slave is Fourth of July?" Douglass helped establish the tradition of dissent and protest of U.S. efforts for imperialism and colonialism and suppression of people of color as a foreign and domestic policy to uphold white supremacy. Fifty-one years later Douglass's son Lewis spoke out against U.S. policy toward Cuba, the Philippines, Hawaii, and Puerto Rico, calling it hypocritical.

Another interesting case is that of Richard Wright, known primarily for his contributions to the American literary tradition and his depiction of the complexities of black life in the United States. Before the Japanese attack on Pearl Harbor on June 6, 1941, Wright gave a speech to the League of American Writers entitled "Not My People's War." In this speech, he argued that World War II was not a war that black Americans should be involved in due to their own oppression and second-class treatment.

Another important figure is Paul Robeson, who like Wright is frequently identified with the Harlem Renaissance and often recollected in narrow ideological terms. Robeson was staunchly opposed to American imperialism and he strongly denounced lynching, racism, and discrimination. In his autobiography, W. E. B. Du Bois asserted that Robeson's treatment by the government was associated with his dissent of U.S. policies.

In the civil rights and post-civil rights eras, there are numerous examples of noninstitutional actors initiating measures to affect U.S. foreign policymaking. Some contemporary illustrations of noninstitutional participation include Martin Luther King, Malcolm X, and Stokely Carmichael, who protested and dissented in regard to the draft of blacks for the Vietnam War. Eventually, it was the loss of support of American citizens, as demonstrated through massive protests and growing opposition to the war abroad, which led to President Richard M. Nixon's decision to end the war.

Perhaps the most prominent example of a noninstitutional actor in the global arena is the Reverend Jesse Jackson. Employing a strategy referred to as "citizen diplomacy," Jackson earned the respect and admiration of governmental leaders and private citizens at home and abroad. Citizen diplomacy has been defined in terms of "the diplomatic efforts of private citizens in the international arena for the purpose of achieving a specific objective or accomplishing constituency goals" (Stanford, 1997, 9). Chief among Jackson's foreign policy credits is his successful December 1983 citizen diplomatic initiative to Syria to negotiate the release of Lt. Robert O. Goodman, Jr. Shot down in an air raid over Syria, Lieutenant Goodman, an African American, eventually was released because of the efforts of Jackson. In addition, on a later mission to Cuba Jackson persuaded Fidel Castro to free scores of political prisoners (Stanford, 1997; Walton and Smith, 2006). Jackson was well situated to articulate and refine the strategy of citizen diplomacy. As a result of his work with Martin Luther King and the civil rights movement, he cultivated a reputation in the United States and around the world as a fighter for justice and freedom. Consequently, he emerged for some time as the mainstream acknowledged spokesperson for the African American community. From this vantage point, Jackson was handed the opportunity to create a strong political persona domestically and globally, as well a chance to develop significant personal relationships with important world leaders. These circumstances allowed him to enjoy considerable influence in the arena of foreign affairs (Walton and Smith, 2006). Although some criticized him for being in violation of the Logan Act, Jackson is largely respected for his accomplishments in foreign affairs. The Logan Act is a federal statute that makes it a crime for a citizen to confer with foreign governments against the interests of the United States. Specifically, it prohibits private citizens from negotiating with other countries on behalf of the United States without authorization. Jackson's work stands as part of the long tradition of noninstitutional citizen diplomacy and activism advanced by others, including Malcolm X and the Reverend Leon Sullivan (Walton and Smith, 2006).

Institutional (Formal) Dissent

Despite their exclusion from the mainstream of U.S. foreign policymaking, there are a number of historical and contemporary examples of African American condemnation and dissent of U.S. foreign policy from inside the system, from the vantage point of elected and appointed positions of power. Several scholars have observed that early on, African Americans used their bureaucratic positions as ministers and ambassadors to African and Caribbean countries to articulate and affect the black interest (Miller, 1978; Skinner, 1992; Walton and Smith, 2006).

Significant progress, though slow and arduous, has been made in the opportunities for African Americans to affect foreign policy decisionmaking through position occupancy, representation, and the exercise of institutional power. For example, among the contemporary institutional dissenters of U.S. foreign policy is Julian Bond, who stood in opposition to the Vietnam War, and consequently was barred from his seat at the time he was elected to the Georgia legislature. Another important example, which illustrates not only dissent but also its consequences, is the case of Andrew Young. As U.N. ambassador, Young chose to meet with representatives of the Palestinian Liberation Organization (PLO) in violation of the policy of the administration of President Jimmy Carter that forbade negotiation with PLO leadership. Despite the fact that officials prior to Young had been in contact with PLO representatives, Young's action created such uproar in the foreign policy establishment that it ultimately led to his resignation. Some black leaders wondered publicly whether there was a double standard applied to Ambassador Young to silence criticism and maximize support from Jewish voters.

More recently, Cynthia McKinney is perhaps the first person to maintain overtly that the U.S. invasion of Iraq was without substantial basis. McKinney, the first African American women elected to represent Georgia in the U.S. Congress, long has been controversial, mostly due to her left-leaning and even radical policy positions with regard to the administration and her colleagues in the House of Representatives. Her critique of the preemptive U.S.-led military strike of Iraq justified her being targeted for defeat by the Republican party and its backers during the campaign for reelection. The bold leadership she demonstrated by suggesting that the Bush administration had advance knowledge of the September 11, 2001, attacks on the World Trade Center and the Pentagon helped galvanize the antiwar movement and heightened in the 2008 presidential race the issue of "bringing the war to an end." McKinney was defeated in 2002, but regained her congressional seat two years later. In 2006 she was defeated in a reelection bid, but more recently as a 2008 presidential candidate for the Green Party, McKinney was able to continue to promote her views against the war in Iraq.

Based on the foregoing overview, African American foreign policy dissenters have operated both inside and outside of formal foreign policy-making organs. While institutional and noninstitutional actors and groups have advanced policies, they operate on different planes, in that formal actors are subject to constitutional as well as bureaucratic constraints.

Analysis and Discussion

The bureaucratic politics model and the foreign policy dissenter framework provide unique lenses for examining Colin Powell's experience as head of the Department of State. In this section, we consider the following hypothesis: Powell's behavior and decisions while secretary of state exhibited a tendency toward foreign policy dissent, frequently conflicting with his own efforts to operationalize a genuine bureaucratic approach to managing the Department of State. These frameworks are employed to investigate Secretary Powell's intranational relationships with bureaucratic actors (that is, the power and role ascribed to his official position within the complex of presidential administration and politics), and their consequences for his ability to exercise power and influence in foreign policymaking. The bureaucratic model and the foreign policy dissenter framework facilitate explanation of the barriers to power that Powell faced while serving as a principal member of the Bush cabinet. An underlying question is whether Powell's apparent disagreements with White House staffers resulted in his relative isolation in the Bush bureaucracy and his resignation from the position of secretary of state.

Powell the Bureaucrat

The bureaucratic model holds that "the decisions and actions of governments are essentially intranational political outcomes: outcomes in the sense that what happens is not chosen as a solution to a problem but rather results from compromise, coalition, competition, and confusion among government officials who see different faces of an issue; political in the sense that the activity from which the outcomes emerge is best characterized as bargaining" (Allison, 1999, 439). This characterization of the bureaucratic operational context paints a picture that implies that government officials, consciously and unconsciously, behave in a manner resulting in the minimization of cooperation among bureaucratic actors and an incoherent approach to defining the national interest. Nonetheless, the bureaucratic model contends that the president and the top foreign policy advisors are at the helm; however, politics and process ultimately work in tandem to dictate the context and constraints imposed on appointed and elected officials.

Allison's Darwinian-like conception of bureaucracy suggests that bureaucratic actors work to bring about foreign policy outcomes commensurate with their own conception or view of the problem and those they represent. The clash of ideas and perspectives, which is inherent to the decisionmaking process, can result in foreign policy decisions that do not squarely speak to a given problem in the form of a practical solution (Allison, 1999). Rather, the process frequently yields ill-focused, incomplete, and generally flawed policies because of issue skewing due to "bargaining, compromise, coalition, competition, and confusion" that take place in the bureaucracy. These activities provide the basis for the formulation of ineffective decisions and foreign policy. Hence, the politics associated with the bureaucracy, by definition, rarely produces tailor-made solutions because of the competition between intranational bureaucratic actors vying for influence in policymaking and, in particular, positioning for influence with the president.

The extrapolation of these dynamics to Secretary Powell's experience may well lead to the conclusion that he did not fare well in the horizontal administrative structure encouraged by George Bush's management style. Similar to other administrations, the competitive administrative environment that evolved rested partially on the personal association one had with the president. Given that, Bush's personal relationships were closer and stronger with others in his administration than with Powell, and it was clear that Powell needed to devise a communication approach with the president that would allow for *objective* consideration of his views about U.S. foreign policy and the operation of the State Department.

As a military man, Colin Powell was accustomed to hierarchy and bureaucratic structure. Notwithstanding the distinctions between military and civilian bureaucracies, his phenomenal success in the U.S. Army suggested that he would be comfortable in this environment. Shortly after being wounded in Vietnam, Powell worked at the Pentagon as an aide in the administration of President Carter. In this role, he began to accumulate the necessary contacts and credentials to catapult him to the head of the Department of State.

Upon accepting his new position as secretary of state, Powell wasted little time making clear that under his foreign policy plans the administration would work closely with China and Russia to iron out areas of disagreement. Powell forcefully declared that "nations that pursued weapons of mass destruction would not frighten us. We will meet them, we will match them. We will contend with them" (DeYoung, 2006, 297). Powell's stature continued to grow domestically and abroad. Although some saw him as an overshadowing figure relative to the new president, Powell's view was that as secretary, he was Bush's number-one foreign affairs advisor. He emphasized this point in major State Department communiqués and in contacts with mass media. To many observers it seemed that while Bush exhibited a relative lack of sophistication, Powell was more knowledgeable, more articulate, and showed more confidence on foreign policy matters. Although this may have been the case in the short run, as time progressed and as bureaucratic forces and foci became more defined and entrenched, Powell's ability to address matters he considered "core" to the articulation of American interests abroad was increasingly sidetracked by his ideological entanglement in matters essentially of a peripheral nature.

In describing the approach to running the Department of State, Kessler (2007) observed that Powell was significantly different from two of his predecessors, James Baker and George Schultz. In comparing the three secretaries, he offers the following analysis:

> In the past two decades, there had been three basic approaches to managing the building: The James Baker model, the Colin Powell model, and the George Shultz model. Baker had a strong seventh floor that essentially ignored the rest of the State Department; he and a handful of aides made the policy, to the resentment of the career staff. The polar opposite to the Baker approach was Powell, who ran the State Department like a military organization, allowing each section to do its task and so permitting ideas to bubble up from the ranks; this made him a popular leader. Shultz's approach was something like a hybrid; he ran the building but he was also respected by it. (26)

Powell's approach lacked consonance with the bureaucracy set in motion by George W. Bush. That he employed "participatory" management strategies, including the division of labor, and recognized the value of specialization contrasted markedly with Bush's tendency to communicate with only a few "trusted" advisors. Powell's bureaucratic style entailed the conscious effort of allowing ideas and suggestions to reach him as secretary from throughout the ranks of the organization. This approach to State Department management, while applauded by some, was threatening to others.

At the outset of his term in office, Powell seems to have miscalculated, erroneously assuming that the president shared his views about organizational management—that ideas be allowed to emerge from within the ranks of the organization. If this is the case, Powell perhaps naively believed that since he was secretary the president would weigh his ideas alongside those of others, and objectively opt for the position demonstrated to be in the best interest of the United States. However, considering the nature of bureaucratic politics, it is fair to wonder whether Powell typically responded in a manner that was appropriately direct and forceful. When the president selected policy options contrary to Powell's position, Powell's power may have been diminished by the tendency to adjust and acquiesce, rather than strategically confront the intranational bureaucratic process. To some extent, this behavior may reflect Powell's extensive military exposure that promotes unquestioned loyalty and commitment.

Although previous studies of secretaries of state employed the bureaucratic framework to understand policy outputs, for obvious reasons, including the absence of high-profile African American foreign policy actors, the proposition that race, ethnicity, and culture are important ingredients in the formulation of intranational bureaucratic interaction has yet to be tested. Given this, one can only speculate that the bureaucracy erected under George W. Bush may have been disproportionately constraining for Powell in contrast to others in the administration, due not only to race and life experiences, but also because of the singular and combined effect of these factors on his ideology and political philosophy. Powell's autobiography provides some insight on this matter:

> Neither of the two major parties fits me comfortably in its present state. Granted, politics is the art of compromise, but for now, I prefer not to compromise just so that I can say I belong to this or that party. I am troubled by the political passion of those on the extreme right who seem to claim divine wisdom on political as well as spiritual matters . . . I am disturbed by the class and racial undertones beneath the surface of their rhetoric. On the other side of the spectrum, I am put off by patronizing liberals who claim to know what is best for society but devote little thought to who will eventually pay the bills . . . I distrust rigid ideology from any direction, and I am discovering that many Americans feel just as I do. The time may be at hand for a third major party to emerge to represent this sensible center of the American political spectrum. (Powell, 1995, 608–609)

This statement provides a perspective on some of the matters that conflicted Powell during the time he served as secretary of state and previously in other foreign affairs-related roles. Apparently, there was some reticence on Powell's part regarding the ideological rigidity of the Democratic and Republican parties. His belief in patience and openmindedness in foreign policymaking and international politics was one of the factors that differentiated him from his contemporaries in the Bush administration. This may have been the result of his military background.

Powell: A Foreign Policy Dissenter?

If as a bureaucrat Powell was only marginally successful, to what extent did his disagreement with the policy positions of Bush and his inner circle affect his tenure at the State Department helm? Perhaps the bureaucratic travails Powell experienced could have been prophesied early on when he interjected himself in the policymaking process and was revealed to be out of sync with the president on the question of whether direct talks should be held with North Korea. That Powell was not in line with Bush on this matter foreshadowed his fate. With the identification of North Korea by President Bush as part of the "axis of evil," which also included Iraq and Syria, the administration's position not to hold direct talks with the country became one of the defining features of Bush's foreign policy.

There is also the suggestion that Powell was openly skeptical about plans advanced in the aftermath of the September 11, 2001, terrorist attacks. For example, he was reluctant to endorse Deputy Defense Secretary Wolfowitz's plans to end "state sponsored terrorism." Consistent with positions he had assumed in the past, Powell expressed serious reservations about Wolfowitz's plans for "regime change" (Hitchens, 2004, 46). Even during the planning phase of the first Gulf War, in contrast to Bush's emerging war strategy, Powell favored the use of diplomacy and a policy that would debilitate Iraq economically and militarily (Gelb, 1991).

In the months following his infamous presentation before the United Nations, Powell indicated in an interview with NBC's Tim Russert that "opportunistic intelligence provided through the Iraqi National Congress" had provided a misleading basis for his belief that there were weapons of mass destruction in Iraq. The apparent juxtaposition of Powell to other foreign policy operatives in the Bush administration, as illustrated by these events and others, led conservatives, including Newt Gingrich, to amplify the charge that Powell was out of step with the Bush administration.

Interestingly, one of the criticisms was that Powell was a puppet, acting on behalf of others in the government in order to maintain his popularity with the public. *The Sowetan,* a South African newspaper, depicted Powell in a cartoon with a forlorn look on his face standing in front of the White House as two African Americans preparing to leave for the conference turn to him and ask: "Coming, Uncle Tom?" Powell replies to this query in exaggerated black dialect: "De massa in de big house says I ain't" (Lusane,

2006, 65). Comments such as these have been made in connection with questions about Powell's loyalty and where it lies. Many citizens, including some in the African American community, apparently believe that his loyalty to Bush was at the cost of progressive policies and positions, some of which were consistent with black global interests.

Still, one reason Powell retained his high standing among blacks despite his close association with the Bush administration was that whatever other positions he adopted, Powell never repudiated affirmative action (Kennedy, 2008, 95). Moreover, Powell departed from the Bush administration position when he "broke with the cautious language that some had been employing and stated in more-or-less terms that the conduct of the racist Arab-Muslim death squads in Darfur conformed to the definition of genocide" (Hitchens, 2004, 42). Powell's attention to and focus on the AIDS crisis in Africa helped earn him enormous respect and admiration from African Americans and other citizens.

It is clear, however, that from the outset Powell was constrained as secretary of state due to the relative "outsider" status he held in reference to the neoconservative structure instituted by Vice President Richard Cheney. Perhaps the most blatant example involves John Bolton. On May 11, 2001, Powell agreed to the appointment of Bolton as secretary for arms control and international security. When it was later uncovered that Bolton was in fact reporting to Cheney, Powell opted not to remove him from the position. In the aftermath, fascinatingly and inexplicably, Powell allowed Bolton to hire David Wurmser, a neoconservative, as a special advisor. Powell's desire to be seen by the president and others as a "team player" may have led him to acquiesce to Wurmser's appointment instead of challenge and confront Vice President Cheney and others in the bureaucracy vying to achieve their aims.

The Iraq situation came to a head when it became clear to Powell that despite his herculean efforts, Bush was unwilling to accept a diplomatic approach. Many of the concrete facts surfaced only after Powell's retirement. At the July 5, 2007, Aspen Ideas Festival in Colorado Powell revealed that he had sought to prevent the Iraq war and that his attempt to convince Bush that the invasion would plunge the nation into the complexities of religion and ideology, which have long existed in Iraq, was to no avail. Powell indicated that he met with President Bush for two and a half hours and that he "took him through the consequences of going into an Arab country and becoming the occupiers" (Baxter, 2007). His efforts were fruitless, and the nation became engaged in an all-out war that threatened national security and the security of the Middle East. Once again, Powell appeared to succumb to the pressure of bureaucratic politics and the demands of presidential loyalty as he construed it. This is substantially demonstrated by the fact that despite his serious reservations, he went on to make "the most cogent presentation of any cabinet member, right in front of the U.N. General Assembly and the entire world, making the case that time had run out for Saddam Hussein" (Hitchens, 2004, 46).

The point that Powell's concept of loyalty may have overreached and been misplaced is reiterated in the February 27, 2003, resignation letter of John Brady Kiesling, an American diplomat who served in the U.S. State Department as political consular at the American Embassy in Greece. In the preface to the entry in the *Congressional Record* (2003), Rep. Fortney Pete Stark of California stated that "Mr. Kiesling's letter is an eloquent expression of principle in opposition to war with Iraq and America's heavy-handed approach to foreign policy under the leadership of President Bush" (Kiesling, 2003, E363). Concerning the Bush administration and Powell's loyalty, in the conclusion of his letter of resignation, Kiesling wrote:

> Mr. Secretary, I have enormous respect for your character and ability. You have preserved more international credibility for us than our policy deserves, and salvaged something positive from the excesses of an ideological and self-serving Administration. But your loyalty to the President goes too far. We are straining beyond its limit an international system we built with such toil and treasure, a web of laws, treaties, organizations, and shared values that sets limit on our foes far more effectively than it ever constrained America's ability to defend its interests. I am resigning because I have tried and failed to reconcile my conscience with my ability to represent the current U.S. Administration. I have confidence that our democratic process is ultimately self-correcting, and hope that in a small way I can contribute from outside to shaping policies that better serve the security and prosperity of the American people and the world we share. (Kiesling, 2003, E364)

In the end, personal ambition may have compounded Powell's loyalty to the president. If personal ambition was a driving force, then Powell may well have been led to avoid confrontation with administration officials, especially those that could become public. However, frequently avoidance behavior intended for the sake of personal ambition projects the appearance of excessive loyalty, when this may not be the case. Given Powell's predicament it is fair to say that he was not only ambitious and concerned about his legacy, but that he genuinely believed himself to be a valued member of the Bush team despite the confrontations and pitfalls.

Conclusion

This chapter focused on Colin L. Powell, the first African American secretary of state, in the first term of the administration of George W. Bush. Specifically of interest was whether Secretary Powell operated in a manner consistent with the bureaucratic model or the foreign policy dissenter framework in the execution of his responsibilities. Although Powell occupied the high-profile formal position of secretary of state inside the neoconservative Bush cabinet, his behavior exhibited a tendency toward the tradition of dissent.

The foregoing discussion shows that Powell had mixed feelings in his role as a bureaucrat, due in part to his inability or lack of desire to evolve a style of bureaucratic management suitable to the civilian sector. To his detriment, he more or less continued to operate in the manner he did while an officer in the military. In the final analysis, Powell was largely unable to assert his own decisions and policy preferences because of his loyalty to Bush, which may have stemmed from both personal ambition and his military training. Although loyalty is essential in military and civilian bureaucracies, the latter demands strong and decisive leadership with the capacity to build consensus through compromise, bargaining, and negotiation. However, the bureaucratic veil set in place by Bush left little room for open debate and objective consideration of the decision and policy options by the president. For Powell, this environment was not necessarily one of optimal fit and comfort. Given that he was an ideological and political outsider operating inside the Bush-Cheney foreign policy structure, Powell's fate was perhaps a predictable one. In contrast to some of his colleagues, Powell's personal association with president was not very strong. For example, one key factor that differentiated Powell from Condoleezza Rice as secretary of state is Rice's long-term association with Bush and members of his family. She was with Bush at the time he made the decision to run for president, and no one ever doubted her ideological compatibility with Bush. The question of Powell's ideological compatibility with the president loomed constantly during his tenure, while party insiders regarded Rice as the stauncher conservative. Addressing the role of the secretary of state in the administrations of George H. W. Bush and Bill Clinton, Kengor (2000) suggests that "if a president decides to allow his vice president a coordinating role in assisting the State Department, he had better ensure that his vice president and secretary of state, as well as their staffs, are politically, ideologically, and personally compatible" (198). Clearly, President Bush failed to heed this sage advice.

However, Powell's political posture and situation in the Bush administration may well be the redeeming feature of his legacy. In December 2003 Powell's public approval rating was at 65 percent, and throughout 2004 it generally remained at that relatively high level. Despite this high percentage, in actuality his rating had declined from above 75 percent the year before, where it had stood since he was appointed to the State Department. Some observers attributed the public's affinity for Powell to his marginalization within the Bush bureaucracy. Christopher Hitchens (2004), for example, wrote that "the bigger factor working in Powell's favor may be his low profile in an administration of more outward, and more hawkish, cabinet members such as Vice President Dick Cheney and Secretary of Defense Donald Rumsfeld, particularly as the fighting in Iraq drones on" (45). Also, Barbara Slavin, a reporter for *USA Today* who covered Secretary Powell, concluded that "most Americans don't blame [Powell] for Iraq, figuring that he did the best that he could to broaden international support for the war and he was bested by Cheney and Rumsfeld" (Hitchens, 2004, 45). This perception helps to explain why many Americans, including some of his critics, see Powell as a "link to a pre-9/11 world in which allies and international institutions mattered" (David Hendrickson, cited in Hitchens, 2004, 45).

Thus, while Powell in many respects has been a pathbreaker, as a bureaucrat in the Bush White House his colleagues, in part due to personal relationships, mostly outmaneuvered him. His loyalty to President Bush may also have undermined his capacity to operate effectively in the civilian bureaucratic setting, consequently neutralizing his foreign policy impact. As secretary, it was incumbent upon Powell to provide leadership, a charge necessitating bargaining and confrontation inside the bureaucracy; however, Powell sometimes appeared to lack the energy, perhaps even the will, to bring his ideas, and ultimately his battles, to fruition. Clearly, personal ambition is not the only factor that might explain why Powell sometimes seemed to stop short. If personal ambition was the critical factor, then Powell neglected to take full advantage of the opportunities at hand to promote himself and his career.

Moreover, Powell was unable to balance the requirements of effective bureaucratic action with his own ideals and positions as secretary. Although Powell was a bureaucrat, he frequently was the lone voice of dissent, although a weak one in the conservative excesses of the Bush bureaucracy. In the end, Powell's notable but relatively lackluster tenure as secretary of the Department of State can be attributed to his inability to manage the tension between his desire to be loyal to the president, and his beliefs about when and how military force should be applied in Iraq.

While history will probably show Powell was not a "good fit" ideologically for the Bush cabinet, it will likely show also his tendency to deviate toward dissent. However, our analysis demonstrates that the nature of dissent from within the foreign policy bureaucracy is quite different from the dissent derived from without. In Powell's case, it is fair to say ideologically he was very much in the mainstream of the liberal wing of the Republican foreign policy establishment, which was skeptical of the war from the beginning, either in its objectives, its execution, or both. The flexibility and strength of a system to challenge itself from within is a hallmark of democracy. However, it remains for the future to foster an American bureaucracy that is compatible with leaders who are able to challenge behavior and policies that have become entrenched and institutionalized.

REFERENCES

Adekeye, A. 2004. "Africa, African Americans, and the Avucular Sam." *Africa Today* 50, no. 3: 93–110.

Allison, Graham T. 1999. "Conceptual Models and the Cuban Missile Crisis." In Ikenberry, 1999, 413–58.

Aptheker, Herbert. 1974. *American Negro Slave Revolts.* New York: International Publishers.

Baxter, Sarah. 2007. "Powell Tried to Talk Bush Out of War." *Times Online,* July 8. Available online: http://www.timesonline.co.uk/tol/news/world/us_and_americas/article2042072 .ece.DeYoung, Karen. 2006. *Soldier: The Life of Colin Powell.* New York: Alfred A. Knopf.

Gelb, Leslie. 1991. "Foreign Affairs: Gen. Powell's Lament." *New York Times,* 9 May. Available online: http://query.nytimes.com/gst/fullpage.html?res=9D0CE1D61239F936A35756C 0A9679582

Halperin, Morton H., and Arnold Kanter. 1992. "The Bureaucratic Perspective." In *International Politics: Enduring Concepts and Contemporary Issues,* 3d ed., ed. Robert J. Art and Robert Jervis, 397–425. New York: HarperCollins.

Henry, Charles P., ed. 2000. *Foreign Policy and the Black (Inter)National Interest.* Albany: State University of New York Press.

Henry, P., and O. Sears. 2002. "The Symbolic Racism 2000 Scale." *Political Psychology* 23: 253–83.

Hitchens, Christopher. 2004. "Powell Valediction." *Foreign Policy* 145:42–51.

Ikenberry, John G. 1999. *American Foreign Policy: Theoretical Essays.* New York: Longman.

Johnson, Benita M. 2007. "Voices in the Wilderness: The Role and Influence of African American Citizens in the Development and Formation of Foreign Policy 1919–1944." *Journal of Pan African Studies* 8:33–51.

Kengor, Paul. 2000. "The Vice President, Secretary of State, and Foreign Policy." *Political Science Quarterly* 115 (Summer): 175–99.

Kennedy, Randall. 2008. *Sellout: The Politics of Racial Betrayal*. New York: Pantheon.

Kessler, George. 2007. *The Confidante: Condoleezza Rice and the Creation of the Bush Legacy*. New York: St. Martin's Press.

Kiesling, John Brady. 2003. *Congressional Record*. Extensions. "Letter of Resignation by John Brady Kiesling." March 4, E363–64. Available online: http://www.fas.org/irp/congress/2003_cr/h030403.html.

Lusane, Clarence. 2006. *Colin Powell and Condoleezza Rice: Foreign Policy, Race, and the New American Century*. Westport, Conn.:: Praeger.

Miller, Jake. 1978. *The Black Presence in American Foreign Affairs*. Washington, D.C.: Howard University Press.

———. 2000. "African American Males in Foreign Affairs." *Annals of the American Academy of Political and Social Science* 569:29–41.

Moss, James A. 1970. "The Civil Rights Movement and American Foreign Policy." In *Racial Influences on American Foreign Policy*, ed. George W. Shepherd. New York: Basic Books.

Powell, Colin. With Joseph E. Persico. 1995. *My American Journey*. New York: Random House.

Skinner, Elliot. 1992. *African Americans and U.S. Policy toward Africa, 1850–1924*. Vol. 1. Washington, D.C.: Howard University Press.

Smith, Steve. 1990. "Perspectives on the Foreign Policy System: The Bureaucratic Politics Approaches." In *Understanding Foreign Policy: The Foreign Policy Systems Approach*, ed. Michael Clarke and Brian White, 109–34. Brookfield, Vt.: Gower.

Stanford, Karin. 1997. *Beyond the Boundaries: Reverend Jesse Jackson in International Affairs*. Albany: State University of New York Press.

Walton, Hanes, Jr., and Robert C. Smith. 2006. *American Politics and the African American Quest for Universal Freedom*. 3d ed. New York: Longman.

SEVEN

Condoleezza Rice and Madeleine Albright

THE CHANGING FACE OF HIGH-PROFILE
U.S. FOREIGN POLICY LEADERSHIP

Michael L. Clemons and Supad Ghose

Women have long been on the sidelines of institutional decisionmaking in the United States, and only recently have they as a group begun to break ground, or as some might say, to shatter the proverbial "glass ceiling." The social exclusion and deprivation of women parallels that experienced by African Americans who suffered the ravages of slavery and Jim Crow. This legacy of the race factor in the operation of American social institutions left an indelible imprint on the lives of a substantial number of American citizens. Further complicating matters is gender, to the extent that African Americans who happen to be women face a double-edged sword. Race, in combination with gender, is an extraordinarily powerful social cue, as indicated by the fact that the political process historically was successful in excluding the participation of women in general and those of color in high-profile foreign policymaking roles.

Madeleine Albright and Condoleezza Rice, each in their own right and excellence, achieved presidential appointment to one of the highest foreign affairs policymaking positions in the United States and in the world. Both of these accomplished women distinguished themselves in the annals of U.S. foreign policymaking by reaching the highest position in the foreign policy bureaucracy, successfully breaking the longstanding gender barrier. As an African American woman and a Republican, Rice has overcome not only gender but also the color barrier, in a country where race and gender continue to influence social resource distribution. Albright overcame the barriers presented by her Jewish ancestry and gender. In the cases of Rice and Albright, it was no minor feat to penetrate the highest level of the formal foreign policymaking establishment, hitherto dominated by white

169

males (notwithstanding Gen. Colin L. Powell's appointment by George W. Bush as the first African American to serve as secretary of state).

In this chapter, we assess the backgrounds, worldviews, and the rise to power of Madeleine Albright and Condoleezza Rice. Specifically of interest is how these women broke gender and racial barriers to reach the highest echelon of the U.S. diplomatic establishment. We focus on each of these leaders as the highest ranking bureaucrat in the nation's foreign policy apparatus—the Department of State. The study necessitates focusing on their education, belief systems, and professional achievements before becoming secretary of state. We also assess their accomplishments following elevation to the position. Underlying this research are the following fundamental questions: (1) What was the role of race and ethnicity in the agendas and policies of Rice and Albright during their terms as secretary, and did these variables in any way distinguish Rice's tenure from that of Albright? (2) To what extent did they face obstacles as women while emerging and serving as secretary of state, and did their relative uniqueness as women of African and Jewish descent, respectively, affect their leadership? (3) Did Rice and Albright have to compromise their gender perspectives to fit in a "man's world"?

Methodology

This research employs the traditional case study method and comparative analysis. For each case, we describe and discuss the background and seek to delineate the lives of Albright and Rice in terms of their education, scholarly life, and other accomplishments. Each case investigation and analysis articulates and illuminates several relevant issue areas. We utilize a comparative approach to shed light on the experiences of these women and to ascertain any differential in the extent to which race, ethnicity, and gender may have influenced their rise to power and its exercise in the context of Democratic and Republican presidential administrations. The similarities and differences between Albright and Rice are explored to make sense of these in the American social and global contexts.

The complexities associated with women's participation in foreign policy-making necessitate a multidisciplinary approach, facilitating the gathering of insights from various disciplines, including intellectual history, gender studies, political science, and sociology. This study employs diverse materials, including books, newspaper articles, scholarly journals, and research monographs published by Rice and Albright. In the following section, we briefly review the history of women's political exclusion in the United States to focus on explanations for their low overall participation rates in the political process. In light of women's political exclusion, it is assumed that those able to achieve success through the route of political appointment followed some relatively clear path to overcome the racial, ethnic, and gender barriers that long precluded participation by certain segments of American society. Especially of interest is *how* Rice and Albright transcended the less-than-favorable social conditions that historically circumscribed women's role in American politics.

Political Participation and Women

For a variety of reasons, research conducted on the role and participation of women in American foreign policymaking has been limited, and the work that has been produced concentrates on examining the noninstitutional support roles they have played in foreign affairs. This is partly because in the United States, only since the 1920s have women initiated organized protest to gain formal inclusion in the political process. Sociological theory suggests that there are explanations derivative of the culture that elucidate the low level of participation by women and the gradual process of their inclusion (Conway, 2001, 231). The slow incorporation of women into the political process generally, and the State Department bureaucracy in particular, did little to stimulate substantial research interest in women, gender, and foreign affairs participation. Recent developments, including the appointments of Albright and Rice, beg for systematic scholarly study to learn the similarities and differences between women and men in their rise, leadership, and impact in foreign policymaking, particularly those in high-profile foreign policy establishment positions. Indeed, within the past two decades women, led by Albright and Rice, have made some important strides in the arena of foreign policymaking.

In addition to women's experience of political exclusion because of the nature of the electoral process and their lack of capacity, including material resources and party support, "gatekeepers" (Burrell, 1993; Norris, 1997; Niven, 1998) have affected the political fortunes of women. Gatekeepers are citizens who occupy various roles, including "voters, party members, financial supporters, or political leaders who select from the pool of applicants" (Norris, 1997, 1). The political recruitment process involves consideration of factors such as social background, resources, and motivations by gatekeepers who make decisions about recruitment and appointment. In addition to these factors, there is the matter of institutional structures and their impact on the recruitment of women (Norris, 1997).

In addition to the negative affect of gatekeepers on women's political participation, there is the problem of the prior selection phase of office seeking. M. Margaret Conway (2001) observed, "In that prior selection process, many potential women candidates may be discouraged from even entering the primary election process" (232). Although the reference here is to the primary election process, the same logic applies to presidential appointments. Women interested in gaining appointment to political office, like those seeking to be elected, need encouragement in the form of support from party leaders and interest groups. They also need the endorsement of the gatekeeper, who likely is the most influential person involved in the appointment decision. In the case of the U.S. Department of State and the appointment of the secretary of state, constitutionally the president has the power to appoint someone to the position, with the advice and consent of the Senate.

Another barrier has been the lack of apprenticeship opportunities for women. This problem has compounded the difficulty that women have had in securing high-level cabinet appointments. Apprenticeship opportunities provide newcomers to the arena with several benefits, including valuable on-the-job training, the advantage of working alongside someone knowledgeable and experienced, and the chance to develop vital networks of support. Without the advantage of the fundamentals associated with comparable apprenticeship opportunities, the selection of women for appointment to high-profile foreign affairs positions has been greatly constrained.

In the sections that follow, we investigate Condoleezza Rice and Madeleine Albright by examining their childhood, education, belief system, and internationalism. Given the African American and Jewish cultural backgrounds, respectively, of Rice and Albright, we assess whether race and ethnicity played a part in their rise to power, leadership, and policies. Also of interest is whether and how gender influenced the work of these two women.

Childhood and Education

As the first female secretaries of state, Rice and Albright were both revered and detested. They have proven that women can effectively represent the United States abroad in the capacity of secretary of state. In light of the resounding achievements of these women, it is instructive to examine their childhood and educational background. These experiences may be particularly instructive given the ongoing role of race, ethnicity, and gender in American society. Examination of the experiences of these women can be beneficial as the United States undergoes a process of social transformation marked by increased diversity, especially the growing proportion of women and people of color who as groups continue to seek access and representation not only at the domestic level but also in the international arena.

MADELEINE ALBRIGHT

Madeleine Albright was born in 1937 in Prague, the capital of what at the time was Czechoslovakia. This was a turbulent period in European history, and two years after her birth, Europe plunged into World War II. Born Marie Jana Korbel, a childhood name that she has retained, Albright was the daughter of Josef Korbel, a young diplomat and an official of the Czechoslovak government. He was highly educated, having received his doctorate in law from Charles University in Prague.

During World War II, the Korbel family took shelter in London and lived in other cities in England as well. Albright received her childhood education in English in Britain and returned to Prague following the end of World War II to begin her schooling. However, she lived in Belgrade, the capital of then Yugoslavia during the time her father served as ambassador for Czechoslovakia. At this time, a governess educated her, since her parents did not want her to attend a communist school in Yugoslavia. Later, Albright was sent to Switzerland for schooling. When the communists assumed power in Czechoslovakia in 1948, her father left the Czechoslovak diplomatic service and took on a new assignment with the United Nations (U.N.) Commission on Kashmir.

The Korbel family eventually left Europe and sought political asylum in the United States, which they achieved, after overcoming a number of obstacles. They settled in Denver, Colorado, where Josef Korbel received a teaching appointment at the University of Denver. Albright attended high school at a private girls' school in Denver, and later enrolled at Wellesley College, an elite women's college in Massachusetts. While at Wellesley, she became politically active and was drawn to the cause of the Democratic party. Later, she met Joseph Albright, from a rich family with an aristocratic background. Albright was the publisher of several newspapers, including the *Chicago Tribune,* the *New York Daily News* and the *Washington Times-Herald* (which later became the *Washington Post* under the ownership of the father of Katherine Graham). The two were married in 1959 upon her graduation from college, and she benefited enormously from the opportunity that marriage gave her to reach the upper echelon of American society.

While in Washington, D.C., where her husband worked as a journalist,

Albright studied on a part-time basis at Johns Hopkins University, earning a master's degree in political science. She later received a doctorate in East European studies under the supervision of Dr. Zbignew Brzezinski at Columbia University in New York during the turbulent times of the Cold War and the radical student protests in the late 1960s.

When President Bill Clinton won a second term in 1992, he named Madeleine Albright secretary of state. This decision for the first time in history elevated a woman to the fourth most powerful post in the U.S. political system. Although Albright was not regarded as a pleasing personality by many, she always served her bosses with unquestioned loyalty. Bill and Hillary Clinton discovered this quality, and the president rewarded her handsomely by appointing her to the highest U.S. foreign policymaking post (Blackman, 1998, 200).

Upon appointment as secretary of state, Albright believed she had made a breakthrough, and felt "she represented all women who had a tough life and [had] not achieved their goal" (Blackman, 1998, 200). It is interesting to note that she had shown virtually no special interest in "women's liberation" in the 1960s. Consistent with this, neither did she question male domination in American society; rather, she took it for granted. Working under strong men and pleasing them in the end seemed to define her career. Albright's reaction to the Monica Lewinski affair helps to shed light on this point. President Clinton's extramarital affair with Lewinski, a young and vulnerable student intern, was not only an act of adultery, but also a flagrant misuse of power in an unequal relationship between a powerful superior and powerless subordinate. Donna Shalala, a cabinet member under President Clinton, risked her career and criticized the president's behavior. In contrast, Albright, a victim of divorce and abuse in a relationship in which her husband abandoned her for a much younger woman, never questioned Clinton's sexual transgressions and supported him even after he admitted adultery.[1] She maintained this posture even after declaring that part of her mission was championing the cause of women.

CONDOLEEZZA RICE

Condoleezza Rice was born on November 14, 1954, in segregated Titusville, Alabama. She was the first African American woman to hold the position of secretary of state, although she is both the second woman and the second African American to hold the post. Prior to this achievement, Rice served as national security advisor to President George W. Bush during his first term. She was the second African American (following Colin Powell) and the first woman to be appointed national security advisor.

Rice attended the University of Denver at age fifteen, and graduated with a degree in international relations at nineteen. Under the guidance of Madeleine Albright's father Josef Korbel, her professor at the University of Denver, she developed an intense interest in international relations and the politics of the Soviet Union. Following undergraduate school, Rice attended the University of Notre Dame, where she earned a master's degree. She later returned to the University of Denver to complete a doctorate in international studies. She then joined Stanford University as an assistant professor.

An accomplished scholar in her own right, Rice published her dissertation, on the loyalty of the Czechoslovak army to the Soviet Union during the Cold War, in book form. To be sure, Rice was a Kremlinologist, but she had not garnered the reputation of some of her male colleagues, including Richard Pipes, one among a galaxy of scholars specializing in the former Soviet Union. Of all her publications, an article on Soviet strategy is regarded as the most sophisticated and scholarly (Rice, 1986, 648–76). In this article, Rice delves into the marxist character of Soviet strategy and its evolution since the Civil War in Russia following the Bolshevik Revolution. As a scholar, she addressed the concept of societal preparation for continuous struggle and the correlation of forces in the former Soviet Union.

In November 2004, President Bush nominated Rice to succeed Colin Powell as secretary of state. She was sworn in on January 26, 2005, and on the same day the U.S. Senate confirmed her nomination by a vote of 85–13. Among the members of the Bush foreign affairs team, Rice possessed the strongest academic background, and because of her race, gender, and youth, she was one of the most distinctive. She was a key Bush ally in the wars against Afghanistan and Iraq, and in the "war against terrorism." Between 1989 and 1991, Rice held several positions that paved the way for her appointment. She served in the administration of President George H. W. Bush as director, and later senior director, of Soviet and East European Affairs in the National Security Council during the period of German reunification and the final days of the Soviet Union. She was also special assistant to the president for national security affairs.

Worldviews of Rice and Albright

In this section, we investigate the contours of the worldviews of Rice and Albright. At issue is whether and how their worldviews informed their work while at the State Department. Under consideration is whether race, ethnicity, and/or gender impinged upon this worldview, consequently affecting their foreign policy positions, programs, and initiatives. Specifically, we raise the question: Did the worldviews of Rice and Albright affect their perceptions, leadership, and policies relative to regions of the world to which they may have felt connected or for which they had a certain affinity? In this section, we seek to shed light on these issues.

MADELEINE ALBRIGHT

Born into a tumultuous world that experienced not only military conflicts but also fierce ideological clashes between Nazism, communism, and capitalist liberal democracy, Albright would predictably develop strong beliefs in favor of one ideology or another. However, since she and her family were victims of Nazism and had lived under communism, Albright developed staunch anticommunist attitudes and these became a pillar in her worldview. Her father, who loathed both Nazism and communism, had an enormous influence on shaping her worldview. In fact, it was "under his tutelage that she absorbed the lessons of Munich" (Blackman, 1998, 111).

During a trip to Czechoslovakia in 1967, Albright met with some distant family friends and relatives. She had conversations with many people that were depressing. They expressed to her the difficulties they had experienced, and the persistence of such problems in their lives. This experience allowed Albright to gain practical insight into two almost completely different systems—liberal capitalist democracy in the United States and communism in Eastern Europe. Like her father, she was attracted to the ideals of freedom and democracy that they both believed they had discovered in the United States. However, as one with Manichaean views (a religious doctrine based on the separation of matter and spirit and of good and evil that originated in third-century Persia), she found that her commitment to democracy encompassed a strange intolerance. Albright, like her father, tended to be intolerant of criticism. She amply exhibited this trait in her role as U.S. ambassador to the United Nations and as secretary of state (Blackman, 1998, 310).

Albright's anticommunist convictions, shaped by both the strong convictions of her father and private schooling, suggested she might have leanings toward the Republican party. However, perhaps, the excesses of the McCarthy era and the anticommunist witch-hunts carried out during the term of President Dwight Eisenhower reminded her father of the same type of anticapitalist tactics at home in Czechoslovakia. This might plausibly explain why she eventually gravitated toward the liberal politics of the Democratic party. As part of her political activism as a student, Albright emphasized liberal values, became a supporter of Robert F. Kennedy, whom she regarded as her political hero, and supported his stand on civil rights and social justice.

Although a student in the 1960s, when radical student protests and the women's liberation movement were erupting in the United States and Europe, Albright was not a party to either. Rather, she concentrated on the pursuit of her doctorate at Columbia University. "I was very motivated to work." She recollected that "I was not part of the sixty-eight stuff" (Albright, quoted in Dobbs, 1999, 214).

Neither did she share the beliefs of students who were cynical about America. Rather, "she remained touchingly grateful to the United States for granting her family political asylum" (Dobbs, 1999, 214). As a child of immigrant parents and refugees from communism, Albright was committed to "her vision of America as a land of freedom and opportunity" (215). As an immigrant, she had "faith in America as a shining beacon for the rest of the world" (257). Indicative of her faith and commitment is that she remained committed to America even when the majority of Americans themselves had begun to reject their own country's involvement in the Vietnam War.

By 1968, Albright began to raise questions about the war. However, her gratitude to America outweighed her reservations. Indeed, even her father's opinion changed following the Tet Offensive in 1968. Nevertheless, "both father and daughter came to view the war as a mistake, but a noble mistake on the part of a country that remained the champion of freedom" (Dobbs, 1999, 218).

Albright found herself drawn to Zbigniew Brzezinski, a professor of political science at Columbia University and foreign policy specialist with whom she shared a worldview that was passionately anticommunist (Blackman, 1998, 149). Since both of them had fled from communism in Eastern Europe and ended up as immigrants in the United States, they connected not only ideologically, but also personally. "America was fighting a corrupt system that they understood from their direct experience" (Blackman, 1998, 149). To be sure, Albright questioned the Vietnam War, but she was never critical of those who defended it. For example, her personal loyalty and friendship with Brzezinski was so strong that even when anti-Vietnam War protesters branded him a war criminal for his staunch support of the war, Albright did not exhibit any differences of opinion with her mentor.

Albright's worldview hinged also on the notion of realism in world affairs. As a realist, she emphasized the primacy of the United States in world affairs and the national interest as the guiding principle in U.S. foreign policy. Along with her strong anticommunist stance, Albright came to believe in political realism or *realpolitik* in world affairs. The academic training she received as a student of politics under her father at Johns Hopkins University and later at Columbia University under teachers such as Zbigniew Brzezinski further consolidated her realist view of world affairs. However, Albright's realism was rather narrow and ethnocentric in its orientation. It not only supported but also legitimized the hegemonic role of the United States in world affairs.[2] Indeed, her realist bent was so strong that while secretary, she emphasized the primacy of national interests and sought to justify the pursuit of two different policies although it bordered on a double standard in light of ongoing calls for democracy. In her own words,

> Neither China nor Burma is democratic, and both take a dim view of dissent. Yet we are engaged in a strategic dialogue with China while maintaining far tougher sanctions, including an investment ban, against Burma. Some accuse us of having a double standard. In reality, we have a single standard based on our assessment of the approach most likely to achieve results that serve U.S. national interest and ideals. (Albright, 1998, 57)

Albright's successful integration within the U.S. power structure was her reward for being loyal to Brzezinski, on the one hand, and for her staunch commitment to anticommunism and *realpolitik,* on the other. Upon gaining the office of secretary, her view that the United States was indispensable in world politics was reinforced.

CONDOLEEZZA RICE

Although Rice was born of African American parents in the Jim Crow South, she traversed an unusual path in the formation of her worldview. Her parents were Republicans who always shielded her from the broader community of African Americans. However, to be Republican in the Democratic-controlled, Jim Crow Alabama was a logical calculation indicative of the family's lack of consonance with the prevailing social relations and structure. In contrast to the poverty and deprivation experienced by many southern blacks of the period, Rice was unequivocally advantaged. She studied piano and ballet, and attended private school. While in college, "she met Professor Josef Korbel, the émigré Czech diplomat who had fled from both Nazism and communism . . . [he] persuaded Rice to switch [her major] to international relations and in particular, to Soviet Studies" (Mann, 2004, 147). She was attracted to Soviet studies because of "Soviet power" (ibid.). She later met with Soviet dissident writer Solzhenitsyn who strengthened her views about Soviet Russia.[3] Hence, through the establishment of important initial contacts while a student of international relations, Rice was brought into the fold of power politics.

Arguably, one of the most important influences on the development of Rice's worldview was Professor Josef Korbel. Rice regarded Korbel as her "intellectual father," since he had sparked her interest in realism. However, apart from Korbel's influence, the study and teaching of international relations in the United States likely influenced Rice's views since only two paradigms—realism and liberalism—have dominated in the United States, with the former having a substantial edge. Since the United States was a superpower in the international configuration of power in the post-World War II bipolar international system, an uncritical stance of the field of study toward both U.S. power and the bipolar international system may have influenced her realist views. Indeed, Rice had been fascinated with President Truman because the former president "gave the U.S. an unprecedented role in international affairs" and "fundamentally reshaped the world and planted the seeds of the Soviet Union's eventual destruction."[4]

Manifestations of Gender

The decline of gender as a problem in American politics has only begun in recent decades as women gain full access and participation in the political process. In view of the institutionalized and systematic nature of the process of women's exclusion, it is reasonable to consider whether and how gender may have influenced the emergence of Condoleezza Rice and Madeleine Albright. Indeed, at various junctures of the careers and experiences of these women, gender seems to have had special implications for their rise to power, their leadership, and the articulation of their worldview.

ALBRIGHT

The pervasiveness of white male dominance in politics, and in foreign affairs in particular, has an important effect on the behavior of individuals seeking to gain entrée into such policymaking circles. For Madeleine Albright, this reality implied the need to know how to navigate in the world of men. Perhaps her parents were instrumental in helping her to form such a perspective. Michael Dobbs has written: "Just as her father and grandfather succeeded in escaping the Jewish ghetto by making themselves indispensable to the majority Christian society, so would Madeleine escape from the female ghetto by making herself indispensable to men" (231). In fact, although conscious of and an aspirant to the role of a woman, she always sought to "fit" in a man's world. While many of her friends were fighting for the rights of women and protesting the inequality of women, Albright was more effective in participating in the "mainstream" rather than protesting (Blackman, 1998, 161). Dobbs (1999) stated that "the politics of confrontation and bra-burning advocated by the radical women's lib were not for her" (231). Certainly, radical feminism, which characterized gender politics in the 1960s and 1970s, was not in her dictionary. According to her friend Emily MacFarquhar, "Feminism wasn't an important cause for her until recently" (quoted in Blackman, 1998, 161).

Michael Dobbs further illuminates this aspect of Albright's career:

> She would climb to the top of America's male-dominated society not by rebelling against that society but by insinuating herself into the ranks and adapting herself to its sometimes archaic rules and rituals. As the rules began to change and pressure grew for women to be admitted to occupations previously reserved for men, the refugee's daughter from Eastern Europe was well placed to take advantage of the new opportunities (321).

Bob Beckel notes:

> The lion in her was always there. The genius of it was that she kept in check knowing full well that if she stepped into that male domain she would have been crushed. There are ways they can crush you, particularly when you are just starting out on that ladder. She completely understood that. Her tongue must have bled a thousand times at night from having to bite it while these guys were stealing her ideas (Beckel quoted in Dobbs, 1999, 272).

Albright grew up under the influence of influential men other than her father (including her husband, Sen. Edmund Muskie, and Brzezinski). However, none was as influential as her father. Dobbs writes, "While there were other influential men in Madeleine's life . . . none of them compared to her father . . . she modeled herself after him" (Dobbs, 1999, 259).

As a protégé of Brzezinski, President Carter's national security advisor, Albright was appointed to assist the White House in establishing a rapport with Congress. Albright played a useful role as a congressional liaison responsible for advising Brzezinski on key issues. She fared well in Congress during her job as a liaison in part due to her success in crossing the aisle to work with conservative Republicans. Albright attempted to solve political problems by resorting to nonpolitical means. She "also learned the importance of stroking the egos of members of Congress" (Blackman, 1998, 178).

In addition to developing highly polished legislative skills and acumen, Albright emerged as a powerful and forceful orator. She learned the importance of strong oratory and communication from her father, and demonstrated her prowess in the various executive positions she occupied. Interestingly, Albright observed the same flaw in President Carter, who she believed did not communicate well with the American people. Though Albright quickly digested the lessons and culture of political Washington, an intimidating barrier she had to confront was the reality that "the world of American foreign policy was still very much the domain of the White male establishment" (Blackman, 1998, 179). This helps to explain why initially "she was not taken seriously on substantive matters as she would have been. She was very sharp and very intelligent and very well-read and studied hard, but she was put into a process role instead of a substantive policy role" (ibid.).

Because of her successful fundraising efforts while with the presidential campaign of Sen. Edmund Muskie, she was later appointed to a part-time position in his senatorial office. He appointed Albright because of her Washington connections and her ability to raise funds for his Senate reelection bid in 1976. In regard to this charge, she performed well, but kept a low profile. However, when she was appointed assistant to Zbigniew Brzezinski to help improve his ties with the Congress, her male colleagues in Muskie's office were surprised because "they failed to take into account her diligence at forming a network of people who would he helpful to her when time came" (Blackman, 1998, 258).

Albright's networks, both personal and political, were enhanced by her appointment as foreign policy advisor to Geraldine Ferraro, the first female vice presidential nominee, during the 1984 Democratic presidential campaign. Albright stated: "The Democratic ticket was obliterated. I hated losing, but the campaign did help me to begin a new life. I made new friends and proved able to hold my own within the highest circles of the Democratic Party" (Albright, 2003, 103). Working for Ferraro "was a psychological boost . . . that helped her overcome the trauma of divorce and rejection. But it also gave her something else that was equally important in her later career: a network of influential women friends on whom she could rely for advice and support" (Dobbs, 1999, 307).

No doubt, Albright had been around influential men like Muskie and Brzezinski, but at the center of her new network were three powerful female politicians: Geraldine Ferraro, Barbara Kennelly, and Barbara Mikulski. Each of these women was a resounding success in her own right, having managed to break the glass ceiling imposed by male domination (ibid.).

Albright not only remained good friends with them but also received their support in different ways. Eventually, she came to terms with the fact that she needed the support of powerful women and women's groups to advance in the male-dominated venue of foreign policymaking. At crucial points in her career, such as her appointment as secretary of state, Albright relied on the lobbying efforts of these women and their organizations to be competitive alongside her male counterparts.

Both as a teacher and as a member of the Georgetown Leadership Seminar, Albright formed policy networks with government specialists, politicians, business leaders, military officers, and journalists across the world. During President Clinton's campaign for a second term in 1996, some political operatives associated with Clinton sought to prevent her appointment. However, Albright's extensive network proved highly effective to her capacity to ascertain and address these developments (Blackman, 1998, 228). Dobbs (1999) concluded that she did succeed not because of her intellect or expertise but rather because of her "political savvy and a gift for handling personal relationships" (267).

RICE

For Rice, gender consciousness apparently was not a component of her realist worldview. During the period of her education in the late 1960s and early 1970s, feminism emerged as a major paradigm on American university campuses. However, Rice hardly seems to have been attracted to feminism, either as a cause or as theory. As a staunch realist, Rice maintained that what matters in world politics is national power. In contrast, feminism stands for "positive peace," a concept embodying "conditions for social justice, economic equity and ecological balance" (Reardon, 1990, 138). Rice's perspective encompasses a masculine conception of peace, which translates into the absence of war and conflict as requisites for a stable world order. For Rice, international security implies the military concept of preservation through armaments, alliances, and the military balance of power, rather than a reliance on reciprocal cooperation.

Rice's success, it seems, hinges not on the fact she is a woman, but that she is a proponent of *realpolitk*, which is generally characterized by the dominant white male culture of the foreign policy establishment as a minimum requirement for entry into its ranks. Her unquestionable loyalty, primarily to President Bush and his family, and secondarily to her mentor Brent Scowcroft, former national security advisor to President George Herbert Walker Bush, provides a second plausible explanation for her successful career. That Rice was an accomplished scholar of international relations does not mean that her success in professional life as a diplomat was necessarily rooted in scholarship. No doubt, her scholarship and expertise in Soviet affairs initially drew the attention of Scowcroft, and was important to her path-breaking success. However, what seems to have principally mattered is her close friendship with President Bush, despite the widely publicized reservations that Bush indicated he had with regard to scholars and intellectuals. However, loyalty and anticipated forthcoming rewards, especially in instances where it is essentially blind, are part of the fabric of the foreign policymaking elite, and more men than women have been the beneficiaries of this arrangement.

Racial and Ethnic Manifestations

In this section, we consider manifestations of race, ethnicity, and culture in the professional lives of Rice and Albright, and assess whether these variables affected the quality and results of their tenure in the U.S. Department of State. Specifically, we consider Rice's African American racial heritage and Albright's Jewish background within the white male-dominated institutional context of foreign policymaking.

ALBRIGHT

Albright, who was of Jewish background, apparently sought to conceal her heritage in one way or another. While visiting Prague in 1967, she met the prominent individual Peter Novak, a survivor of the Holocaust. Reportedly, during this visit, she deflected questions about her Jewish heritage in various ways. One explanation for her behavior might be that communism created information barriers between the East and West during the Cold War. This may have helped Albright's family to hide their Jewish identity, and thus "build a new identity for themselves in America" (Dobbs, 1999, 207). Also, Josef Korbel's pragmatic ideals about the potential difficulty that a Jew might have in navigating a career in a Christian-dominated world may have been a factor. This sort of thinking was not at all far-fetched, given historical patterns of discrimination against the practitioners of Judaism. Korbel went so far as to convert to Catholicism during World War II in Britain, perhaps reflecting on the future career prospects of his children in America. This may be the most plausible explanation for his attempt to hide the Jewish past of his family (ibid., 211).

Albright's conversion to Protestantism as a result of her marriage to Joseph Albright perhaps sheds some light as well. Since her husband's family could not tolerate a Catholic relation, her future husband suggested she change her religious affiliation prior to marriage, and Albright readily agreed. As a practical thinker, "she [was] very operationally oriented and achievement oriented" (Ann Platt, quoted in Blackman, 1998, 163). She may have believed that concealing her Jewish identity and converting from Catholicism to Protestantism, the religion of the majority of Americans, would help pave the way for greater success in her career.[5]

Yet in contrast to the concealment of her Jewish heritage, Albright was open about her background as a Czechoslovak immigrant. Immigrant status has often been a barrier in politics; however, Albright apparently was not disadvantaged by this factor. Her immigrant background meant a lot personally, and she always focused on it to define who she had been in life and who she had become. Although an immigrant, Albright inherited from her family the great talent and ability to adapt to new circumstances. Her steely determination allowed her to avail herself of every opportunity for acceptance as an American. As a result, "her adjustment was so complete that it seemed effortless. She became indistinguishable from millions of other Americans. She lost her accent, and thanks to her marriage to Joseph Medill Patterson Albright, she even lost her ethnic-sounding name with which she was born" (Dobbs, 1999, 262).

Albright had a burning desire to be part of the American establishment. It is clear that her immigrant background and adjustment to American society, even acculturation, were two fundamental aspects of the character she publicly projected. That upon her appointment by President Clinton as U.S. ambassador to the United Nations, she "referred to herself as a Czech immigrant, spoke of her father, and said how proud she would be to sit at the United Nations behind the nameplate that reads 'United States of America,'" lends further support to this assertion. Her words moved many who were present, including her daughters and the president-elect (Blackman, 1998, 229–30).

RICE

Growing up in Birmingham, Alabama, in the 1960s would seem to lend greater authenticity to one who had transcended the challenges posed by de jure and de facto segregation; however, there are many who wonder aloud about this matter when it comes to Condoleezza Rice. Although regarded by many as one of the most powerful African Americans in the United States, the salient question often posed is how much has Rice been able to relate to the black community as a whole? Since she was born and raised in segregated Alabama and experienced racial discrimination herself, it is reasonable to think that race consciousness would be a formative part of her being, and therefore reflected in her administration of the State Department. However, during her term at the State Department, there was little if any indication that she considered herself part of the African American community and little to indicate that blacks or whites regarded her as a member of that community. No doubt, she understands the pitfalls of society and its inglorious past in terms of its treatment of her black ancestors, but on balance, this does not seem to have been translated into her work at the State Department. Eugene Robinson, a Pulitzer Prize-winning columnist for the *Washington Post,* explains:

> When Rice was growing up, her father stood guard at the entrance of her neighborhood with a rifle to keep the Klan's nightriders away. But that was outside the bubble. Inside the bubble, Rice was sitting at the piano in pretty dresses to play Bach fugues. It sounds like a wonderful childhood, but one that left her able to see the impact that race has in America—able to examine it and analyze it—but not to feel it (Robinson, 2005).

Thus, upbringing might help explain why Rice on one occasion did not show any visible emotion when she ruminated about her childhood friend Denise McNair, one of the young girls killed in the bombing of Birmingham's Sixteenth Street Baptist Church by Klan members in 1963. It is significant also that the hardheaded realist worldview that Rice represents does not accommodate emotion. Mary Riddell, a columnist for the *London Observer,* stated that "Dr Rice is an unemotional woman who failed to cry at her mother's funeral, explaining that they would meet again in heaven" (Riddell, 2006).

J. L. Chestnut, a black clergyman from Alabama who knew the Rice family, not only corroborated what Eugene Robinson (2005) wrote in the *Washington Post,* but elaborated further. He stated that Rice's parents not only sheltered her from Jim Crow racism, but also misled her. Chestnut wrote:

> The truth is they did a lot more than shelter Rice. They misled her about the justice of the civil rights movement, misled her about the courage of Rev. Fred Shuttlesworth, misled her about the greatness of Rev. Martin Luther King, and misled her about all the dedicated people risking their lives in the streets and jails in Birmingham. Rice and most upper middle class blacks in Birmingham were misled in the 1960s about the black struggle and they were taught that the civil rights movement represented what black folks should not do.[6]

These revelations substantiate that the sheltered, upper-middle-class upbringing in Birmingham, Alabama, that Rice experienced affected her political socialization. During her tenure as secretary of state as well as in various other positions, race consistently was a nonfactor in her interpretation of global affairs, and it seems to have had little to no impact on her decisions.

Nonetheless, Rice is an important figure in the history of U.S. foreign policy in the sense that she not only broke racial barriers as an African American but also gender barriers as a woman. Colin Powell's appointment to the position of secretary during the first term of the Bush administration was not such scintillating news, since President Clinton following his election to the presidency in 1992 had offered Powell the same position. However, when President Bush named Rice secretary of state following his 2004 presidential election, it was construed as a major breakthrough in American politics.

A not so subtle irony, however, is that Rice represents neither the African American community nor women, despite her outward physical features. Apparently, she has never been a part of the black community in any sense that suggests an ongoing connectedness. As shown previously, she was shielded by her parents from the lived experience of African Americans. Nevertheless, far worse was that her parents not only rejected the greater cause of the community during the civil rights movement, but also as J. L. Chestnut observed, they had disdain for the progressive causes of the community. Despite citizens' and leaders' efforts within and outside the foreign policy mainstream, neither Africa nor the African Diaspora materialized as a substantial part of the interests and worldview of Rice. However, by some measures the Bush administration was more involved in Africa than any other administration in history. We might therefore conclude that Rice (as well as Powell) was also involved. However, behind the laudable efforts of the Bush administration's increased budget to fight AIDS in Africa may be a smokescreen for the pursuit of geopolitical objectives stemming from the increasing dependence of the United States on African oil.

Analysis and Discussion

Rice and Albright share some important similarities, yet they are different in other respects. One similarity is that both studied politics, international relations, and East European politics. Their specializations, however, are different: Albright is known for her East European expertise and Rice for her Soviet expertise. Although Albright and Rice both were active in political life, Albright was a Democratic party activist; Rice, an active scholar and affiliated with the Republican party. Her scholarly achievements are more substantial than Albright's, and this is shown by Rice's status as a full professor. In contrast, Albright served as an adjunct professor.

A parallel is that Josef Korbel, professor of international relations at the University of Denver, influenced the worldview and ideology of these women. Although Korbel is the biological and intellectual father of Albright, Rice also acknowledged Korbel as her intellectual father because he introduced her to the study of international relations and was a significant influence on her thinking.

Albright and Rice subscribed to the tenets of realism in the articulation of their worldviews and belief systems, perhaps because realism has long been a litmus test for entry into the male-dominated U.S. foreign policy establishment. In addition, both hold strong anticommunist views, although anticommunism has been more of a defining principle for Albright because of the timing of her service and her life experience. Nonetheless, Albright's and Rice's belief in realism accommodated the hegemonic power of the United States in world affairs and its self-professed mission to fight the forces of evil.

Moreover, Rice and Albright evolved professionally and experienced changes in their belief systems. For example, Albright initially had some faith in internationalism and in international institutions like the United Nations. However, she seems to have sacrificed internationalism and her faith in the U.N. because her career goals demanded such change. However, without this evolution, she could never penetrate the U.S. foreign policy establishment. One could argue that Albright nakedly pursued her career while sacrificing her faith in the United Nations, as evidenced by the fact that she joined the Republicans in bashing the organization and its secretary general Kofi Annan.

Notwithstanding the similarities between Albright and Rice, we can draw some important differences. Perhaps the pattern of difference most striking and perplexing is in reference to these leaders' relationship to their respective racial and ethnic groups and to the cause of women. Albright, who shunned feminism in early life, later sought to address issues related to the welfare of women and formed networks with powerful women. Albright applied "tactical" or "opportunistic feminism," while in contrast Rice appears oblivious to women's causes. Moreover, Albright was a champion of the cause of Eastern Europe and her native land and the Czech Republic. In Rice's case, however, there is little evidence that the black community and the African Diaspora exist in her worldview or consciousness, although many African Americans see her as one of the most influential Americans of the modern era.

Albright and Rice were the public face of U.S. foreign policy in their respective terms, the Clinton and Bush administrations. Both women were highly popular with the American people. Of all the cabinet members of the Clinton administration, Albright enjoyed the highest popularity ratings in public opinion surveys. Similarly, Rice emerged as the most popular cabinet member of the Bush administration. Nevertheless, Albright and Rice are different in their public persona. Whereas Albright was regarded as a rabble-rouser, tough-talking and combative, Rice is more affable, sociable, gracious, and noncombative in her dealings with friends and foes. To be sure, Albright was viewed as ambivalent because of her loyalty, even subservience, and her unfriendliness toward those she did not need to be in company with for any reason at all.

Loyalty has been a defining characteristic for many rising elites, including Albright and Rice. Loyalty is important in the business of politics not only for women, but for anyone seeking to achieve higher office. In fact, both enjoyed unprecedented success in their careers because they served their male bosses with unquestioning loyalty. Albright, a tough and determined person, grew up under influential men like her father Josef Korbel, her mentor and supervisor Zbigniew Brzezinski, Edmund Muskie, and Bill Clinton. She served them without questioning their authority. Her successful career and finally her elevation to the position of the U.S. secretary of state were aided by her absolute loyalty to powerful men she happened to serve. Although Albright might have developed some sort of feminist consciousness in the 1980s and 1990s, when it was expedient to advance her career in the male-dominated foreign policy establishment in the United States, she was willing to sacrifice the perspective.

Although she is recognized as one of the most intellectually gifted and sophisticated members of the Republican establishment, the pinnacle of Rice's success came with her promotion to the positions of national security advisor and later U.S. secretary of state. Her appointment by Bush was due mostly to her absolute and unquestioning loyalty. Some might even argue that as a woman she could only reach the highest echelon of the U.S. foreign policy establishment, dominated by white males, by serving them not only loyally, but also submissively. Even so, in the final analysis, in the bastion of men, both Albright and Rice achieved the highest position in the field of U.S. foreign policy.

Conclusion

Although the foreign policy establishment has enunciated the ideals of democracy, liberty, and freedom from time to time as declaratory principles of U.S. foreign policy, the reality is that the underlying goal of U.S. foreign policy has always been an irreducible national interest informed by *raison d'état,* or reason of state. As a result, American foreign policymakers have practiced a variant of political realism, or *realpolitik,* as their guiding principle. This was the arena of foreign policymaking for which Madeleine Albright and Condoleezza Rice had prepared for much of their lives. They were not insulated, like other students of U.S. foreign policy, from the pervasive realist consensus that emerged in the period following World War II (Falk, 1992, 218).

In the end, it seems that Albright and Rice are far more likely to be viewed in history as transcendent figures of race, ethnicity, and gender than as advocates for their respective racial and ethnic groups, and for women. The capacity to transcend race, ethnicity, and gender cannot be demonstrated unless the political actor involved is able to like and accept who they happen to be, as well as understand how others perceive them and why. Neither Rice nor Albright, based on this assertion, can be characterized as "transcendent." Despite the institutional constraints, both women obtained positions, and we would hypothesize, articulated their role as secretary of state, largely in the same way as their male counterparts. Moreover, it is unequivocal that Albright's and Rice's ticket to the zenith of the U.S. foreign policy establishment was paid for not only with their hard work, dedication, knowledge, and perseverance, but also by their adherence to the realist worldview, and their commitment to serve mostly white men in authority with unconditional and absolute loyalty.

This research has implications for the articulation of U.S. foreign policy in an era of growing diversity. An important question for the future is whether African Americans and other racial and ethnic groups, and women, can resist the temptation to conform to the existing norms and challenge existing approaches, policies, and dogma to bring about dynamic global change and improvement along social, economic, and political dimensions. As increasing numbers of women and racial and ethnic group members serve in high-profile and other roles in the U.S. foreign policy establishment, this question will need to be addressed in an affirmative manner that exploits all the advantages associated with the wonderful diversity of the American citizenry.

NOTES

1. Madeleine Albright admits that had she remained married, she would never have become U.S. secretary of state. However, overall she is ambivalent about the effect of her divorce on her career. For details, see her autobiography, especially p. 107.

2. On the study of international relations in the United States from the standpoint of realism, see Smith, 2002.

3. For details, see Nordlinger, 1999.

4. Rice, quoted in Nordlinger, 1999.

5. Albright's Jewish ancestry created many controversies once she became secretary of state in 1997. She had denied having known it until it became public knowledge. Despite her strong public denials, the research of *Washington Post* correspondent Michael Dobbs suggests that she may well have known. Nevertheless, Albright's side of the story suggests that she might not have known since her parents did not inform her. It is plausible that her Jewish ancestry was concealed in the aftermath of family's conversion to Christianity.

6. For details see Chestnut, 2005.

REFERENCES

Albright, Madeleine K. 1998. "The Testing of American Foreign Policy." *Foreign Affairs* 77:50–64.

———. 2003. *Madam Secretary*. New York: Miramax.

Blackman, Ann. 1998. *Seasons of Her Life: A Biography of Madeleine K. Albright*. New York: Scribner.

Boutros-Ghali, Boutros. 1999. *Unvanquished: A U.S.-U.N. Saga*. New York: Random House.

Brown, Seyom. 1994. *The Faces of Power: United States Foreign Policy from Truman to Clinton*. New York: Columbia University Press.

Burgess, F. Stephen. 2001. *The United Nations under Boutros Boutros-Ghali 1992–1997*. Lanham, Md.: Scarecrow Press.

Burrell, Barbara C. 1993. "Party Decline, Party Transformation, and Gender Politics: The USA." In *Gender and Party Politics*, ed. Jon Lovendusk and Pippa Norris. London: Sage Publications, 291–308.

Carpenter, Ted Galen. "Roiling Asia." *Foreign Affairs* 77:2–6.

Chestnut, J. L. 2005. "Condi Rice's Disdain for Civil Rights Movement." *Catholic New Times*, December.

Cohn, Carol. 1987. "Sex and Death in the Rational world of Defense Intellectuals." *Sign* 12:687–718.

Conway, M. Margaret. 2001. "Women and Political Participation." *PS: Political Science and Politics* 34: 231–33.

Dobbs, Michael. 1999. *Madeleine Albright: A Twentieth Century Odyssey*. New York: Henry Holt.

Ellison, Ralph. 1952. *Invisible Man*. New York: Random House.

Falk, Richard A. 1992. *Explorations at the Edge of Time: The Prospects of World Order*. Philadelphia: Temple University Press.

Felix, Antonio. 2002. *Condi: The Condoleezza Rice Story*. New York: New Market Press.

Goldstein, Joshua S. 2001. *International Relations*. New York: Longman.

Hollander, Paul. 1978. *Soviet and American Society: A Comparison*. Chicago: University of Chicago Press.

Lasch, Christopher. 1965. *The New Radicalism in America: The Intellectual as a Social Type*. New York: Alfred. A. Knopf.

Lippman, W. Thomas. 2000. *Madeleine Albright and the New American Diplomacy.* Boulder, Colo.: Westview Press.

Mann, James. 2004. *Rise of the Vulcans: The History of Bush's War Cabinet.* New York: Viking.

Niven, David. 1998. *The Missing Majority: The Recruitment of Women as State Legislative Candidates.* Westport, Conn.: Praeger.

Nordlinger, Jay. 1999. "Star-in-Waiting." National Review, August 30. Located at http://www.nationalreview.com/flashback/nordlinger200411170605.asp (accessed December 7, 2009).

Norris, Pippa. 1997. "Introduction: Theories of Recruitment:." In *Passages to Power*, ed. Pippa Norris. Cambridge: Cambridge University Press, 1–14.

Powell, Colin. With Joseph E. Persico. 1995. *My American Journey.* New York: Random House.

Reardon, Betty A. 1990. "Feminist Concept of Peace and Security." In *A Reader in Peace Studies*, ed. Paul Smoker, Ruth Davies, and Barbara Munske. Oxford: Pergamon Press.

Rice, Condoleezza. 1984. *The Soviet Union and the Czechoslovak Army, 1948–1983: Uncertain Allegiance.* Princeton, N.J.: Princeton University Press.

———. 1986. "The Making of *Soviet Strategy.*" In *Makers of Modern Strategy From Machiavelli to the Nuclear Age,* ed. Peter Peret, 2d ed. Princeton, N.J.: Princeton University Press, 648–76.

———. 1999. "Campaigning 2000: Promoting the National Interest." *Foreign Affairs* 79: 45–62.

Robinson, Eugene. 2005. "What Rice Cannot See." *Washington Post,* October 25.

Rourke, T. John. 2003. *International Politics on the World Stage.* New York: McGraw-Hill.

Smith, Steve. 1989. "Paradigm Dominance in International Relations: The Development of International Relations as a Social Science." In *The Study of International Relations: The State of the Art*, ed. Hugh C. Dyer and Leon Mangasarian. New York: St. Martin's Press.

———. 2002. "The United States and the Discipline of International Relations: Hegemonic Country, Hegemonic Discipline." *International Studies Review* 4:67–85.

Walton, Hanes, Jr., and Robert C. Smith. 2006. *American Politics and the African American Quest for Universal Freedom.* New York: Longman.

EIGHT

The Rise and Fall of Black Influence on U.S. Foreign Policy

Charles P. Henry

I don't believe we can have world peace until
America has an "integrated" foreign policy.

—MARTIN LUTHER KING, JR.

As I write, U.S. foreign policy is being constructed and implemented by its second consecutive black American secretary of state. While Condoleezza Rice is known for her extraordinary access to President George Bush, her predecessor, Colin Powell, was a widely respected military leader. Although both have linked their racial experiences to their work, neither has raised the status of Africa (excluding Egypt) as a foreign policy priority or moved aggressively to solve any of the continent's many problems. On the contrary, they have been the most visible spokespersons for a foreign policy that many Africans and many African Americans reject.

For most of their history in America, blacks have generally worked for and were perceived as working for subjugated communities of color in Africa, the Caribbean, and South America. While the actions of black Americans, especially in the nineteenth century, were often paternalistic, they generally did oppose the antidemocratic and unjust dimensions of U.S. foreign and military policies. Today not only do they help shape these policies, but a disproportionate number of the U.S. troops carrying out these policies in some sixty-five countries worldwide are black.

At a time when African Americans enjoy unprecedented wealth and political access, this work critically examines the decline in a progressive foreign policy agenda for Africa. Tavis Smiley's book *Covenant with Black America* totally ignores foreign policy. The Congressional Black Caucus Foundation report for 2004 ignores Haiti, Colombia, the International

Criminal Court, the World Trade Organization, the Israel-Palestine conflict, aid and trade with Africa, the environment, and the war on terrorism. Neither Powell nor Rice's nomination to the position of secretary of state received organized opposition from the black community.

This work contends that the rise and fall of a progressive black voice in foreign policy may be attributed to a decline in political Pan-Africanism. More specifically, the cases of South African divestment and the Rwandan genocide represent the peak and nadir of black international influence. Finally, Darfur illustrates the continuing absence of an effective and progressive black voice in foreign policy.

Identity, Ethnicity, and U.S. Foreign Policy

Perhaps the first question to ask is whether ethnicity/race should play a role in U.S. foreign policy. To some extent the question is moot because ethnicity and race have always influenced U.S. foreign policy, whether overtly or covertly. Still, the question can be raised of whether the mobilization of particular groups around questions related to their countries of origin is always in the national interest.

Of course, the response to this question is another question: who determines the national interest? Foreign policymaking, more than any other area of government, has traditionally been restricted to elites. With the United States isolated from the historic conflicts on the European continent and America's individualistic liberalism devoted to the cause of material progress, for much of U.S. history many Americans were content to let the elite guide foreign affairs.

Still, as a multicultural democracy with relatively fluid class hierarchies, the United States was more vulnerable to ethnic influence than most nation-states. While much lobbying remained dominated by for-profit professionals, on certain occasions ethnic consciousness played a role. After all, most social change in the United States has come from social movements and not political parties.

Most scholars see foreign policy as being shaped by two competing camps—realists and idealists. Realists hold that the United States should avoid any entanglements or alliances that are not in the national interest. They define national interest as almost exclusively security and economic needs. For realists, the United States needs to maintain its superiority in military or "hard" power. If applied consistently, this thesis means that the United States has no permanent friends or enemies, only permanent interests. Idealists believe it is in the national interest to promote "American values" globally. Those values have historically included democracy, capitalism, and human rights. These values, "soft power," are conveyed through American popular culture, diplomacy, academic exchanges, missionaries, and democracy and human rights training programs. If the concept were applied consistently, the United States would reward regimes that promote American values and punish those that do not.

Obviously, the realist-idealist dichotomy fails to explain U.S. support for countries that are undemocratic or violate human rights, such as apartheid South Africa and Saudi Arabia, for example, or opposition to countries that are not military or economic threats, such as Vietnam in the 1950s and 1960s and Cuba today. The concept of "kin countries" provides some insight lacking in the two standard models.

Samuel Huntington says that

> Groups or states belonging to one civilization that become involved in war with people from a different civilization naturally try to rally support from other members of their own civilization. As the post–Cold War world evolves, civilization commonality, what H. D. S. Greenway has termed the "kin-country" syndrome, is replacing political ideology and traditional balance of power considerations as the principal basis for cooperation and coalitions.[1]

While Huntington's "clash of civilizations" thesis has been hugely influential and widely attacked, it does bring the question of culture to the foreground in a way that earlier works on ethnicity and foreign policy ignored.[2] Richard Payne, building on Huntington, states that multiculturalism in the United States challenges the notion of a consensual political culture. He believes that the national interest is influenced by a cultural reservoir that is an accumulation of goodwill and understanding stemming from a set of values, beliefs, attitudes, historical experiences, and racial and ethnic links that two or more countries have in common.[3] Thus the U.S.–Israel link is different from the U.S.–Bosnia link, which is further distinct from the U.S.–Rwanda link. The United States finally ratified the U.N. Convention on the Elimination of All Forms of Racial Discrimination (CERD) in the early 1990s in response to the ethnic violence in Bosnia, not Africa.

These links may or may not be in the broader national interest; however, they appear to be increasing in importance with the rise of "civic society" and the diasporic notion of "host country" versus "homeland." In *Foreign Attachments,* Tony Smith cites three stages of ethnic group influence. First, from the 1910s to the 1930s Germans, Scandinavians, Irish, and later Italians promoted U.S. isolationism and sank the League of Nations.

During the Cold War, the second stage, all ethnic groups were internationalist and anticommunist except African Americans during the Carter administration. Third, from 1989 to the present ethnic groups are internationalist but there is no consensus on the national interest. Smith argues that the influence of such groups has grown given decreasing bipartisanship in Congress and an increasing division between the executive and legislative branches of government. The most successful ethnic organizations are the American Israel Political Action Committee (AIPAC) and the Cuban American National Fund (CANF)—both started with government assistance. However, Smith believes the rigid policy agendas promoted by these two organizations, among others, are not in the national interest. These groups should not be able to dictate U.S. policy in specific regions of the world. Moreover, says Smith, the only groups that can claim priority of ethnic rights over national obligations are African Americans and Native Americans.[4]

The very exemption Smith provides for privileging African American identity over national identity highlights the extraordinarily complicated relationship black Americans have with Africa. Africa is a geographical construct that bears none of the European ethnic groups' cultural attachments to their lands of origins.[5] Thus, the shifting conceptions of Pan-Africanism in both its cultural and political forms have presented unique challenges.

Despite Smith's exemption, African Americans have fought in all of America's wars. Their loyalty, however, did not pay dividends in terms of foreign policy influence. From the Nationality Act of 1790, which limited naturalization to free white persons, to the recognition of Haiti and Liberia to the Atlantic Charter on decolonization to the Byrd Amendment on Rhodesian Chrome, the black voice in foreign policy has been suppressed. As late as 1925, only one black, Clifton Wharton, Sr., was serving in a professional position in the State Department. Not until 1959 was a black representative, Charles Diggs, placed on the House Foreign Affairs Committee.[6] Virtually everyone who studies Africa agrees that it has always ranked at the bottom of the regions of the world in which the United States has a national interest. How can that be when historically 10–20 percent of all Americans come from Africa?

Obviously, the lack of citizenship rights in general and the right to vote in particular have played a key role in the absence of black influence on foreign policy, but it is not the whole story. While white Americans have emotional and affective ties to specific homelands, African Americans lack similar particular roots. In addition, if African Americans lacked full citizenship rights in America, neither did they want to embrace an Africa that often seemed foreign and hostile to them. In his definitive work on African Americans and early U.S. policy toward Africa, ambassador and scholar Elliott Skinner states:

> Africa was never universally viewed by the descendants of the bonds-persons as a land of bliss. Many took a dim view of an ancestral land whose military and political weaknesses permitted its inhabitants to be carried off and enslaved. They were scorned when Africa was conquered and colonized by outsiders who convinced of the sub-humanity of its inhabitants, felt called upon to Christianize and civilize them. More-over, some African Americans, though certainly not a majority, re-mained ashamed of Africa's legacy, their black skin, which remained a badge of low status despite individual accomplishments.[7]

These reasons, among others, account for the widespread rejection of at-tempts to colonize free blacks during the antebellum period. And even with the rise of back-to-Africa movements in the late nineteenth and early twentieth centuries, the emphasis was on the "civilizing and christianizing mission" of the more advanced New World black. Still, black leadership seemed to agree that the rise of at least one powerful state in Africa would benefit blacks in the Diaspora as well.

In *The Big Sea,* Langston Hughes tosses his academic books overboard as his ship sails for Africa, in a symbolic rejection of Columbia College and Eurocentric knowledge in general. Although the Africans considered Hughes "a white man" and the renowned poet spent most of his search for African identity in Harlem, he is perhaps best remembered for his poem "The Negro Speaks of Rivers," linking the flow of black history from the Nile and Congo to the Mississippi. The Harlem Renaissance, the Garvey movement, the Italian-Ethiopian War, and the Pan-African Congresses are just the best known phenomena of many events, persons, and organiza-tions that reflected a new Pan-African consciousness among blacks in the Diaspora in the early twentieth century.

The global race consciousness that W. E. B. Du Bois, Ralph Bunche, George Padmore, C. L. R. James, Paul Robeson, and others promoted in the first half of the twentieth century was suppressed during the McCarthy era. A host of new scholarly works by James Meriwether, Mary L. Dud-zick, Jeff Woods, Brenda Gayle Plummer, Kevin Gaines, Gerald Horne, Penny M. Von Eschen, and others have documented the difficulty of sup-porting the anticolonial struggle abroad while avoiding being labeled a communist at home.[8] The decoupling of these dual struggles for racial equality is perhaps best seen in the condemnation of Martin Luther King, Jr., for his public opposition to the war in Vietnam by almost the entire civil rights establishment.

By the time of King's 1967 Riverside Church speech, leadership of the Pan-African movement had shifted to the leaders of the newly emerging African nations. Names like Kwame Nkrumah, Julius Nyerere, Amilcar Cabral, Sekou Touré, and Jomo Kenyatta were as familiar to African American activists as the names of Du Bois, Garvey, and Robeson had been to the African activists of an earlier generation. Yet it would be another twenty years before African Americans asserted decisive influence on U.S. foreign policy toward Africa.[9] The Comprehensive Anti-Apartheid Act of 1986 represents the highpoint of black influence on U.S. foreign policy.

Yet that success did not carry into the 1990s. Keith Richburg, East African Bureau chief of the *Washington Post,* had come to Africa to make a difference. As one of the few black reporters working for an influential national newspaper, his first African assignment in Somalia became an obsession. Convinced that the suffering of Africans was as newsworthy as the suffering of Bosnians, he pressured his bosses to give increasing coverage to the disaster that was unfolding in Somalia. Richburg said the U.N. secretary-general, Boutros Boutros-Ghali, was deluged with daily phone calls from European heads of government about the Bosnia crisis, but on Somalia, "the phones were largely silent . . . Boutros-Ghali said (Bosnia) was 'a rich man's war.'" The disaster became personal when four of Richburg's friends and colleagues were killed by a crowd of Somalians enraged by civilian deaths caused by missiles fired into a residential neighborhood by U.N. forces.[10]

By the time Richburg took on his next assignment in Rwanda, his view of Africa had been turned on its head. The hope that sprang up from the end of the Cold War and the rise of South Africa, the ending of conflicts in Mozambique and Angola, and the stepping aside of "big men" in countries such as the Ivory Coast, Malawi, and Zambia was crushed. For Richburg the "African Renaissance" was over. Now for the *Washington Post* reporter Rwanda represented the despair and chaos that was postcolonial Africa. The corruption, violence, tribalism, and disease seemed endemic, and Richburg wanted no part of it. The uprooting of his identification with Africa is best symbolized by the title of his 1997 book *Out of America: A Black Man Confronts Africa.*

Richburg's viewpoint is similar to those of nineteenth-century black Americans who distinguished themselves from Africans through the institution of slavery that brought them out of the "dark" continent. Whether it was the Pan-Africanism of Paul Cuffee, Lott Carey, Martin Delany, Alexander Crummel, Henry McNeal Turner, or Booker T. Washington, it was a paternalistic and one-way Pan-Africanism that sought to take the blessings of Western civilization to the less developed people of Africa.[11] Only with the rise of colonization beginning with the Berlin conference in 1884–85 do we get the development of a political Pan-Africanism.

The development of a political Pan-Africanism focused on colonialism did not go unnoticed by the U.S. government. Government efforts to keep W. E. B. Du Bois from attending the first Pan-African Congress, called by him in Paris in 1919, are fairly well known. Also known is the government's refusal to let Marcus Garvey back into the United States after a successful tour of the Caribbean promoting his Black Star Line enterprise in the early 1920s. Less well known are the U.S. efforts to keep language promoting racial equality out of the charter of the League of Nations and its successor, the United Nations. The first Asian-African global conference meeting at Bandung, Indonesia, in 1955 was greeted with hostility and suspicion by the United States despite the conference's full support for the U.N. Charter and the Universal Declaration of Human Rights.[12] More recently the United States at first opposed and then refused to attend the U.N. World Conference Against Racism in 2001 and the follow-up meeting in Geneva in April 2009. Neither did it attend either of the two previous world conferences against racism, in 1978 and 1983.

Not only did Richburg disconnect from Africa, but African Americans in general seemed to join him. From the widespread mobilization of blacks and others forcing local, state, and national action on South Africa in the mid-1980s, Rwanda drew only a comparative whisper of concern in the mid-1990s. What accounts for these varying responses, and what does it portend for the ongoing crisis in Darfur?

Public opinion polls appear to support the perception of African American ambivalence toward Africa. On the one hand, black Americans are significantly more likely than white Americans to support improving the standard of living in less-developed countries (38 percent vs. 20 percent); defending human rights (45 percent vs. 33 percent); and combating world hunger (65 percent vs. 55 percent). On the other hand, fewer blacks than whites see Egypt as a country "vital" to U.S. interests (31 percent vs. 58 percent).[13]

Nikongo BaNikongo reports that a 1991 survey found only 35.8 percent of respondents recognized the name of Nelson Mandela, and not surprisingly only 15.1 percent knew what "constructive engagement" was. An amazing 70 percent had no opinion on U.S. African policy. By contrast, the

1993 National Black Political Survey found that 70 percent of respondents believed black children should study an African language.[14]

The ambivalence of black public opinion on Africa is shared by African American members of Congress:

> Congresswoman Eva Clayton says her interest in Africa was initially sparked from "a sense of pride, and a sense that Africa was part of [her] history as a black American." Representative Floyd Flake, from New York's Sixth Congressional District, cites his connection with the African Methodist Episcopal church as the primary impetus motivating his interest in African affairs. Congressman William Jefferson, second district, New Orleans, characterized his initial interest in Africa as "remote, romantic, [and] the same type of interest that most African Americans exposed to some information about Africa would have."[15]

Despite these positive feelings toward Africa, none of these representatives sees their work on Africa as part of a worldwide struggle for racial justice. All place primary emphasis on serving their local constituents, and none was motivated to serve on the House Committee on International Relations.[16]

African Americans' ambivalence toward Africa may be returned by African states. Masipula Sithole reports that there is a lack of solidarity between African elites and African Americans. Most Africans see African Americans as Americans first; however, they expect African Americans to influence U.S. policy toward Africa.[17] In 1995 Rep. William Clay (D-MO) investigated who Africans hired to represent their interests in Washington. Clay's study reported that of the fifty-three African nations recognized by the United Nations, only six were represented by black-owned firms: Gabon, Nigeria, Sao Tome and Principe, and the republics of Benin, Mauritania, and Cameroon.[18] Clay responded to the data by saying, "Africans have never wanted to be identified with black Americans. They feel superior to black Americans."[19] Ironically, for a long time the situation was the reverse.

South Africa

With the exception of Liberia, no country in Africa has had more extensive ties with African Americans than South Africa. By the 1880s, early black resistance to white domination in the form of religious Ethiopianism was inspired by American black churches established earlier.[20] Whites in South Africa, especially the Afrikaners, did not know how to deal with African American visitors. Although they were not accorded equal status with whites, they were placed above indigenous blacks. When the McAdoo Minstrels were permitted to perform in the Orange Free State, it generated pride in local blacks because it furnished proof to them that given an opportunity, people of African origin could excel. This led to the formation in 1891 of an African Choir that toured South Africa, Great Britain, and the United States. The group's success led to several of the members attending Wilberforce University in Xenia, Ohio. When Bishop Henry McNeal Turner traveled to South Africa to formalize links between his own African Methodist Episcopal Church and the Ethiopian Church, he was granted the status of "honorary white," as were other African American visitors. Rev. Joseph Booth, a white missionary, with Booker T. Washington's cooperation sought to establish "industrial missions" for black South Africans. Both Turner and Washington supported the British in their struggle with the Boers for control of South Africa. Some African Americans then in South Africa actually fought on the side of the British during the Boer War.[21]

This early contact continued as both Marcus Garvey and W. E. B. Du Bois took up the cause of racial justice in South Africa. The National Association for the Advancement of Colored People (NAACP) and the African National Congress (ANC) were established at roughly the same time, and the founders of the former provided advice to their South African counterparts. Attending the Silver Jubilee of the ANC, Ralph Bunche criticized the organization's inertia and reliance on whites. By 1940, younger members agreed with Bunche, electing Dr. Xuma president and drawing in young activists including Nelson Mandela, Oliver Tambo, and Walter Sisulu.[22] This new militancy was also reflected in the United States, as Paul Robeson and Max Yergan established the Council on African Affairs (CAA), the first American anti-apartheid organization, in 1937. Yergan had lived in South Africa between 1921 and 1936, serving as secretary of the "native" branch of the Student Christian Association. Robeson, the main fundraiser and policymaker of the council, became interested in Africa after meeting African nationalists, such as Jomo Kenyatta, Nnamdi Azikiwe, and Kwame Nkrumah, while living in London in the 1920s and 1930s. Even before apartheid became the official policy in South Africa in 1948, the CAA and India campaigned for international sanctions at the first U.N. General Assembly meeting in London in 1946.[23]

Just as the anti-apartheid movement began to emerge, the onset of McCarthyism convinced many mainstream black activists to abandon anticolonialism, while leftists like DuBois and Robeson were severely harassed by the FBI and Justice Department. Withdrawal of Robeson's passport meant the cutoff of CAA's major funding source and its collapse in 1955. Replacing the CAA as the most visible black-led organization focusing on African policy was the American Committee on Africa (ACOA), organized by George Houser in 1954. ACOA reflected a Cold War perspective, referring to African liberation fighters as "terrorists." While such leaders as Roy Wilkins called the Mau Mau primitive and unacceptable, Malcolm X held them up as "freedom fighters." The young Martin Luther King, Jr., reached out to support Albert Luthuli as his father had done in the 1940s. King endorsed ACOA's Declaration of Conscience campaign as a nonviolent protest over the arrest for treason of 156 black southern liberation leaders.[24]

The Sharpeville massacre on March 23, 1960, forced a rethinking of the utility of nonviolence against the South African state. The murder of at least seventy-two men, women, and children who were nonviolently protesting against pass laws also sparked a mobilization of public support in the United States. By 1962, George Houser of ACOA was able to organize the founding conference of a new organization, the American Negro Leadership Conference on Africa (ANLCA). Participants in the founding conference included Martin Luther King, Jr., Whitney Young, A. Philip Randolph, and Roy Wilkins.[25]

International opinion also shifted sharply against South Africa. Rather than viewing apartheid as an internal matter, the United Nations now saw apartheid as a threat to international peace. In 1962, the U.N. General Assembly called for diplomatic and economic sanctions against South Africa and established the Special U.N. Committee on Apartheid as a monitoring agency. In the same year the U.N. Security Council called for a voluntary embargo against sales of military items to South Africa. In these actions and others, the United States consistently supported South Africa and criticized the competence of the United Nations to deal with the domestic human rights of sovereign states.[26]

The South African government responded to this pressure by increasing the repression on black South Africans. Prime Minister Hendrik Verwoerd's white minority regime withdrew from the British Commonwealth and then launched its plan for "separate development" of blacks into Bantustans or "homelands" constituting only 13 percent of the country's total area. Black activists in the ANC reacted to the government's banning of liberation organizations by forming Umkontho we Sizwe (Zulu for "Spear of the People"), an armed wing led by Mandela, Tambo, and Sisulu. At its founding conference in May 1963, the Organization of African Unity not only asked the United States to choose sides in the anticolonial struggle but also condemned racial discrimination in America.[27]

By the late 1960s, the anti-apartheid movement had grown to include black and white church groups as well as student communities. The new strategy was to attack the economic linkages undergirding South African apartheid. In 1967 James Forman, former executive director of the Congress of Racial Equality (CORE), introduced the first stockholder resolution involving financial relationships with South Africa at the national meeting of Morgan Guaranty Trust. As the divestment movement grew, the Interfaith Center on Corporate Responsibility and the Washington Office on Africa were established to help coordinate movement activities.[28]

The stockholder strategy was complemented by a more direct assault on corporate activity in South Africa by the Polaroid Revolutionary Workers Movement. With the assistance of ACOA, workers at Polaroid attempted to initiate a global boycott of Polaroid products.[29] Black athletes also joined the anti-apartheid movement, starting with the 1964 effort to expel South Africa from the Tokyo Olympics and extending through Arthur Ashe's attempt to play in the South African Open in 1970.[30]

Jimmy Carter's election as president and his appointment of Andrew Young as ambassador to the United Nations led many activists to shift to an "insider" strategy in their attempts to influence U.S. foreign policy. During the Nixon administration it was clear that government policy supported the apartheid regime. Under Henry Kissinger, the National Security Council had produced the infamous Study Memorandum 39 (NSSM 39). The memorandum concluded that "the Whites are here to stay and the only way that constructive change can come about is through them."[31] Nixon also relaxed sanctions against Rhodesia and approved legislation allowing the importation of Rhodesian chrome. Efforts by the newly formed Congressional Black Caucus (CBC) to meet with Nixon were ignored until the caucus boycotted his 1971 State of the Union address, forcing him to hear their concerns.[32]

Not everyone pursued an insider strategy. Perhaps the most significant outside pressure came from the development of the African Liberation Support Committee (ALSC), which grew out of Owusu Sadukai's (Howard Fuller) idea for an African Liberation Day to celebrate the anniversary of the founding of the Organization of African Unity (OAU). At the 1972 African American National Conference on Africa, leaders of the Congress of African People joined with representatives of the CBC, including Charles Diggs, Jr., chair of the congressional subcommittee on Africa, to criticize Nixon's support of the white minority regimes in southern Africa. The ALSC was able to mobilize some 15,000 demonstrators in Washington and another 15,000 in rallies across the country for the first African Liberation Day on May 25, 1972.[33]

South Africa's government again shocked the world in 1976, murdering fifty-four unarmed schoolchildren who were protesting the imposition of Afrikaans as the language of instruction in black schools. By the end of what came to be called the Soweto uprising, the official death toll was 377 and the unofficial count was nearly 700. Outrage over Soweto helped provide the impetus for the CBC's "African American Manifesto on Southern Africa" the same year and the formation of TransAfrica in 1977. Working closely with the CBC, TransAfrica and its director Randall Robinson became the most important black-led lobby for Africa and the Caribbean. By the end of the decade, TransAfrica, along with student and religious groups, had pressured twenty-six higher education institutions to divest approximately $87 million in stocks from corporations with ties to South Africa.[34]

Although anti-apartheid activists often had a contentious relationship with the Carter administration, the election of Ronald Reagan meant a return to the policy of "constructive engagement" outlined in NSSM 39—a policy applauded by the *Washington Post,* among others. Shortly after his election, Reagan told Walter Cronkite of CBS News, "we cannot abandon a country that has stood by us in every war we ever fought—a country that is strategically essential to the free world in its production of minerals we must all have."[35] Conveniently setting aside the Nationalist Party's support for the Nazis in World War II and excluding the South African regime from his call for democracy in Eastern Europe, Reagan turned back the clock. Jeanne J. Kirkpatrick, Reagan's ambassador to the United Nations, famously made a distinction between dictatorships, saying "racial dictatorship is not as onerous as Marxist dictatorship."[36] Under Reagan the United States increased military and nuclear collaboration, eased restrictions on the exports of U.S. goods to South African security forces, colluded with South Africa against U.N. Security Council Resolution 435, supported IMF loans to South Africa, and blocked a censure of South Africa for bombing Angola.

Reagan's support for the white racist regime in the face of almost universal global opposition bolstered the anti-apartheid movement domestically. Jesse Jackson inserted South African policy into his 1984 campaign for president, giving it unprecedented visibility and forcing Democratic candidates to address the issue. Around the same time, Randall Robinson, Rep. Walter Fauntroy (D-DC), U.S. Civil Rights Commission member Mary Frances Berry, and former Carter administration official Eleanor Holmes

Norton began a sit-in at the South African Consulate in Washington, D.C. This was the beginning of the Free South Africa Movement (FSAM), involving a host of celebrities and politicians in sit-ins in some two dozen cities and hundreds of college campuses. Within a year over 5,000 people had been arrested for participating in the sit-ins.[37]

By 1985, six states and a number of cities had passed divestment legislation. On June 5, 1985, the House of Representatives passed a sanctions bill sponsored by Rep. William Gray (D-PA). The following month the Senate overwhelmingly passed a weaker sanctions bill. Seeking to forestall congressional action, Reagan reversed his anti-sanctions stance and issued an Executive Order imposing limited economic sanctions on South Africa falling far short of the goals of anti-apartheid activists. The administration continued to directly support the South African government at the United Nations.

Reagan's maneuvers failed to deter congressional interest in strong sanctions, and Congress passed a Comprehensive Anti-apartheid Act in the summer of 1986. Ignoring Republican members' warnings that they would support the bill, Reagan vetoed it on September 26, claiming it would hurt the black majority in South Africa. Both houses of Congress overrode the veto, with thirty-one Republican senators voting against the president. It was Reagan's first major foreign policy defeat.[38]

What accounts for this remarkable black-led policy turnaround over a popular U.S. president? First, nearly fifty years of organized black opposition to apartheid and nearly twenty years of black activity on divestment produced a broad-based movement encompassing leftists, nationalist, religious leaders, politicians, labor organizations, students, and civil rights leaders. Beginning with the black leftists of the CAA in 1937 and expanding to the more moderate activists of the ANLCA in 1962 and TransAfrica in 1977, blacks presented a vocal and united force for change. Moreover, the focus on divestment provided a concrete, easily understood action involving the private sector as well as state, local, and national government.

A second factor was the almost universal condemnation of the South African regime. No issue received more attention from the United Nations after 1948 than the apartheid regime in South Africa and its illegal occupation of Namibia. In its numerous resolutions, special committees, and decades of action against South Africa, the United States, often joined by Great Britain, was South Africa's only defender. When in 1974, for example, ten members of the Security Council voted to expel South Africa from the United Nations, it was saved by vetoes from the United States, Britain, and France. The General Assembly then took the unprecedented step of suspending South Africa from any participation in its deliberations.[39]

Undoubtedly race played a major role in mobilizing both African American opposition and U.N. condemnation of the South African regime. The southern region of Africa anchored by the Union of South Africa represented the last bastion of a hundred years of colonialism.[40] Its existence directly contradicted the founding principles of the United Nations, and its support by the United States ran counter to the objectives of the civil rights and black power movements.

While a majority of Americans eventually supported U.S. efforts to end apartheid, public opinion polls reveal a racial gap in that support. A Carnegie Endowment for International Peace survey in 1979 reported that "Black Americans emerge as much more interested in Africa than are Whites, more emphatic about applying pressure on South Africa to change, and along with Jews, they identified world news as their principal interest." The report adds that "Blacks and Jews exhibited particularly great concern for discrimination in the world but, surprisingly, the latter voiced the strongest opposition to U.S. action to bring about change in South Africa."[41]

A National Election Studies survey covering the period from 1986 to 1992 found that 45.8 percent of blacks as compared to 26. 5 percent of whites favored sanctions against South Africa.[42] In a 1994 survey on the use of U.S. troops in hypothetical situations of conflict, a Chicago Council of Foreign Relations survey reported that 38 percent of blacks favored using U.S. troops in a civil war in South Africa and only 16 percent of whites supported military action.[43] Given the lack of strong support for sanctions on the part of white Americans, it would appear that African American activism was the driving force in passage of the Comprehensive Anti-Apartheid Act of 1986.

Rwanda

Less than eight years after the success of the divestment campaign, the most intense genocide in human history occurred in Rwanda. In about 100 days, some 800,000 persons—mostly members of the Tutsi group—were murdered, primarily by Hutu wielding clubs and machetes. The genocide spurred the largest refugee flow in human history, with some 1.5 million people fleeing for their lives. Not only did a Democratic administration and the most powerful military in the world stand by, in crucial instances they actually impeded action by others. Barely a whisper was heard from African Americans.

The most densely populated nation on the continent of Africa, Rwanda is part of the Great Lakes region of Africa, which has never been a high priority on the U.S. foreign policy agenda. Further, U.S. African policy has historically received less attention than its foreign policy for any other region of the world. When Rwanda burst onto the public consciousness in April 1994, the secretary of state had to look up its location in an atlas.[44]

The two largest population groups in Rwanda, known as Hutu and Tutsi, settled the region over a period of two thousand years. They developed a single and highly sophisticated language, called Kinyarwande; created a common set of religious and philosophical beliefs; and practiced a common oral culture that celebrated the same heroes. Throughout their history agriculture was the primary means of support, along with a few pastoralists who raised cattle. Rwanda emerged as a major state in the eighteenth century, and by the end of the nineteenth century the ruler governed the central regions closely through multiple hierarchies of competing officials, leaving powerful lineage groups to dominate the periphery. Hutu and Tutsi sometimes intermarried, but as the governing elite grew in power its members began to think of themselves as superior to the masses. The name Tutsi first described the status of an individual—a person rich in cattle— and then became the term that referred to the elite as a whole. "Hutu," in contrast, changed from a term describing a subordinate or follower to a reference for the masses in general.[45]

The Germans established colonial administration over Rwanda at the turn of the twentieth century, and the Belgians replaced them at the end of World War I. Seeking administrative efficiency, the Belgians began to simplify the complex, competing hierarchies that had balanced Rwandan life. As they centralized power, they also decreed that only Tutsi should be officials. Hutu were removed from positions of power and excluded from higher education. It was not so much a "divide and rule" strategy as the implementation of their racist beliefs, which saw the Tutsi as more like themselves and therefore more capable rulers. In fact, during the 1920s and 1930s a new mythical history was constructed that made use of the "Hamitic hypothesis," stating the Tutsi were descended from a "Caucasoid" race in northeastern Africa (the builders of the pyramids). Once the Belgians decided only the Tutsi would receive higher education and would be allowed to rule, they needed to distinguish exactly who was Tutsi. They did so by using physical characteristics. All Rwandans were required to declare their group identity, with 84 percent identifying as Hutu, 15 percent as Tutsi, and 1 percent as Twa.[46] In short, the Belgians injected race into what had been at worst ethnic or class differences.

After World War II and feeling pressure from the United Nations, Belgium began to provide more opportunities for Hutu. These minor reforms did not satisfy the Hutu but frightened the Tutsi who hoped to remain in power with approaching independence. Following the death of the long-time Tutsi monarch Mutara Rudahigwa in 1959, a series of conflicts erupted, leading to the proclamation of a republic in January 1961, which was later confirmed by a vote. This "Hutu Revolution" was assisted by the Belgians, and their former allies, the Tutsi, were driven to peripheral areas or out of the country. By 1967 some 20,000 Tutsi had been killed and more than 300,000 had fled the country.[47]

In a military coup in July 1973, Gen. Juvenal Habyarimana replaced Gregoire Kayibanda, Rwanda's first president, to restore order among competing Hutu groups, declaring a second republic. Two years later he made Rwanda a single-party state controlled by the National Revolutionary Movement for Development (MRND). As leader of the state, the military, and the party, Habyarimana was able to control the intellectual elite and enjoyed the support of the hierarchy of the Catholic Church, to which 62 percent of Rwandans belonged. Although the majority of clergy and religious brothers and sisters were Tutsi, the church switched sides even before the Hutu Revolution.[48]

As Habyarimana consolidated his position in Rwanda with the help of European and American "development" donors, the exiled Tutsi population—now numbering 1 million—became more of a threat. Organized as the Rwandan Patriotic Front (RPF), they helped overthrow Ugandan dictator Milton Obote and launched a full-scale invasion of Rwanda in 1990. The attack created anti-Tutsi hysteria in Rwanda, leading to "the Hutu Ten Commandments" that were published and widely circulated.[49] The Hutu government was able to repel the invasion with the help of the French. Still, European, American, and African diplomats pressured Habyarimana to negotiate with the RPF. The resulting 1993 Arusha Accords allowed for the return of Tutsi refugees, the integration of the RPF into the Rwandan armed forces, the establishment of a broad-based transitional government, and a timetable for elections. Hutu hardliners saw the accords as a sellout imposed by outsiders, and the agreement polarized the two groups rather than bringing them together.[50]

To monitor implementation of the Arusha Accords, the U.N. Assistance Mission to Rwanda (UNAMIR) was dispatched at the end of 1993. The 2,500 troops from twenty-six countries—the United States had fought against sending 5,000—were commanded by Canadian Gen. Romeo Dallaire. Dallaire immediately requested better equipment and new rules of engagement that would permit UNAMIR to disarm hostile groups, among other things. These requests, as well as the earlier recommendations by

U.N. special rapporteur Waly Bacre Ndiaye, were refused or ignored. The Hutu-led government set up militias, called the Interahamwe, which began attacking Tutsi, and the government radio station began broadcasting anti-Tutsi propaganda, even inciting murder of the "cockroaches." By early 1994 a high-level Interahamwe source had provided Dallaire with detailed plans of how the mass murder would be carried out, including the killing of Belgian peacekeepers. When Dallaire cabled Kofi Annan, the head of U.N. peacekeeping operations, with his warning of "genocide," he was told to take no action because it went beyond UNAMIR's mandate under Resolution 872. In fact, Dallaire was told to share his information with President Habyarimana![51]

On April 6, 1994, the plane carrying the presidents of both Rwanda and Burundi was shot down on approach to Kigali airport. By the next morning Prime Minister Agathe Uwilingujime, a Tutsi who had taken refuge at a U.N. compound in Kigali, had been assassinated and the Belgian U.N. peacekeepers guarding her, slaughtered. Belgium instantly began an international campaign to withdraw all UNAMIR troops to cover its own withdrawal and the United States quickly agreed. As the crisis grew, U.N. Secretary-General Boutros-Ghali offered the Security Council three options: immediate and massive reinforcement of UNAMIR; downsizing the force from 2,500 troops to 270; or a complete withdrawal. The first option, which Dallaire believed could have stopped the genocide, was moot since no countries were willing to commit more troops. Total withdrawal would be humiliating and would endanger other peacekeeping missions. The result was 270 peacekeepers left in the middle of a genocide.[52]

Even as the genocide unfolded, there were key points at which the United States could have limited the killing. After advocating the withdrawal of most U.N. troops in April, U.S. officials delayed a U.N. decision in May to send new peacekeeping troops as deaths mounted. Repeated pleas from relief workers and human rights experts to shut down the propaganda radio broadcasts that were inciting and sustaining the genocide were turned down by U.S. officials, who cited concerns over international law. During the entire campaign of genocide, the U.S. government continued to grant diplomatic recognition to Rwanda's self-declared "interim government." U.S. officials supported a French military intervention that—given RPF's distrust of the French—ensured the RPF would push for total military victory as it entered Rwanda, resulting in a refugee crisis in Zaire. The Clinton administration's refusal to acknowledge that "genocide" was indeed occurring hampered efforts to mobilize public support for humanitarian intervention by private relief agencies.[53]

On several occasions later in his administration, Clinton expressed regret over the lack of response by the United States during the Rwanda genocide. Yet Samantha Power argues that Clinton followed standard U.S. foreign policy procedure in reacting to genocide. Power states that the United States has never intervened to stop genocide and rarely condemns it, citing the cases of Armenia, the Jewish Holocaust, Cambodia, Kurds in Iraq, and Rwanda. She cites four factors that contribute to the lack of action. First, despite graphic media coverage, Americans assume rational actors will not inflict seemingly gratuitous violence, and once the violence starts, they assume civilians will not be targeted. Second, U.S. political leaders interpret society-wide silence as public indifference, meaning there will be no cost for noninvolvement but possible risk if they engage in action. Third, the United States tends to frame involvement as sending troops versus noninvolvement, ignoring less extreme measures. Finally, U.S. officials themselves encourage the public to see two sides to the violence or to see U.S. action as futile or harming the victim.[54]

Power's analysis clearly applies to the Rwandan genocide. First reports of the scope and intensity of the genocide were either dismissed or downplayed as exaggerated. Many media representatives were stationed in Nairobi, which contributed to gaps in their coverage. At the height of coverage of the killings the number of reporters present never exceeded fifteen.[55] Still, by mid-April newspapers such as the *Washington Post* and the *New York Times* were reporting corpses piling up on Kigali's streets. Moreover, U.S. and U.N. officials had knowledge of the plans for the genocide as early as January 1994.

Political leaders from the president on down felt little political pressure to become involved. Not only did the United States not have any "vital" interests in Rwanda, few officials could even locate the country on a map. Senate minority leader Bob Dole, who helped lead the fight for U.S. action in Bosnia, said, "I don't think we have any national interest there." He added, on April 10, "The Americans are out, and as far as I'm concerned, in Rwanda, that ought to be the end of it."[56] When Sen. Paul Simon (D-IL), chair of the Senate Foreign Relations Subcommittee on African Affairs, criticized USAID administrator J. Brian Atwood for inaction, he responded, "I did not hear any voices up here suggesting that the U.S. should insert its forces in the midst of a hot civil war."[57]

On May 13, Simon and Sen. James Jeffords (R-VT), ranking minority member on the subcommittee, sent an urgent, hand-delivered note to the White House requesting that the United States get the Security Council to authorize the deployment of the troops for which General Dallaire had pleaded. The White House never responded. When a Human Rights Watch staff member asked NSC director Anthony Lake how they could alter U.S. policy, he responded, "You will have to change public opinion . . . you must make more noise."[58]

Indeed, public opinion polling on Rwanda found both ambivalence and indifference. A Time/CNN poll on May 16 found that 45 percent of respondents favored the use of U.S. armed forces as part of a U.N. mission to try to stop the violence in Rwanda, while 41 percent opposed using U.S. troops. However, when asked in the same poll whether the United States should do more to reduce the violence in Rwanda, only 34 percent responded positively and 51 percent responded negatively.[59] Another poll conducted in May by NBC News/Wall Street Journal asked respondents how well they thought Bill Clinton handled the "civil war" in Rwanda. Four percent thought Clinton was doing well and 27 percent said somewhat well. However, 16 percent of respondents said not very well and only 15 percent responded not at all well. Tellingly, some 38 percent were not sure about the president's response. This ambiguity about the president's response is reflected in a Times Mirror poll the same month that found only 34 percent of respondents followed the "tribal massacre" in Rwanda either very closely or fairly closely, while 64 percent said not too closely or not at all closely.[60]

In June 1994 an NBC News/Wall Street Journal poll asked whether the United States should take the lead, take an equal part with other countries, or not be involved at all in ending the "civil war" in Rwanda. Only 7 percent of respondents thought the United States should lead, 42 percent favored an equal role with other countries, and 46 percent opposed any involvement.[61] After the violence had subsided in August, a Time/CNN poll found that 69 percent of respondents favored sending U.S. military forces to provide humanitarian aid to citizens of Rwanda, while 24 percent opposed U.S. assistance.[62] Perhaps reflecting this pro-assistance opinion, the United States played an active role in the effort, providing some $527 million in relief in the eighteen months following the genocide.[63]

As reflected in the questions asked in the public opinion polls, the use of U.S. troops was a major concern. Lesser actions, such as jamming the Hutu-sponsored hate radio station, withdrawing diplomatic recognition of the "transition" government, or providing logistic support for additional U.N. troops, were not part of the public discussion. That the United States did not take those relatively easy steps provided reassurance to Hutu leaders that they could carry out their genocidal plans without outside interference. On the few occasions when the civilian militias were challenged, they usually backed down.

As in the previously mentioned comments by Atwood and in the public opinion polls, officials and the media consciously framed the conflict as "civil war" or "tribal warfare." Framed this way, U.S. action would seem futile as Hutu and Tutsi would continue killing each other as they had done for centuries. Calling it a civil war helped the United States avoid labeling the massacre "genocide." The assistant secretary of state for democracy, human rights and labor, John Shattuck, said, "I wanted to deliver a statement both in private meetings and in public that stressed the 'personal responsibility of the Rwandan military leaders for genocide,' but I could not get clearance to use this language."[64] He was told that an official pronouncement that genocide had been committed might have been understood not simply to be a statement of fact, but to have policy implications. In fact, Susan Rice (now U.S. ambassador to the United Nations), an NSC staffer who worked on Africa, asked at an interagency teleconference in late April: "if we use the word 'genocide' and are seen as doing nothing, what will be the effect on the November [congressional] election?"[65] The United States and Britain also insisted on excluding the word *genocide* from a U.N. Security Council statement. Finally, six weeks and hundreds of thousands of deaths after the killing began, State Department officials were authorized to say only that "acts of genocide" had occurred.[66] Had the conflict been framed from the start for the public by the government and the media as "genocide" instead of "civil war," it might have generated the political pressure to act that Anthony Lake claimed he wanted.

While Power's provocative thesis holds that it is U.S. policy *not* to respond in a meaningful way to genocide in any part of the world, it does not fully explain what happened in Rwanda. Specifically, it does not address two factors that were of critical importance in the U.S. response to events in Rwanda: Somalia and Haiti.

The U.S. response to Rwanda was directly affected by what has come to be known as the "Somalia syndrome." In Somalia a U.N. humanitarian mission supported by the United States and designed to deliver food to starving people had quietly shifted to a campaign to rid the country of warlords and build democracy. When eighteen U.S. soldiers were killed and publicly humiliated in their efforts to capture Mohammad Farah Aideed, public and congressional support for Clinton's foreign policy plummeted. Instead of better preparing for future humanitarian crises through clear criteria and new rules of engagement for peacekeepers, the United States retreated to a new isolationism. Ironically, President George H. W. Bush had sent U.S. troops to Somalia at the very end of his term in office to counter criticism that the United States had not intervened in Bosnia because the Bosnians were Muslims. "Somalia gave us the ability to show they were wrong," said NSC advisor Brent Scowcroft, "it was a Southern Hemisphere state; it was black; it was non-Christian; it was everything that epitomized the Third World."[67]

As a direct result of the Somalia humiliation and at the very height of the atrocities in Rwanda, President Clinton issued a new Presidential Decision Directive (PDD 25), authored by Richard Clarke of the NSC, that required the United States to actively oppose the establishment or continuation of any U.N. peacekeeping mission where hostilities were occurring. For Clarke, who would later play a major role in the Iraq conflict, the news from Rwanda only confirmed his negative views about U.N. peacekeeping. Clarke's views trumped those of African specialists who believed the United States should do more.[68]

Events in Haiti were unfolding at the same time as the Rwanda genocide. Yet in contrast to Rwanda, the "Somalia syndrome" and PDD 25 were overcome as President Clinton chose active intervention in Haiti. What accounts for the difference?

As the massacre was under way in Rwanda, President Clinton, according to one Democratic Party insider, was about to embark on "a preposterous adventure in the Caribbean in which no U.S. interest is even remotely involved."[69] The *National Journal* article went on to say that Clinton had shown no enthusiasm for military action against Haiti's dictators and had embraced the "let's just fence off our borders" policies of the Reagan and Bush administrations. His primary goal, the article stated, "has been to try to ensure that refugees fleeing that dictatorship don't wipe out his chances of competing for Florida's 25 electoral votes in 1996."[70]

One answer to the question of why Clinton reversed his own policy and that of previous administrations as well as the "Somalia syndrome" is the mobilization of black foreign policy influence. At the very time events began to reach crisis in Rwanda, Randall Robinson of TransAfrica began a hunger strike over Clinton's Haiti policy. Shortly after Robinson began his protest, six members of Congress were arrested in front of the White House for protesting the administration's decision to turn back Haitian refugees on the high seas. Robinson was hospitalized for dehydration on May 4, and five days later Clinton officially changed his policy on repatriation. Anthony Lake, who claimed he was powerless to do anything in Rwanda, spearheaded the effort to overturn the Powell-Weinburger "all or nothing" doctrine on the use of military force and escape the limits imposed by PDD 25. On September 19, the U.S. Army led a multinational force into Haiti, restoring deposed president Jean-Bertrand Aristide without firing a shot.[71]

Using human rights to justify his actions, Clinton overcame congressional and Pentagon opposition, as well as a lack of public support. A May
1994 Washington Post/ABC News poll found only 33 percent of whites,
compared to 50 percent of blacks, saw Haiti as a vital interest of the United
States. Seventy-one percent of whites believed the United States should
turn back Haitian refugees, but only 43 percent of blacks agreed. On military force, neither a majority of whites (36 percent) nor a majority of blacks
(48 percent) agreed that it should be used to restore democratic government to Haiti.[72]

Pressure from TransAfrica and the Congressional Black Caucus would
appear to be crucial variables in forcing U.S. government intervention. In
talking about American's Haitian refugee policy, Randall Robinson said, "I
can't remember ever being more disturbed by any public policy than I am
by this one. I can't remember any American foreign policy as hurtful, as
discriminatory, as racist as this one. It is so mean, it simply can't be toler-
ated."[73] The discriminatory nature of the policy, especially when compared
to the treatment of Cuban refugees, appears to be reflected in the black-
white public opinion gap on Haiti policy.

Black representatives in Congress also responded to the pressure. Rep.
Ronald Dellums (D-CA), who played a key role in promoting sanctions
against South Africa and who organized the congressional protest against
Clinton's Haiti policy, mentions Rwanda only once, in passing, in his autobiography.[74] Rep. Alcee Hastings (D-FL), in comparing the reaction to
Haiti to the lack of response on Rwanda, said, "In my constituency, I'm the
first to admit that the primary focus is on Haiti. You have to remember that
I come from south Florida, and . . . we have suffered the mega shocks of refugee influx. Africa seems so far away, and there is no vital interest that my
constituency sees."[75] Rep. Maxine Waters (D-CA) was even more blunt: "I
don't know whether the Hutus or the Tutsis were correct. I couldn't tell any-
body what I thought they should do." She added, "a lot of people were like
me; they didn't know from crap."[76] Thus, as roughly 8,000 Tutsi were murdered every week, America's black leadership focused on Haitian refugees.

Darfur

Over three years, a war in the Darfur region of Sudan killed at least 200,000
people and left 2.5 million homeless. The United Nations called it "the
world's worst humanitarian crisis" and U.S. Secretary of State Colin Powell
officially labeled it genocide. Kofi Annan, then secretary general of the
United Nations, classified the conflict in Darfur as a threat to international

peace and security, providing international legal justification for intervention. Yet the Sudanese government rejected or refused to implement U.N. recommendations and the slaughter continued, claiming by some estimates 10,000 lives per month.[77]

Following Rwanda, political elites including President George W. Bush vowed such atrocities would "not occur on my watch." Scholars attempted to establish clear criteria for humanitarian intervention. These include: (1) the existence of gross, systematic, and pervasive human rights abuses; (2) posing a threat to international peace and security in the region; (3) military intervention must be feasible and used as a last resort; and (4) the region in question must be of a vital interest, for cultural, strategic, or geopolitical reasons to one powerful nation and not opposed by another powerful nation.[78] The crisis in Darfur easily meets the first three criteria; however, the fourth—often implicit—criterion seems to present an insurmountable obstacle.

Although most Americans would not label Darfur as vital to the national interest, and only about one-third follow events there closely,[79] a series of public opinion polls shows majority support for military intervention. A PIPA–Knowledge Networks survey in December 2004 found 74 percent of Americans favored U.N. intervention with military force to stop the genocide in Darfur. Sixty percent believed the United States should be willing to contribute troops to a U.N. operation. The figures were nearly the same for a July 2004 poll.[80] In April 2007, a World Public Opinion poll reported that 68 percent of Americans favored military intervention including U.S. troops, but the figure fell to 45 percent two months later.[81]

Despite public support and congressional pressure, the U.S. government has not embraced military intervention. Sudan, which was host to Osama bin Laden in the 1990s, cut its ties after the terrorist attacks of September 11, 2001, and became a U.S. ally in the "war on terror." The CIA reopened its Khartoum station, and General Gosh who controls the Janjaweed (the Sudanese paramilitary responsible for major human rights violations) also commutes to Washington on CIA airplanes for intelligence meetings. Thus the United States does appear to have a vital interest in maintaining the current government in Khartoum.[82]

The United States also has a national interest in maintaining good relations with China. China, and to a lesser extent Russia, has major oil interests in Sudan and has blocked stronger U.N. action on Darfur. In addition, the Arab and Islamic bloc have strongly supported Sudan, unlike their position in the Bosnian war.[83]

Conclusion

What lessons can we draw from South Africa and Rwanda for Darfur? Donald Culverson has ascribed the success of the anti-apartheid movement to three factors: (1) structural economic changes in the United States that magnified the value of critical expertise on Africa; (2) the expansion of a socio-demographic base of activism; and (3) the diffusion of resources and constituencies across borders.[84] Yet all these factors were present in 1994 and still failed to influence U.S. policy toward Rwanda.

Black action on Haiti provides an answer. David Dickson focuses on such ethnic variables as ethnic constituency mobilization and electoral impact in his examination of lobbying on foreign policy.[85] It seems clear from the examples of South Africa and Haiti, and the counter-case of Rwanda, that a sense of racial injustice is the key to mobilizing both black elites and the rank and file. Darfur would appear to resemble Rwanda in that it represents black-on-black human rights violations. Moreover, when combined with the absence of longstanding personal or institutional links to African Americans, there is no consensus to act. The noticeable lack of African American involvement in the unfolding tragedy in Darfur raises real questions about Pan-African solidarity in particular and African American commitment to human rights in general.

Even with a historical connection to black America, mass action to pressure the U.S. government to act does not appear to be decisive. When civil war led to massive human rights violations in Liberia and Sierra Leone in the 1990s, the United States was largely silent. The black lobbying that occurred was primarily on the wrong side. Rev. Jesse Jackson and Rep. Donald Payne (D-NJ), then CBC chair, for example, encouraged President Clinton to support Charles Taylor's efforts to control Liberia.[86] Taylor is currently on trial in The Hague for gross human rights violations.

Literally millions of African Americans are descended from the ethnic groups in Sierra Leone and Liberia—two countries established for, and for most of their histories controlled by, ex-slave elites. The noticeable lack of African American involvement in these two countries with so many historic ties to the United States does not bode well for mass black pressure to end the tragedy unfolding in Darfur.

Ironically, at a time when cultural Pan-Africanism is as widespread as ever in the form of world music, hip hop, and Afrocentrism, progressive political Pan-Africanism is in a state of flux. It remains to be seen whether the Kenyan roots of Barack Obama will translate into a new sense of Pan-African consciousness among African Americans. Even in the humanitarian efforts directed toward Africa, the black faces of 1985's "We Are the World" concert have been largely replaced by white entertainers. The most visible black representatives on foreign policy—Powell and Rice—have supported policies that undercut development, democracy, and human rights. Powell was the foremost American voice in selling the Iraq war at the United Nations and Rice was the major author of the Bush administration's doctrine of military preemption. Powell was booed at the 2002 World Summit on Sustainable Development, and only one one-hundredth of one percent of the U.S. budget is spent on aid to sub-Saharan Africa. Powell also headed the Presidential Commission for Assistance to a Free Cuba. Rice even backed away from Powell's declaration of genocide in Rwanda, stating that the issue must be studied to see if acts of genocide had occurred. Rice sat on Chevron's board of directors and chaired its Committee on Public Policy from 1999 to 2000, opposing any resolutions dealing with the environment and human rights concerns in Nigeria. She undercut Haiti's Aristide by threatening Jamaica and other Caribbean governments that offered to harbor him. Yet in November 2007 *Ebony* magazine ran a flattering story on Rice, interviewing her at the State Department. Right-wing black Republican organizations such as Project 21 provided cover for Rice and Powell and attacked black leaders such as Jesse Jackson. Other conservative black Republicans, such as Ohio's Ken Blackwell, served the Bush administration in key human rights posts in Geneva.[87]

What is needed is a new self-critical Pan-Africanism—the type of Pan-Africanism promoted not by Richberg but by Walter Rodney that analyzed the class nature of state power. One that takes into account the perspective from below rather than the elite level.[88] A Pan-Africanism that includes the 150 million South Americans of African descent. Only this kind of Pan-Africanism can generate the will to do anything about events such as those in Darfur or in Africa as a whole.

NOTES

1. Samuel P. Huntington, "The Clash of Civilizations," *Foreign Affairs* 72, no. 3 (Summer 1993): 8.
2. See, for example, Abdul Aziz Said, *Ethnicity and U.S. Foreign Policy* (New York: Praeger, 1981); Paul Y. Watanabe, *Ethnic Groups, Congress, and American Foreign Policy* (Westport, Conn.: Greenwood, 1984); George W. Shepherd, Jr., ed., *Racial Influences on American Foreign Policy* (New York: Basic Books, 1970); Alexander DeConde, *Ethnicity, Race, and American Foreign Policy* (Boston: Northeastern University Press, 1992).
3. Richard Payne, *The Clash with Distant Cultures* (Albany: State University of New York Press, 1995), 5.

4. Tony Smith, *Foreign Attachments: The Power of Ethnic Groups in the Making of American Foreign Policy* (Cambridge, Mass.: Harvard University Press, 2000), passim.

5. Following the lead of the late Cheikh Anta Diop, who argued for the cultural unity of black Africa, Afrocentrists have extended the cultural reach of Egypt to include African Americans. If true, these cultural ties remain subconscious since African American public opinion does not demonstrate affective links to Egypt. See Cheikh Anta Diop, *The Cultural Unity of Black Africa* (Chicago: Third World Press, 1978), and Molefi Kete Asante, *Kemet, Afrocentricity and Knowledge* (Trenton, N.J.: Africa World Press, 1990).

6. Kenneth Longmyer, "Black American Demands," *Foreign Policy* 60 (Fall 1985): 6–7. As late as 1998 only 2.8 percent of the Foreign Service Corps was African American. See Hanes Walton, Jr., and Robert C. Smith, *American Politics and the African American Quest for Universal Freedom* (New York: Longman, 2000), 280.

7. Elliott P. Skinner, *African Americans and U.S. Policy toward Africa 1850–1924* (Washington, D.C.: Howard University Press, 1992), 10.

8. See Brenda Gayle Plummer, *Rising Wind: Black Americans and U.S. Foreign Affairs, 1935–1960* (1996); Mary L. Dudzick, *Cold War Civil Rights: Race and the Image of American Democracy* (2000); Penny M. Von Eschen, *Race against Empire: Black Americans and Anticolonialism, 1937–1957* (1997); Gerald Horne, *Black and Red: W. E. B. Dubois and the Afro-American Response to the Cold War* (1986); Jeff Woods, *Black Struggle, Red Scare: Segregation and Anti-Communism in the South, 1948–1968* (2004); Kevin L. Gaines, *American Africans in Ghana: Black Expatriates and the Civil Rights Era* (2006); and James H. Meriwether, *Proudly We Can Be Africans: Black Americans and Africa, 1935–1961* (2002).

9. Athletes and entertainers were often asked to do diplomatic work in Africa. When President Jimmy Carter sent Muhammad Ali to an important meeting of African leaders in Tanzania, President Nyerere cited his presence as inappropriate and refused to recognize him.

10. Keith B. Richburg, *Out of America: A Black Man Confronts Africa* (New York: Basic Books, 1997), 49. See also James Campbell, *Middle Passages: African American Journeys to Africa 1787–2005* (New York: Penguin, 2006), 382.

11. See Tunde Adeleke, "Black Americans and Africa: A Critique of the Pan-African and Identity Paradigms," *International Journal of African Historical Studies* 31, no. 3 (1998): 505–36; and Wilson Jeremiah Moses, *The Golden Age of Black Nationalism, 1850–1925* (New York: Oxford University Press, 1978).

12. See Paul Gordon Lauren, *Power and Prejudice: The Politics and Diplomacy of Racial Discrimination* (Boulder, Colo.: Westview Press, 1996).

13. Robert C. Smith and Richard Seltzer, *Contemporary Controversies and the American Racial Divide* (Lanham, Md.: Rowman & Littlefield, 2000), 42–44.

14. Nikongo BaNikongo, ed., *Leading Issues in African-American Studies* (Durham, N.C.: Carolina Academic Press, 1997), 624.

15. Alvin B. Tillery, Jr., "Black Americans and the Creation of America's Africa Policies: The De-Racialization of Pan-African Politics," in *The African Diaspora: Old World Origins and New World Self-Fashioning*, ed. Carol Boyce Davies et al. (Bloomington: Indiana University Press, 2001).

16. Ibid., 518.

17. Masipula Sithole, "Black Americans and United States Policy towards Africa," *African Affairs* 85, no. 340 (July 1986): 325–50.

18. Tillery, "Black Americans and the Creation of America's Africa Policies," 518.

19. Ibid.

20. Anthony W. Marx, *Making Race and Nation: A Comparison of South Africa, the United States and Brazil,* (Cambridge: Cambridge University Press, 1998), 195. See also George M. Fredrickson, *Black Liberation* (New York: Oxford University Press, 1995).

21. Skinner, *African Americans and U.S. Policy toward Africa 1850-1924,* 181–94.

22. Charles P. Henry, *Ralph Bunche: Model Negro or American Other?* (New York: New York University Press, 1999), 83.

23. Francis Njubi Nesbitt, *Race for Sanctions: African Americans against Apartheid, 1946– 1994* (Bloomington: Indiana University Press, 2004), 4–6. See also Paul Gordon Lauren, *Power and Prejudice: The Politics of Diplomacy and Racial Discrimination* (Boulder, Colo.: Westview, 1996), 180–83.

24. Nesbitt, *Race for Sanctions,* 30–32.

25. According to Nesbitt, the new organization was more broadly based but more conservative than the CAA. Ibid., 46. See also Frederic I. Solop, "African Americans Confront Apartheid," in *Minority Group Influence,* ed. Paula D. McClain (Westport, Conn.: Greenwood, 1993), 59.

26. Lauren, *Power and Prejudice,* 276. Of the three U.N.–sponsored global conferences on racism—1978, 1983, and 2001—the United States has not attended any. In 1978 and 1983, it objected to the emphasis on South African apartheid. In 2001, the post-apartheid South African government hosted the conference, and the United States refused to participate due to a focus on reparations and Palestine.

27. Nesbitt, *Race for Sanctions,* 51.

28. Solop, "African Americans Confront Apartheid," 60–61.

29. Nesbitt, *Race for Sanctions,* 78–85.

30. Ibid., 83.

31. Ibid., 73.

32. Tillery, "Black Americans and the Creation of America's Africa Policies," 507. After his appointment as a full delegate to the U.N. General Assembly in 1971, Charles Diggs, Jr., created a sensation by becoming the first U.S. delegate to resign his post. Nesbitt, *Race for Sanctions,* 94.

33. Komozi Woodard, *A Nation within a Nation* (Chapel Hill: University of North Carolina Press, 1999), 175–76.

34. Ibid., 97–99; and Solop, "African Americans Confront Apartheid," 62–63.

35. Woodard, *A Nation within a Nation,* 114.

36. Lauren, *Power and Prejudice,* 284.

37. Nesbitt, *Race for Sanctions,* 133. See also Robert E. Edgar, ed., *Sanctioning Apartheid* (Trenton, N.J.: Africa World Press, 1990); and Winston P. Nagan, "Sanctions, Black America, and Apartheid," in *Foreign Policy and the Black (Inter)national Interest,* ed. Charles P. Henry (Albany: State University of New York Press, 2000), 119–30.

38. In addition to economic sanctions, the bill also prescribed political action, including the end to the state of emergency and release of political prisoners such as Nelson Mandela; the unbanning of liberation organizations; the revocation of the Group Areas Act and the Population Registration Act; full citizenship for blacks; and international

mediation leading to a power-sharing arrangement with the black majority. See Nagan, "Sanctions, Black America, and Apartheid,"126. The administration was slow to enforce the act, and stronger legislation was not approved by the next Congress.

39. Lauren, *Power and Prejudice,* 280.

40. See Shepherd, *Racial Influences on American Foreign Policy,* 225–27.

41. The poll found 67 percent of blacks and 51 percent of whites favored U.S. government action to end apartheid. Given Israel's links to the apartheid regime, the opposition of Jews to action may not be so surprising. See Milfred C. Fierce, "Black and White American Opinions towards South Africa," *Journal of Modern African Studies* 20, no. 4 (1982): 677 and 683.

42. Donald R. Kinder and Lynn M. Sanders, *Divided by Color: Racial Politics and Democratic Ideals* (Chicago: University of Chicago Press, 1996), 30.

43. Smith and Seltzer, *Contemporary Controversies and the American Racial Divide,* 43.

44. Samantha Power, *A Problem from Hell: America and the Age of Genocides* (New York: Harper Collins, 2002), 352.

45. Alsion Des Forges, *Leave None to Tell the Story: Genocide in Rwanda* (New York: Human Rights Watch, 1999), 31–33.

46. Ibid., 34–37.

47. Ibid., 39–40.

48. Ibid., 43.

49. An abridged version of the ten commandments includes the following elements: (1) suggests all Tutsi women are traitors and any Hutu who has relations with them is a traitor; (2) promotes the value of Hutu women; (3) encourages Hutu women to bring their husbands, brothers, and sons back to reason; (4) labels any Hutu who does business with a Tutsi a traitor; (5) entrusts all strategic positions to Hutu; (6) entrusts a majority of the education sector to Hutu; (7) says the Rwandese Armed Forces should be exclusively Hutu; (8) states Hutu should have no mercy on Tutsi; (9) calls for Hutu solidarity; and (10) calls for the teaching of Hutu ideology at every level. See Power, *A Problem from Hell,* 338–39.

50. John Shattuck, *Freedom on Fire: Human Rights Wars and Americas Response* (Cambridge, Mass.: Harvard University Press, 2003), 30–31; and Rene Lemarchand, "Managing Transition Anarchies," *Journal of Modern African Studies* 32, no. 4 (December 1994): 591–92.

51. Power, *A Problem from Hell,* 43; and Adam Le Bor, *Complicity with Evil: The U.N. in the Age of Modern Genocide* (New Haven: Yale University Press, 2006), 167–69.

52. Ibid., 176. LeBor reports that even the small number of remaining U.N. forces were able to save hundreds of lives.

53. Testimony of Jeff Drumtra of the U.S. Committee on Refugees, Subcommittee on African Affairs of Senate Foreign Relations Committee, Washington, D.C., July 26, 1994, p. 3.

54. Power, *A Problem from Hell,* xvii–xviii.

55. Ibid., 325.

56. Ibid., 352.

57. J. Brian Atwood, quoted in "U.S. Steps Up Rwandan Relief as Lawmakers Assail Race," *Congressional Quarterly,* July 30, 1994, 2158.

58. Power, *A Problem from Hell,* 377.

59. Time/CNN, Rwanda Poll, May 16, 1994, accessed at http://poll.orspub.com.

60. Times Mirror, Rwanda Poll, May 19, 1994, accessed at http://poll.orspub.com.

61. NBC News/Wall Street Journal, Rwanda Poll, June 1994, accessed at http://poll.orspub.com.

62. Time/CNN, Rwanda Poll, August 8, 1994, accessed at http://poll.orspub.com.

63. Shattuck, *Freedom on Fire*, 25.

64. Ibid., 43.

65. Power, *A Problem from Hell*, 359.

66. Ibid., 361–63.

67. Ibid., 293.

68. PDD 25 lists eighteen factors for U.S. policymakers to consider when determining whether to support a U.N. peacekeeping resolution in the U.N. Security Council. Nine guidelines are for when no U.S. soldiers are involved and nine more rigorous guidelines would allow U.S. participation. Shattuck, *Freedom on Fire*, 342. Clarke's negative views on peacekeeping were shared by Colin Powell, former NSC administrator and chair of the Joint Chiefs of Staff under George H. W. Bush.

69. Dick Kirschten, "Focus—OK, Back in the Bottle!" *National Journal*, July 23, 1994, 1.

70. Ibid.

71. Shattuck, *Freedom on Fire*, 99–109.

72. Smith and Seltzer, *Contemporary Controversies and the American Racial Divide*, 57.

73. Power, *A Problem from Hell*, 375.

74. Ronald V. Dellums and H. Lee Halterman, *Lying Down with the Lions* (Boston: Beacon Press, 2000), 187.

75. Power, *A Problem from Hell*, 374.

76. Ibid.

77. See, for example, "A New Sudan Action Plan," International Crisis Group, Africa Briefing No. 24, Nairobi/Brussels, April 26, 2005; Dinaw Mengestu, "The Tragedy of Darfur," *Rolling Stone*, September 21, 2006; "Report of the High-Level Mission on the Situation of Human Rights in Darfur," U.N. Human Rights Council, A/HRC/4/80, March 7, 2007; and LeBor, *Complicity with Evil*.

78. Michael Ignatieff, *Human Rights as Politics and Idolatry* (Princeton, N.J.: Princeton University Press, 2001), 40. See also Debra L. Delaet, *The Global Struggle for Human Rights* (Belmont, Calif.: Thomson Wadsworth, 2006), 150–53.

79. Pew Research Center, Darfur, Sudan Poll, December 6–10, 2006, accessed at http://poll.orspub.com.

80. PIPA/Knowledge networks, "Three Out of Four Americans Favor UN Military Intervention in Darfur," July 2004 and December 2004, accessed at http://poll.orspub.com.

81. World Public Opinion, Darfur, Sudan Poll, April 2007 and June 2007, accessed at http://poll.orspub.

82. LeBor, *Complicity with Evil*, 224.

83. Ibid., 205–6.

84. Donald R. Culverson, "From Cold War to Global Interdependence," in *Window on Freedom*, ed. Brenda Gayle Plummer (Chapel Hill: University of North Carolina Press, 2003), 221–38.

85. David A. Dickson, "American Society and the African American Foreign Policy Lobby," *Journal of Black Studies* 27, no. 2 (November 1996): 139–51.

86. James Campbell, *Middle Passages: African American Journeys to Africa, 1787–2005* (New York: Penguin, 2006), 417.

87. See Clarence Lusane, *Colin Powell and Condoleezza Rice: Foreign Policy, Race, and the New American Century* (Westport, Conn.: Praeger, 2006), passim.

88. See Walter Rodney's introduction to *Resolutions and Selected Speeches from the Sixth Pan African Congress* (Dar es Salaam: Tanzania Publishing House, 1976), 21–34.

PART III

Transnational Activism and Globalization

NINE

The Looming Quest for Global Reparations

AFRICAN AMERICANS AND
THE WORLD CONFERENCE AGAINST RACISM

Ife Williams

Ever since the first African was ripped from the shores of the continent, the global aspirations of people of African descent have been characterized by two perennial themes: returning to a pre-holocaust state and unification of all Africans who underwent a similar fate. At present, that politic is evidenced in "global reparations," the utilization of Pan-Africanism, "the total liberation of African people everywhere they live on the face of the earth" (Clark, 1973, 32), and the provision of reparations as the economic, social, and spiritual means to sustain development. African descendants throughout the Diaspora have historically participated in international conferences to elucidate the contradictory nature of human rights atrocities of the slave trade, slavery, colonialism, segregation, apartheid, and genocide.[1] By focusing attention on those actors who proclaim democracy, freedom, and fraternity, it was hoped that the aggressors would be pressured to abandon such practices and make restitution for the present dire social, political, and economic conditions that exist as a direct consequence of those gross violations of humanity. The World Conference against Racism, Xenophobia, and Related Intolerance (wcar) in 2001 offered that opportunity. Even more, at the conference the issue of reparations for African descendants was debated and legitimated by the international community. The significance of addressing this issue is that the effects of the transatlantic slave trade, slavery, and colonialism persist at present and continue to be sources of systemic discrimination, marginalization, poverty and exclusion that still adversely impacts African descendants throughout the Diaspora."[2]

This chapter examines the role of African Americans, via the African

225

Descendants Caucus (ADC) at WCAR, in having the transatlantic slave trade and slavery declared crimes against humanity, thus establishing the legal foundation to move into the next phase of "compensation." Under investigation here is the process that informed this historic mandate, the guiding definitions of reparations that were advanced, the nature of the opposition, and the political navigation of the caucus to establish this universal precedent for global reparations.

Background to Conference

In the early 1990s, several nongovernmental organizations (NGOs) dominated by African Americans, including the December 12th Movement (D-12), along with selected African governments, successfully lobbied the United Nations to hold the Third World Conference against Racism. It is believed that those African governments shifted the reparations movement "from a demand of Diaspora blacks for restitution in their own countries to a new worldwide crusade for reparations for the African and black world as a whole" (Mazrui, 1994, 4). In 1993, the Organization of African Unity (OAU) charged a group of persons, under the chairmanship of Chief Bashorun M. K. O. Abiola, to investigate reparations for enslavement, colonialism, and its aftermath. Their findings delineated two forms of reparations, nonmonetary and financial (primarily through debt forgiveness). The major goal and related strategy concerned empowerment of African states, inclusive of women, to become stronger, autonomous players in the global community. They also recommended the "Middle Passage Plan": skills transfer, direct power transfer or power sharing, and giving African countries in total a veto on the Security Council of the United Nations that would facilitate including "Africa in the mainstream of global decision-making after centuries of deprivation" (Mazrui, 1994, 7). In 1998 the African Group unanimously called for a U.N. resolution declaring the transatlantic slave trade and slavery crimes against humanity. As such, statutes of limitation would not apply. The Senegalese chair of the group withdrew the resolution after international pressure, but the group resolved to have it reintroduced at WCAR (Wareham, 2003). The major difficulty here that evolved up through the 2001 world conference in deliberations with the African governments was their reliance on the West to provide "freedom for opposition" that is inherently antithetical to Western interests. The International Secretariat of D-12, as reported by Roger Wareham, began their efforts for a world conference on racism at the U.N. Commission on Human Rights in 1989 and at the U.N. World Conference on Human Rights in 1993. During this process colonialism was added as constituting many crimes against humanity (Wareham, 2003, 231).

Historically, the United Nations has served as the international venue to organize around redress from racism because of its proclamations against human rights violations. Opting to use the structures, guidelines, and language of the West to remedy harms inflicted in the pursuit of their interests automatically compromises the analysis of the causes of oppression and strategic maneuvers for redress. An underlying principle of liberalism holds that the process of dividing functions creates some semblance of a democracy (Parenti, 1973). U.N. conferences are segmented into a number of preparatory meetings that are document driven, thus resulting in notable disconnects and replications. The name of the proceedings alone suggested an epistemological concern that shaped the efforts of the Conference against Racism, Xenophobia, and Related Intolerance. It blurred the distinction between those victimized by specific economic historical circumstances, such as the transatlantic slave trade, slavery, and colonialism, with those alienated by cultural, social, and inherent physical limitations. The name also represented a compromise by the West to allow the proceedings in an effort to dilute the race question (Wareham, 2001).

Preparation for the U.N. World Conference against Racism, Xenophobia, and Related Intolerance (WCAR) spanned a two-year period beginning in 1999 and culminated in Durban, South Africa, with over seven thousand participants.[3] One year prior to Durban there was a press conference in Washington, D.C., led by U.S. African American government spokesperson Deborah Carr, who presented an optimistic posture for U.S. involvement, complete with the offering up of Colin Powell as the diplomatic liaison for the U.S. government at the conference. In attendance were representatives from NGOs, the civil society, the academy, and the media who came together to discern the U.S. position. Although this was the third world conference on racism, it was the first one in which the United States agreed to participate.[4] President Bush inherited this agreement from President Clinton, and it became clear that the Bush administration wanted to distance itself from the outset.

This U.N. conference on racism was also the first that garnered massive involvement by NGOs from throughout the world. Formal world political institutions had shifted away from "grassroots" participation in international affairs; however, the United Nations altered its usual protocol and opened up to NGOs without consultative status (Lusane, 2004). The Non-Governmental Organizations Forum was charged with developing documents assessing the issues and a program of action to address the conference themes that could assist the governments.[5] The civic community was presented with a one-year time constraint to educate, mobilize, and ensure participation of their constituents. The American Friends Service Center (AFSC), through its Third World Coalition Office, was one of the few NGOs that went beyond raising their issues to serving as an agency to unite other NGOS. AFSC established a global network through an NGO coordinating committee that met at every juncture of the process to strategize, and later it served to facilitate the mandate of the African Descendants Caucus.

The African/African Descendants Caucus

An ad hoc meeting was organized at the First Preparatory Conference (Prepcom) session in Geneva, Switzerland, in May 2000 at the behest of December 12th Movement, Black United Front, National Coalition of Blacks for Reparations in America (N'COBRA),[6] and other NGOs[7] in which the African/African Descendants Caucus was formed. Its members were drawn from NGOs in continental Africa, Europe, Canada, United States, Latin America, Central America, and the Caribbean, and claimed representation of "approximately 200 million persons in the Americas and Europe whose ancestors were victims of the transatlantic slave trade, slavery and colonialism."[8] The group "worked valiantly to overcome differences of language and culture" that could have been divisive, as they adhered to the principle of unity, "recognizing that . . . similarities outweigh any differences that may exist."[9] Most of the African Descendants were new to the U.N. process, so in addition to following the mandates of the particular represented interests, there was a humbling factor of having to learn and navigate proper protocol. Those who were familiar with the United Nations assumed a position of leadership in briefing the group but had little impact on the agenda.

One critique of the caucus was that African Americans dominated it particularly in terms of logistics, as the meetings and all the ensuing documents were in English and the majority of the participants were from the United States. In an effort to make the caucus more responsive to African descendants throughout the Diaspora, a motion was made to have the meetings and documents translated into French, Spanish, and Portuguese and to be more inclusive of representatives from those countries; however, those members never gained full ownership of the caucus and were challenged when incorporating their country-based concerns (Cabral, 2007).

The discussions regarding the depth and manifestations of racism took into consideration geographical location, historical era, resource imperatives, and strategic viability.[10] These debates induced a sensitivity to resist imposition of the U.S. race model on other countries and ethnic groupings

by the caucus. Although the methods and timing of race-based global oppression differed according to nation-states, the impact was/is the same,
thus rendering a common remedy, reparations.[11] Some African descendants who did not reside in the United States generally viewed reparations
as a U.S. issue. For example, the Afro-Brazilians were focused on the extension of civil rights through affirmative action.

The guiding theory developed through the entire process was linking
the present crisis of African descendants to the slave trade, slavery, and
colonialism in general, and then explicitly detailing the vestiges of exploitation in the criminal justice system, education, housing, employment,
health, media, environment, and the condition of the youth. The caucus
emphasized the lasting effects on the Africans and African descendants, in
psychological spheres as well as economic, social, political, and cultural
ones.

Much of the debate concerning reparations among the social activists
revolved around definition. If presented as a singular issue, would it be able
to withstand incorporating all other issues within it or should it be woven
into those identified areas? The tendency lent itself to the creation of a
mono-issue that led to antagonism and competition with other ethnic
groups, in particular indigenous populations, where the weighing of subjugation occurred. This process was referred to as "Oppression Olympics,"
when in essence all the African descendants suffered and established the
baseline for the oppression of other people.[12] The narrow definition of reparations, as opposed to compensatory measures, led to theoretical problems of analyzing race and the intersection of poverty, gender, historical
context, and so forth. Another quandary was present-day slave trade and
slavery in Sudan, Chad, and Mauritania, and the desire to merge this with
the transatlantic slave trade. Also, by definition, would not human trafficking and migratory labor be considered under the rubric of the slave trade?
Further, would the conditions under which forced labor is extracted be
indicative of contemporary manifestations of slavery?

Throughout the process the caucus worked closely with government del-
egations from Africa, especially South Africa, Ghana, Nigeria, and Kenya.[13]
"At the request of the Africa group, a short document was prepared . . . that
summarized the history of the use of reparations and its importance to the
success of WCAR.[14] Two committees were later organized that functioned
for the duration of the conference: the Drafting Committee and the Strategy and Lobbying Committee.[15] Research ensued on former U.N. resolutions around racism to extract related protocol and proceedings that were
then translated for non-English-speaking African descendants.

The caucus was briefed by D-12 concerning its activities to have the transatlantic slave trade, slavery, and colonialism declared crimes against humanity, as it later became the major focus. The companion issue was the provision of "reparations and compensatory measures" for the Africans and African descendants for resultant injuries suffered.[16] It was agreed that the caucus would lobby member states around these defined issues, monitor all the proceedings, have representation on speaker lists, and schedule report-back sessions to the larger body and align with other NGO caucuses.

Historical, regional, and strategic factors were involved in forming alliances with groups that did not particularly identify themselves as African Descendants, but who suffered from extreme race-based discrimination. These groups, particularly the Dalits and Palestinians, saw the African Americans as a strong lobby and believed their success in raising their issues was contingent upon support from that caucus. A statement by Fundación Ideas, an NGO representing Latin America and the Caribbean, proclaimed: "it is the indigenous people and the people of African descent who need to lead the struggle against racism."[17] Meetings were held with representatives from the African descendants, indigenous populations, Dalits, Palestinians, Btwah, women, Afro-Brazilians, the Sudanese, and other groups around the question of compensation. In practically every meeting there were government representatives posing as civic organizations (so-called "gongos"), in full denial of any racism or unequal treatment in their countries. Some African American participants believed their positions were relegated to the demands and interests of competing constituencies. One of the more emotionally charged meetings took place with the indigenous people of North America, where the legacy of African Americans' collusion with whites to exterminate their populations remains.

Compensation vs. Reparations

The next meeting of the full caucus was held at the Americas Preparatory Conference in Santiago, Chile, in December 2001. The level of analysis became more poignant as it informed strategic lobbying to incorporate language into the NGO and government documents. The Americas meeting was originally scheduled to be held in Brazil, but after massive protests against Christopher Columbus Day, the government withdrew in alignment with its denial of racism in Brazil. However, the Brazilians had over 160 representatives under the coordinative social activist group, Alianza Estratejeca Afro Latino y Caribena in Santiago. Meetings were held where common objectives and accompanying strategies were developed to lend communal support in their attainment. The first formal act was in response to theme number four of the conference, which stated: "Provision for effective remedies, recourses, redress, [compensatory] and other measures at the national, regional and international levels."

A written request was made by Adjoa Aiyetoro, a representative of the Women's International League for Peace and Freedom (WILPF), endorsed by thirty-nine NGOs and eleven individuals from the Caribbean, Central America, North America, and South America, to remove the square brackets around the word "compensatory," an indication that a consensus could not be reached by the government representatives to allow for a full exploration of all forms of remedies, including reparations. U.N. recognition of compensatory remedies for groups was cited as the legal precedent, and to limit dialogue of such "belies this history and severely restricts a full and meaningful discussion of effective remedies." The request also linked current oppression to historical enslavement that further diminished fundamental rights and freedoms, thereby holding that "it is critical that the delegates be able to fully examine and recommend appropriate and adequate remedies for these egregious human rights violations." A bibliography on the "importance of compensatory remedies to fully and adequately redress the violations of human rights that flow from racism" was also provided.[18] It was at this juncture that the ADC claimed full membership as an integral part of the process. The heightened passion in the collaboration that ensued is evidenced in the positions of the ADC in the first three of ten points for inclusion in the Declaration and Program of Action.[19]

1. We call for the recognition that the slave trade, slavery and colonialism are crimes against humanity.
2. We call for the recognition of Reparations for Africans and African Descendants as essential to ending the inequality derived from the Slave Trade, Slavery and Colonialism.
3. We call for the recognition of the economic basis of racism as a continuation of the economic basis of the Slave Trade, Slavery and Colonialism.[20]

The African descendants were further encouraged by Pitso Motwedi, political counselor from the Permanent Mission of South Africa, who stated that the African governments had made global reparations a priority. Motwedi requested the assistance of African Americans to provide more historical and empirical data to support the position of compensation since "reparations" were severed from the historical experience of the slave and colonial eras at the African expert meeting, held in Addis Ababa, Ethiopia, October 4–6, 2000. One of the many obstacles facing the African governments was the question of the categorization of "tribal warfare" and civil strife as evidence of internal racism, thereby negating reparations. Those phenomena were then dissociated from the former colonizers by not taking into account underlying cleavages that caused ethnic conflict.[21]

It was clear that there would be strong opposition from the United States and European countries over the issue of compensation; however, the caucus believed its coalitions with African and Caribbean governments and NGOs could provide a formidable offense. "At the outset some of the major European nationalists led by Belgium were open to the idea of formally apologizing to those victimized by slavery. However, Britain, backed by three other former enslavement nations, Holland, Spain, and Portugal, officially objected to a formal apology, stating that it could leave the government open to a lawsuit" (Christian, 2002, 181). Wareham holds that the United States in alignment with Canada changed its tactics to pressure Latin America and the Caribbean countries to weaken language around compensatory measures, in exchange for U.S. agreement to a consensus document (Wareham, 2003, 233).

The opposition to redressing those victimized by slavery, slave trade, and colonialism was successful in altering the definition of reparations as distinct from compensatory measures and making the two synonymous. The significance is that any formal government efforts directed toward racism, such as civil rights legislation, affirmative action, or truth and reconciliation could be considered reparations. There was even an attempt by the United States and its allies to view the aforementioned as models of "best practices," those actions to remedy injustices of a nation-state that can be replicated throughout the world. The context of the language was further deranged by an attempt to separate compensatory measures from the African holocaust. The African American U.S. ambassador, Betty King, announced, "the U.S. could not support discussion of the term compensatory measures if used in the same context as the transatlantic slave trade, slavery and colonialism." "The United States urge[d] the governments and us to accept the revisionist view that these reprehensible systems of murder, torture, kidnap and physical, emotional and spiritual defilement were not at the time of their commission crimes against humanity."[22]

This dissociation and contextual manipulation of language became major obstacles to the African Descendants Caucus, which viewed the transatlantic slave trade, slavery, and colonialism as the legitimate justification for redress. The basis of the analysis is that the present conditions of those victimized by such heinous acts were caused and are maintained by those horrific practices. However, "the governments and their allies" remained "consistent in blocking any language that would characterize the[se] tragedies . . . as the crimes against humanity that noted historians, political leaders and national and international forums have acknowledged these practices were."[23]

African NGO Forum

In order to assist in provision of language to the governments and to align with African NGOs, the caucus decided to have representation at the Non-Governmental Organization Forum in Botswana and the African Governments meeting in Dakar in January 2001. The role of the United Nations Non-Governmental Organizations liaison office in quelling the radicalization of the process became painfully evident in Botswana. The African NGOs invited were politically moderate and had their travel financed by the U.N. NGO office, thereby facilitating an unofficial allegiance to their directives. It was clear that the NGOs were not informed of the conference, the proceedings to date, and what was expected of them at that juncture. More progressive African NGOs had not been contacted by the U.N. NGO liaison officer; only select NGOs and others with Internet access were notified. The first order of business, as defined by the U.N. NGO representative, was to discard the African government document and dismiss the question of reparations. The reticence of the African NGOs towards reparations was twofold: first, they were wary of corruption by African governments, as this could be a scheme for them to further enrich themselves. Second, was the questionable nature of relationships between African governments and the West: how would such an endorsement affect already tenuous alliances? These concerns were shared by the caucus, as evidenced in the statement that "the right to life and freedom of African people is being regularly violated with complete indifference in Western countries and by African dictators who are very often supported and protected by Western countries."[24] Reparations was then minimized as a subordinate issue but after much lobbying was included in the Botswana African NGO document as such:

> ACKNOWLEDGE the traumatic effects of historical trans-Atlantic slave trade, traditional and contemporary forms of slavery and bondage that continue to haunt the victims and arrest their ability to achieve their full potential as equal citizens of the world and condemn the attitudes and indifference of the international community who continue to ignore the practice of contemporary forms of slavery.[25]

What is interesting here is that the African NGOs merge transatlantic slave trade with present-day slave trade and slavery, with the former being a precipitant of current atrocities. In their recommendations, they state:

> Accept the right of the African peoples of the continent and in the Diaspora, to just and fair compensatory measures that include reparations, apologies, and pledges of non-repetition of outrages suffered by Africans, regardless of who the perpetrators were and call for international cooperation in the achievement of these goals.[26]

A proposal was offered, and defeated, to boycott the upcoming African government meeting in Senegal because of the interchange between the Senegalese government and the United Nations on scheduling and venue. The meeting was held at the same time as the Paris-to-Dakar rally, and the government only guaranteed housing to the African governments, making NGO participation almost impossible.

The African Governments Meeting

In Senegal, in January 2001, President Wade opened the African governments meeting by announcing, "there is no racism in Senegal" against a backdrop of the notorious "door of no return" on Goree island, now a haven for affluent whites. President Wade's assessment indicated that the present conditions of Africans are "human rights" violations and are not a consequence of, or related to, racism. The onus is on the victim to "stop worrying about a practice that has passed" and therefore discard the idea of reparations. He added that he had never personally experienced racism and that France is his friend. The role of Africans in the slave trade was pointed out in order to conclude that it is "Africa [that] has to take responsibility for the slave trade." President Wade called for a compromise on reparations as he made a plea not to let the conference fail over one issue. In spite of President Wade, the African governments, with input from the NGOs, penned the historic Dakar Declaration that held: "the consequences of (slave trade, slavery, colonialism and apartheid) have resulted in substantial and lasting economic, political and cultural damage to African peoples and are still present in the form of damage caused to the descendants of the victims by the perpetuation of prejudice against Africans on the continent and people of African descent in the Diaspora."

In the African governments' Recommendations for a Program of Action, they devised an elaborate international plan to implement reparations through establishment of a fund for colonized countries, having the world conference define the modalities of "reparation and compensation" and "the form that policies by states and private interests that benefitted from said practices should take."[27] It was also at this meeting that we learned of the introduction of NEPAD-New African Initiative: Merger of the Millennium Partnership for African Recovery.[28] This was a pledge by African leaders, spearheaded by Thabo Mbeki of South Africa, to eradicate poverty and participate actively in the world economy by "extricating themselves and the continent from the malaise of underdevelopment and exclusion in a globalizing world." The endorsement of NEPAD corresponded with a retreat by the African governments on the issue of reparations. African descendants refer to this effort as "kneepad," as the African leaders will have to get on their knees for the West to effectuate this plan. After much politicking, the call for reparations remained, but only for the transatlantic slave trade and slavery. Colonialism was taken off the table.

By not appropriating colonialism the status of crime against humanity, ADC suffered a major future litigation defeat, as it is on the African continent that we most witness the disastrous impact of global racism. "The philosophical and tactical brilliance of reparations lies in its synthesis of moral principles and political economy." African subjugation in colonialism and present neocolonialism best exemplify direct economic exploitation and the moral ineptitude of the West to claim responsibility (Biondi, 2003, 5). A statement by the representative of Trinidad and Tobago reads as follows:

> The world conference should acknowledge that differences in ethnic identities have long manifested themselves in diverse ways, but should recognize that the racism of the colonial era constituted an unprecedented system of thought and action that has a specific historical origin in the transatlantic slave trade and the consequent development of the global racial chattel enslavement of Africans. Consequently, doctrines of racial hierarchy were developed that facilitated the commercial and social exploitation of enslaved persons.[29]

The African Descendants penned a section entitled "Restoring Africa, The Motherland," where they addressed the current "plundering of Africa" through the debt crisis; the violations of "life and freedom of African people"; and the negation of African history and values through "cultural imperialism."[30] The present challenge is examination of the causes of socioeconomic subordination as firmly established in the scholarship of underdevelopment analysis (Rodney, 1973; Amin, 1974; Wallerstein, 1986).

African Descendants Vienna Conference

The Caucus realized that beginning with the preparatory meetings in Geneva up to the meeting in Chile, the issue of antiblack racism was being diminished and attention was lent to other forms of discrimination. In order to fully strategize and respond, an African Descendants Coordinating Committee was organized and met in Vienna, Austria, in April 2001.[31] There were approximately 100 participants in attendance, with a strong showing by African Americans. The Vienna Declaration document attests to an in-depth investigation of the ongoing questions. It is at this meeting that contemporary trans-Saharan and trans-Indian Ocean slave trade was incorporated as distinct from transatlantic slave trade and slavery:

> CONDEMNS AFRICAN SLAVERY in all its manifestations (trans-Atlantic, trans-Saharan and trans-Indian Ocean) and calls on the United Nations and the governments of the World to do likewise;
>
> DEMAND THAT THE Governments of the World condemn the trans-Saharan and Indian Ocean slave trade which, like the trans-Atlantic slave trade, brought serious damages to Africa. Unlike the trans-Atlantic slave trade, vestiges of the trans-Saharan slave trade continues this day unabated (specifically in Mauritania and Sudan); and, call on the governments of Mauritania and Sudan to recognize this problem and to eradicate it completely.

They also expanded and specified victims from World War II who have yet to receive compensation for their internment and losses.[32]

> CALL on the German and Italian Government to ask for forgiveness for the exactions and genocide committed during the World War by the Nazis and Fascists against Africans and African descendants; recognizing that African and African descendant victims of Nazism have the same right to compensatory measures as Jews or Romas.

The final nuance of the Vienna Document is its insistence on having those victimized "reserve the right to determine the form and manner of reparations."[33] From the spirit of H.R. 40, legislation introduced in the U.S. Congress by Rep. John Conyers, the African descendants devised in detail the research methodology that would minimize at best racial bias, and offered an accurate appraisal of their overall status. The collection of data through provision of linkages with existing public policy research institutions is also imperative to oversee the implementation and fulfillment of WCAR goals.[34] In the final government document, states were urged to "collect, compile, analyze, disseminate and publish reliable statistical data . . . to assess regularly . . . individuals who are victims of racism."[35]

Expansion of the Caucus Mandate

By May 2001 membership and representation increased as the caucus developed working relationships with African descendants from throughout the Diaspora. The Strategies and Lobbying committees that were organized coordinated meetings with government groups, received documents from other caucuses for endorsement by the African descendants, developed alternative language for government documents, and "added language for topics not covered."[36] African Americans, who represented diverse constituencies, were able to integrate their specific issues, such as women, criminal justice systems, death penalty, environmental racism, cultural restoration, and so forth. In the May 2001 document, women of African descent are highlighted:

> We affirm that the transatlantic slave trade, slavery and colonization has uniquely impacted African and African descendant women whose bodies, familial roles and reproductive ability have been used as a tool of oppression and exploited for the production of economic wealth and whose forced labor under inhumane circumstances and the use of specific negative stereotypes all have been and continue to be used to maintain the subordinate position of African and African descendant women on the bottom of the social, economic, cultural and political system.[37]

This resolution was encompassed in the final document as the member states were convinced of the differential impact on racism for women and girls and recognized the "need to integrate a gender perspective into relevant policies, strategies and programmes of action against racism."[38] Further, it was stated that policies aimed at combating racism be "based on quantitative and qualitative research, incorporating a gender perspective."[39] Additionally, the platform called for the release of those wrongfully imprisoned because they exercised their right to speak out against race, racism, xenophobia, and other intolerances. They also noted the "multiplicity" of racism toward African descendants and held that they cannot be separated from discrimination on other grounds, in particular, sexual orientation.

> The World Conference against Racism, urges States to enact laws that prohibit discrimination and explicitly guarantee and promote the equal

rights of all persons without distinction on any ground including sexual orientation and to adopt programs to implement this guarantee of
equality.

In the African/African Descendants Caucus Proposal for Non-Negotiable
Language appears the concept of "unjust enrichment," a major legal precedent for cases of redress when a group, government, or private interest benefits materially from the oppression of others. This was the argument used
against the Nazis and against the United States for Japanese internment.

> We urge States, institutions, companies and individuals which benefited
> materially and were unjustly enriched from the transatlantic slave trade,
> slavery and colonialism, to contribute to policies, program and measures
> at the institutions, to compensate and repair the damage inflicted on
> the affected communities of Africans and African descendants.

Another dimension of the negative ramifications of the transatlantic slave
trade, slavery, and colonialism is evident in societal relationships "that have
created structural distortions in relationships between them and the descendants of the Americans and Europeans who engaged in these practices."[40] "As a result of this history the superficial differences between ethnic and racial identities have led to deep-seated conflict, lasting distrust
and hatred, guilt and shame."[41]

Durban

A Third Preparatory Conference was held in Geneva, Switzerland, in August 2001, a few weeks before the Non-Governmental Organizations Forum
and the full conference in Durban. The decision was made to form a Coordinating Committee with representatives from the United States, Latin
America, Africa, and Europe.[42] The members wanted the December 12th
Movement on the committee, but that group had been working independently and formed its own coalition called the "Durban 400." The committee met daily from August 27 to September 9, finalizing language and planning activities for the upcoming conferences.

In addition to following the prescribed strategies, the ADC attended a
Maafa ceremony on the edge of the Indian Ocean where libations were
poured and homage paid to the ancestors who were torn from the continent. This was followed by a major demonstration and a candlelight vigil
with the theme "'United against Global Racism' and the slogan of 'Reparations Now' [with] Danny Glover as the celebrity speaker."[43] The leadership

of ADC met with members of the U.S. Congressional Black Caucus and other dignitaries, such as Dorothy Height, President Wade of Senegal, the ambassador from the Sudan and its delegation, and David Commissiong from Barbados to obtain their support on reparations.

On September 6, as deliberations of the conference were breaking down, a joint statement was released to the press by the African Descendants and Durban 400, urging "the governments to not sacrifice language on slavery and the slave trade as crimes against humanity and reparations for the victims."[44] The caucus also publicly denounced the United States for abandoning the conference with Israel under the formulated nonissue of equating Zionism with racism. This is what was offered in the final draft of the NGO Forum:

> We declare that the slavery and servitude of peoples descended from Africans, Caribbeans, indigenous peoples and other ethnic groups and sectors of society, the effects of which continue to exist under the wing of racist and colonialist ideology were crimes against humanity. This Conference recalls the right of the affected peoples to reparation and signals States as responsible for initiating reparation as a moral and ethical obligation which should guide their national and international policies, and signals international agencies as responsible for administering and issuing such reparation.[45]

The ADC did have a major impact on the overall proceedings, as evidenced in the Final Declaration and Program of Action by the governments. In spite of the efforts by the Caribbean and African governments to have reparations as a core agreement, the member states went only as far as to condemn transatlantic slave trade and slavery. The group "acknowledge and profoundly regret the massive human suffering and the tragic plight of millions of men, women and children caused by slavery, the slave trade, the transatlantic slave trade, apartheid, colonialism and genocide, and call upon States concerned to honour the memory of the victims." They conceded the underlying claim for reparations that those practices "have led to racism, racial discrimination, xenophobia and related intolerance."[46] A call was made to the international community to find "appropriate ways" to "restore the dignity of the victims." As a means of reconciliation and healing, "those dark chapters in history" need to be closed."[47] Being aware of the "moral obligation" of states, they are relieved of reparations for the transatlantic slave trade, slavery, and colonialism, and are requested to "take appropriate and effective measures to halt and reverse the lasting consequences of those practices."[48]

In the "Programme of Action II. Victims of Racism, Racial Discrimination, Xenophobia and Related Intolerance, Africans and People of African Descent" drawn up by the member states, they:

6. Call upon the United Nations, international financial and development institutions . . . to develop capacity-building programmes.
7. Consider establishment of a working group . . . to study the problems of racial discrimination faced by people of African descent living in the African Diaspora . . .
8. (a) to assign particular priority, and allocate sufficient funding, within their areas of competence and budgets, to improving the situation of Africans and people of African descent . . .
8. (b) To develop programmes intended for people of African descent allocating additional investments to health systems, education, housing, electricity, drinking water and environmental control measures and promoting equal opportunities in employment as well as other affirmative or positive action initiatives;
9. Requests States to increase public actions and policies in favour of women and young males of African descent, given that racism affects them more deeply, placing them in a more marginalized and disadvantaged situation.
10. Urges States to ensure access to education and promote access to new technologies . . . further urges States to promote the full and accurate inclusion of the history and contribution of Africans and people of African descent in the education curriculum;
11. Encourages States to identify factors which prevent equal access to, and the equitable presence of, people of African descent at all levels of the public sector. . . . take appropriate measures to remove the obstacles identified and also to encourage the private sector to promote equal access to, and the equitable presence of people of African descent at all levels within their organizations.[49]

Although the member states acknowledged, condemned, deplored, and "profoundly regretted" the transatlantic slave trade, slavery, and colonialism, they are not obliged to make amends beyond voluntary apologies, for those "past" injustices. The European and other states recognized the "immense suffering" of slavery, the most "reprehensible aspects of colonialism," and admitted "regrettably" that those practices "have led to racism, racial discrimination, xenophobia and related intolerance." They then absolved themselves of any responsibility to redress. The representative of Belgium made the following statement on behalf of the European Union:

> The Declaration and the Programme of Action are political, not legal documents. These documents cannot impose obligations, or liability, or a right to compensation, on anyone. Furthermore, the European Union has joined consensus in a reference to measures to halt and reverse the lasting consequences of certain practices of the past. This should not be understood as the acceptance of any liability for these practices, nor does it imply a change in the principles of international development cooperation, partnership and solidarity. It will not change the nature of current national and international development cooperation criteria.

The Durban conference has been discredited, and thus the work to be done as defined in the Program of Action is yet to be addressed (Lawyers Guild, 2002). However, the victory for the African Descendants is stated in paragraph 13 of the U.N. World Conference against Racism Declaration and Program of Action:

> We acknowledge that slavery and the slave trade, including the transatlantic slave trade, were appalling tragedies in the history of humanity not only because of their abhorrent barbarism but also in terms of their magnitude, organized nature and especially their negation of the essence of the victims, and further acknowledge that slavery and the slave trade are a crime against humanity and should always have been so, especially the transatlantic slave trade.

Conclusion

Although the transatlantic slave trade and slavery were deemed "crimes against humanity," no conventional definition prevails and "human rights conventions are silent about the duty to punish violators." International human rights law provides thresholds for violations, distinguishing between gross, that is, cruel or extreme degree of depravity, and systematic, that is, official, widespread pattern or practice, and then is expected to adjust remedies in accordance (Shelton, 1999, 321–22). What is to take place is some type of collective amnesia about the past while acknowledging its impact on the present and moving forward by providing judicial access for redress of current individual claims of discrimination. Two basic problems are (1) individualizing racist acts as distinct from institutional and corporate acts, thereby absolving those entities as a whole, and (2) "juridifica-tion," the transfer of political conflict into legal disputation. Both processes "privileges lawyers over citizens and courtrooms over more public sites of debate and deliberation . . . also [the movement becomes] vulnerable to being hijacked by unscrupulous people pursuing their own objectives, par-ticularly where those political aims concern primarily economic matters" (Torpey, 2004, 171).

The incorporation of "unjust enrichment" and transgenerational post-traumatic slave syndrome (Leary, 2005) as resultant of the atrocities has reframed the reparations legal strategy to repair and does not rely on in-dividual rights and remedies. In this way, a nexus is formed between his-torical wrongs committed by one group, and present harm to both the material and psychological well-being of African descendants, as well as damaged relations between the groups and the society at large. Add to this "underdevelopment" data that affirms the unbridled exploitation leaving African societies to degenerate, then isolate the "cultural psychic scars," further injuring the African Diaspora populations and "without remedy" and the case is fully substantiated (Yamamoto, 2003, 1297; Hewitt, 2004). The legal strategy is thereby shifted from the reparation claim of redress, that is, a final, indeterminate monetary amount or gesture, to repair, that is, a prolonged process that identifies specific areas to undergo restoration.

"Shielding people from personal responsibility for large scale injustices by suggesting that one's personal role in great collective wrongs is subsumed in a more diffused, general and impersonal 'civil' duty'" will not suffice (Hughes, 2004, 253). Compensation is important as it offers acknowledgment of wrongs done, deters future abuses, and allows healing to take place. The recipients should not be regarded as victims, for the labor provided by Afri-cans, on which the wealth of this present economy rests, should be viewed as gifts. It is "illegitimate to ask Black people to recreate wealth at this ad-vanced stage of capital accumulation" (Hewitt, 2004, 1002). "We require nothing that we did not create through our own devices. We will make our way, we will take what is only our due for services rendered, and lives lost and hope deferred" (Coates, 2004, 862). Acknowledgment and disclosure would have a major impact psychologically and emotionally on those de-scendants. "Victims may better become survivors if some part of the legacy of the past is addressed . . . Justice, even if long delayed, is reparative" (Shel-ton, 1999, 331). The world community has yet to address the present ravages of the transatlantic slave trade, slavery, and colonialism, and it is only within that framework that the discussion of reparations can become normalized and the full investigation of white supremacy can be addressed.

NOTES

1. During slavery Frederick Douglass, Sojourner Truth, Zumbi dos Palmares, Joaquim Nabuco, Harriet Tubman, and Luiza Mahin attended anti-slave trade and antislavery conventions in Europe. Ida B. Wells traveled extensively throughout Europe to highlight the issue of lynching in the United States. Later W. E. B. Du Bois made remarkable strides toward Pan-Africanism by organizing three international conferences. Of course, these examples represent civil society and are different from those African Americans enlisted on behalf of the state, such as Ralph Bunche. In April 1955 a conference was staged in Bandung, Indonesia, by African and Asian nations to promote economic and cultural cooperation and to oppose colonialism. Adam Clayton Powell, Jr., went to represent the imperialist interest of the United States, by alluding to the progress of the Negro. Also see Carol Anderson, *Eyes Off the Prize: The United Nations and the African American Struggle for Human Rights, 1944–1965* (Cambridge: Cambridge University Press, 2003).

2. Documents from the conference can be accessed at http://academic.udayton.edu/race/06hrights/wcar2001/index.htm..

3. UN.org/wcar.

4. Following are the U.N. conferences that have been held: First Decade to Combat Racism and Racial Discrimination, 1973–82; First World Conference to Combat Racism and Racial Discrimination, Geneva, 1978; Second World Conference to Combat Racism and Racial Discrimination, also in Geneva, 1983; Second Decade for Action to Combat Racial Discrimination, l983–92; Third Decade to Combat Racism and Racial Discrimination, 1994–2003.

5. The conference themes included the following:

    Theme 1: Sources, cause, forms, and contemporary manifestations of racism, racial discrimination, and related intolerance

    Theme 2: Victims of racism, racial discrimination, and related intolerance

    Theme 3: Measures of prevention, education, and protection aimed at the eradication of racism, racial discrimination, and related intolerance at the national, regional, and international levels

    Theme 4: Provision for effective remedies, recourses, redress, [compensatory] and other measures at the national, regional, and international levels

    Theme 5: Strategies to achieve full and effective equality, including international cooperation and enhancement of the United Nations and other international mechanisms in combating racism, racial discrimination, and xenophobia

6. The National Coalition of Blacks for Reparations in America is a grassroots coalition organized for the sole purpose of obtaining reparations for African descendants in the United States. N'COBRA's founding meeting, September 26, 1987, was convened for the purpose of broadening the base of support for the longstanding reparations movement. Organizational founders of N'COBRA include the National Conference of Black Lawyers, the New Afrikan Peoples Organization, and the Republic of New Afrika. N'COBRA has individual members and organizational affiliates. It has chapters throughout the United States and in Ghana and London. It is directed nationally by a board of directors. Its work is organized through nine national commissions: Economic Development, Human Resources, Legal Strategies, Legislation, Information and Media, Membership and Organizational Development, International Affairs, Youth, and Education.

7. The International Coordinating Committee of African and African Descendants Caucus, formally organized at the May 2001 African Descendants Caucus in Geneva, Switzerland, includes the following members: Annie Davies, Development Information Network, Nigeria; Marian Douglas, Macedonia; Bahati Mildered Jawara, Citizens For Environmental Justice USA; Mutombo Kanyana, Groupe de Réflexion et d'Action Contre le Racisme Anti-noir (Forum suisse contre le Racisme), Switzerland; Vernellia Randall (declaration drafting coordinator), University of Dayton, Ohio, USA; Cikiah Thomas, African Canadian Legal Clinic, Canada; Eleonora Wiedenroth, Initiative of Black People in Germany (ISD-Bund), Germany.

8. Response of the African and African Descendants Caucus to the Africa group Non-Paper (the minority opinion of a subgroup of the African descendants that disagreed on reparations), August 10, 2001, 1.

9. Press release of the African Descendants Caucus, August 9, 2001.

10. See Asante, 2003.

11. Press release of the African Descendants Caucus, August 9, 2001.

12. Statement by Angela Davis at the World Conference against Racism, NGO Forum, September 2001.

13. http://academic.udayton.edu/race/06hrights/VictimGroups/AfricanDescendants/WCAR01.htm.

14. African and African Descendants Caucus, World Conference against Racism, summary of focus and activities, July 2001, 1–2.

15. http://academic.udayton.edu/race/06hrights/VictimGroups/AfricanDescendants/WCAR01.htm.

16. African and African Descendants Caucus, World Conference against Racism, summary of focus and activities, July 2001, sec. II.A.

17. Department of News and Information, Durban, September 6, 2001.

18. Request That Compensatory Remedies Be Part of the Theme for the World Conference against Racism, submitted September 2000, 2.

19. "Ten Priority Action Points of Consensus-African and African Descendants Caucus," Chile, December 2000.

20. African and African Descendants Caucus, General Intervention, Second Preparatory Meeting, WCAR, May 31, 2001.

21. See the works of Shelby Faye Lewis and her discussion of the divisive impact of colonialism and the economic, social, and political "cleavages" created.

22. Press release of African Descendants, August 9, 2001.

23. Press statement by African Descendants Caucus, August 9, 2001.

24. Vienna document, April 2001.

25. African Regional Conference for the World Conference against Racism, Racial and Ethnic Discrimination, Xenophobia, and Related Intolerance, Dakar (Senegal), January 20–21, 2001. Declaration of the African NGO Forum, 2.

26. Declaration of the African NGO Forum, 3.

27. See Dakar Declaration.

28. www.nepad.org.

29. Working Group Papers, final document, 115.

30. See Martin Carnoy, *Education as Cultural Imperialism* (New York: D. McKay, 1974).

31. The Vienna document is available at: http://academic.udayton.edu/race/06hrights/VictimGroups/AfricanDescendants/WCAR01.htm.

32. See Clarence Lusane, *Hitler's Black Victims: The Historical Experience of Afro-Germans, European Blacks, Africans and African Americans in the Nazi Era* (New York: Routledge, 2002).

33. Vienna Document, April 2001, xxv. Available at: http://academic.udayton.edu/race/06hrights/VictimGroups/AfricanDescendants/WCAR01.htm.

34. African and African Descendants Caucus, May 25, 2001 (Proposal for the Draft Declaration and Program of Action for the Second International Prepcom of the World Conference on Racism [summary of main points]).

35. Final government document. Available at http://www.un.org/wcar/coverage.htm.

36. African and African Descendants Caucus, World Conference against Racism, summary of focus and activities, July 2001, 1–2.

37. Draft of Main Points, May 25, 2001. Available at http://www.un.org/wcar/coverage.htm.

38. Final government document, Resolution No. 69, 17.

39. Final government document, Resolutions Nos. 92–94, 42.

40. Press release by the African Descendants Caucus, August 9, 2001.

41. WCAR final document, 115 (documents the statement of the representative of Trinidad and Tobago).

42. Members of the Coordinating Committee included the following: Alioune Tine; a representative from Europe, Maluza Martin; a youth representative, Amani Olubanjo Buntu, from Norway now living in South Africa; a representative from Canada, David Onyalo, who could not serve (Sandra Carnegie-Douglas was substituted); a representative from Latin America, Romero Rodriquez, who designated Humberto Brown to represent him; a representative from the drafting committee, Barbara Arnwine; and a representative from the United States, Adjoa A. Aiyetoro.

43. The Maafa ceremony was endorsed and supported by the African Descendants Caucus.

44. Press release by African Descendants, August 6, 2001.

45. Final Draft Conference of Citizens against Racism, Xenophobia, Intolerance, and Discrimination: Forum of NGOs and Civil Society Organizations of the Americas, December 3–4, 2000, Santiago de Chile. Report of the World Conference against Racism, Racial Discrimination, Xenophobia, and Related Intolerance, Durban, August 31-September 8, 2001. A/CONF.189/12. A. 57. Declaration A. 4, United Nations Document Office.

46. Final government document, Resolution No. 99, 21.

47. Ibid. Resolution No. 101, 22.

48. Ibid. Resolution No. 102, 22.

49. Program of Action II, Victims of Racism, Racial Discrimination, Xenophobia, and Related Intolerance, Africans and People of African Descent, in final government document, 27.

REFERENCES

African and African Descendants Caucus. May 25, 2001. Proposal for the Draft Declaration and Program of Action for the Second International Prepcom of the World Conference on Racism (summary of main points).

———. May 31, 2001. General Intervention-Second Preparatory Meeting, WCAR.

———. August 9, 2001. Press release on World Conference against Racism, Xenophobia and Related Intolerances.

African Regional Conference for the World Conference against Racism, Racial and Ethnic

Discrimination, Xenophobia and Related Intolerance, Dakar (Senegal), January 20–21, 2001. Declaration of the African NGO Forum.

Aiyetoro, Adjoa. December 3–7, 2000. "Statement on Reparations: The Importance of Compensatory Remedies for Victims of Racism." Santiago, Chile.

Alkalimat, Abdul. 2004. "Rethinking Reparations: Rebuilding for Reform and Revolution." *Black Scholar* 3: 34–41.

Amin, Samir. 1974. *Neocolonialism in West Africa*. New York: Monthly Review Press.

Anderson, Carol. 2003. *Eyes Off the Prize: The United Nations and the African American Struggle for Human Rights, 1944–1965*. New York: Cambridge University Press.

Asante, Molefi. 2003. *Afrocentricity: The Theory of Social Change*. Sauk Village, Ill.: African American Images.

Balfour, Lawrie. 2003. "Unreconstructed Democracy: W. E. B. Du Bois and the Case for Reparations." *American Political Science Review* 97, no. 1: 33–44.

Barbados Protocol. November 2002.

Biondi, Martha. 2003. "The Rise of the Reparations Movement." *Radical History Review* 87: 5–18.

Brooks, Roy L., ed. 1999. *When Sorry Isn't Enough: The Controversy over Apologies and Reparations for Human Injustice*. New York: New York University Press.

Cabral, Amilcar. 1974. *Return to the Source: Selected Speeches*. New York: Monthly Review Press.

Cabral, Bahia. 2007. Interview with author. Philadelphia, April.

Christian, Mark. 2002. "An African-Centered Perspective on White Supremacy." *Journal of Black Studies* 33, no. 2: 179–98.

Clarke, John Henry. 1991. *African World Revolution*. Trenton, N.J.: Africa World Press.

Coates, Rodney. 2004. "If a Tree Falls in the Wilderness: Reparations, Academic Silences, and Social Justice." *Social Force* 83, no. 2: 841–64.

Dymski, Gary. 2000. "Illegal-Seizure and Market-Disadvantage Approaches to Restitution: A Comparison of the Japanese American and African American Cases." *Review of Black Political Economy* 27, no. 3: 48–79.

Forde-Mazrui, Kim. 2004. "Taking Conservatives Seriously: A Moral Justification for Affirmative Action and Reparations." *California Law Review* 92.

Forum of NGOs and Civil Society Organizations of the Americas. December 3–4, 2000. Conferencia Ciudadana Contra el Racismo, la Xenofobia, la Intolerancia y la Discriminacion . . . Documento de trabajo/Final Draft, Conference of Citizens against Racism, Xenophobia, Intolerance and Discrimination. Santiago de Chile.

Fosu, Augustin Kwasi. 1999. "An Economic Theory of Pan Africanism." *Review of Black Political Economy* (Fall): 7–12.

Gifford, Lord Anthony. 1993. "The Afrocentric Experience of Reparations: Legal Arguments in Support of Reparations." Paper presented to the First Pan-African Congress on Reparations, Abuja, Federal Republic of Nigeria, April 27–29.

Hewitt, Cynthia Lucas. 2004. "One Capital Indivisible under God: The IMF and Reparation for Slavery in a Time of Globalized Wealth." *American Behavioral Scientist* 47, no. 7 (March): 1001–27.

hooks, bell. 1990. *Yearning: Race, Gender, and Cultural Politics*. Canada: Between the Lines.

Hughes, Paul M. 2004. "Rectification and Reparation: What Does Citizen Responsibility Require?" *Journal of Social Philosophy* 35, no. 2 (Summer): 244–55.

Leary, Joy. 2005. *Post Traumatic Slave Syndrome: America's Legacy of Enduring Injury and Healing.* El Segundo, Calif.: Upton Books.

Legg, Michael. 2002. "Indigenous Australians and International Law: Racial Discrimination, Genocide and Reparations." *Berkeley Journal of International Law* 20: 387–416.

Lusane, Clarence. 2001. *Shift Happens: Contemporary Racism and African Americans.* Silver Spring, Md.: International Possibilities Unlimited.

———. 2003. *Hitler's Black Victims.* New York: Routledge.

———. 2004. Interview with author. Philadelphia, July.

———. 2006. "What Color Is Hegemony? Powell, Rice and the New Global Strategists." Paper presented at the annual meeting of the National Conference of Black Political Scientists, March.

MacLean, Frank. 1918. *Towards Extermination: Germany's Treatment of the African Natives.* St. Albans, U.K.: Campfield Press.

Marcuse, Peter. 2004. "Are Social Forums the Future of Social Movements?" Unpublished paper.

Mazrui, Ali. 1994. "Global Africa: From Abolitionists to Reparationists." *African Studies Review* 37, no. 3 (December): 1–18.

Osabu-Kle, Daniel Tetteh. 2000. "The African Reparation Cry: Rationale, Estimate, Prospects and Strategies." *Journal of Black Studies* 30 (January): 331–50.

Parenti, Michael. 2007. *Democracy for the Few.* Boston: Wadsworth Publishing.

Podur, Justin. 2002. "Non-Reformist Reparations for Africa: Repairing the Damage." *Z Magazine* (February): 45–48.

Rodney, Walter. 1973. *How Europe Underdeveloped Africa.* Dar-Es-Salaam: London and Tanzanian Publishing House.

Rufai, Misbahu. 1998. "Making a Case for International Reparation Campaign." *Muslim Journal* 23, no.16 (January).

Shelton, Dinah. 1999. *Remedies in International Human Rights Law.* New York: Oxford University Press.

Torpey, John. 2004. "Paying for the Past? The Movement for Reparations for African-Americans." *Journal of Human Rights* 3, no. 2 (June): 171–87.

United Nations. September 2001. World Conference against Racism, Xenophobia and Related Intolerances. Programme of Action.

U.S. Department of Foreign Affairs. May 24, 2002. A New African Initiative: Merger of the Millennium Partnership for the African Recovery Programme (MAP) and Omega Plan, July 2001.

Vasarhelyi Istv'an. 1964. *Restitution In International Law.* Budapest: Publishing House of the Hungarian Academy of Science.

Wallerstein, Immanuel.1986. *Africa and the Modern World.* Trenton, N.J.: Africa World Press.

Wareham, Roger. 2003. "The Popularization of the International Demand for Reparations for African People." In *Should America Pay?* ed. Raymond Winbush. New York: Amistad Press.

Williams, Ife. 2005. World Conference against Racism, Xenophobia and Other Forms of Intolerance: Assessment of Participation of American Friends Service Center.

Winbush, Raymond, ed. 2003. *Should America Pay?* New York: Amistad Press.

Women's International League for Peace and Freedom. September 2000. Request That

Compensatory Remedies Be Part of the Theme for the World Conference against Racism.

Woodly, Deva R., Brandi Thompson Adams, and Cathy J. Cohen. 2003. "Black Reparations in a Time of Terror." Unpublished paper.

World Conference against Racism, Racial Discrimination, Xenophobia and Related Intolerance. August 31-September 8, 2001. Report. A/CONF.189/12.

Yamamoto, Eric, Sesuai Serrano, and Michelle Navidad Rodriguez. 2003. "American Justice on Trial Again: African American Reparation, Human Rights and the War on Terror." *Michigan Law Review* 101 (March): 1269–1336.

TEN

The Emergence of a Legislative Caucus of Afro-Descendant Legislators in the Americas

CONTEXT, PROGRESS, AND AGENDA SETTING

Minion K. C. Morrison

This chapter provides an update and contextual setting for the organization of Afro-descendant legislators. The group had its organizational meeting in 2003 with the major goal of bringing together all elected legislators of African descent in the Americas and the Caribbean. Its target membership therefore is those representatives from South and Central America, the United States, and the Caribbean. The working assumptions of the organizers have been that these legislators have a great deal in common: an African background that lends cultural affinities across the region; similar experiences in a racialized world where they suffer degradation and oppression as a group; and a belief that the group can benefit from solidarity of purpose and action in altering political and social isolation in the Americas. The Afro-descendant legislators movement can therefore be placed in the context of a long tradition of strivings for unity using the African background as a symbolic and practical tool for identity, mobilization, and political action.

The context for this movement is Pan-Africanism, a historical movement that sought first to gain the liberation of continental Africa from colonialism, but which was organized by unified African descendants in the Americas. Its primary assumptions were that the oppression suffered by Africans everywhere was so general that little short of a common movement was required to fight these conditions. The focus of the movement for African liberation has thus always been intensely political, seeking self-determination for a people excluded from ordinary public participation and economically exploited. Therefore, the fundamental purpose of the organization of Afro-descendant legislators is to achieve full political participation for blacks wherever they are located in the Americas and to regularize the terms of community membership in countries where they have been relegated to second-class citizenship or rendered invisible as an identity group. This chapter proceeds from that assumption in updating and contextualizing the work of the organization of the Afro-Descendant Legislators.

The analysis is divided into three broad sections. The first section considers the background and history of the Pan-African movement. It describes the theory of Afro-Diasporan unity, the history of the movement, and how it relates to continental African unity efforts. The second section considers mobilization efforts in the Americas, focusing principally on the United States and Brazil. This discussion is framed around the concept of representation and how elected officials who form a caucus fit into it. The last section focuses exclusively on the first two meetings of the Afro-descendant legislators, sketching their goals and accomplishments in slightly less than two years of operation.

African Unity and Afro-Diasporan Unity

There is a long history of African peoples seeking means for solidarity in the face of oppression, dispossession, and misrepresentation of their social and political interests. They, like others in history, have expressed the fundamental human desire to pursue their own ends in light of felt needs, core cultural expressions, and feelings of community owing to historical experiences. In the peculiarities of their relations with Europeans, African peoples have been particularly insistent and persistent about the preservation of their independence and freedom. This is not without justification. In the long history of relations between Europeans and Africans, the latter have had to contend with efforts to denigrate their cultural modes, humanity, and territorial space.

There are spectacular markers of their interactions that serve to structure the African persistence in seeking independence. Perhaps the most notorious of these interactions was the enslavement of Africans and their transport across the Atlantic to the Americas (Du Bois, 1965; Curtin, 1969) It was a forced migration that so severely depopulated the continent that a full recovery has not been made to this day. A close second in symbolic/representative encounters was the colonization of the African continent by the Europeans. This was reflected by a virtually complete alienation of Africans from their land and their complementary political domination (Balandier, 1965). Under these conditions it is reasonable to contemplate the continuous African striving for self-determination, and the contentious nature of relations between the two entities. This same striving characterizes the descendants of Africa in the Americas, the victims of the forced migration and the degradation of a system of chattel enslavement that awaited them upon arrival.

The continuity of the striving has most often been borne out in several realms-solidarity, resistance, and adaptations wrought out of the interactive experiences with Europeans. These continue to be constitutive elements of the modern-day Africans and those in the American Diaspora. The efforts to achieve solidarity in the form of organizations are the subject of this chapter. The focus is on the recent organization of Afro-descendant legislators that emerged in the southern part of the Americas, whose aim is to bring together lawmakers who self-identify as such. While there have doubtless been any number of organized fora in which these Afro-descendants have tried to achieve solidarity, my specific focus is on a group that had its beginnings in Brazil and which acquired a formal status in a maiden meeting of legislators, activists, and scholars in November 2003 in Brasilia. Its leader and founder was Luiz Alberto dos Santos, a deputy in the Brazilian legislature. That this is a group of Afro-descendants who are public officials gives it an immediate base and structure for operation that is reminiscent of a legislative caucus. That fact forms another part of the contextual analysis that is framed around the model of the Congressional Black Caucus (CBC) in the United States.

History of Pan-African Movements

The organization of Afro-descendants in the Americas is hardly a new means of aiming for solidarity among continental Africans or those in the Diaspora. Perhaps the series of Pan-African Congresses organized under the leadership of African descendants in the United States and the Caribbean best reflects this tradition. The Pan-African Congresses were a series of six, intermittent meetings that took place between the two World Wars. They were fora for the preparation and public articulation of a view favoring continental African independence, which sought to draw together variant strands of African communities in the Americas and the continent for common action against colonialism. W. E. B. Du Bois (regarded as the father of Pan-Africanism) and Sylvester Williams organized the first of these meetings, which remained dominated by descendants in the Americas until the last conference at Manchester, England, in 1945 (Legum, 1962; R. Moore, 1971). Du Bois spoke forcefully about the goals of this movement: "The African movement means to us what the Zionist movement must mean to the Jews, the centralization of race effort and the recognition of a racial front. . . . Any ebullition of action and feeling that results in an amelioration of the lot of Africa tends to ameliorate the condition of the colored peoples throughout the world" (*Crisis*, November 19, 1919). And so the loosely organized group of leaders and spokesmen sought both to redeem the African continent and the status of its sons and daughters in the various places to which they had been dispersed. The initial energy was to be directed toward the achievement of continental independence, a matter to be taken up at Versailles, where the notion of self-determination of nation-states was being affirmed per the ideas of U.S. president Woodrow Wilson. But at the outset the movement had a well-wrought ideology of solidarity aimed at inclusiveness of all African descendants. Indeed, the Diaspora base of the early proponents suggests as much-all African descendants had a virtual obligation to be engaged for the alleviation of the problem of continental African oppression. Those in the Diaspora were simply better placed for moving the project along. Their suitability was deemed to rest on the relative openness of their societies, which provided even blacks opportunities, albeit measured, to challenge the policies and practices that hamstrung indigenous Africans. Those in the Diaspora could use their routine strategies of protest and mobilization, licensed by their democratic processes, to challenge colonization, for example, while Africans could not. At the same time those in the Diaspora, in their coming together, could advance their own political organization for making claims against local discrimination.

A remarkable amount of development and communication for the times actually occurred between and within these diasporic communities. In the United States, for example, Du Bois was developing a parallel organization dedicated principally to issues relating to U.S. blacks, the NAACP. He often used the more bureaucratically organized NAACP to provide information about the situation of continental Africa. But more important, the organization provided a vehicle through which information and political positions could be disseminated to a broad Pan-African audience (Lewis, 1994, 386; Lewis, 2000). At the same time, the African descendants from the Caribbean were equally active in developing their own organizations and cementing contacts with related groups in the United States. It was a framework that was exploited by blacks in their disparate locations in North and South America to the end that much of the "elite" leadership class was aware of its counterparts (Williams, 1970; Harris, 1982; Padmore, 1953). The Pan-African Congresses provided a venue where they could meet occasionally. And they had other means-writing letters, programming each other in locally arranged events, reading and exchanging political writings and ideas, and participating in publicly advertised protest campaigns. In short, a remarkable number of them consorted with each other, achieving a ready solidarity in this modest and influential group with many shared experiences and sentiments. Writers in the Harlem Renaissance, for example, were widely read in the Caribbean and vice versa (Harris, 1982; Hughes, 1940; Butler, 1998).

The Pan-African movement got its stimulus in the Diaspora and ultimately had a defining influence on the idea when it emerged on the African continent. In large measure this occurred because many African students who were expatriates in Europe and the United States came to political maturity during their studies there. Many of them did so as organized groups of African intellectuals working in concert with African descendants who were active in the Pan-African community. Many of those who became prominent postindependence leaders in Africa were so engaged: Kwame Nkrumah, who became a protégé of Du Bois at the Manchester conference, studied in the United States and made many contacts among African American political leaders. He remarks that he was especially influenced by this experience, beginning with his undergraduate studies at Lincoln University, a black college. He worked with the NAACP, read and was influenced by Marcus Garvey. Meanwhile, he also came into contact with other important African nationalist thinkers as a product of his choice to study in the United States. The most notable of these was Nnamdi Azikiwe, who himself became an important postindependence leader. Later Nkrumah went on to London and met still others like Jomo Kenyatta (Nkrumah, 1957; Birmingham, 1998).

Africans from French colonies who were resident in France matched Nkrumah's experience. Even before they organized themselves into a collective, the French colonial system allowed a number of Africans to have a presence in government positions. This official status gave them an ability to communicate broadly with counterparts from other French colonized territories, but it also allowed them to communicate with African descendants in the Americas. Some of this contact was routine for communication with "Départements" in the Antilles, overseas colonies in the Caribbean. After all, a number of these island entities had their own students resident in France, such as Aimé Césare or Leon Damas (Kesteloot, 1974; Jahn, 1968). But contact was much broader. Blaise Diagne, for example, facilitated the travel of Du Bois to Paris in hopes of making a representation before the conference at Versailles (Lewis, 1994). Some of the Harlem Renaissance artists, such as Langston Hughes, had direct communications with and were sources of inspiration for emerging African writers in France. Eventually, of course, these expatriates established their own literary movement, dubbed Negritude. It was at its inception far more than merely a literary society of writers. Its affiliates were intensely political with their urgings in support of reconnections to precolonial traditions and cultural tropes, all the while propounding a vision of resistance to colonial oppression and a critique of authoritarian rule (Kesteloot, 1974; Jahn, 1968).

History of African Unity

Subsequently the Pan-African movement did shift its center to the African continent. This became inevitable when the African presence reached a critical mass at the 1945 conference and when African independence became the prime agenda item. This coincided with the emergence of salient nationalist movements in virtually every colony after World War II. But its real impetus was the speed of the nationalist campaign and subsequent independence of Ghana led by Kwame Nkrumah. The role of Nkrumah ultimately earned him the title of "father of African nationalism" (Birmingham, 1998). He became head of government business in Ghana in 1951 and led the country to independence in 1957. Then the very next year he called the Conference of Independent African States. This really was the first continental Pan-African Congress, so to speak, insofar as invitation went to other independent states. The expressed goals of the event were to work as a unified group to attain the full independence of other African colonies. Nkrumah invoked a number of principles that he asserted were essential to self-determination: the fundamental right of Africans to control their own affairs ("Africa for the Africans"), and the insertion of the "African Personality" (or worldview) into public discourse (Nkrumah, 1963).

Later Nkrumah's ideas formed the basis for what became the continental organization aimed at unifying all independent African states. The first proposal along these lines was for a "commonwealth" of African states made at another 1958 conference sponsored by Nkrumah in Ghana, the All African Peoples Organization. Legum (1962, 42–43) has called this conference "the high water mark of the Pan-Africanist idea. At last the peoples of Africa gathered in Africa to talk about how to change the European social order that had been fostered upon them." While the pressure to first achieve territorial independence subsequently outran the notion of a continental organization, a watered-down version of the grand idea of a continent-wide organization of African states did become a reality. The Organization of African Unity (OAU) was founded in 1963. And while it hardly lived up to being a strong entity for continental government, it did provide a useful vehicle for communication among young leaders and spoke with a more or less unified voice on certain measures that inserted the African worldview into international affairs and in reference to some continental issues, such as apartheid (Clapham, 1999).

Many regional entities have been spawned by the essentially national-ist vision that Nkrumah propounded for solidarity and efficiency in the face of neocolonialism. Nkrumah himself orchestrated several of these regional entities: among them, the Mali Federation that linked several French- and English-speaking territories in West Africa. At the same time regional entities sprang up widely elsewhere, some with quite remarkable success at organizing members states in various common market and other economic ventures. The Economic Community of West African States (ECOWAS) certainly has become a major player in the regional economic and political organization of West Africa. The old East African Federation has also enjoyed some success in its various iterations as Kenya, Tanzania, and Uganda have tried to obtain unity. And a later regional group, SADAC, has sprung up to accommodate states in the southern African region.

The strivings for an organization that does speak with some force on continental political issues may be better realized in the latest entity—the African Union (AU). This organization has been in the planning since the Treaty of Abuja in 1992 specified certain changes and expansion of the guid-ing concepts for the OAU. The evolving organization looked to the EU as a kind of model of what African states might achieve. The process of creating the AU has been very measured, becoming a formal reality only in 2002. Its nurture has been provided largely by the interest and influence of the lead-ers of Africa's two largest states, Nigeria and South Africa, one of which was an object of scorn at the organization of the OAU. One early assessment of the promise of this organization sums it up as follows:

> The re-invention of the OAU as the AU marks a qualitative break with earlier attempts at African unity. Compared to 1963, the situation at the dawn of 2003 was much more favourable to continental unification. Many African leaders show commitment to democracy and develop-ment. A stronger civil society in many countries, the ICT revolution, continental corporations and NGOs, all deepen inter-governmental links between countries. South Africa, the continent's strongest econ-omy, is now a democratic leader. Nigeria, the largest nation, is today a co-driver of continental unity. Unlike all the other regional economic communities in Asia and the Americas, the AU aims at EU-level insti-tutionalisation of integration, including a continental parliament, court, central bank, common market, plus a peace-keeping military and po-

lice force. This is the most ambitious project of its kind in the world outside the EU. Treaties obligate it to culminate in a single market of 800 million people. (Gottschalk, 2005, 22–23)

The driving forces for these African efforts at unification are very similar to those that inspired early efforts. Control of continental African affairs and that of its independent states remain substantially out of the hands of indigenous people and indigenous governments. Among other things, individual countries remain in the ambit of the former colonial powers because of the strong economic and political linkages and legacies that were bequeathed in the negotiations that led to independence. This form of relationship was labeled "neocolonialism" by Nkrumah (1965) well before the carefully articulated theory of dependency was laid out (Cockcroft et al. 1972). And beyond dependency, the new globalization has reduced the capacity of Africans to bid in a market where capital and the terms of capital flow and investment are dedicated to interests outside those most desirable for the conditions of African states and economies. Equally significant in driving the Africans toward continental unity is the transition to a new wave of democratization after the almost universal betrayal of the first wave of open political participation at the transfer of power at the time of decolonization in the early 1960s. A heavy premium is now placed on African agency in the alleviation of a dependent status that may well have been orchestrated by external forces, but was surely sustained by local corruption in the first democratic phase (Bratton and van de Walle, 1997). The Pan-African imagination invested in this continuing effort is hardly lost on the African descendants in the Americas. The OAU was lauded as an important symbol, however modest, of the dream that African peoples would unify to defeat their former enslavers and colonizers, and that a kind of redemption of the "African Personality" would occur in the process. Similarly, the AU has been regarded with the same interest and hope. The African descendants have sought and received acknowledgment of their claims for some official status within the organization on the strength of their continuing reality of displacement and discrimination that mirrors that of the African continent.

Mobilization Movements in the Americas

African descendants in the Americas have ironically been in the business of mobilizing and organizing for the purpose of solidarity around their claims for rights protection longer than continental Africans have in modern times. Perhaps this is no irony at all. The African descendants were forcibly transported to the Americas and enslaved in a chattel system— totally separated from their homeland and their humanity debased, with the aim of halting the routine production and reproduction of the associated cultures. Therefore, their first efforts at group organization were as forces of resistance, large and small, to eliminate their servitude. Haiti succeeded in a total overthrow of its captors and established an independent state (James, 1963); maroons were active throughout the Caribbean and Latin America in establishing safe havens for the practice of an independent African style of life (Price, 1979; Thelwell, 1980; Fausto, 1999). Even the United States was susceptible to this kind of organized resistance, despite the minority status of the African population in most places (Aptheker, 1942). And even under the spectacular conditions of violence and other means of brutality exerted to obliterate cultural production, an equally powerful energy was exerted by the displaced Africans to sustain cultural communities and memories (African survivals) (Thelwell, 1980; Counter and Evans, 1981; Siqueira, 1998; Knight, 1970; Turner, 1949; Blassingame, 1979).

After the emancipation (a process that moved at deliberate speed across the Americas—1865 in the United States and 1888 in Brazil), organized efforts for African descendant unity were continuous and voluminous. And they occurred all over the Americas, ebbing and flowing with broader political conditions in the various host countries. The formal end to enslavement was a marker for increased solidarity campaigns everywhere. The United States had a relatively short-lived Reconstruction that resulted in a profoundly significant and rapid amount of electoral participation among blacks. The emancipation itself in Brazil did not inspire the same immediate burst of directed energy because a significant amount of titular freedom occurred before the event. However, the new conditions directly contributed to an emerging movement among urban workers that gave the country its national, race-based fervor in the 1920s and 1930s (Butler, 1998). A wholly different element was added elsewhere with the achievement of decolonization for much of the Caribbean (Williams, 1970).

What may be termed a significant political mobilization has occurred in the areas in the Americas with the largest communities of African descendant populations—the United States and Brazil. In the former, a slowly growing movement congealed over twenty-five years or so to become known as the civil rights movement of the 1960s. After a substantial portion of the black population moved away or was displaced from the traditional rural, plantation-based existence, their political activism in the

North helped to create new opportunities for challenging the virtual peon-age system that replaced enslavement in the South. Between 1940 and 1965 challenges to discrimination and racism escalated into a comprehensive organized campaign for civil rights. This period represented the greatest flowering of organizations and contention for social and political change in history by blacks in the United States. The NAACP perfected its strategies of lobbying and legalism, effectively challenging unconstitutional practices and laws. Martin Luther King, Jr., became the single most effective charis-matic leader in U.S. history in his nonviolent campaign.

And even students organized their own campaign via Student Non-violent Coordinating Committee (SNCC) that focused on the development of local leadership and power. Their radical critique of the democratic sys-tem and its capitalist economic partner brought the movement full circle into a symmetry with African events or a Pan-African vision. In a conflu-ence of events in the United States and Africa, this civil rights campaign and the nationalist movements had a mutually stimulating and reinforcing effect. African descendants in the United States were watching and sup-porting the nationalist African campaigns, holding out their success as a symbol of hope and redemption. From the point of view of SNCC activists, the continental African cause was the same as that in the United States, and they argued for the establishment of direct organizational and other link-ages. A major feature was the adaptation of indigenous African symbols, ideas of a national African community, and cultural elements of dress for a strong "black pride" movement.

Elements of this movement tapped into a well-worn tradition of har-kening to the African continent as a symbol of redemption and possible escape from the throes of repression in the United States. SNCC was far from the first organization to invoke these principles. Throughout the Af-rican presence in the United States, Africa has been utilized in this fashion. In the precolonial period African Americans of means and education looked to Africa as a potential base for economic ventures, repatriation for salvation, and Christian proselytizing (Cuffee). Throughout the enslave-ment there were also movements designed to repatriate Africans by na-tionalist thinkers and moral leaders within the group (Turner and Crum-mell) (Uya, 1971), as well as private and public organizations (the American Colonization Society and Abraham Lincoln) (Franklin and Moss, 1994). And, of course, perhaps the most renowned was the twentieth-century movement led by Marcus Garvey that focused on Liberia as both a place of salvation and a market (Cronin, 1955).

African descendants in the Southern Hemisphere were equally active in utilizing the African background as a means for identity and group progress in a racialized environment. In this case there were much more obvious markers of African continuities on the ground. Brazil, Jamaica, Haiti, Suriname, and Cuba sustained near pure versions of African community life in the West. This was perhaps most prominent in replications of religious experience, such as the adaptation of African deities in everyday usage. Brazil and Cuba, for example, continue to have deities represented in religious practice. It occurs in two forms—as indigenous religious communities, such as Candomble and Santeria, and as syncretic features of Catholicism (Siqueira, 1998). In Suriname there are replications of West African languages and communal patterns of social organization among rural elements of the population (Counter and Evans, 1981). This is a condition similar to what was reflected in "maroon" communities in Jamaica (Thelwell, 1980). Kim Butler sums this up effectively:

> The year was 1910 and in the hillsides of northeastern Brazil that once harbored fugitive slaves, Eugenia Ann dos Santos inaugurated a sacred community so that African ancestors and deities could give direction and strength to their children in the diaspora. Assisted by a *babalawo*, a diviner trained in Nigeria, she dedicated the land to Zango, the patron deity of the kings of the Oyo Empire. In ritual learned from elders on both sides of the Atlantic, the first of many generations of spiritual children entered this special land to become African. (Butler, 1998, 1)

Moreover, as in the United States, African descendants in South America often invoked Africa as a reference for salvation because it was the original homeland, the repository for cultural rudiments, and the symbol of the racialized animus that generated group solidarity. Just as the maroons or other runaway groups sought to replicate Africa, other African descendants in South America sought to use it as a source for identification and a way to negotiate improved status in the new environment. This was especially indicative of efforts after the formal end to enslavement. Brazilian groups adopted what they remembered to be African signs and symbols for their organizations, even as they sought to secure a place in the organized social and political order of individual countries. This development has been tracked in a number of the South American countries, but nowhere has it been of the force of that in Brazil because of the size of the African descendant population there. Many of the former enslaved blacks who moved to the cities in Brazil began to utilize their common experience of discrimination and oppression as a base for organization and identity. Between 1888 and the 1930s a major movement essentially based on African descendant solidarity developed in São Paulo, where the group organized its own political party, the Brazilian Black Front (Butler, 1998, 59). Meanwhile, there was a similar, albeit divergent, redefinition of the terms of African descendant relationships in Bahia, where their number constituted the largest proportion of any major city. These rudiments had all of the elements of a campaign for the negotiation of access and stability of rights for local community membership that have occurred in the United States. Its evolution also followed a similar, if muted, path—the development of a broad raced-based critique of the social order. It became known as the United Black Movement (MNU) and effectively mobilized a group of African descendants who labeled themselves Afro-Brazilians as they contested the racialized social order that systematically relegated African descendants to a lower status. It was a movement that referenced Africa in many ways—reemphasizing cultural elements long present in the society, and adopting styles and an ideology focused on solidarity in racial identity and self-determination.

So all over the Americas organizing and negotiating social and political rights based on solidarity obtained from repression as African descendants is nothing new. It is a constant and part of a long tradition. This long tradition was consistent with the Africa-centered options proposed during the civil rights movement of the 1960s in the United States. But it is also indicative of a continuing strain of interest on the part of African descendants in the Americas in general—building on the commonality of a racialized experience as Africans, and adopting African unity as a strategy for identity and group progress. It is little wonder that when African descendants have successfully negotiated terms of engagement with the existing political and social order in the West, they have often bargained within those processes and structures with a race-based African identity.

Elective Representation

The subject of this chapter is elective representation insofar as we are describing the organization of African descendant legislators as solidarity entities in the legislative process. It is therefore critical to reflect on the meaning of representation. Despite the appearance of clarity of meaning, "representation" is a slippery concept. Recent research focuses on at least four varieties of it: *formal representation*, the mere acquisition of a formal office with the authority to act within that body; *descriptive representation*, one who reflects the social characteristics of constituents; *symbolic representation*, a representative whose views are deemed to be at one with those of the constituents; and *substantive representation*, where the representative is deemed to act responsively to the opinions and interests of the constituents (Pitkin, 1967; Whitby, 1997). These dimensions of representation become critical because of the manner in which African descendant legislators manage to win election and/or how they are able to respond to the special needs of African descendant peoples in their districts. They are frequently elected in districts where there is a large black population, especially in the United States. When they are not elected from such districts, there is always the question of how effectively they can respond to the interests of African descendants who may reside in the district in a minority status. In both instances questions arise about how these legislators function with regard to African descendant constituents since the former are almost always in a minority status in the lawmaking body. Can they deliver the goods? Are they mere symbols of the general condition of African Americans, and if so, how does that translate for the distribution of benefits to other blacks?

Largely because of the range of problems attendant to representation for African descendant legislators in bodies where they are a voting minority, they have often sought to make gains by mobilizing their strength as a solidarity bloc. The model example of this has been the CBC in the U.S. Congress. After the considerable gains of the civil rights movement that reenfranchised blacks in the United States, there was significant growth in the number of blacks in Congress, almost all in the House of Representatives. Their numbers increased from the three elected in the 1950s to the twelve members who first established a "Select Committee" in 1969 that subsequently became the CBC in 1971 (Barnett, 1982).

The purpose for organizing the CBC was to "facilitate communication among black representatives and between those representatives and the House leadership" (Barnett, 1982, 30). As the organization evolved, it came to be see itself as "representative at-large for 20 million black people" (Barnett, 1982, 33), focusing on such activity as "provision of casework services, gathering and disseminating information, administrative oversight, articulation of the interests of a specialized group within the black community, and the development of legislative proposals (Barnett, 1982, 34). But in an evolutionary process the group also recognized that they had individual constituencies and that it was equally necessary to be assiduous in representing those interests, especially as reelection depended on it. This reality has sustained an organization that sees itself performing the function of representing African descendants in the United States writ large, at the same time that its individual members look after routine constituency affairs in their districts. As these are largely black-majority districts, it puts the legislators in the position of playing an essentially ethnic interest group game (Barnett, 1982). However, since most legislators and most of their black constituents affiliate with the Democratic Party, another unexpected role has emerged. As legislators became more involved in party leadership and attained more seniority in their relatively "safe districts," significant energy has been dedicated to shoring up the fortunes of the party. This has become more and more critical as the party lost its legislative majority and had to fight for its very existence (Tate, 2003).

The organizational status of the CBC has changed significantly since its founding. At its inception the Caucus, one of the most substantial among a plethora of groups calling themselves caucuses, was a formal organization of the House of Representatives. It had an office and a staff in the Capitol buildings and was led by a member elected from among the group. It was reasonably well supported by a membership fee of $4,000 received from each of its members. As the membership grew, the support base for its secretariat also grew, However, when the Democratic Party lost its majority in 1994, the Republicans withdrew formal congressional recognition and space, and barred use of public funds to support such caucuses. This was a blow to the organization as it was forced to organize itself as a private foundation and to raise money to continue its business (Walton and Smith, 2003, 173).

Despite the diminished formal standing of the CBC, its public persona has not suffered significantly. It has succeeded in sustaining itself and continues to have a voice in public debate. It and its members individually are a significant presence in the legislative body, thus assuring black constituents symbolic representation, a variety of benefits often underestimated, but ubiquitous in the general representative process in the United States (Tate, 2003). Also, the Caucus continues to perform many of the functions it set for itself at the outset. Among other things, it continues to offer an alternative budget each year and to seek coalitions with other representatives on legislation deemed important to the broad interests of blacks across the country. Its members sponsor legislation and perform about average in getting laws passed, and they continue to sketch out a substantive program that seems consistent with the particular interests of blacks in each given session. The following goals are cited in the CBC website for the 108th session:

- Expanding employment and building wealth
- Affordable, high-quality health care for every American
- Ensuring equity in the education of our children
- Strengthening and enforcing our civil rights laws
- Providing both homeland and hometown security

The First Afro-Descendant Legislators Meeting

Since African descendant legislators in the United States have arguably been the most successful in attaining representative power in a lawmaking process, where they constitute a numerical minority, they have become an important model for African descendants in South America. The legislators in the Southern Hemisphere have observed blacks in the United States use their votes as a bloc in their largely racially exclusive electoral districts to elect their own to Congress, and they have watched the elected representatives struggle to effectively represent their constituents in the general context of legislative work. And as the "invisible" communities of African descendants in the South American countries revive their movements for greater participation, they too have elected a small number of representatives who identify themselves as reflective of these aspirations. They are found in virtually all of the countries and have had varying degrees of success negotiating the slippery terrain of race for elective positions. Provisionally (in 2003) there were twenty-six members representing eight countries:

BRAZIL

Deputados

Luiz Alberto Silva dos Santos
Carlos Santana
Gilmar Machado
João Batista dos Santos
Francisca Trindade
Vicente Paulo da Silva
Alceu Collares
Reginaldo da Silva Germano

Senadores

Paulo Paim
Eurípedes Camargo
Sebastião Machado Oliveira
Ideli Salvatti

ECUADOR

Rafael Erazo

PANAMA

Haydee Milanes De Lay

URUGUAY

Edgardo Ortuño

COLOMBIA

Diputados

Wellington Ortiz
Maria Isabel Urrutia

Senadora

Piedad Cordoba Ruiz

COSTA RICA

Epsy Campbell
Edwin Patterson Bent
Julián Watson Pomear

HONDURAS

Luis Flores
Olegario Lopez

PERU

Jose Luis Risco
Martha Moyano
Cecilia Tait

It is not clear when legislators in South America began to actively plan for a region-wide organization, though clearly the idea is not new. The first organized efforts with the intent of bringing together the legislators can be dated to July 2001. At that time the National Conference of Brazilian Black Legislators, already a loosely formed caucus, took the first steps. The group responded to one of its deputies, Luiz Alberto Silva dos Santos (Salvador), who "called for a regional meeting of Afro-Descendant legislators." Subsequent to this "the group of Black Legislators in the Brazilian National Congress designated a commission that took the first steps towards organizing the regional meeting." While it took two years of laying the foundation, that Pan-South American meeting took place in Brasilia in November 2003 under the sponsorship of the Brazilian National Congress and was organized by Deputy Luiz Alberto and his legislative counterparts.

The conference billed itself as a Conference of Afro-Descendant Legislators of the Americas, but it was at inception much broader. The first audience that the Brazilian Commission sought to engage was indeed black legislators from all over the Americas and Caribbean. A considerable effort was exerted, unsuccessfully, to get representation from the CBC, for example. Though there was a presence of African descendants from the United States, elected congressional representatives were not among them. Beyond lawmakers, the invitation list included civil society organizations and was open to a variety of other activists, intellectuals, and advisers. Among the latter, an invitation was sent to African governments and/or diplomatic missions. And aside from the legislators from Central and South American countries, a sizeable contingent of local NGOs and activists, largely from Brazilian communities, did attend. Aides and staff from the CBC attended, as did members of the Race and Democracy Project, a collection of scholars, activists, and students from the United States and Brazil.

The goals of the first meeting were substantive, having to do with some of the central issues in the countries from which members came. The first goal was just such a broad concern—the socioeconomic conditions of blacks. Then the statements continued to focus on means by which legislators could use their offices to structure a legislative agenda that was inclusive of issues and sentiments shared by Afro-descendants. To this end they looked to establish a network, perhaps a caucus, though that language was specifically avoided. The complete list of goals was as follows:

1. To raise the visibility of the socioeconomic conditions of Afro-descendants in the Hemisphere
2. To strengthen the debate on ways in which Afro-descendant issues can be incorporated into the legislative agenda

3. To create a network of Afro-descendant legislators and civil society organizations dedicated to Afro-descendant communities in the Hemisphere
4. To elaborate a legislators' plan of action aimed at racial equality
5. To discuss the human rights legislation throughout the Hemisphere and its role in elimination of racial discrimination

There was little doubt that the Afro-descendant legislators saw themselves as operating within the context of the international Pan-African movement. The broad reach of their appeal for participation is the first sign that this movement sought to build on a well-wrought plan of action for unifying peoples of African descent for altering racial discrimination and exclusion. The initial statement of identity affirmation referred to their Africaness—an emphasis on the essential nature of the African origins for giving them a place and a claim. Acknowledgment of the role of the ancestors in traditional African life is clarified by an early reference to the ancestors who provided the "path." And there is an immediate reference to the continuous resistance to the European domination and enslavement. As the meeting took place in Brazil, it was perhaps appropriate that a local model was used—"the land of Zumbi of Palmares . . . whose struggles of liberation . . . inspir[ed] . . . Afro-Brazilian . . . and Afro-Descendants in the Diaspora." And the statement went on to link this resistance to an expanded conflict—allies among other racialized and/or oppressed peoples around the world. Here they invoked declarations against racial discrimination, calling special attention to the U.N.-sponsored conference on race held in Durban, South Africa.

The issues focused on in the Brasilia Declaration were broad, encompassing the full range of exclusions that Afro-descendants encountered in their societies. There was a constant focus on policymaking and the policy process. It was noted that Afro-descendants are largely excluded from participation in the policy process or in setting the policy agenda. Therefore, the group first sought an expansion of their participation in this arena. It seems clear that the legislators were especially concerned about their exclusion from policy debate, which then made it easy for their interests to be excluded from policy decisions. A major bone of contention was the continuing debate about the Free Trade Area of the Americas. Afro-descendants asserted that the discussions were dominated by the United States and therefore left South Americans with an a priori disadvantage. For the black communities, this disadvantage was deemed even more egregious since the most negative impact of free trade across the Americas would be on the most fragile, localized markets. Therefore, there was some urgency in the exhortation of the black legislators to boost the general role of their individual governments, at the same time that more directed attention should be given to the differential impact on Afro-descendant communities. Similarly, they called for legislation to be targeted to particular problems of race and gender, and demanded that an affirmative action program be developed to expand the participation of such underrepresented elements across the Americas and Caribbean. And in the hope of generating a body of legislation and policies that would have a region-wide impact, the legislators called for international cooperation between governments, with special attention to developing market links to continental Africa.

There were also a number of practical decisions about the management of the emerging legislative "caucus." Considerable attention was given to the question of continuity. The long-range interest was for the development of an Afro-descendant Parliament of the Americas. They established a working group to develop appropriate plans. Moreover, they announced plans for development of a website to be used as a clearinghouse for information, where legislative developments and other relevant material could be transmitted and exchanged with the target audience.

The summary statement of the hopes of the Afro-descendant legislators set into bold relief their concern with the fundamental exclusion of blacks as a racial group, where the consequence was a reduction of the peoples to invisibility—denigrating their humanity and their culture, the very core from which claims might be made on public resources and regular community membership. They put it this way: "The set of commitments signed in Brasilia revolves around the social insertion, the defense and preservation of the culture and tradition of Afro-Descendants in the Americas. In this context, we will dedicate ourselves to making the demands, repressed for centuries by material, spiritual and symbolic exploitation and debilitation, part of the political agenda of our countries, in order to ensure the well being of our peoples."

Second Meeting of Afro-Descendant Legislators

The second meeting of the legislative group occurred six months later under the auspices of the National Legislature of Colombia. The events took place May 19–21, 2004, in the capital city of Bogotá. Its co-sponsors were the Ministry of Justice and the Externado University of Colombia. As with the meeting at Brasilia, legislators were not the only representatives invited. A wide range of NGOs, activists, scholars, Colombian government representatives, and diplomats were present. The program included formal presentations by legislators focusing on matters of law and political issues (local and regional); panel discussions by NGOs and activists regarding project descriptions, implementation, and results; and academic presentations by scholars. These were organized into a series of plenary sessions under the themes of "General Description of Conditions and Problems of the Americas and the Caribbean" and "International Accords and the Promotion of Afro-Descendant Politics." A substantial portion of the activity was dedicated to workshops on subjects including "Rights of Afro-Descendants in the Americas and the Caribbean"; "Identity, Culture and Education"; "Plans for International Cooperation"; "Legislative Experiences and the Future of Afro-Descendants"; and "Census and Land Issues of Afro-Descendant Communities."

The attendees included many of the participants from the first conference. There were twenty-one legislators, representing nine countries in Central and South America. The official delegation also included diplomatic representatives from two African countries: two from Morocco and another from Nigeria. Once again, despite considerable effort, no members of the U.S. CBC attended. However, there were two legislative staff members representing their congressional employers, and a representative from the Rainbow—PUSH organization of Jesse Jackson. Scores of representatives of NGOs and local activists from Colombia and a few others from member countries participated, as did four representatives of the Race and Democracy Project—three from the United States and one from Brazil. Here is the list of participants:

BRAZIL
Luiz Alberto dos Santos
João Grandão Batista dos Santos
Isaias Silvestre
Carlos Santana

COLOMBIA
Edgar Ulises Torres Murillo
Piedad Córdoba Ruiz
Maria Isabel Urrutia
Francisco Wilson Córdoba
Julio Gallardo Archbold
Julio Rufino Córdoba
Wellington Ortiz
María Teresa Uribe

COSTA RICA
Epsy Campbell
Edwin Patterson Bent

ECUADOR
Rafael Erazo

HONDURAS
Olegario Lopez

PANAMA
Samuel Binns Villagra

PERU
José Luís Risco
Martha Moyano

URUGUAY

Edgardo Ortuño

VENEZUELA

Adela Muñoz

MOROCCO

Mohamed Njib Boulif

M'Barak Bouhida

NIGERIA

Usman Bagaje

The conferees first noted their achievements with regard to the goals of the first conference. First was that the second meeting was under way with good participation. The planning group was working toward the creation of a Parliament of Afro-descendant legislators; a website was operational, becoming a repository for the dissemination of important information; and a video presentation had been produced of the first meeting and was actively being used as a tool for bringing visibility to the legislators' project.

Another achievement, not noted in the official document per se, but very evident during the proceeding, was the value of the interaction. These individual members were clearly attaining a knowledge of each other in these close encounters that generated an ease of communication between them. The three days of concentrated time together also gave them a rare opportunity to trade ideas, share experiences, and build rapport for collaborative ventures. And the relatively short time span between the first and second conferences afforded them the rare opportunity of continuity in conversations (picking up where they left off, so to speak) with short-term reflection. Otherwise, because of the similarity of their legislative experiences across the region, they had a wealth of information to exchange and a ready rubric that allowed them to "cut to the chase." Consequently, they were able to also acquire considerable information about the other countries in their region. And they were able to conduct this business together with the relative comfort of a secure and supportive environment, outside their routinely exposed positions as a small minority in their home legislative setting.

The range of issues considered at the meeting can be divided into six broad and somewhat overlapping areas: economic policy, democratic norms, international conventions, social issues, Pan-Africanism, and topical country issues. The economic policy questions continued the concern about the major free trade negotiations that were occurring in Colombia concurrent to the Afro-descendants meeting. The free trade measures were seen as a threat especially to Afro-descendant communities, and the governments did not seem attuned to the matter. This was largely attributed to an absence of voices from the affected Afro-descendant communities in the policy process and to the weaknesses and irresponsibility of the South and Central American governments with regard to the United States.

However, the legislators went beyond mere discussion of the implications of the free trade negotiations. They also took up the question of the debt burden of the Latin American countries. Instead of simply asking for debt forgiveness, as many Third World states do with excessive debts, they issued a novel challenge. The legislators proposed that there should rather be a debt exchange, which would require that the proceeds acquired in debt forgiveness arrangements be invested in Afro-descendant communities toward the alleviation of racial disparities.

A considerable amount of discussion continued to be devoted to democracy. The legislators expressed an abiding interest in securing democratic norms in the region. Participation and access were seen as the basic alternative to elite-dominant governments all over the region, whose membership was exclusive of Afro-descendants, notwithstanding policy influence. The group alluded to its own method of participation in its events as a model for what true participation required. They noted that each of their meetings had been a collaborative effort for civil society agents—what the legislators termed an alliance.

As in the first meeting, a good deal of emphasis was placed on international protocols affirming the rights of oppressed and racialized groups. Article 14 of the Santiago convention against racial discrimination, the U.N. conference on race held at Durban, South Africa, and the Organization of American States convention against racial discrimination were all invoked. The legislators saw these protocols as important tools for forcing their local governments into action. There were two reasons for this. In the first place, most of their governments had signed the declarations and conventions, which they observed in the breach; and second, the protocols in and of themselves sustained the claims of the aggrieved and expanded their conflict to a large international community of allies. And with the increased involvement of international actors in putting pressure on countries that violate human rights, the Afro-descendants were hedging a bet that such support could be mobilized against their governments.

The Pan-African focus that was evident in the Brasilia meeting was perhaps more prominent in the iteration for the Bogotá venue. The notion of the Diaspora as a direct and formal part of the African Union was put forward. These legislators proposed that the African descendants in the Americas be considered a sixth region of the membership of the continental union. It was the expression of a desire that had long been prevalent among Pan-Africanist political groups who argued that this membership was natural given historical circumstances—their forced removal from Africa and subsequent enslavement. All this was orchestrated, it is argued, on claims of African inferiority. This negative evaluation of continental Africans has also been transferred to the descendants in the West, which has led to mass oppression of African peoples wherever they are. So the similarity of conditions makes it reasonable to assume that solidarity and unity of Africa and all of its descendants is desirable. That this position is articulated so strongly suggests its symbolic power for the legislators, but it also has a practical benefit. In several other instances, reference was made to arranging trade relations with African countries as a means of creating a Third World alternative to the assumed exploitative market arrangements with the dominant Western capitalist nations.

Social issues remained prominent at Bogotá. A major emphasis was placed on measures that would integrate Afro-descendants into the routines of daily life in their home countries. A good deal of this focus referred to the racial and class exclusions that left most African descendants outside of the educational system, with inadequate housing, and suffering an array of health maladies due to lack of access to medical care. The general view was that because there was almost no public acknowledgment of the racialization of Afro-descendant communities, this identity was repeatedly rendered invisible by the authorities and the general population. Yet the reality of their everyday existence redounded to isolation in racialized enclaves, almost always within the lowest social class sector of the society. The legislators called for an acknowledgment of this racialized identity as a means of throwing sunshine on its consequences, and in order to take affirmative steps for its alteration.

Finally, the meeting called attention to a variety of topical issues in individual countries. Perhaps the most visible local issue was the status of Afro-descendant communities in the host country of Colombia. Among other things, serious displacements were occurring among north and northwestern coastal communities because of the ongoing violent civil conflict between drug lords and rightwing militias. Some of the most vulnerable citizens were blacks in these faraway rural, agricultural communities. A number of local politicians, NGOs, and activists called attention to the serious displacement wrought by the narco-traffic in their local areas. They worried about the violence that forced people from their homes and caused their land to be confiscated, and about crop destruction due to chemical spraying to destroy supposed illegal drug cropping. Thus, the issue was not merely a local one, but had international implications, too. The Colombia government was widely seen as colluding with the United States in an effort to eliminate the narcotics traffic, with little or no concern for its costs to innocent indigenous, largely Afro-descendant populations settled in these areas. The legislators called on the host government to provide greater resources to the displaced families, and to provide better support for security in the long term.

Conclusion

The Afro-descendant legislators group has a challenging agenda and faces a complex of logistical and other issues in achieving its goals. Yet it has generated a remarkable amount of energy and resources in a mere two years. It has managed to acquire significant support from its general legislative bodies that have helped to underwrite the first two meetings and to provide facilities for doing so. But the most prominent feature of the fledgling organization is in the human resources it has marshaled from the Afro-descendant legislators themselves and from a wide range of community affiliates and allies. While no single member can take full responsibility for the success of the first two outings, surely a first among equals here is Luiz Alberto dos Santos. This deputy from Salvador worked tirelessly to bring together members of his own legislative body in Brazil and then extended that effort to bringing those from other countries on board. His leadership provided the model for how local funds might be generated to support meetings, and his steady hand guided the conceptualization of the project around its major themes of Afro-descendant identity and Pan-Africanism. The latter is a notable achievement under regional conditions where the leadership of virtually all of these governments deny such identity and disparage claims for Diaspora affinities.

Perhaps the most serious failings so far have been the efforts to engage Afro-descendants in the United States and the Caribbean. Each of these has special conditions that make the efforts problematic. The U.S. CBC, which is a kind of model for the Afro-descendant legislators, while having certain strengths, may not be as well positioned to contribute to the new organization as is supposed. One of its strengths, of course, is its size. It represents the largest single minority body of Afro-descendant legislators in the most powerful legislature in the world. Their longstanding organized caucus makes them the most experienced, giving them a degree of expertise and savvy that might be shared and transferred to Afro-descendant legislators elsewhere. Also, they have an ideological stance and status little different from those of their South American counterparts; they have a social change orientation based on participatory democracy and are largely bound together as a racialized entity. Indeed, they are subject to a kind of super-racialization with regard to their southern counterparts. They, too, see continental Africa as an important part of the racialized identity and in general espouse support for solidarity with the continent and its similar sociopolitical conditions. And there are all manner of indications that CBC members value the opportunity to collaborate with their legislative kinfolk in Latin America.

Yet the marriage of these two entities with so much to lend to each other has not been consummated. A part of the difficulty for the CBC is that it is not the organization it used to be. While its public visibility has not waned, because the number of members has actually held fairly constant, its internal capacity is much diminished. In its original iteration the CBC was supported by public funds and had an ability to organize projects and programs. When the Democratic Party, to which the overwhelming majority of Afro-descendants is aligned, lost its congressional majority, the CBC suffered. The new majority quickly barred use of public funds and public space to caucus organizations (Walton and Smith, 2003). Since the CBC was by far the best organized and most elaborate of these caucuses, the impact was profound (Barnett, 1982). In any case, having to privatize its operations leaves the CBC in a precarious position. Under these conditions, as an example, it could hardly host a meeting of the legislators' group. But the reverberations are far broader. The partisan circumstances, being a part of the congressional minority, now heightens the responsibility of the CBC members as party members versus articulation of its race agenda. That happens at a time when there is increasing pressure for these representatives to look after local, district-based issues and reelection (Tate, 2003). This combination of factors weakens the potential for participation and influence in a Western hemispheric organization of Afro-descendants.

The Caribbean is an area that raises a set of different but equally interesting questions. For the most part, these are governments where the legislative majority is and has always been a racial majority. Notwithstanding that the countries are all subject to the same conditions of racialization and its consequences of oppression, partisan agendas are likely to be defined in terms that do not necessarily match those in the United States and South and Central America. And so far, there has been no success in engaging prominent states among those in the Caribbean region to participate in the conferences. One supposes that this is both a product of lack of outreach to them, their lack of independent resources, and some quandary about their ability to influence the agenda. This deserves much further investigation than has been done to date.

There are nevertheless many features of the agenda of the Afro-descendant legislators that are consistent with presumed agenda items for Caribbean countries. Many of the latter certainly have Pan-African affinities and direct connections that often rival those in South America and the United States. The independent governments in the Caribbean have had longer direct government-to-government relations with African countries. And many of the independence leaders in the Caribbean came into their own in metropolitan Europe, together with African nationalists then present there. The alliances between them were many and complex. So that part of the Diaspora agenda is similar, and the Caribbean nations can bring a considerable amount of experience to it. The range of social issues is the same, too—poverty and flawed practice of democratic norms, among others. In this instance, however, the government culprit is as likely to be an Afro-descendant leader as a neocolonial agent. Even so, there is likely to be some interface with other countries in the presence of an expatriate entrepreneur. And from this point of view, some of the topical issues that concern the Afro-descendant legislators in South and Central America very likely resonate in the Caribbean.

APPENDIX A

Meeting of Afro-Descendant Legislators of the Americas and the Caribbean Brasilia Declaration

After reuniting in Brazil in the First Meeting of Afro-Descendant Legislators of the Americas and the Caribbean, organized by the Parliamentary Front in Defense of Racial Equality, from the 21st to the 23rd of November of 2003, legislators of the region, accompanied by representatives of the Black Movement and civil society organizations, decided to subscribe the present Brasilia Declaration.

We reaffirm our identity as Afro-Descendants. We recognize the path of our ancestors, the commitments assumed by our governments with our people and communities contained in the Declarations and Plans of Action of Santiago and Durban.

We recognize that we are in the land of Zumbi of Palmares, ancestral hero who led struggles of liberation from slavery and who should serve as a model of inspiration for the Afro-Brazilian community as well as for all Afro-Descendants in the Diaspora.

Considering that:

The Afro-Descendant people and communities have contributed enormously to the construction of all American and Caribbean societies;

In the Americas and in the Caribbean, there cannot be true democracy without the inclusion of Afro-Descendant men and women;

We Afro-Descendants account for more than 150 million in the Americas and the Caribbean, the majority of which live in poverty, a situation disproportionately affecting Afro-descendant women;

Our governments have signed the Declarations of Durban and Santiago, although the majority of them have not fulfilled the commitments assumed by these declarations;

We Afro-Descendants are scarcely represented in the government, particularly in Congress and Parliament; hence we must double our efforts and our work. This lack of representation has an even greater effect on Afro-descendant women;

The efforts aimed at including our people and our communities should consist of both universal and targeted policies. On the one hand, general policies to eradicate poverty in our countries that embody gender and ethno-racial perspectives should be promoted, on the other, public policy and legislation that specifically target Afro-descendant populations must also be promoted;

Our countries are immersed in a process of integration through agreements such as Mercosur, Pacto Andino, Caricom, Sica. One of the most important expressions of this process is in the Free Trade Area of the Americas (FTAA) in which the general situation of exclusion of wide sectors of the population is not present, especially in light of the historic neglect of our people and communities. Thus, as Afro-Descendants legislators, we should participate in this important debate in which the regional legislators have been practically absent;

Brazil is on the brink of approving the Statute for Racial Equality, which represents a qualitative and historic jump in terms of addressing the socioeconomic conditions of Afro-Brazilians;

Colombia, as well as other countries, has promoted legislative and constitutional reforms that promote the inclusion of Afro-Descendants. However, we do not have mechanisms for the exchanging of experiences on this legislation or public policy originating from them;

Substantive programs of cooperation or strong international relations do not exist between countries in Africa and the countries of our region. Brazil is taking important steps towards this goal;

The preservation of religions of African origin is a fundamental premise in the reaffirmation of the identity and culture of Afro-Descendants.

We commit to:

Drive a new form of policymaking based on respect for and inclusion of Afro-descendant men and women and all historically excluded people;

Create a working group of Afro-Descendant legislators of the Americas for the promotion and construction of an Afro-Descendant Parliament of the Americas and Network of Afro-Descendant Legislators;

Demand that the legislators of the Americas maintain active participation in the political control and in the debate of negotiations with FTAA, in which we will participate in order to incorporate the vision and the perspective of Afro-Descendant communities;

Demand that our governments fortify the regional blocks and promote popular consultation regarding FTAA in order to make decisions that truly consider the situation of the majority and not just one small segment of the population;

Actively participate in discussions leading to social, economic and fiscal reforms, including in them the development of legislative proposals that promote racial and gender equality;

Promote affirmative action legislation and policies based upon the Statute of Racial Equality of Brazil and Law 70 of Colombia, among others;

Promote among the Congress and Parliament of our respective countries the necessity to deepen the horizontal cooperation efforts between Latin America, the Caribbean and Africa, which contribute to social, economic and cultural development for the countries of both continents;

Elaborate a joint publication that refers to legislation and public policy in favor of Afro-Descendants as a tool for regional development;

Open an information portal on the Internet that increases the visibility of the actions and the proposals of the Afro-Descendant legislators, as well as posts information about policies and legislation;

Participate as Afro-Descendant legislators in the Summit of the Americas and in the Ibero-American Summit, which will occur in 2004;

Demand that our governments designate financial and human resources for the implementation of the Santiago and Durban agreements, especially those related to the Afro-Descendant people and communities and that the governments guarantee a process of evaluation in the Santiago +5 Conference;

Demand that the Brazilian National Congress approves the Statute of Racial Equality, guaranteeing financial resources for its implementation, which should serve as a benchmark for the countries of Latin America;

Demand that the Congress of Ecuador discuss and approve the project about collective rights of the Afro-Ecuadorians. In the same token, we demand that all congresses of the region that have pending legislation in favor of their Afro-Descendant populations discuss and approve them;

Organize the Second Meeting of Afro-Descendant Legislators of the Americas and the Caribbean in Colombia in 2004.

The First Conference of Afro-Descendant Legislators of the Americas and the Caribbean poses itself as an important element in the international political articulation of Afro-Descendants in the region. It does so in order to give the racial issue in the continent the necessary visibility for the rupture of the ideology of subjugation that still maintains more than 150 million people of African descent in exclusion.

The set of commitments signed in Brasilia revolves around the social insertion, the defense and preservation of the culture and tradition of Afro-Descendants in the Americas. In this context, we will dedicate ourselves to making the demands, repressed for centuries by material, spiritual and symbolic exploitation and debilitation, part of the political agenda of our countries, in order to ensure the well being of our peoples.

Câmara dos Deputados
BRASILIA, NOVEMBER 23, 2003

APPENDIX B

Second Meeting of Afro-Descendant Legislators of the Americas and the Caribbean

BOGOTÁ, COLOMBIA, 19–21 MAY, 2004

BOGOTA DECLARATION

Holding to our political responsibilities as Afro-descendant legislators of the Americas and Caribbean and in response to our commitments set forth in the first meeting in Brasilia, November 21–23, 2003, we came together on May 19–21 in Bogotá, Colombia to hold the Second Meeting of Afro-descendant Legislators of the Americas and the Caribbean.

We would like to highlight that the Second Meeting of Afro-descendant Legislators of the Americas and the Caribbean was organized with great success by the Ministry of the Interior and of Justice, the House of Representatives of the Republic of Colombia, and Externado University of Colombia with the objective of reuniting legislators, Afro-descendant civil society leaders, government officials and academics from the region.

We have chosen to subscribe to this Bogotá Declaration that reaffirms our identity as Afro descendants, recognizes the paths of our ancestors and reiterates the commitments of our governments to the actions outlined in the declarations and plans of action of Santiago and Durban.

We recognize that we have also met here in Colombia with the goal of joining in the commemoration of "Afro-Colombian Day" and to support the Afro-Colombian communities that have been seriously affected by the internal armed conflict in Colombia, and especially as it relates to their displacement and further marginalization.

We start by declaring that we have advanced on the following agreements set forth by the Brasilia Declaration from the First Meeting:

The realization of the Second Meeting of Afro-Descendant Legislators before the date outlined in which we ensured broad and diverse participation.

The launching of a web site that serves as an instrument of communication and the exchange of information between Afro-descendant legislators. This web site will be reviewed and finalized hereafter (www.afrolegis .com).

The creation of a Working Group to be in charge of the creation and the promoting of the Network of Afro-Descendant Legislators of the Americas and the Caribbean.

The production of a video of the First Meeting that serves as a tool for divulgation and to make our organizational efforts more visible.

Considering that:

Our efforts as legislators are important as we represent a community that is over 150 million people.

We also realize that the governments of the region do not concretize their legal and political commitments to Afro-Descendant communities thereby leading to a situation of continual exclusion and abandonment of Afro-descendant people.

Our active participation in politics, social movements and in opening democratic spaces in the Americas and the Caribbean has driven the participation of Afro-descendants in governmental agencies and in the decision making processes in the region; however, this participation is still limited and insufficient, especially the participation of Afro-descendant women.

The inclusion of Afro-Descendants in the national censuses and other statistical data is essential. Afro-descendant children and youth do not enjoy the necessary opportunities that would guarantee their basic rights of education that would allow them to enjoy equal living conditions in our Latin-American societies.

It is essential that our governments, congresses and parliaments of states that are members of the Organization of American States support processes that formulate and implement the Inter-American Convention against All Forms of Racism and Discrimination.

We value alliances with civil society and legislative, judicial and public powers in order to eradicate racial discrimination, xenophobia and intolerance in all of its forms in Latin America and the Caribbean.

We should continue the national efforts that call attention to the issues affecting Afro-descendant populations' inclusion in the decision-making processes and the implementation of national public policy initiatives especially as they relate to the fight against exclusion and marginalization.

Our countries are immersed in bilateral and multilateral free-trade negotiations without an in-depth discussion by legislators or the Afro-descendant movement about the impact not only on our countries, but also on our peoples and communities.

We recognize that the preservation of a democratic environment, which includes the respect for institutional norms and autonomy of each country, are a fundamental part of the development of our countries and of Afro-descendant communities.

Colombia faces a special situation of the forced displacement of Afro-descendant communities without effective actions that allow them to enjoy their most basic human rights, and in many cases in addition to their up-rooting, leaving them in a situation of abandonment.

Whatever action to expedite the achievement of peace and the fight against narco-traffic should ensure the active participation of communities of African descent that have been effected by the conflict.

We commit to:

Continue the process of the creation of the Afro-descendant Parliament of the Americas and the Caribbean to assure that in the next two years it will become a political space of reference throughout the region. The Parliament will contribute to the implementation of international conventions and accords and policies targeted at Afro-descendants. We also commit to nominate a coordination commission to continue this process which will consist of Brazil, Colombia and Costa Rica.

Consider the formal denouncements made by social movements in international forums that condemn our countries for not fulfilling their commitments to laws and international conventions in favor of Afro descendants.

Drive initiatives that permit states to negotiate with international financial institutions about exchanging their external debt for effective investment in Afro-descendant communities.

Continue opening the space for the participation of representatives of diverse state bodies and civil society organizations that are committed to fighting against racial discrimination.

Promote legislation and policies in favor of Afro-descendant youth and children.

Incorporate the special situation of exclusion faced by Afro-descendant women in our discussions and propositions.

Foster the inclusion of the issues raised by Afro-descendants participating in regional forums (Andean Parliament, Central American, Latin American, Parliamentary Confederation of the Americas). In addition, we commit to create a special commission to deal with Afro-descendant issues within the Andean Parliament.

Monitor the Andean Plan of Social Development to ensure that Afro-Andean issues are incorporated, as this plan will be debated in the next Andean Presidential Summit.

Promote policies in favor of Afro-descendants through affirmative action in areas of ethno-education, quality and level of education in Afro-descendant communities, quotas in universities, fiscal incentives for the hiring of Afro-descendants, quotas in hiring, earmarked funds in government budgets, among other initiatives.

Optimize the use of communication mechanisms such as video, teleconferencing and virtual dialogues to address the issues affecting our communities.

Elaborate a joint publication that compiles the legislation and policies in favor of Afro-descendants and foster exchanges of experiences between the different countries in the Americas and the Caribbean.

Insist that governments in the region implement Article 14 of the International Convention on the Elimination of Racial Discrimination that will create a process by which complaints can be made regarding racial discrimination.

Urge states to call "Santiago +5," a meeting to evaluate the fulfillment of the accords of the Regional Conference against Racism, Racial Discrimination and Xenophobia.

Encourage the participation of Afro-descendant legislators in the effort to reconceptualize the African diaspora as the Sixth African Region in order to have active participation in topics related to the development of the African continent.

Promote all of the actions necessary to guarantee the respect of land and territory of Afro descendants who are victims of armed conflict. At the same time, we commit to promote development policies that utilize science and technology that validate traditional knowledge and that permit the amelioration of the quality of life for Afro-descendants.

Promote holistic social programs for displaced people and the communities to which they relocate while at the same time providing the conditions for them to return safely to their communities.

Hold the Third Meeting of Afro-descendant Legislators of the Americas and the Caribbean in 2005 in either Costa Rica or in the United States in accordance with the conditions, political definitions and logistics that will be outlined in the preparatory process.

Urge the National Congress of Brazil to approve the Statute of Racial Equality that serves as a fundamental reference point for the other countries in the region.

Demand that the government of Colombia effectively implement the provisions set up by Law 70.

Urge the Colombian government and international institutions to concretize the definition of the Colombian government's policy on the pacific region based on the Pacific Agenda 21 and allocate economic resources for its execution. Develop a regional administrative structure to divulge these plans within the region and the rest of the country.

Urge the government of President Alvaro Uribe to make the Presidential Council on Afro-descendant Issues, which was established in the National Development Plan 2000–2006, more functional with a greater role.

Finally, we Afro-descendant legislators of the Americas and the Caribbean, reunited for the Second Meeting of Afro-descendant Legislators of the Americas and the Caribbean and committed to facing the challenges of our time reaffirm our struggle to overcome the substandard living conditions of our peoples and the elimination of all forms of discrimination and intolerance.

We take on the collective challenge of economic and social development on our continent while claiming the richness of its diversity. We know that this will achieve better relationships among people, communities, which will foster respect, solidarity and cooperation. This will undoubtedly create a better world in the new millennium, one in which there will be equal opportunities for everyone.

ELÍPTICO SALON

HOUSE OF REPRESENTATIVES OF THE REPUBLIC OF COLOMBIA

NATIONAL CAPITOL BUILDING

BOGOTÁ, COLOMBIA, MAY 21, 2004

REFERENCES

Aptheker, Herbert. 1942. *American Negro Slave Revolts*. New York: International Press.

Balandier, Georges. 1965. "The Colonial Situation." In *Africa: Social Problems in Conflict and Change*, ed. Pierre van den Berghe, 36–57. San Francisco: Chandler.

Barker, Lucius, et al. 1999. *African Americans and the American Political System*. Saddle River, N.J.: Prentice-Hall.

Barnett, Marguerite Ross. 1982. "The Congressional Black Caucus: Illusions and Realities of Power." In Michael B. Preston et al., *The New Black Politics: The Search for Political Power*. New York: Longman.

Birmingham, David. 1998. *Kwame Nkrumah: The Father of African Nationalism*. Rev. ed. Athens: Ohio University Press.

Blassingame, John. 1979. *The Slave Community*. New York: Oxford University Press.

Bratton, Michael, and Nicolas van de Walle. 1997. *Democratic Experiments in Africa*. New York: Cambridge University Press.

Butler, Kim. 1998. *Freedoms Given, Freedoms Won: Afro-Brazilians in Post-Abolition São Paulo and Salvador*. New Brunswick, N.J.: Rutgers University Press.

Clapham, Christopher. 1999. *Africa and the International System: The Politics of State Survival*. New York: Cambridge University Press.

Cockcroft, James, et al., eds. 1972. *Dependence and Underdevelopment: Latin America's Political Economy*. New York: Anchor Books.

Counter, S. Alan and David Evans. 1981. *I Sought My Brother*. Cambridge, Mass.: MIT Press.

Cronin, E. David. 1955. *Black Moses: Marcus Garvey and the United Negro Improvement Association*. Madison: University of Wisconsin.

Curtin, Philip. 1969. *The Atlantic Slave Trade*. Madison: University of Wisconsin Press.

Du Bois, W. E. B. 1965. *The Suppression of the African Slave Trade*. New York: Russell and Russell.

Fausto, Boris. 1999. *A Concise History of Brazil*. New York: Cambridge University Press.

Fontaine, Pierre-Michel, ed. 1985. *Race, Class and Power in Brazil*. Los Angeles: Center for African American Studies.

Franklin, John Hope, and Alfred A. Moss. 1994. *From Slavery to Freedom*. 7th ed. New York: McGraw Hill.

Gottschalk, Keith. 2005. "Things Fall Together: The Founding of the African Union." Unpublished paper.

Hanchard, Michael, ed. 1999. *Racial Politics in Contemporary Brazil*. Durham, N.C.: Duke University Press.

Harris, Joseph, ed. 1982. *Global Dimensions of the African Diaspora*. Washington, D.C.: Howard University Press.

Hughes, Langston. 1940. *The Big Sea*. New York: Hill and Wang.

Jahn, Janheinz. 1968. *Neo-African Literature: A History of Black Writing*. New York: Grove Press.

James, C. L. R. 1963. *The Black Jacobins: Toussaint L'Ouverture and the San Domingo Revolution*. New York: Vintage.

Kesteloot, Lilyan. 1974. *Black African Writers in French: A Literary History of Negritude*. Philadelphia: Temple University Press.

Knight, Franklin. 1970. *Slave Society in Cuba during the Nineteenth Century*. Madison: University of Wisconsin Press.

Legum, Colin. 1962. *Pan-Africanism: A Short Political Guide*. New York: Praeger.

Lewis, David Levering. 1994. *W. E. B. Du Bois: Biography of a Race, 1868–1919*. New York: Henry Holt.

———. 2000. *W. E. B. Du Bois: The Fight for Equality and the American Century 1919–1963*. New York: Henry Holt.

Marx, Anthony. 1998. *Making Race and Nation: A Comparison of the United States, South Africa and Brazil*. New York: Cambridge University Press.

Moore, Carlos. 1988. *Castro, the Blacks, and Africa*. Los Angeles: Center for African American Studies.

Moore, Richard. 1971. "Du Bois and Africa." In *Black Brotherhood: Afro-Americans and Africa,* ed. Okon Edet Uya. Lexington, Mass.: D. C. Heath.

Nkrumah, Kwame. 1957. *Ghana: The Autobiography of Kwame Nkrumah.* New York: International Publishers.

———. 1963. *Africa Must Unite.* New York: International Publishers.

———. 1965. *Neo-Colonialism: The Last Stage of Imperialism.* New York: International Publishers.

Padmore, George. 1953. *The Gold Coast Revolution.* London: Dobson.

Pitkin, Hanna. 1967. *The Concept of Representation.* Berkeley: University of California Press.

Price, Richard, ed. 1979. *Maroon Societies: Rebel Slave Communities in the Americas.* Baltimore: Johns Hopkins University Press.

Siqueira, Maria de Lourdes. 1998. *Agô Agô Lonan: Mitos, Ritos e Organização em Terreiros de Candomble da Bahia.* Belo Horizonte, Brazil: Mazza Edições.

Tate, Katherine. 2003. *Black Faces in the Mirror: African Americans and Their Representatives in the U.S. Congress.* Princeton, N.J.: Princeton University Press.

Thelwell, Michael. 1980. *The Harder They Come.* New York: Grove Press.

Turner, Lorenzo. 1949. *Africanisms in the Gullah Dialect.* Chicago: University of Chicago Press.

Uya, Okon Edet, ed. 1971. *Black Brotherhood: Afro-Americans and Africa.* Lexington, Mass.: D. C. Heath.

Walton, Hanes, and Robert Smith. 2003. *American Politics and the African American Quest for Universal Freedom.* 2nd ed. New York: Longman.

Whitby, Kenny. 1997. *The Color of Representation.* Ann Arbor: University of Michigan Press.

Williams, Eric. 1970. *From Columbus to Castro: The History of the Caribbean 1492–1969.* London: Andre Deutsch.

ELEVEN

African Americans, Transnational Contention, and Cross-National Politics in the United States and Venezuela

Sekou M. Franklin

Introduction

On September 1, 2005, shortly after Hurricane Katrina struck New Orleans, Louisiana, and the Mississippi Gulf Coast, Rev. Jesse Jackson, the founder and president of the Rainbow/PUSH Coalition, held a press conference at the Baton Rouge command center. Accompanying Jackson were Louisiana governor Kathleen Blanco and Felix Rodriguez, the president of CITGO, a subsidiary of Petróleos de Venezuela, S.A. (PDVSA), Venezuela's state-owned, oil company. At the conference Rodriguez announced that Venezuela would provide an assortment of aid to Katrina survivors: 1 million barrels of gasoline, $5–6 million in cash, medical supplies, and 50 tons of canned goods.[1] Venezuela was one of seventy countries that initially offered humanitarian assistance to Katrina survivors, and within a week Venezuela reconfirmed its offer at the Rainbow/ PUSH Coalition's Chicago headquarters.[2] Yet, due to mounting tensions between the United States and Venezuela, President George W. Bush rejected most of the aid package. Venezuela redirected the aid to the American Red Cross and Louisiana state government, and more than a year after the hurricane, Venezuela assisted organizations such as the People's Hurricane Relief Fund and Oversight Coalition, which have carried out social justice-oriented reconstruction initiatives in New Orleans.[3]

Coincidentally, Jackson traveled to Venezuela a few days before the hurricane battered the Gulf Coast, at the invitation of President Hugo

Chávez Frías (generally referred to as Hugo Chávez). Jackson's delegation, which included a Texas state senator, Rodney Ellis, discussed a number of issues with Chávez: immigration policy, Chávez's petroleum diplomacy, and which U.S. "markets" or jurisdictions would be receptive to coordinating domestic social programs with Venezuelan officials.[4] The delegation also met with other government officials as well as activists from the Network of Afro-Venezuelan Organizations, the foremost black social movement organization in Venezuela.

The highlight of Jesse Jackson's trip was his thirty-minute speech before the Venezuelan National Assembly on August 28, perhaps the first of its kind by an African American leader. During the speech, Jackson linked Chávez's populist social programs—what Chávez refers to as twenty-first-century socialism or the Bolivarian revolution (named after Simón Bolivar, the nineteenth-century, Venezuelan-born independence leader)[5]—with the social justice orientations of Rev. Martin Luther King, Jr., Coretta Scott King, and Rosa Parks.[6] These programs include urban land committees, community councils, cooperative economic initiatives, subsidized supermarkets in poor neighborhoods, and social missions (government institutions that provide free health care, eye surgery, literacy development, adult education, and food security to the country's poor and working class).[7] Jackson gave additional praise to the Venezuelan government for institutionalizing participatory democracy and antidiscriminatory protections for women and Amerindians (indigenous/Native Venezuelans) in its 1999 constitutional reforms. Finally, he encouraged the assembly to implement the civil rights proposals recommended by the Network of Afro-Venezuelan Organizations.[8]

The Rainbow/PUSH Coalition's visit was part of a series of dialogues involving African American activists and elected officials, Venezuelan government leaders, and Afro-Venezuelan activists. For example, TransAfrica Forum, a U.S.-based social justice group that lobbies for African and African Diaspora issues, sent a delegation to Venezuela in January 2004. Traveling with the group were entertainer-activists Danny Glover, the chair of TransAfrica's board of directors, and board member Harry Belafonte, both of whom are staunch allies of Hugo Chávez.[9] Two years later, TransAfrica sent another contingent of activists to Venezuela, which included scholar-activist Cornel West; Dolores Huerta, formerly of the United Farm Workers; Malia Lazu, a young voting rights activist; and Daniel "Nane" Alejandrez of the antigang organization Barrios Unidos.[10]

This chapter examines African American/Venezuelan alliances and social movement activities, or what I refer to as transnational contention.

Transnational contention involves cross-national sociopolitical activism, consciousness-raising activities, international solidarity work, cultural and political exchanges, the allocation of resources from one country to another (or resource exchange between civil society groups from two or more nations), the formation of social and political networks, and initiatives targeting the foreign policies of constituent (African American/Venezuelan) nations or global/supranational institutions.[11] From the standpoint of African American/Venezuelan relations, transnational contention is dissident political behavior because the aforementioned initiatives do not comply with the established norms and rules of the U.S. foreign policy establishment. Moreover, African Americans use transnational contention to interrogate black identity and the interdependence between African Americans and Afro-Latinos. This is worth noting since there are between 130 million and 150 million people of African descent in Latin America, and at least 15 percent (and perhaps as much as 30–40 percent) of Venezuela's population has African lineage.[12]

This chapter lays out a theoretical framework for evaluating the efficacy of black transnational contention. This is followed by a detailed discussion of three forms of black transnational contention. First, *state-focused transnationalism* entails cross-national initiatives by government officials, either in Venezuela or the United States. *Development-oriented contention*, the second type of transnationalism, consists of coalition-building and consciousness-raising activities that occur at networking sites such as international forums, rallies, and conferences, in solidarity campaigns, and during cultural and political exchanges. Additionally, *race-oriented (Pan-African) transnationalism* is central to African American and Afro-Venezuelan alliance building and antidiscrimination initiatives.[13]

Transnational "Bridge" Building

Much of the research on transnational contention in the Americas has focused on the antiglobalization movement and cross-national dissent against neoliberal austerity programs.[14] Despite the utility of the antiglobalization/antineoliberalism arguments, they do not adequately explain why some forms of transnational contention are successful and why others are not, and how transnational contention is uniquely shaped by race and identity politics.[15] In this section, I identify four factors that help to explain the trajectory and efficacy of black transnationalism, especially pertaining to Venezuela and Latin America.

First, transnational contention allows black progressives (and other progressives) to advance internationally based, or cross-national, social justice claims that may be marginalized inside the formal U.S. foreign policy apparatus. Indeed, when domestic policymaking opportunities are limited, aggrieved populations will look to the transnational sphere for allies and political support.[16] Robnett's research, despite focusing exclusively on the U.S. civil rights movement, is instructive for describing why and how transnationalism takes place. She says that an informal tier of leadership emerged during the civil rights movement composed mainly of women, youth, and low-income blacks. This leadership sector (or what she calls "bridge" leadership) was excluded from formal leadership positions in traditional civil rights organizations that were mostly headed by middle-class men.[17] Bridge leaders subsequently used their informal positions within the civil rights movement to cross boundaries and mobilize other informal or dissident activists who, because of their gender, age, or class predispositions, did not conform to the mores of the civil rights establishment.

Robnett's research is applicable to this discussion of black transnationalism. It explains how some political actors use nontraditional or informal policymaking methods to shape public opinion and global relations when they are shut out from established political channels. The U.S. foreign policy establishment's defense of capitalism and backing of pro-Western foreign leaders have forced many progressive activists to find alternative or creative ways to influence global affairs. This is exemplified in Stanford's research on Jesse Jackson's "citizen diplomacy" initiatives.[18] Jackson's solidarity with Palestinian and (black) South African independence movements, and insistence that the United States should normalize relations with left-leaning Latin American governments, conflicted with the official positions of U.S. foreign policy analysts. Yet as Stanford notes, Jackson was not deterred from trying to shape U.S. public opinion about foreign policy or from using transnational contention to cultivate cross-border relations. Accordingly, Jackson and progressive transnationalists were able to build a bridge—that is, they used nontraditional methods to affect cross-national issues and opinions—between their constituents' interests and progressive movements outside the United States.

Another factor influencing the efficacy of black transnationalism is the availability of indigenous resources. Indigenous resources are preexisting infrastructures, organizations, and networks that facilitate movement activism, even in the absence of monetary resources or the granting of legitimacy by political elites.[19] Although attention is given to the influence of movement organizations and activists during the height of movement activities, in reality, movements are successful because they are facilitated by groups and activists (indigenous resources) that were busy long before the most intense periods of movement campaigns. Transnational contention involving African Americans and Venezuelans has been successful because of the longstanding work of indigenous activists. This indigenous resource base is fairly diverse and draws from varied sectors of black civil society and leadership networks. A multi-sector field of indigenous activists and networks—a social movement field that appeals to a broad section of indigenous activist and allies—enhances the efficacy of transnational alliances. It decentralizes contentious claims and creates multiple entry points for a diverse group of activists and allies to support transnationalism.[20]

Indigenous groups in Venezuela and Latin America have been critical to promoting transnational dialogue between African American and Venezuelan activists. Activists from Afro-America 92, Afro-America 21, the Afro-Venezuelan Foundation, the Black Women's Union, and the Afro-Araguan Foundation had been involved in international solidarity campaigns and consciousness-raising activities since the early 1990s.[21] Some of these activists eventually created the Network of Afro-Venezuelan Organizations (also referred to as La Red or the Net) and cemented a relationship between African Americans and Afro-Venezuelans.

In the United States, as early as 1998, the Organization of Africans in the Americas (OAA), co-founded by Michael Franklin, engaged in alliance-building initiatives with Afro-Venezuelans and other blacks throughout Latin America.[22] Other U.S.-based indigenous groups, such as Hunter College's Global Afro-Latino and Caribbean Initiative (GALCI), Trans-Africa Forum, and the Rainbow/PUSH Coalition have forged ties with Afro-Venezuelans.

The third factor influencing black transnational contention is an available political opportunity structure. *Political opportunity structure* generally refers to favorable political conditions that are receptive to social movement campaigns. Some examples of favorable political opportunity structures are the emergence of political elites who are sympathetic to movements, political instability and/or divisions among elites that can be exploited by activists, and the transition from one regime to another that is sympathetic to social movement demands.[23]

Chávez's election victory in 1998 created a host of political opportunities for progressive-left activists and black transnationalists. As president of a top-five oil-producing country that provides the United States with at least 11 percent of its oil,[24] Chávez helped to reenergize the Organization of Petroleum Exporting Countries (OPEC), restructured business contracts with Western oil companies to give Venezuela greater control over oil distribution, and used the country's burgeoning oil profits to redistribute wealth and fund antipoverty programs within and outside of Venezuela. (This is referred to as *petro-diplomacy*.)[25] Additionally, he joined Cuba's Fidel Castro to revitalize the Non-Alignment Movement as a counterbalance to U.S. influence in the Global South.

Furthermore, Chávez has paid off Venezuela's debt to the International Monetary Fund and World Bank, and "refinanced a portion of Argentina's IMF debt."[26] As an alternative to U.S.-backed free trade agreements, such as the Free Trade Agreement for the Americas (FTAA)—a South American version of the North American Free Trade Agreement (NAFTA)—Chávez pushed Latin American countries to endorse the Bolivarian Alternative for the Americas (ALBA). If implemented in its original form, ALBA would create a social emergency fund, literacy and free health care plans, and a development bank for South America.[27] As part of his international economic program, Chávez has lobbied for Venezuela's admittance to the Southern Common Market (Mercosur), South America's powerful economic integration body, and has advocated for the creation of a Latin American currency that could compete with the U.S. dollar.[28]

Chávez's unflinching criticisms of the West/Global North are partially fueled by what he believes was the Bush administration's aggressive attempts to destabilize Venezuela. On September 20, 2006, Chávez delivered a speech before the U.N. General Assembly denouncing the Bush administration's military ventures in the Middle East and the U.S. "anti-democratic veto mechanism" in the U.N. Security Council. Referring to Bush as the "Devil" and "Mr. Imperialist Dictator," he stated that the United States had made "desperate efforts to consolidate its hegemonic system of domination" in Latin America and the Global South.[29] Some political commentators from the United States criticized Chávez's speech, and after he made biting criticisms about Bush the next day in a visit to Harlem, New York, Rep. Charles Rangel admonished Chávez. Still, Chávez's speech was warmly received by the U.N. General Assembly and underscored his attempt to reshape Latin America's geopolitical landscape.

Chávez's own rise to power was influenced by a radical populist tradition in Venezuela.[30] It also resulted from shifting political opportunities in the late 1980s and early to mid-1990s and disillusionment with neoliberalism among the country's rank and file.[31] This included a failed coup attempt by Chávez in 1992, followed by his two-year prison sentence. The unrest convinced members of the Punto Fijo—the indistinguishable two-party system composed of Acción Democrática and the Social Christian Party of Venezuela (COPEI)[32]—to decentralize political authority. Previ-

ously, candidates for parliamentary and gubernatorial elections were selected through a closed party list chosen by Punto Fijo elites.[33] Once he was
released from prison in 1994, Chávez and his political party, Revolutionary
Bolivarian Movement—200 (later renamed the Movimiento Quinta Re-
pública), convincingly articulated the discontent of Venezuela's poor and
working-class groups who continued their criticisms of the government's
support for neoliberal programs. Finally, in 1998, Chávez won the presidency and the Punto Fijo's forty-year reign came to an end.

   The important point is that Chávez's rise to power, as well as the efforts
by African Americans and progressive activists in the United States to develop cross-national linkages with Venezuela, were augmented by favorable political conditions. Further, the Bush administration's hostility toward
Chávez inadvertently created more opportunities for African American/
Venezuelan transnationalism. Many political observers believed the coup,
combined with the oil workers' strike by Chávez's opponents in 2003 that
destabilized the nation's economy, and the failed presidential recall referendum a year later, were all backed by the Bush administration.[34] Hence,
there is a belief that because blacks are among the most liberal-progressive
cohorts in the United States, they would be receptive to amicable diplomacy between the United States and Venezuela. Jody Nesbitt points out,
"For leftist leaders, support of the African American community in the
[United] States is just as important as the support of the masses at
home . . . pressure from Black America is now necessary to reverse jingo-
istic perceptions in favor of support for Venezuelan sovereignty."[35] Black
progressives and radicals, whose antipoverty orientations are similar to
those promoted by Chávez, were seen as particularly receptive to his social
programs. Moreover, currying favor among black America's civil rights
and social justice activists was essential to countering the aggressive posture toward Venezuela by Condoleezza Rice and Colin Powell, both high-
ranking black officials in the Bush administration.[36]

   Finally, identity formation, or what Kevin Gaines calls "contested citizenship," is central to black transnational contention. Contested citizenship "is based on the idea that meaning and content of U.S. citizenship is
subject to debate, and open to a range of possibilities for political behavior."[37] Gaines believes transnationalism is attractive to African Americans
because they see their fate and political-economic predicament as similar
to those of other underdeveloped communities in the Global South.[38] This
interpretation of contested citizenship is similar to Cunningham's description of "globalized identity," which asserts that global politico-economic
forces cultivated kinship ties among social justice activists from different

countries.[39] It also parallels Michael Dawson's discussion of linked fate,[40] and reinforces Vargas's belief that African American/Afro-Latino alliances gave birth to a "transnational black politics" in the Western Hemisphere.[41]

Taken together, these factors—bridge building, indigenous resources, favorable political conditions, and identity formation/contested citizenship—lay the groundwork for explaining black transnationalism. The remainder of this chapter examines the three forms of transnational contention (state-focused, development-oriented, race-oriented) and explains the linkages between African Americans and Afro-Venezuelans.

State-focused Transnational Contention

State-focused transnational contention entails cross-national initiatives that are started by or are closely linked to the work of government officials in Venezuela or the United States. These initiatives include petro-diplomacy social programs, alliance-building activities, election monitoring, and solidarity campaigns. Although these initiatives may involve nongovernmental or social justice groups, they were propelled by public officials from one of the participating countries.

TransAfrica Forum has been at the vanguard of state-focused transnationalism with Venezuela. Toward the end of 2003, Chávez extended an invitation to TransAfrica Forum to attend a commemoration and school-naming ceremony honoring Rev. Martin Luther King, Jr., in Venezuela. Earlier, TransAfrica's president, Bill Fletcher, expressed an interest in visiting Venezuela to learn about the Bolivarian project and meet with Afro-Venezuelan activists. Fletcher believed this conversation was essential to the "on-going work [of TransAfrica] to strengthen relationships with the African Diaspora in the Western Hemisphere."[42] TransAfrica routinely links with progressives and African-descended communities in Western Hemisphere countries. Shortly before Fletcher's arrival, Randall Robinson, TransAfrica's founder, organized a delegation to Cuba, and was instrumental in mobilizing blacks behind prodemocracy initiatives in Haiti.[43]

Traveling to Venezuela in January 2004, the delegation consisted of Glover and Belafonte; intellectuals/academicians Julianne Malveaux, Sylvia Hill of the University of the District of Columbia, and James Early, a Smithsonian Institution specialist in Latin American and Caribbean affairs; labor activist Patricia Ford; and Malika Asha Sanders of the Selma, Alabama-based Twenty-first Century Youth Leadership Movement. Upon their arrival, the activists met with Chávez at the presidential palace, held discussions with other government leaders, met with Afro-Venezuelan activists, and even met with anti-Chávez groups such as Democratic Coordinator and the Central Venezuelan Workers (CTV).

The delegation was impressed by Chávez's antipoverty agenda and the practice of participatory democracy in Venezuela. Malveaux wrote, "It is hard to quibble with the way Chávez has embraced poor Venezuelans and focused on eliminating poverty through education—in some ways, more than our own government has done here."[44] Sanders recalled traveling with the delegation to Veroes, Yaracuy, for Chávez's weekly radio address, Aló Presidente, and seeing masses of people, primarily low-income and "dark"-skinned Venezuelans walking to the event.[45] This experience, she believes, indicated that a "mass movement" was taking place in Venezuela. James Early, the delegate who knew the most about Latin American culture and politics, had made several visits to Venezuela dating back to his first trip in the early 1970s. Yet during TransAfrica's trip, he noticed major changes in the body politic since Chávez's presidential victory. One of the most dramatic changes, Early explained, was "the radical, democratic step essentialized in the concept of participatory democracy, which has set a new framework for civic and governance dialogue throughout Latin America."[46] After the trip, he joined TransAfrica's board of directors and later served on the board of Telesur, a regional television project that models itself after a Latin American version of the British Broadcasting Corporation. Although Telesur is owned by several Latin American countries, with Venezuela owning 51 percent of the station, it is coordinated by representatives of different civic groups.[47] Telesur attempts to counter the elite and racial bias of Latin America's television networks. In 2007 the media network allocated $18 million to the Haitian revolutionary project for a film to be directed by Danny Glover, a member of Telesur's advisory board.[48]

Petro-Diplomacy Initiatives

Venezuela has implemented a host of petro-diplomacy initiatives in coordination with U.S.-based social justice leaders and elected officials. Through the Venezuelan-owned CITGO corporation, Venezuela's consulate offices worked in coordination with grassroots organizations and elected officials to deliver discounted fuel for low-income families facing expensive energy bills during the winter and summer months. The Venezuelan government accelerated this program in 2005 after the U.S. Congress and the Bush administration approved funding cuts to the Low Income Energy Assistance Program.[49]

The discounted energy program was negotiated by members of Congress, CITGO and Venezuela's consulate offices, state and local officials, and civic organizations. CITGO then delivered the fuel at below-market rates to local agencies and civic groups that worked with families in need of energy assistance. In 2005, CITGO collaborated with Rep. José Serrano and three nonprofit organizations in the Bronx to deliver oil for residents in seventy-five apartment buildings. This came after Chávez met with seventeen community groups in the Bronx while visiting the U.N. annual meeting.[50] A year later, Rep. Charles Rangel proposed a pilot program for oil to be delivered to Harlem residents through the organizations Hope Community, Inc. and the Community League of the Heights. A similar agreement was brokered for 25,000 Philadelphia residents by Pennsylvania state senator Vincent Hughes, Rep. Chaka Fattah of the Congressional Black Caucus, and the Community Legal Services of Philadelphia.[51] Another agreement was arranged for 45,000 southeastern Massachusetts residents by Rep. William Delahunt (D-MA), Joseph Kennedy's Citizens Energy Corp., and the Mass Energy Consumer Alliance.[52] Other programs have been proposed in Milwaukee, San Francisco, Detroit, and New Haven, Connecticut.

In addition, Venezuela offered the Chicago Transit Authority (CTA) a 70 percent discount for 7 million gallons of diesel fuel to help reduce transportation costs.[53] The proposal, which came amidst a fare increase by the CTA, was rejected by CTA president Frank Kruesi, who cited the "U.S. government's strained relationship with Chávez" as the one of the reasons why the CTA could not accept the offer.[54] Kruesi's rebuff angered state legislators, city council representatives, and Rep. Luis Gutierrez who had worked with Venezuela's consulate office in Chicago to broker the deal. Omar Sierra, Venezuela's deputy consul, believed the two sides were close to an agreement, but U.S.-Venezuelan tensions may have discouraged Kruesi from accepting it.[55] Afterward, Rep. Dennis Kucinich recommended that the Cleveland RTA should approach CITGO with a similar proposal, but this also faced strong opposition.[56]

Another example of transnational contention concerns the collaboration between Venezuelan officials and Mike McGee and Joe Davis, black members of the Milwaukee common council. Between 2005 and 2007, the aldermen partnered with Sierra on several cross-national initiatives. Sierra arranged a meeting in Venezuela between the aldermen and Luis Reyes, the governor of the state of Lara. Reyes is a black Venezuelan who used to live in the United States. The officials discussed establishing a Sister Cities program between Milwaukee and Carora, Lara's capital city.[57]

In July 2006, McGee and Davis invited Mayor Julio Chavez of Carora to speak before the Milwaukee common council's Sister Cities committee.

Chavez said his city would provide eye surgery for as many as 400 elderly and low-income Milwaukee residents. He informed the committee that his city had "already established facilities and doctors and they are available to Milwaukee low-income residents."[58] The program would be administered by Venezuela's eye surgery mission, the Miracle Mission, which would arrange for the transportation of the Milwaukee patients. He also informed the committee about investment initiatives in Carora that would be available to Milwaukee business leaders.

A month before Mayor Chavez's visit, a Venezuelan delegation, led by Ambassador Bernardo Herrera Alvarez, traveled to Detroit and Lansing, Michigan. The delegation, intent on building relations with state and local officials, met with Detroit Mayor Kwame Kilpatrick, Rep. Carolyn Kilpatrick, Detroit city council representatives, and black state legislators.

Before leaving Michigan, the Michigan Welfare Rights organization hosted a ceremony celebrating Alvarez's visit.[59] Alvarez expressed additional interest in establishing a social development fund for Detroit health clinics and local economic cooperatives. Afterward, his delegation traveled to Milwaukee to meet with city officials and community activists at several health facilities, including the Martin Luther King Heritage Health Center.[60] The meetings were designed to shore up support for the Sister Cities program.

Electioneering in Venezuela

Venezuela further solidified ties with African Americans by requesting their participation as election monitors in the 2006 presidential election, which pitted Chávez against opposition leader Manuel Rosales. Black state and local officials from Michigan and Wisconsin participated as election monitors,[61] as did Henry Hamilton, a former magistrate judge in Iowa and member of the Milwaukee NAACP. Hamilton traveled to Venezuela with a delegation of Midwest judges. He was "pleased to find out about the social programs [in Venezuela]," and found that "a lot of aspects of their democracy surpass some of the practices that we [election observers in the United States] see."[62] After the trip, the delegation published a document, "Final Statement by State Supreme Court Judges,"[63] that validated the fairness of the presidential election.

In addition, the NAACP's International Affairs Department sent an eight-member delegation to monitor the election. The delegation was organized by Peter Graham Cohn, a San Francisco Bay area attorney. In early 2006, Cohn initiated discussions about the trip with the NAACP executive board.[64] Upon the delegation's return to the United States, the NAACP dispelled any rumors of election irregularities. Afterward, Cohn continued to bridge African Americans and social justice activists with Venezuelan officials. For example, he organized a lecture in San Francisco by Ambassador Alvarez.

Chávez's ascendancy expanded the opportunity structure for blacks and antipoverty activists to engage in petro-diplomacy and international election monitoring. As evidenced in this discussion, African American progressives (and other progressives) looked to Venezuela for assistance at a time when the U.S. body politic was lukewarm to antipoverty social programs. This suggests that "blocked channels of grievance articulation between domestic groups and the government spur activists [and dissident elected officials] to look elsewhere for support."[65] Black activists were further impressed with Venezuela's model of participatory democracy and electioneering process, especially considering the election irregularities and disenfranchisement of black voters in the 2000 and 2004 presidential elections.

Adding to the success of state-focused transnationalism was its appeal to a diverse segment of blacks. Earlier, I argued that effective transnational bridge building is shaped by how well U.S.- and Venezuelan-based activists appeal to multiple sectors of indigenous blacks. Chávez's social programs appealed to progressive black activists, while election monitoring was attractive to black elected officials and civil rights groups. Petro-diplomacy assisted nonprofit organizations as well as black elected officials, as long as they could be delivered through formal policy channels.

Another factor shaping the efficacy of state-focused transnationalism was its specific race-conscious appeal. In their visits to Venezuela, even those initiated by the Venezuelan government, African Americans held separate meetings with Afro-Venezuelan activists who educated them about racial politics in the country. TransAfrica Forum's trip was highlighted by the opening of a school dedicated to Rev. Martin Luther King, Jr. The Rainbow/PUSH Coalition visited with community leaders in the predominantly black region called Barlovento where they participated in political dialogues and cultural activities.

Countering the Counterinsurgency against Venezuela

The participation of African Americans in cross-national alliances with Venezuela was particularly significant during George W. Bush's presidency. Many journalists documented the Bush administration's destabilization campaign in Venezuela.[66] In addition, the Bush administration accused Chávez of abetting narcotics traffic.[67] In what Frank Furedi calls the "social construction of a terrorist,"[68] conservative intellectuals, republican lawmakers in Congress, and the Bush administration also tried to link Chávez with terrorism.[69]

Notwithstanding the support Chávez has among some members of the Congressional Black Caucus (CBC), Alcee Hastings (D-FL), a member of the House Permanent Select Committee on Intelligence, criticized Chávez. In June 2003, he introduced a House resolution that stated, "[Venezuela] seems to be slipping once again into an era of 'strong man' rule, and a state that embraces socialist dogma."[70] The National Endowment for Democracy and the AFL-CIO's American Center for International Labor Solidarity (ACILS) also funneled resources to anti-Chávez organizations.[71]

Black transnationalists viewed the U.S. destabilization campaign as an attack on their interests and the policy objectives of Afro-Venezuelans. In response, Afro-Venezuelan activists urged African Americans to actively oppose U.S. policy toward Venezuela. The Network of Afro-Venezuelan Organizations wrote to black American social justice activists in 2004, requesting their assistance in offsetting U.S. aggression. Written by the organization's three leading activists (Jesus "Chucho" Garcia, Nirva Camacho, and Jorge Guerrero Veloz), the letter stated, "You [African Americans and Afro-Latinos] can enter this struggle with us, by doing what you can do in your country, to ensure that Venezuela's right to determine its political direction is respected without U.S. interference, or intervention directly or indirectly."[72] Although it is difficult to ascertain the impact of this letter, African American groups and leaders intensified their defense of Venezuela between 2005 and 2007.

LaMar Lemmons introduced a resolution before the Michigan legislature urging the United States to respect Venezuela's sovereignty.[73] Over a year earlier, he sponsored a similar resolution (Resolution 06–64) that was adopted at the National Black Caucus of State Legislators annual convention.[74] In November 2006, Jesse Jackson and Cornel West coauthored a petition with Dolores Huerta and social justice activist Tom Hayden, defending Venezuela from U.S. attacks.[75] Joining them were Afro-Venezuelan activist Professor Alejandro Correa and Willie Thompson, a Pan-Africanist writer for the prominent Bay Area online newspaper, sfbayview.com, who co-authored an essay urging African Americans to pay close attention to events in Venezuela.[76]

Certainly, African American leaders were not the only ones who attempted to curtail U.S. hostility toward Venezuela. Latino activists in the

United States, Native American groups, and white leftists challenged U.S. interventionism. Yet African Americans were actively involved in this effort because they viewed the anti-Chávez sentiment as an attack on social justice programs, which if fully implemented in the United States, would be beneficial to marginalized African Americans. Further, Afro-Venezuelan indigenous leaders encouraged African Americans to counter U.S. intervention in their country.

Development-oriented Transnationalism

Development-oriented transnationalism, or the cultivation of social and political ties and agenda-setting initiatives, is facilitated by activists at international gatherings, rallies, human rights conferences, and within solidarity campaigns. These venues provide opportunities for activists within and outside the United States and Venezuela to share ideas about pertinent political issues.[77] These activists have created an alliance structure that uses consciousness-raising activities to counteract U.S. aggression against Venezuela and dialogue about racial politics in Venezuela.

International conferences and forums created opportunities for interaction between activists from Venezuela and the United States. From 2004 to 2007, Venezuela hosted the World Social Forum, the Fourteenth Congress of the Women's International Democratic Federation, and the World Youth Festival. African American activists attended all these events. For example, Nellie Hester Bailey, cofounder of the Harlem Tenants Council, attended the Women's Congress, and youth from Georgia's Benjamin E. Mays Youth Center, the Clayton County Village 100 Black Men of America, Inc., and Project South attended the World Youth Festival.[78]

Several groups, including Global Exchange and Witness for Peace, also coordinate politico-tourism trips to Venezuela. Although Global Exchange is a white-led, progressive organization, it has an exchange program, "Afro-Venezuela: The San Juan Cultural Festival," which allows the participants to meet with Afro-Venezuelan activists and public officials. During the 2006 exchange, Marcus Bellamy, a Howard University student, had the opportunity to inform junior government officials about the tensions surrounding an oil pipeline extending from Venezuela into a region in Colombia heavily populated by Afro-Colombians. Bellamy warned that the Afro-Colombians would be subject to exploitation and abuse by multinational corporations and paramilitary groups that wanted to control the pipeline once it crosses into Colombia.[79] Global Exchange also organized a speaking tour in 2004 for Jesus "Chucho" Garcia, a popular Afro-Venezuelan activist, to discuss the ill effects of the U.S.-backed Free Trade for the Americas Agreement.

Another set of networking opportunities has been provided by Venezuelan solidarity gatherings. In October 2005, the Rainbow/PUSH Coalition sponsored an exhibit and panel, "Venezuela Matters," in Chicago, which pulled together activists from Venezuela and the United States.[80] Additional gatherings were sponsored by students and faculty from the University of Illinois at Champaign-Urbana and Macalester College in St. Paul, Minnesota. In March 2006, two dozen groups organized the Venezuela Solidarity Conference in Washington, D.C. Over 400 activists attended the conference, including representatives from the Network of Afro-Venezuelan Organizations, the All-African People's Revolutionary Party (A-APRP), the People's Hurricane Relief Fund and Oversight Coalition, and the Malcolm X Grassroots Organization. At the conference, Bob Brown, a veteran social activist and a leading member of the A-ARPP, proposed the creation of the solidarity organization called the People of African Descent in Solidarity with Venezuela.[81]

Cultural anthropologist Sheila Walker has been instrumental in facilitating gatherings on black identity in the Americas. She contends that black transnationalism must broaden the conceptual interpretation of "African American" to include a Pan-American/Pan-African understanding of the term—one that culturally and politically links African-descended communities throughout the Americas. Historically, this has been difficult to achieve because Pan-Africanism has privileged alliances between U.S. blacks, Caribbeans, and Africans.[82] While at Spelman College, Walker organized "Afro-Latin American Week" in October 2003 and a parallel conference, "Generating Knowledge from the Inside," that emphasized "the contributions of Africans in creating the Americas."[83] In 2004, she participated in the Network of Afro-Venezuelan Organizations 150-year anniversary commemoration of slavery's abolition in Venezuela.

Additional opportunities for Afro-Latinos and African Americans to address critical race issues that are marginalized in Latin America have occurred at international gatherings sponsored by the United Nations (the U.N. Millennium Summits or the World Conference against Racism, Racial Discrimination, Xenophobia and Related Intolerance), the U.N. Economic Commission for Latin America, the Inter-American Dialogue, the Inter-Agency Consultation on Race in Latin America, the Interamerican Foundation, the U.N. Educational, Scientific and Cultural Organization (UNESCO), and the Global Afro-Latino Caribbean Initiative (GALCI). Until the 1990s and early 2000s, Central and South American governments failed to respond to the demands of civil rights and antidiscrimination activists. Yet the aforementioned gatherings created a context for mobilizing international pressures against racially conservative regimes. International events, as Carmin and Hicks contend, can "give movement actors in closed political systems more international attention, potentially buffering them from repression."[84] These conferences had little impact on U.S. race relations, but they legitimatized black-led antidiscriminatory campaigns in Latin America.

An important initiative addressing race and gender in Latin America has been organized by a coalition of Afro-Latina and Afro-Caribbean women, who eventually formed the Network of Afro-Caribbean and Afro-Latina American Women. The women first came together in the early 1990s to develop a political agenda in advance of the 1995 Fourth World Conference on Women in Beijing, China.[85] After several meetings between the mid-1990s and the early 2000s, the group met in 2006 in Managua, Nicaragua, and approved a set of resolutions called the "Managua Declaration." The resolutions condemned racism and sexism, and said the network would be used as "a space for discourse and as a political instrument for reflection, exchange, denunciation and proposals for the defense of the human development of Afro-descendant women."[86] Another set of resolutions endorsed sexual and reproductive rights—a fairly radical position in Latin America's Catholic-dominated countries—and expressed a desire to combat HIV/AIDS. The group also passed a resolution in support of women who were displaced by Hurricane Katrina.

Participating in the Managua meeting were Afro-Venezuelans Nirva Camacho, the most prominent living Afro-Venezuelan woman activist, and Blanca Escalona Rojas. Camacho and Rojas are members of the Network of Afro-Venezuelan Organizations and are founding members of the Afro-Venezuelan feminist group, Cumbe de Mujeres Afrovenezolanas. Activists from the United States were involved in some of the network's meetings. Yvette Modestein, a black Panamanian residing in the United States, served on the regional board of the group. Hunter College's GALCI, headed by Humberto Brown, served as a clearinghouse, or what Aldon Morris calls a "movement center,"[87] for the Managua meeting. In May 2005, Brown attended the International Afro-Descendent Conference in Caracas. His group also organized a series of dialogues inside the United States assessing relations between African Americans and Latinos.

As the Managua experience points out, development-oriented transnationalism has been used to interrogate gender identity and feminism in the Americas. For example, in January 2006, New York's Alberto Lovera

Bolivarian Circle sponsored a panel of half a dozen Venezuelan women to explore gender politics and society. Traveling with the delegation was Reina Arratia, a member of Venezuela's Presidential Commission to Prevent and Eliminate Racial Discrimination and a former member of the Network of Afro-Venezuelan Organizations and the Union of Black Women (this group no longer exists). Andree-Nicola McLaughlin, the founder of the Black Women's Institute, also spoke at the gathering.[88] In addition, Danny Glover brought to San Francisco Nora Castaneda, the head of Venezuela's Women's Development Bank, during her speaking tour in the United States.[89] While in San Francisco, Castaneda was honored by Tom Ammiano, a city supervisor who put forward a resolution declaring January 29 "Nora Castaneda Day."

Development-oriented transnationalism has provided African Americans and Afro-Latinos the political space to engage in consciousness-raising activities about black identity and citizenship. The Managua group approved a resolution urging Latin American countries to formally recognize the concept of "African-descended" people. This was the fruition of a long history of Afro-Latino/a organizations pressuring international organizations such as the United Nations to recognize the term. Another component of this identity formation has been a reassessment of the concept "African American." Jorge Guerrero Veloz, a leading Afro-Venezuelan activist who has traveled to the United States on a number of occasions, is adamant about extending the African American concept to include African-descended people in the Americas.[90] GALCI also broached the subject in a February 2006 panel in New York, Redefining African American: What's at Stake?[91]

Finally, development-oriented transnationalism has produced a multiracial alliance structure of blacks, whites, Native American groups, and Latinos. Yet, African American involvement in development-oriented transnationalism with Venezuelans and Afro-Latinos is distinctly wedded to their sense of shared fate and the belief that both (African Americans and Africans/Latin Americans) are adversely affected by the same political, economic, and social forces. Harry Belafonte, for example, praised his friendship with Venezuela's ambassador because they had the chance "to sit, to talk, to strategize, on what we can do in mutual assistance and reciprocity, not just for poor people of color, Hispanics, Blacks, indigenous people, women, [but for] all poor."[92] This sentiment was echoed by Lucius Walker, the founder of Pastors for Peace, an international social justice group, and Chris Silvera, chair of the Teamsters' National Black Caucus organization. Both were invited speakers at the November 8, 2005, town hall meeting, Evening in Solidarity with Bolivarian Venezuela, in New York sponsored by the International Action Center and the Alberto Lovera Bolivarian Circle. Walker later explained that "Venezuela's political perspective under Chávez's leadership takes into account a responsibility to relate to people who are economically marginalized, including black folk and Latinos in the U.S. and throughout the Americas."[93] Silvera also emphasized that "it's important that we [African Americans] support the liberation struggle" in Venezuela.[94] Nellie Hester Bailey, the cofounder of the Harlem Tenants Council and a delegate to the Fourteenth Congress of the Women's International Democratic Federation in Caracas in April 2006, further believes Venezuela provides African Americans the opportunity to align themselves with Global South social movements.[95] Ojette Brundage, an African American expatriate who lives outside Caracas, traveled to Venezuela for the 2005 World Social Forum and for a Global Exchange excursion program in 2006. She believes Venezuela provides an opportunity for evaluating how "we [U.S. residents] plan to deal with the people of the world and what concessions we are willing to make to make this world more equitable."[96] Her migration to Venezuela was partially a result of her disappointment with (white-led) progressive and antiwar movements in the United States that were unwilling to take the necessary risks to fight for poor communities.

Race-oriented Transnationalism

Race-based contention is the third type of transnationalism. Since the 1990s, African Americans have been active participants in discussions and lobbying initiatives designed to promote racial equality in Venezuela and throughout Latin America. These dialogues, carried out in solidarity with Afro-Venezuelan and Afro-Latino activists, attempted to shape U.S. policy toward African-descended Latinos, and encouraged Latin American governments to implement antidiscriminatory protections for African-descended communities.

As in most Latin American countries, race is somewhat of an enigma in Venezuela. Unlike the United States, where racial hierarchy was institutionalized in the legal, social, and economic framework of the country and penalized all blacks, including those of hypo-descendant or mixed ancestry, Latin America's racial history is more complex. Latin America's cosmic or mixed identity, defined by a triple heritage (European, Amerindian, African) or mixed ancestry, thwarted attempts by African-descended communities to develop race-centered or black consciousness movements.[97]

Venezuelan political elites implemented "whitening" policies—policies that recruited white European immigrants to the country and allowed some mixed-race descendants to legally identify with racial classifications other than black[98]—in order to deracialize Venezuela and limit the influence of nonwhite groups. Further complicating matters was that Venezuelan elites perpetuated the myth (or lie) that the country was not divided along racial lines, and that its cosmic or mixed identity precluded the imposition of racist practices against African-descended Venezuelans and Amerindians.[99] This myth of racial democracy permitted elites to institutionalize their influence with the support of middle- and upper-middle class, mostly white Venezuelans.

Venezuela's racial complexity produced several challenges for Afro-Venezuelan activists. First, it diminished the import of race as a mobilizing variable for Afro-Venezuelans. Many Afro-Venezuelans, accordingly, explain their marginal status not in terms of racism, but mainly as a result of their class (impoverished) predispositions. Many Afro-Venezuelans, or black and brown Venezuelans, refuse to identify with the black cause, and in some cases, reject the notion that racism exists in Venezuela. Some Afro-Venezuelans even believe in the superior beauty of light-skinned and white Venezuelans. Race-conscious Afro-Venezuelan activists contend that internal racism (*endo-racismo*), or the rejection of black identity, is actually worse than institutionalized racism in Venezuela.[100] This is complicated by the fact that most darker-skinned (African-descended) Venezuelans are poor, and the media, as well as other sectors of Venezuelan society, continue to perpetuate racial stereotypes and overt forms of discrimination against blacks.

This debate points to two strategies regarding how Afro-Venezuelans and their allies, including African Americans, should go about advancing race-based claims in Venezuela. First, some Afro-Venezuelan activists believe they should channel their energies within the Bolivarian revolution instead of making hard, and potentially disruptive, demands for civil rights protections. Proponents of this strategy insist that because of their working-class and impoverished status, black and brown Venezuelans will continue to benefit from the class-based, socialist-oriented initiatives of the Bolivarian revolution. Subsequently, Afro-Venezuelans should join in solidarity with Chávez's Bolivarian project, which is beneficial to poor Afro-Venezuelans. Then, once Afro-Venezuelans have institutionalized their influence within Chávez's governing coalition, they can advocate for problack, civil rights protections. This position is advocated by the Movimiento Cimarrones Afrodescendientes por la Revolución (Afro-descendent Maroon Movement for the Revolution), a group of Afro-Venezuelan activists allied with Chávez.[101]

The second viewpoint contends that race-based initiatives or civil rights protections should be at the forefront of the Bolivarian revolutionary project, even if this causes some discomfort among Chávez supporters and the Venezuelan left. Willie Thompson, a San Francisco Bay area activist and founder of the Organization of African North Americans, first visited Venezuela in the early 1960s. He is a Chávez supporter and has facilitated dialogues between African Americans and Afro-Latinos. Yet he claims that "international solidarity work [in Latin America and Venezuela] has to have an African component," and that antiracist measures should be at the forefront of socialistic-oriented programs in Venezuela.[102]

The Network of Afro-Venezuelan Organizations (also called La Red) has pushed for the second strategy. La Red's core leadership worked closely with the Chávez administration, but advised the president to use his bully pulpit to aggressively attack racism in the country.[103] Although La Red was excited about Chávez's public embrace of his African ancestry when he was first elected, it was disappointed with the National Assembly's refusal to approve of civil rights protections for Afro-Venezuelans. In addition to their struggle for civil rights protections, La Red has pushed for a national census of Afro-Venezuelans.[104] It has further pressured the Venezuelan government to incorporate Afro-Venezuelan history and culture in its educational curriculum.

La Red has won support among Afro-Latinos and African Americans for their initiatives. When TransAfrica Forum visited Venezuela in 2004, La Red urged the delegation to focus on the government's willingness to attack racism. James Early said that "Chávez readily responded to the critical observations of the lack of formal recognition of Afro-Venezuelans."[105] TransAfrica held a press conference at the end of the trip proclaiming that even though it approved Chávez's Bolivarian revolution, the government needed to give more attention to attacking racism. Interestingly, media conservatives in Venezuela used racist imagery and cartoons to characterize the group,[106] thus highlighting the entrenched racism in the country.

U.S.-based nongovernmental organizations and members of the Congressional Black Caucus (CBC) provided additional credence to racial justice movements in Latin America. In February 2006 the Inter-Agency Consultation on Race in Latin America and the Inter-American Dialogue organized the "Race Counts" conference, which addressed racial inequality in the Americas. The CBC, which began working with the Inter-American

Dialogue's Race Program in 2003, participated in the conference and hosted a reception for the attendees on Capitol Hill.[107] In 2003, CBC members Charles Rangel, Gregory Meeks, Donald Payne, William Jefferson, and Barbara Lee introduced House Concurrent Resolution 47, "Commemorating Africans' Descendants in the Americas." The resolution expressed solidarity with Afro-Latinos and urged the United States to actively promote racial equality in the Americas.[108]

Congress did not pass the resolution, but a year later, Representative Meeks submitted House Concurrent Resolution 482, which urged Latin American governments "to promote the visibility of Afro-descendants."[109] This was followed by a House resolution in 2005 (H.Con.Res. 175) recognizing the crimes committed against Afro-Latinos as a result of the transatlantic slave trade. CBC members were also involved in the Afro-Descendant Legislators of the Americas and the Caribbean, a regional black parliament that advocates for antidiscriminatory protections on behalf of Afro-Latinos.

Chávez also formed a presidential commission to study racial discrimination and xenophobia, and created offices inside the National Institute for Women, the National Institute for Youth, and the Ministry of Culture to study the status of Afro-Venezuelans. In June 2007, Venezuela began the long process of conducting its first census of African-descended people with 2010 set as the target date for completion.[110] These reforms, according to Jose Guerrero Veloz and Norma Blanca, a member of La Red, would not have been implemented if not for international pressures, including pressure from African Americans.[111]

Interestingly, racist attacks against the Chávez government probably caused him to devote more attention to addressing racism in Venezuela. Shortly after his presidential victory and after the 2002 coup, opposition leaders, media personalities, and elite activists criticized Chávez for drawing much of his support from black and brown communities.[112] Opposition leaders and the media used racially derogatory language to describe Chávez supporters and his association with blacks.[113] According to La Red members, the white elite uses the term *Chávista*—a universal term used to describe Chávez's political base—as a pseudonym to describe dark-skinned Venezuelans.[114] Thus, as Jesus "Chucho" Garcia points out, the coup and attacks against Chávez underscored the fact "that racism in Venezuela is now something that the government knows we have to do something about."[115] The anti-Chávez fervor and its association with racism contradicted Venezuela's myth as a racial democracy, and in some respects vindicated La Red's insistence that race and class are intricately intertwined in Venezuela.

Conclusion

Transnational contention is an important dimension of African American politics. Black transnationalism is exemplified in the participation of African Americans in the Pan-African Congresses during the first half of the twentieth century; the black radical internationalism of the 1960s and 1970s; black opposition to African and Caribbean colonialism, neocolonialism, and imperialism; the citizen diplomacy initiatives of Jesse Jackson; and African Americans' involvement in international conferences such as the World Social Forums and the U.N. conferences against racism and sexism.

Transnational contention allowed African American activists and elected officials to build a programmatic bridge between their constituents' interests and those of Venezuelans. Furthermore, transnational contention and cross-national initiatives, such as election observation, petro-diplomacy programs, and networking, have been influenced by a favorable political opportunity structure—most notably, Hugo Chávez's 1998 presidential victory—and shaped by an array of indigenous activists from Venezuela and the United States.

Race (identity)-based claims are another factor shaping black transnationalism toward Venezuela. African American activists and elected officials are receptive to cross-national linkages with Venezuelans because they believe their fate is linked to the material conditions of underdeveloped communities outside the United States. Black activists insist that U.S. aggression against Venezuela is an attack on social programs that are improving the lives of Afro-Venezuelans. They further believe these programs, if adopted in the United States, would benefit low-income communities and poor African Americans. The Network of Afro-Venezuelan Organizations has been central to educating African Americans and other progressives about race, class, and gender concerns in Latin America and Venezuela. The network is also a principal benefactor of race- and gender-based solidarity initiatives involving African Americans.

Finally, it is worth mentioning that African Americans are not alone when it comes to transnational contention and cross-national dissidence pertaining to U.S.-Venezuela relations. Yet black transnationalism stands out because African Americans remain among the most liberal/progressive subgroups in the United States, and their attention to global affairs in the

Americas is critical to counterbalancing the hostile U.S. stance toward Venezuela and other left-leaning governments.

NOTES

1. Citizens for Responsibility in Ethics, "Crew's Hurricane Katrina International Offers of Assistance Matrix," Washington, D.C., 25.
2. Cristóbal Valencia Ramirez, "Venezuela in the Eye of the Hurricane: Landing an Analysis of the Bolivarian Revolution," *Journal of Latin American Anthropology* 11, no. 1 (2006): 173.
3. Kali Akuno, "VZ Aid for Katrina: The Government said NO; The People say YES" (Media Advisory), People's Hurricane Relief Fund and Oversight Coalition, May 14, 2007.
4. Butch Wing, Interview by Sekou Franklin, May 24, 2007. Wing is a speechwriter for Rev. Jesse Jackson.
5. Marta Harnecker, *Understanding the Venezuelan Revolution* (New York: Monthly Review Press, 2005); Richard Gott, *Hugo Chavez and the Bolivarian Revolution* (New York: Verso, 2005).
6. Adalberto Trejo, "Rev. Jackson Durante Homenaje al Dr. King en la AN: Visión de Chávez da Respuesta al Imperative Moral de Nuestros Tiempos," August 28, 2005, available at http://www.aporrea.org/tiburon/n65183.htm and http://www.aporrea.org/imprime/n65183.html.
7. Michael A. Lebowitz, *Build It Now: Socialism for the Twenty-first Century* (New York: Monthly Review Press, 2006).
8. I use the term *Afro-Venezuelan* to describe Venezuelans of African descent. Yet, because of Venezuela's complex racial history, which suppressed racial identity, most Afro-Venezuelans do not identify with the concept, and many use the terms *negro/negra* (black), *moreno/morena* (brown), or *mestizaje* (mixed-blood).
9. Edgar A. Hernandez, "TransAfrica Forum Delegation Left Venezuela with a Very Positive Image of the Bolivarian Project," January 22, 2004, available at www.venezuelanalysis.com/articles.php?artno=1093.
10. Gregory Wilpert, "Delegation of Prominent U.S. Progressive Leaders Visits Venezuela," January 8, 2006, available at http://www www.venezuelanalysis.com/news.php?newsno=1862.
11. Chadwick F. Alger, "Transnational Social Movements, World Politics, and Global Governance," in *Transnational Social Movements and Global Politics: Solidarity beyond the State*, ed. Jackie Smith, Charles Chatfield, and Ron Pagnucco (Syracuse, N.Y.: Syracuse University Press, 1997), 260–75; Sanjeev Khagram, James V. Riker, and Kathryn Sikkink, "From Santiago to Seattle: Transnational Advocacy Groups Restructuring World Politics," in *Restructuring World Politics: Transnational Social Movements, Networks, and Norms*, ed. Sanjeev Khagram, James V. Riker, and Kathryn Sikkink (Minneapolis: University of Minnesota Press, 2002), 6; Marc Edelman, "Transnational Peasant Politics in Central America," *Latin American Research Review* 33, no. 3 (1998): 49–86; Mangala Subramaniam, Manjusha Gupte, and Debarashmi Mitra, "Local to Global: Transnational Networks and Indian Women's Grassroots Organizing," *Mobilization: An International Journal* 8, no. 3 (October 2003): 335–52; Robert Rohrschneider

and Russell J. Dalton, "A Global Network? Transnational Cooperation among Environmental Groups," *Journal of Politics* 64, no. 2 (May 2002): 510–33.

12. For a discussion of the Afro-Latino and Afro-Venezuelan populations, see James Early and Jesus "Chucho" Garcia, "The Political Status of Afro-Venezuelans in the Bolivarian Revolution: A Democratic Measure for Venezuela and Hemispheric Imperative," in *The Venezuelan Reader: The Building of a People's Democracy*, ed. Olivia B. Goumbri (Washington, D.C.: EPICA, 2005), 51; Clare Ribando, *Afro-Latinos in Latin America and Considerations for U.S. Policy* (Washington, D.C.: Congressional Research Service, 2005), 3.

13. For a similar discussion, see Joel S. Migdal, *Strong Societies and Weak States: State Society Relations and State Capabilities in the Third World* (Princeton, N.J.: Princeton University Press, 1988).

14. Paul Almeida and Hank Johnston, "Neoliberal Globalization and Popular Movements in Latin America," in *Latin American Social Movements: Globalization, Democratization, and Transnational Networks*, ed. Hank Johnston and Paul Almeida (Lanham, Md.: Rowman & Littlefield, 2006), chap. 1.

15. Deborah J. Yashar, "Resistance and Identity Politics in an Age of Globalization," *Annals of the American Academy of Political and Social Science* 610, no. 1 (March 2007): 160–81.

16. Margaret Kick and Kathryn Sikkink, "Transnational Advocacy Networks in the Movement Society," in *The Social Movement Society: Contentious Politics for a New Century*, ed. David S. Meyer and Sidney Tarrow (Lanham, Md.: Rowman & Littlefield, 1998), 217–23; Jackie Smith and Dawn West, "The Uneven Geography of Global Civil Society: National and Global Influences on Transnational Association," *Social Forces* 84, no. 2 (December 2005): 621–52.

17. Belinda Robnett, "African-American Women in the Civil Rights Movement, 1954–1965: Gender, Leadership, and Micromobilization," *American Journal of Sociology* 101, no. 6 (May 1996): 1661–93. In a collection of articles on black-Latino relations, *Black Enterprise* also uses the concept "bridge" to describe black/Latino alliances. See Milca Esdaille and Alan Hughes, "The Afro-Latino Connection: Can This Group Be the Bridge to a Broadbased Black-Hispanic Alliance" (Special Report), *Black Enterprise* 34, no. 7 (February 2004): 110–18.

18. Karin L. Stanford, *Beyond the Boundaries: Reverend Jesse Jackson in International Affairs* (Albany: SUNY Press, 1997), 107–37.

19. Aldon Morris, *The Origins of the Civil Right Movement: Black Communities Organizing for Change* (New York: Free Press, 1984).

20. See Marshall Ganz, "Resources and Resourcefulness: Strategic Capacity in the Unionization of California Agriculture, 1959–1966," *American Journal of Sociology* 105, no. 4 (January 2000): 1003–62; Mara Loveman, "High-Risk Collective Action: Defending Human Rights in Chile, Uruguay, and Argentina," *American Journal of Sociology* 104, no. 2 (September 1998): 477–525.

21. Jorge Guerrero Veloz, Interview by Sekou Franklin, June 13, 2007 (Caracas).

22. Willie Thompson, Interview by Sekou Franklin, May 22, 2007.

23. Donatella Della Porta and Mario Diani, *Social Movements: An Introduction* (Malden, Mass.: Blackwell, 1999), chap. 8.

24. Jim Wells et al., *Energy Security: Issues Related to Potential Reductions in Venezuelan Oil Production* (Washington, D.C.: U.S. Government Printing Office, June 2005).

25. Miguel Tinker-Salas, "Fueling Concern: The Role of Oil in Venezuela," *Harvard International Review* 26 (Winter 2005): 50–54.

26. Ramirez, "Venezuela in the Eye of the Hurricane," 181.

27. Michael Fox, "Defining the Bolivarian Alternative for the Americas—ALBA," August 4, 2006, available at http://www.venezuelanalysis.com/articles.php?artno=1790.

28. Samuel A. Arieti, "The Role of MERCOSUR as a Vehicle for Latin American Integration," *Chicago Journal of International Law* 6, no. 2 (Winter 2006): 761–73.

29. Hugo Chávez Frias, "Statement by H. E. Hugo Chávez Frias, President of the Bolivarian Republic of Venezuela at the 61st United Nations General Assembly," September 20, 2006.

30. Julia Buxton, *The Failure of Political Reform in Venezuela* (Burlington, Vt.: Ashgate Press, 2001), chap. 6; Steve Ellner, "Revolutionary and Non-Revolutionary Paths of Radical Populism: Directions of the *Chavista* Movement in Venezuela," *Science and Society* 89, no. 2 (April 2005): 160–90.

31. Marguita Lopez May and Luis Lander, "Popular Protest in Venezuela: Novelties and Continuities," in *Latin American Social Movements: Globalization, Democratization, and Transnational Networks,* ed. Hank Johnston and Paul Almeida (Lanham, Md.: Rowman & Littlefield, 2006), 43–56.

32. Kenneth Roberts, "Social Correlates of Party System Demise and Populist Resurgence in Venezuela," *Latin American Politics and Society* 45, no. 3 (Autumn 2003): 35–57; Harry Kantor, "The Development of Acción Democrática de Venezuela," *Journal of Inter-American Studies* 1, no. 2 (April 1959): 237–55.

33. Brian F. Crisp and Daniel H. Levine, "Democratizing the Democracy? Crisis and Reform in Venezuela," *Journal of Interamerican Studies and World Affairs* 40, no. 2 (Summer 1998): 44–50; Michael Coppedge, *Strong Parties and Lame Ducks: Presidential Partyarchy and Factionalism in Venezuela* (Stanford, Calif.: Stanford University Press, 1994); Richard S. Hilman, *Democracy for the Privileged: Crisis and Transition in Venezuela* (Boulder, Colo.: Lynne Rienner, 1994).

34. See Eva Golinger, *The Chávez Code: Cracking U.S. Intervention in Venezuela* (Havana, Cuba: Publicaciones en Lenguas Extranjeras, 2005); Deborah James, *U.S. Intervention in Venezuela: A Clear and Present Danger* (San Francisco: Global Exchange, 2006).

35. Jody Nesbitt, "African Americans and Venezuela," June 13, 2006, available at www.venezuelanalysis.com/articles.php?artno=1751.

36. For an insightful discussion of Condoleezza Rice's and Colin Powell's positions toward Venezuela, see Clarence Lusane, *Colin Powell and Condoleezza Rice: Foreign Policy, Race, and the New American Century* (Westport, Conn.: Praeger, 2006), chap. 7.

37. Sean Jacobs, "American Africans and Citizenship" (Interview), *Journal of the International Institute* 14, no. 1 (Fall 2006): 4.

38. Kevin Gaines, *American Africans in Ghana: Black Expatriates and the Civil Rights Era* (Chapel Hill: University of North Carolina Press, 2006).

39. Hilary Cunningham, "The Ethnography of Transnational Social Activism: Understanding the Global as Local Practice," *American Ethnologist* 26, no. 3 (August 1999): 583–604.

40. Michael C. Dawson, *Behind the Mule: Race and Class in African-American Politics* (Princeton, N.J.: Princeton University Press, 1995).

41. João Costa Vargas, "The Inner City and the Favela: Transnational Black Politics," *Race and Class* 44, no. 4 (April–June 2003): 19–41.

42. Bill Fletcher, Jr., "A New Chapter in Venezuela?" TransAfrica Forum, October 2004, available at www.transafricaforum.org.

43. Randall Robinson, *The Debt: What America Owes to Blacks* (New York: Dutton Adult, 2000), chap. 6.

44. Julianne Malveaux, "King's Legacy Lives On—In Venezuela," *USA Today*, January 16, 2004, A13.

45. Malika Asha Sanders, Interview by Sekou Franklin, June 4, 2007.

46. James Early, Interview by Sekou Franklin, June 6, 2007.

47. Nikolas Kozloff, *Hugo Chavez: Oil, Politics, and the Challenge to the United States* (New York: Palgrave Macmillan, 2006).

48. Most accounts in the press said that Venezuela allocated funds to Danny Glover. Yet this assertion was disputed by James Early, who said funds were given to a project in Latin America that commemorates the Haitian revolution and Glover was assigned to direct the movie. Early, Interview by Sekou Franklin.

49. National Energy Assistance Directors' Association, "States Plan for Deep Cuts in Low-Income Energy Assistance," December 13, 2002, 1–6; National Energy Assistance Directors' Association, *2005 National Energy Assistance Survey* (Washington, D.C.: NEADA, 2005).

50. Michelle Garcia, "Politics or Not, Bronx Warmly Receives Venezuelan Heating Oil," *Washington Post*, December 8, 2005, A8.

51. Thomas Fitzgerald, "Philadelphia's Unlikely Energy Source," *Philadelphia Inquirer*, January 27, 2006, A1; Betsey Piette, "Venezuelan Oil Flows to Philly," January 31, 2006, available at http://www.workers.org/2006/us/venezuela-philly-0209/.

52. Michael Levenson and Susan Milligan, "Thousands in Mass. to Get Cheap Oil: Delahunt, Chavez Broker Deal," *Boston Globe*, November 20, 2005, A1.

53. Mark J. Konkol, "CTA Kruesi under Fire for Passing Up Discount," *Chicago Sun-Times*, January 5, 2006, 10.

54. Ibid.

55. Omar Sierra (Deputy Consul at Venezuela's Consulate Office in Chicago), Interview by Sekou Franklin, May 29, 2007.

56. James Ewinger, "RTA Foresees Deficits, Weighs Fare Increases," *Plain Dealer Reporter*, March 22, 2006, B1.

57. Alderman Joe Davis, Sr., "Media Advisory," City of Milwaukee News Release, Common Council City Clerk Communications Center, November 30, 2006; Gregory Stanford, "Whatever the Motives, Aid from Chavez a Good Thing," *Milwaukee Journal Sentinel*, January 21, 2007.

58. Sister Cities Committee (Milwaukee Common Council), "Meeting Minutes," Milwaukee, Wisconsin, July 21, 2006, 1.

59. Prensa Consulado de Venezuela en Chicago, Estadounidenses de Michigan y Wisconsin Reciben Calurosamente a Diplomáticos Venezolanos, June 21, 2006, available at http://www.aporrea.org/imprime/n79561.html; News Hits Staff, "Venezuelan Eye Opener," *Metrotimes: Detroit's Weekly Alternative*, June 21, 2006, available at http://metrotimes.com/editorial/printstory.asp?id=9350.

60. Consulado de Venezuela, "Estadounidenses de Michigan y Wisconsin Reciben Caluro-

samente a Diplomaticaos Venezolanos," June 21, 2006, available at www.aporrea.org/venezuelaexterior/n79561/html.

61. Voces Urgentes, "Delegación Afro-Estadounidense Visita Lara: El Proceso Bolivariano es la Concreción del Sueño de Martin Luther King," December 4, 2006, available at http://www.medioscomunitarios.org/pag/index.php?id=33&idn=218.

62. Henry Hamilton, Interview by Sekou Franklin, June 7, 2007. Hamilton also conveyed these sentiments in an opinion column, "U.S. Could Learn from Venezuelan Voting," *Milwaukee Journal Sentinel,* December 10, 2006.

63. "Final Statement by State Supreme Court Judges," available at http://www.rethink venezuela.com/downloads/judges.htm.

64. NAACP, *An Observational Briefing on the 2006 Venezuelan Presidential Election* (Washington, D.C.: NAACP Research Department, February 2007), 7.

65. Julia Stewart, "When Local Troubles Become Transnational: The Transformation of a Guatemalan Indigenous Rights Movement," in *Latin American Social Movements: Globalization, Democratization, and Transnational Networks,* ed. Hank Johnston and Paul Almeida (Lanham, Md.: Rowman & Littlefield, 2006), 199.

66. Numerous studies detail the Bush administration's active involvement in the 2002 coup, the 2003 oil workers' strike, and the 2004 recall referendum against the Chávez administration. See Golinger, *The Chávez Code;* Richard Gott, "Racist Rage of the Caracas Elite," *The Guardian,* December 10, 2002, available at http://www.guardian.co.uk/print/0,,4564317-103677,00.html; Gregory Wilpert, "The Meaning of 21st Century Socialism for Venezuela," July 11, 2006, available at www.venezuelanalysis.com/aticles.php?artno=1776; Marta Harnecker-Abiven, "Venezuela: Blows and Counterblows," July 4, 2007, available at www.venezuelanalysis.com/articles.php?artno=2088.

67. Tiffany Isaacs, "Drug Wars: Bush Launches Attack on Venezuela," *The Council on Hemispheric Affairs' Washington Report on the Hemisphere* 26, nos. 20–21 (November 1, 2006): 1, 6.

68. Frank Furedi, *The New Ideology of Imperialism: Renewing the Moral Imperative* (London: Pluto Press, 1994), 34–56.

69. Frank C. Urbancic, "Venezuela: Terrorism Hub of South America?" Principal Deputy Coordinator for Counterterrorism, Statement before the House Committee on International Relations, Subcommittee on International Terrorism and Nonproliferation, Washington, D.C., July 13, 2006; Rep. Mark Kirk, "Fight Poverty, Not Colombia," *Congressional Record—House,* July 11, 2005, H5608; Rep. Cliff Stearns, "Chavez Begins Third Term in Venezuela," *Congressional Record—House,* January 12, 2007, H440.

70. Rep. Alcee Hastings, "A Resolution to Condemn the Political Unrest and Political Leadership in Venezuela and Calling on the Government to Hold New National Elections in Accordance with the Venezuelan Constitution," *Congressional Record—House,* January 28, 2003, E77.

71. Kim Scipes, "The AFL-CIO Foreign Policy Program and the 2002 Coup in Venezuela," September 28, 2006, available at http://www.venezuelanalysis.com/print.php?artno=1836.

72. Jorge Veloz, Nirva Camacho, and Jesus "Chucho" Garcia, "Afro Venezuelan Network Letter to African American Organizations," July 2004.

73. House Resolution No. 43, House Journal 24, March 13, 2007, 278.

74. National Black Caucus of State Legislators, *Seeing Beyond Investing in State Leadership: Improving Communities* (2006 Ratified Resolutions) (Washington, D.C.: Na-

tional Black Caucus of State Legislators, December 9, 2005), 80–81. (See Resolution 06-64, "Forbidding Any Incursion upon Venezuelan Sovereignty.")

75. Rev. Jesse Jackson et al., "Petition to Respect the Democratic Electoral Process in Venezuela," November 30, 2006, available at http://www.blackcommentator.com/208/208_petition_electoral_process_venezuela.html, Issue 208.

76. Alejandro Correa and Willie Thompson, "African Venezuelans Fear New U.S. Coup against President Chavez," June 14, 2006, available at http://www.sfbayview.com/092502/africanvenezuelans092502.shtml.

77. Keck and Sikkink, "Transnational Advocacy Networks in the Movement Society," 228–35; Ann Mische, "Cross-Talk in Movements: Reconceiving the Culture-Network Link," in *Social Movements and Networks: Relational Approach to Collective Action* (Oxford: Oxford University Press, 2003), 250–80.

78. "Benjamin E. Mays Goes to Venezuela," July 25, 2005, available at http://www.dogonvillage.com/benemays/archives/11-Benjamin-E.Mays-Goes-to-Venezuela.html.

79. I witnessed this exchange in Venezuela. Later, Marcus Bellamy outlined his arguments in an email correspondence. Bellamy, "Venezuela Research," June 13, 2007, email correspondence.

80. Ramirez, "Venezuela in the Eye of the Hurricane," 174.

81. Abayomi Azikiwe, "Gathering Establishes Network to Support the Bolivarian Revolution" (Pan-African News Wire), March 6, 2006, available at http://www.lasolidarity.org/ConfReport.html; W. T. Whitney, Jr., "Activists Form Venezuelan Solidarity Network," March 16, 2006, available at http://www.pww.org/article/articleview/8757/1/144/.

82. Elisa Larkin Nascimento, *Pan-Africanism and South America: Emergence of Black Rebellion* (Buffalo, N.Y.: Afrodiaspora, 1980).

83. Renita Mathas, "Afro-Latin Week Celebrates African Heritage of South America," *Black Issues in Higher Education*, November 20, 2003, 21.

84. JoAnn Carmin and Barbara Hicks, "International Triggering Events, Transnational Networks, and the Development of Czech and Polish Environmental Movements," *Mobilization: An International Journal* 7, no. 3 (2002): 305–24.

85. Beatríz Ramirez, "Red de Mujeres Afrolatinas y Afrocaribeñas (1992–2006): Una Evaluación Necesaria," in Memoria del Tercer Encuentro de la Red de Mujeres Afrolatinoamericanas, Afrocaribeñas y de la Diáspora, 2006, available at http://www.movimientos.org/mujerafro/.

86. See "Declaración de la Red de Mujeres Afrocaribeñas y Afrolatinoamericanas en el contexto de la Conferencia Regional de las Américas, Santiago + 5, sobre los Avances y Desafíos en el Programa de Acción contra el Racismo, la Discriminación Racial, la Xenofobia y las formas Conexas de Intolerancia," in Memoria del Tercer Encuentro de la Red de Mujeres Afrolatinoamericanas, Afrocaribeñas y de la Diáspora, 2006, available at http://www.movimientos.org/mujerafro/. Translation provided by Hunter College's Global Afro Latino & Caribbean Initiative, available at http://www.hunter.cuny.edu/galci/pdfs/archives/07.14.06/Santiago_mas_5_DeclarationEng.pdf.

87. Aldon Morris, "Black Southern Student Sit-in Movement: An Analysis of Internal Organization," *American Sociological Review* 46, no. 6 (December 1981): 746.

88. Minnie Bruce Pratt, "Women and the Bolivarian Revolution," February 5, 2006, available at www.workers.org/2006/world/women-0209/.

89. Rachel West, "Nora Castenada, Head of Venezuela's Women's Bank Coming to San Francisco," June 14, 2006, available at http://www.sfbayview.com/012104/nora012104 .shtml.

90. Veloz, Interview by Sekou Franklin.

91. Global Afro Latino & Caribbean Initiative Presents, "What's at Stake? Redefining African American" (Flyer), March 2, 2007, Franklin H. Williams Caribbean Cultural Center, African Diaspora Initiative.

92. Harry Belafonte, "I Will Continue to Serve the African World," Acceptance Speech, TransAfrica Forum's Amilcar Cabral International Freedom Award, March 31, 2006, available at www.transafricaforum.org.

93. Lucius Walker, Interview by Sekou Franklin, June 6, 2007.

94. Chris Silvera, Interview by Sekou Franklin, June 7, 2007.

95. Nellie Bailey Hester, Interview by Sekou Franklin, June 7, 2007.

96. Ojette Brundage has a private blog, "Draft Life in Venezuela!" August 11, 2006.

97. Marilyn Grace Miller, *Rise and Fall of the Cosmic Race: The Cult of Mestizaje in Latin America* (Austin: University of Texas Press, 2004); Peter Winn, *Americas: The Changing Face of Latin America and the Caribbean* (Berkeley: University of California Press, 1999 [1992]); and Jesus Maria Herrera Salas, "Ethnicity and Revolution: The Political Economy of Racism in Venezuela," *Latin American Perspectives* 32, no. 2 (March 2005): 73–79.

98. Jesus "Chucho" Garcia (Interview by Gregory Wilpert), "Racism and Racial Divide in Venezuela," January 21, 2004, available at www.venezuelanalysis.com/articles.php?artno =1091.

99. Salas, "Ethnicity and Revolution."

100. Nirva Rosa Camacho, *Familia Afrovenezolana Endorracismo y Autorreconocimiento* (Caracas: Cultural Ministry, 2005). Ojette Brundage has written insightfully about racism in Venezuela. See Brundage, "Racism in Venezuela" (no publisher, 2007).

101. See Movimiento Cimarrones Afrodescendientes, "Movimiento Cimarrones Afrodescendientes por la Revolución. Declaración de Caracas," November 23, 2006, avalaible at http://www.aporrealos.org/actualidad/a27531.html.

102. Willie Thompson, Interview by Sekou Franklin.

103. Luis Perdomo, Lecture (Barlovento Region, Miranda State, Venezuela) to Global Exchange, June 26, 2006.

104. Jorge Guerrero Veloz, *Afrovenezolanidad y Subjectividad* (Caracas: Cultural Ministry, 2005), 47.

105. Early, Interview by Sekou Franklin.

106. Fletcher, "A New Chapter in Venezuela?" 6. Writing for the anti-Chávez outlet vcrsis. com, Gustavo Coronel disagreed with Fletcher's commentary and said he misunderstood the media's criticisms of TransAfrica and its board chairman, Danny Glover. TransAfrica's chief critic was "Zapata," a dark-skinned Venezuelan cartoonist who also referred to Glover as "quemado" (burned). Coronel says *quemado* really means "politically burnt out" and has no racial connotation. However, this was disputed in my discussions with members of the Network of Afro-Venezuelan Activists. The group said that, notwithstanding Zapata's dark-skinned features, he has a history of attacking Chávez supporters and using racially vitriolic imagery and language. See Gustavo Coronel, "TransAfrica Forum Pontificates about Venezuela," October 11, 2004, available at http://www.vcrisis.com/index.php?content=letters/200410111507.

107. Tianna Pachel, "Constitutional Provisions and Legal Actions Related to Discrimination and Afro-Descendant Populations in Latin America," *Race Report* (Washington, D.C.: Inter-American Dialogue, August 2004), 6.

108. Ibid., 7.

109. Ribando, *Afro-Latinos in Latin America and Considerations for U.S. Policy*, 20.

110. Humberto Márquez, "Venezuela: Afrodescendientes Tras la Verdad Numérica," Interpress News Service Agency, June 22, 2007, available at http://ipsnoticias.net/print.asp?idnews=41303.

111. Veloz, Interview by Sekou Franklin; Norma Romero, Interview by Sekou Franklin, June 13, 2007. Caracas.

112. Statistical data for Chávez's support in communities heavily populated by people of African descent are nonexistent because Venezuela has yet to conduct a census or population count of Afro-Venezuelans. Yet election and political observers almost universally conclude that Chávez's political base is in these communities. Salas, "Ethnicity and Revolution"; Hisham Aidi, "Chavez and the Black Cause," *New African*, March 2003, 58–60; Roy Levy Williams, "Venezuela's Black Vote," reprinted from *The New York Amsterdam News*, December 25, 2006, available at www.zmag.org/content/print_article.cfm?itemID=11701&sectionID=1; Vinod Sreeharsha, "Is There a "Black Vote" in Venezuela?" available at www.venezuelanalysis.com/articles.php?artno=1899 (reprinted from www.slate.com).

113. Karen Juanito Carillo, "Completing the Chavez Revolution," available at http://www.seeingblack.com/2006/x070105/garcia.html. Also see Gott, "Racist Rage of the Caracas Elite."

114. Blanca Escalona Rojas, Interview by Sekou Franklin, June 14, 2007; Argenis Delgado, Interview by Sekou Franklin, June 18, 2007. Caracas.

115. Karen Juanita Carrillo, "Completing the Chavez Revolution," July 1, 2005, available at www.seeingblack.com/2005/x070105/garcia.shtml.

TWELVE

The Assault of the Monkey King on the Hosts of Heaven

THE BLACK FREEDOM STRUGGLE AND CHINA—
THE NEW CENTER OF REVOLUTION

Robeson Taj P. Frazier

In every town and city we went to the opera, and can never
forget the assault of the Monkey King on the Hosts of Heaven,
facing God and the angels. A night sleeping train took us over
the 30-hour trip from Peking to Wuhan. There I saw the bridge
that had been miraculously thrown across the Yangtze.

—W. E. B. DU BOIS, *THE AUTOBIOGRAPHY OF W. E. B. DU BOIS* (1959)[1]

We have been like the "Monkey King Upsetting Heaven" in
the old play. We have thrown away the Heavenly Rule Book.
Remember this. Never take a Heavenly Rule Book too seriously.
One must always go by one's own revolutionary rules.

—MAO ZEDONG, (1964)[2]

In the Fall of 1949 the Chinese Communist Party (CCP) established the
People's Republic of China (PRC), an act that challenged U.S. visionary globalism and shifted the Cold War to East Asian terrain.[3] The CCP's model of
revolution blended communism and radical nationalism, a standpoint that
presented a stark contrast to the bipolar new world order advocated by the
United States and the Soviet Union. Ten years after the establishment of the
PRC, ninety-one-year-old scholar and activist W. E. B. Du Bois traveled to
China and summed up the nation's challenge to Western interests. Du Bois,
in the epigraph that opens this chapter, referred to a classic Chinese fable,
Journey to the West, and cast the Chinese as the tale's protagonist, the Mon-   **313**

key King, and the West as its adversary.[4] He surmised that China's "assault" on Western civilization signified a momentous shift in the logic and force behind Euro-American hegemony and the colonial and imperial crucible faced by people of the Third World. It is no coincidence that CCP leader Mao Zedong also made this same pronouncement throughout his reign.

A good number of blacks in the United States shared Du Bois's outlook and attraction to China. After World War II, more and more of them situated China as an important global force and Third World model that could assist them in the struggle against U.S. racial capitalism. Several publications have probed this little known history of black internationalism.[5] These works relay that Mao and the CCP's platform provided black radicals and internationalists with a useful lens to consider and view global relations, national development, modernization, and Third World socialism.

Chinese communism offered an Asian example of revolution and development, and a useful and progressive reconceptualization of Marxism-Leninism. While Soviet leaders V. I. Lenin, Leon Trotsky, and Joseph Stalin designated the Soviet Union as the vanguard leader of the world socialist revolution, Mao pointed to the Third World. Mao's "Theory of the Three Worlds" argued that it was up to the colonized populations in Asia, Africa, and the Americas to "combat imperialism, colonialism and hegemonism."[6] Mao also moved away from the Soviet theory of "permanent revolution" and offered his own conceptualization of revolution, "the new democratic revolution," which posited that it was not vital to have a stage of bourgeois capitalism before the emergence of socialism. Instead, Mao argued that a nationalist patriotic united front could defeat imperialism, spurring a national democratic revolution that would ultimately develop into a socialist revolution. Moreover, Mao asserted that it was not Marxism that fueled revolution; it was how revolutionaries cultivated and applied Marxism to their specific circumstances, histories, and localities that determined its impact on any revolution. Mao also insisted that the creativity of the most downtrodden populations best informed and cultivated a socialist revolution. Consequently, Mao celebrated China's peasant masses, as opposed to the revolutionary intellectual vanguard or the working class, as the guiding social force of the Chinese Revolution. The peasants' creativity, he pointed out, was what carried the revolution into the superstructure, that is, the national culture. Ultimately, these concepts displayed Mao's ability to engage Marxism with nationalism and create what seemed like the possibility of a cultural movement and revolution that did not prioritize class over race and culture.

Part of what historian Besenia Rodriguez terms the "tricontinental" spirit and political culture of the 1950s through 1970s, Chinese communism and Maoist thought supplied black activist intellectuals with a triple-threat attack and critique of capitalism, imperialism, and racism.[7] Some proclaimed themselves as "Maoist" in belief and political sensibility, while others barely regarded themselves as Marxist, never mind Maoist. Black radicals studied and found relevance in Maoist concepts such as "the united front," "protracted revolution," "power is in the barrel of a gun," and "the importance of contradiction," and engaged these ideas with the local conditions and dilemmas of their struggles. Certain groups cultivated innovative ideas, strategies, and practices that were directly influenced by Maoist thought and CCP policy. However, for a number of these radicals, Chinese communism and Maoist thought were far from perfect.

Mao Zedong's policy, depending on the time period, often contradicted his past positions. Those who looked to him for revolutionary guidance often found themselves in the tough position of correlating Mao's writings and ideas to Chinese foreign diplomacy and current events in China. Time and time again it proved tasking and strenuous, frequently impossible, to connect the two. The limited amount of news updates, information, and literature that filtered from China into the United States left pro-China black radicals and internationalists without stable legs to stand on. They often lacked honest and critical engagement of how Chinese communism was or was not being translated into sustained practice in China. In addition, the U.S. government's portrayal of China as an enemy of the state put China supporters on the defensive. As a result, black internationalists speciously defended Mao-sanctioned atrocities such as the Great Leap Forward and Cultural Revolution. Consequently, they found themselves, their endorsement of China, and their espoused communist faith, like Mao, in deep contradiction.[8] Nonetheless, they believed in the principles of democratic socialism and desired to establish a more evolved and humane American public.[9] What these internationalists obtained from China was not a direct line of political thinking, but one model that helped them envision and develop change.

This chapter provides a concise examination of African American interest in Chinese communism during the Cold War and investigates how one activist intellectual linked Maoist thought to the fight for black power in the United States. This chapter is divided into two sections. The first section begins with a historical account of China's entrance into the politics of the Cold War and U.S. efforts to thwart the expanding influence of the CCP. The U.S. government did not take communist hegemony in Asia lightly. It responded with a right-wing anticommunist China crusade that aimed to contain and isolate China, and uncover and reprimand Americans who endorsed the CCP. The section concludes with analysis of African Americans' engagement of Chinese policy and Chinese communism from the 1940s through the 1960s. Despite the rampant anti-China discourse in U.S. policy, the American media, and popular culture, increasing numbers of African Americans and other groups of color became drawn to Chinese communism.

The second section details the efforts of Detroit autodidact socialist and black power theoretician James Boggs to link the Chinese Communist Revolution with the then emerging black power movement. This section asserts that a synthesis of revolutionary nationalism and Mao Zedong's ideas informed aspects of Boggs's analysis. Boggs felt that several of the same questions and dilemmas that Mao encountered during the Chinese Revolution were also present in the fight for black power. Mao's essays, such as "On Practice," "On Contradiction," and "On the Correct Handling of the Contradictions among the People," as well as his "build as you fight" strategy of revolution, were a stimulus to Boggs's analysis.[10] Reading Boggs's writings alongside Mao's philosophical thought, one finds an American counterpart to Mao's ideas on revolution, redefining social relationships and activities, and the value of politics and political engagement. Ultimately Boggs's analysis displays the heterogeneity of black nationalism and black Marxism, the role that nonstate actors play in engaging and translating foreign nations' theories and policies into local demands and strategies of activism, and the saliency of transnational discourses in the politics of the post-World War II black freedom struggle.

I.

In 1945, the Allied Powers' defeat of Japan and Germany was a decisive victory. With this triumph and the end of World War II, the United States supplanted the economically depleted powers of Western Europe, most especially Britain and Germany, as the paramount economic and political force and global hegemonic force. U.S. political officials, policymakers, and businessmen grew excited about a shift of global geo-economics and geo-politics in favor of U.S. interests. The interwar rise of Germany and Japan made clear the challenges that foreign nationalism and ultra-nationalism, like fascism, presented to U.S. trade interests and access to overseas markets. The U.S. government rationalized that this growing tide of nationalism and the sectarianism it produced among nation-states, as well as the financial collapse of the Great Depression, forced many countries to draw inward. As nations separated themselves into self-sustaining trading blocs during the 1930s, the U.S. economy, as well as those of other nations, regressed. World War II provided the United Statees with an opportunity to eliminate these trading blocs. By instituting a world financial system and new global political order, the United States established itself as the leader of a world globalism and capitalism that would connect nations to one another and expand the international market. Asian studies scholar Richard C. Kagan describes it this way: "The concerns of American political elites in the 1950s were thus no longer with domestic economic politics, but with the creation of Pax-Americana."[11]

No nation posed a greater challenge to U.S. globalism than the Union of Soviet Socialist Republics (USSR). The United States primarily valued its easy access to international markets and its ability to have constant unregulated access to these markets. The Soviet Union's quest to build its own political and economic empire and its indisputable, although sluggish, support of national liberation movements in Africa and Asia, alongside the prospect of further bilateralism and state trade, threatened U.S. prospects of unrestricted entry into Western and Eastern Europe, Asia, and Africa. U.S. officials asked themselves: if the world were split into two separate political and economic spheres, where new markets and trade expansion were limited, how would the United States navigate another economic crisis? In what came to be known as the Cold War, the United States and the Soviet Union struggled with one another to expand their spheres of influence, win allies, and sway foreign nations' national policies.[12]

A key issue for both powers was the future of China. The U.S. government envisioned a postwar Asian order with China serving as its junior partner. U.S. foreign policy considered China the centerpiece of a U.S.-based global police force in Asia. Walter Lafeber asserts, "American diplomatic plans during most of the war revolved around hopes for China. China would emerge as their closest ally in the region. Chiang Kai Shek and his people were to join the United States, Great Britain, and the Soviet Union as one of the world's 'four policemen' . . . China could be used as a useful counterpoise to the Soviet Union."[13] China's vast economic potential also increased the U.S. appetite for trade and industry. Japan's World War II surrender ended Japanese expansionism in northern China and other parts of East Asia. U.S. government officials assumed that the elimination of European and Japanese imperialism in China would open China and other parts of Asia to the interests of U.S. capital.

Yet as World War II came to its conclusion, a civil war began in China between the Chinese Nationalist Party, better known as the Guomindang/

Kuomintang (GMD), and the Chinese Communist Party (CCP). This Chinese civil war exacerbated the U.S.-USSR conflict. The GMD and the CCP had deep ties to the United States and the Soviet Union, respectively, and the war's winner would determine China's future and the Cold War superpower with which China would align itself.[14] At the war's end, it was the CCP that was victorious. On October 1, 1949, the CCP established a sovereign and independent Chinese national government, the People's Republic of China (PRC). Overpowered and ousted, the GMD took refuge in Taiwan, a small group of islands off China's coast.

The U.S. government was critical of the CCP's mix of communism and radical nationalism.[15] As communists, the CCP aligned ideologically with the Soviet Union and attacked the U.S. international economic agenda and foreign policy. In addition, the entrance of China onto the Cold War's main stage coincided with the decolonization and liberation movements occurring in Asia and Africa. The CCP's defeat of the GMD, a U.S. ally, was regarded by newly independent and colonized nations as proof that the United States was not an omnipotent power. The U.S. government was alarmed by China's size and the CCP's focus on modernizing China and developing the nation into a world power. A communist-led China reduced U.S. influence in the East and placed Chinese markets and Asian markets in the control of either a Chinese-Soviet alliance or the Chinese themselves. Historian Chen Jian argues that communist China "altered the orientation of the Cold War by shifting its actual focal point from Europe to East Asia . . . [a] shift, as it turned out, [that] would make East Asia *the* main battlefield of the Cold War."[16] The CCP's support for communist revolutions and clashes with the United States in Korea in 1953, in Indochina in 1954, and in the Formosa Straits in the Fall of 1954 brought this shift to the fore.

The U.S. government responded by generating an anti-China campaign that smeared the CCP as "enemies of freedom" so as to contain and isolate China. To encourage the American public to perceive possible U.S. aggression against China and other U.S. opponents as justified, the U.S. government and the American media cultivated a skewed depiction of communism wherein the ideology became synonymous with being in "opposition to freedom" and unpatriotic.[17] The McCarthy hearings and public attacks on suspected communists and their supporters stigmatized communist ideology in the United States and helped foster an all-out national denunciation. "Freedom" became the word, discourse, and strategy of U.S. patriotism and imperialism. It asserted that the opening and expansion of the international market to greater freedom and free trade would create more competition, cooperation, and wealth among nations, whereas communism and the elimination of private property were the antithesis to such an international environment.[18]

A network of GMD officials and businessmen, right-wing U.S. politicians, hired American agents, and American businesses assisted in fostering anticommunist and anti-CCP sentiment. During the 1950s and 1960s, this coalition made every effort to influence the U.S. president, Congress, and the American public to regard the CCP and communism in Asia as detrimental to American national security and the collective security of U.S. allies.[19] Pro-GMD newspapers and periodicals such as *Young China*, the *Chinese Nationalist Daily*, and the *China Monthly: The Truth about China*; top American newspapers and magazines like *Time, American Mercury, Collier's, Human Events, Life, New Leader, Reader's Digest, Saturday Evening Post,* and *US News & World Report*; as well as organizations like the American China Policy Association, the China Emergency Committee, and the Committee to Defend America by Aiding Anti-Communist China depicted Americans who critiqued the GMD as either communists or communist sympathizers.[20] According to these media outlets, "to be critical of the Nationalists was tantamount to giving 'aid and comfort to the enemy'— an accusation of treason as defined in the U.S. Constitution."[21] In addition, travel to China on a U.S. passport was outlawed until 1959 and business relations with Chinese enterprises were frowned upon. In the mainstream where most Americans received their news, the U.S. public was not presented with critical portrayals of the Chinese government; thus, most Americans lacked a comprehensive view of China. Pro-China and pro-CCP writings by American writers Edgar Snow, William Hinton, Anna Louise Strong, Jack Belden, foreign-service officer John S. Service, world traveler Agnes Smedley, and historian Graham Peck were given little consideration or mainstream attention.[22]

Negative and racist statements made by U.S. political officials legitimated this anti-CCP discourse. George Kennan, U.S. diplomat and Department of State adviser, lambasted the CCP as "embittered fanatics" and "ruthless men consumed with ambition."[23] President Dwight Eisenhower argued that Chinese people's race and culture prevented them from having reason: "We are always wrong when we believe that Orientals think logically as we do."[24] He juxtaposed the Chinese and the Soviets and tacitly asserted that the Soviets' white skin and European identity distinguished them from the Chinese: "No matter what differences in culture and tradition, values or language, the Russian leaders were human beings and they wanted to remain alive."[25] Eisenhower's statements conveyed a common misperception held by other Americans. They believed that the CCP did not win the Chinese revolution and develop its policy independently, but rather was successful due to dependence on "white" Russia. This tendency to frame "yellow" China's policy as dictated by "white" Moscow stemmed from the notion that "America did not regard Russia as an Asian power."[26] Evidently the Soviets were not stereotyped and racialized in the same negative manner as the Chinese. Nowhere was the U.S. valuation of Soviet humanity over Chinese humanity more clear than at the 1954 Geneva Conference. There, U.S. Secretary of State John Foster Dulles refused to shake Chinese Premier Zhou Enlai's hand, yet minutes later shook the hand of the Soviet delegate, another ironic moment that displayed the hypocrisy and racism of U.S. foreign policy.[27]

Black internationalists, like the U.S. government, also perceived that China had an important role to play in world affairs, but for different reasons. In the 1930s, they revered Japan—even as Japan increased its colonization of China. By the 1940s blacks, who had remained silent about Japanese imperialism in China in the 1930s, began to distance themselves from Japan after Japan's bombing of Pearl Harbor in December 1941. They subsequently designated China as the "new champion of the darker races."[28] A growing number of blacks connected China's struggle against imperialism and foreign influence to their own struggle against racial discrimination. What became clear was that despite the differences between black internationalists and the U.S. government's stances on China, each used China to wage battles for their own interests. During the Chinese Civil War, groups of blacks initially aligned with the GMD rather than the CCP. From 1942 to 1946, white and black liberals, like novelist Pearl Buck and NAACP executive secretary Walter White, labored to reshape the GMD's image among African Americans. In presentations and speeches throughout the country, Buck worked to create a stronger cultural connection between blacks and the GMD, all while the NAACP and black newspapers heralded the GMD as the saviors of China. In 1943 White championed GMD leader Chiang Kai-Shek (Jiang Jièshí) as the new "leader of the colored world" and solicited Kai-Shek's wife to denounce racial discrimination at an NAACP-sponsored event at Madison Square Garden. Two years later, at the founding of the United Nations, the Chinese delegation, represented by GMD officials, briefly proposed creating a clause on racial equality in the U.N. charter; they ultimately abandoned the proposal due to U.S. prodding and influence.[29]

Nonetheless, the imagined community between black America and China was not as stable or concrete as White, Buck, the NAACP, the black press, or white liberals depicted it. In fact, the image of black American-GMD solidarity was predicated on a set of illusions and contradictions. Despite efforts by Chinese journalist Liu Liang Mo to expand blacks' viewpoints of China in his regular column in *The Pittsburgh Courier*, and black activists' support of repealing the Chinese Exclusion Act, Chinese citizens and black Americans during the 1940s knew little about each other.[30] For instance, black newspapers published orientalized, negative depictions of Asians. In the *Baltimore Afro-American*, an article differentiated between various Asian ethnic groups by using stereotypes and sweeping generalizations.[31] At the same time, Chinese American shop owners' discriminatory treatment of black patrons countered black and white liberals' claims that the Chinese lacked race prejudice. Lastly, in 1943 and 1944 GMD leader Chiang Kai-Shek's refusal to allow black American GIs into China to complete construction of the Stillwell Road provided further evidence of Chinese racism. It moreover displayed the GMD's lack of interest in defending black Americans' human rights and its overall allegiance to the U.S. racial status quo.[32]

Although some black Americans elected the GMD as their ally against American racism during the 1950s, it was the CCP that took a solid stance on the issue of American racial inequality throughout the decade. In black newspapers, CCP officials linked Jim Crow racism to the GMD's oppression of ethnic minorities.[33] Furthermore, on August 12, 1963, more than 10,000 Chinese citizens and representatives of Chinese people's organizations and democratic parties gathered for a mass rally in Beijing. There, they proclaimed their support for blacks' struggle against racial discrimination and condemned U.S. imperialism. At the rally, Mao Zedong issued a statement that connected the plight of black Americans to the larger anticolonial fight and called for universal support for black Americans' cause. Mao stated:

> I call on the workers, peasants, revolutionary intellectuals, enlightened element of the bourgeoisie, and other enlightened persons of all colors in the world, whether white, black, yellow or brown to unite to oppose the racial discrimination practiced by U.S. imperialism and support the American Negroes in their struggle against racial discrimination . . . I am firmly convinced that with the support of more than 90% of the people of the world, the American Negroes will be victorious in their just struggle. The evil system of colonialism and imperialism arose and throve along with the enslavement of Negroes and the trade of Negroes, and it will surely come to its end with the complete emancipation of the Black people.[34]

This statement was prompted by militant Robert Franklin Williams's calls for international support for black Americans' struggles against racial discrimination. Williams, living in exile in Cuba, for over a year waged a letter-writing campaign to international Third World leaders pleading them to align with the civil rights movement, and it was Mao who first honored Williams's request. Consequently, in the period thereafter, black radicals and internationalists took Mao's statement as a sign of China's opposition to Western imperialism and racial capitalism. As a result, they deemed Mao's leadership as special and refreshing.

Black internationalists were also impressed by the CCP's efforts to build a bridgehead between Asia and Africa. At the Bandung Conference of 1955, the Chinese delegation articulated an international policy of alliance among the nations of the Third World. Black Americans linked China's call for Third World unity to their own domestic struggles against institutional racism. The conference empowered them on the global stage by critiquing Western expansion and Western hegemony. After the conference, Egypt opened the first Chinese embassy in Africa in 1956, and this began a period of increased economic and diplomatic relations between China and the emerging independent African nations. Sino-African relations flourished over the course of the next twenty years and resulted in African support for the admission of China to the United Nations in 1971. By supporting and training African revolutionary groups, and financing loans for extravagant African infrastructure projects, China established stronger ties with Africa—another factor that prompted black American interest in China.

W. E. B. Du Bois first visited China in 1936. In February 1959 he returned with his wife, Shirley Graham Du Bois, to view the new communist regime's impact on the nation. The couple traveled throughout China for two months and visited Beijing, Shanghai, Hankou, Guangzhou, Chongqing, Chengdu, and Nanjing. During these travels, Du Bois collected honorary degrees, honors denied to him in his home country. Although Du Bois described this trip as "the most fascinating eight weeks of travel and sightseeing, I have ever experienced," he affirmed that "China is no utopia."[35] However, he was impressed with Chinese people's efforts to advance and reshape Chinese society. Du Bois heralded how this "land of colored people" labored in its "planning of a nation and a system of work" while "rising over the entrails of dead empire."[36] He asserted, "What is the secret of China in the second half of the 20th century? It is that the vast majority of a billion human beings have been convinced that human nature in some of its darkest recesses can be changed, if change is necessary . . . I have never seen a nation which so amazed and touched me as China in 1959."[37]

In the period thereafter, Du Bois was not alone in his endorsement of the PRC. His wife Shirley was so struck by Chinese culture and China's development that she spent the last years of her life as a Beijing resident.[38] In 1967 and 1968 she accepted a temporary position with the Permanent Bureau of the Afro-Asian Writers located in Beijing, and later made China one of her homes throughout the 1970s as she fought to be allowed visa entry into the United States. "No American can feel the suffering of China more keenly than does the American Negro," she remarked.[39] Freedom fighter Robert F. Williams, editor of the radical periodical *The Crusader* and host of transnational radio show *Radio Free Dixie*, traveled to China on several occasions during the early 1960s. He and his family were so impressed with the nation and its government that they opted to abandon their life of exile in Cuba and live as American expatriates in China from 1966 to 1969.[40] William Worthy, journalist and foreign correspondent for the *Baltimore-Washington Afro-American*, first traveled to China in late 1957 and was one of the first American journalists to interview Chinese premier Zhou Enlai. When Worthy returned to the United States, the media hounded him with offers to publish the interview, whereas the U.S. State Department confiscated his passport.[41] In 1958 black communist Harry Haywood, a former member of the African Blood Brotherhood and one of the leading black voices in the U.S. Communist Party, helped found the New Communist Movement, an organization that modeled itself after the CCP. Haywood asserted:

> A great deal has been learned from the People's Republic of China, its Communist Party and its great leader, Mao Zedong. The emphasis on testing ideas in practice, care and flexibility in applying united front tactics, of relying upon and serving the people, realism in dealing with power relationships, respect for integrity of national minorities and for the rights of the third world nations against great nation chauvinism, the concrete analysis and application of Marxist-Leninist principles to one's own country, and the pursuing of the two-line political struggle inside the party are all part of China's great legacy. For me, this has been a cause for great optimism for the future.[42]

At the end of the day, the relationships of Haywood, W. E. B. and Shirley Graham Du Bois, Williams, and Worthy with the Chinese government helped push black American radicals in the direction of China.

During the late 1960s and early 1970s, as black Americans' struggle for racial equality was transformed into a larger clash with the U.S. power structure over power—what blacks poignantly called "black power"—black American interest in Chinese communism surged. Individuals and organizations such as the Revolutionary Action Movement, the California Communist League, the Black Panther Party for Self-Defense, the Black Workers Congress, the Youth Organizations for Black Unity, the League of Revolutionary Workers, the Congress of African People, and the African Liberation Support Committee read and studied Mao Zedong's writings. The remainder of this chapter examines one example of this history—the theory and writings of black revolutionary nationalist James Boggs.

II.

In the 1960s deindustrialization had a colossal effect on Detroit's workforce, primarily affecting the black working class, the black working poor and the black unemployed. Economic recessions in 1957–58 and 1960–61 decreased the number of black new hires. From 1947 to 1963, Detroit industry lost 134,000 jobs and the unemployment rate skyrocketed to 10 percent, almost double the national rate, with unemployment among black men more than double the rate among white men. The Vietnam War briefly stimulated job growth in 1965, but thereafter jobs for black workers decreased rapidly.[43] Liberal attempts to respond to Detroit's decline and transform it into the "Great Society" were meaningful yet unsuccessful. They failed to confront the economic and social challenges faced by the black working class and the unemployed, and sidestepped an opportunity to produce significant change in the city.[44] By the decade's end Detroit was the site of one of the largest insurrections in U.S. history. Over the course of four days during July 1967, looting, arson, and conflicts between the police and local citizens ravaged the city. The chaos, referred to as "The Great Rebellion" by Detroit locals, signified the severity of the effects of deindustrialization, unemployment, poverty, and racial inequality on the city and its inhabitants.

Four years before the rebellion, James Boggs, an electrical equipment operator for Detroit's Chrysler-Jefferson auto plants, forecast the uprising in a letter to the editors of *Monthly Review*. He proclaimed to the editors, "The American revolution has begun, while of course, most people don't even know it has begun."[45] Boggs contextualized the struggles faced by black workers, blacks searching for work, and those blacks who would never obtain work. Moreover, he situated them in a dynamic global economy that had little interest in their survival. He contended that the oppression that blacks faced due to Detroit and other American cities' epidemics of mass unemployment, deindustrialization, and poverty forced them to mount an increasingly radical and revolutionary challenge against U.S. racial capitalism. He added that the civil rights movement and blacks' demands for power were indications of this black resistance. Intrigued by Boggs's claim, *Monthly Review* in late 1963 published Boggs's first book, a short work entitled *The American Revolution: Pages from a Negro Worker's Notebook.*[46]

Boggs and his wife and activist-intellectual partner and collaborator, Grace Lee, from the 1940s onward were two of Detroit's most notable writers, activists, organizers, and educators. In the context of the black power movement, the Boggses continuously problematized and advanced what black power meant intellectually and theoretically and how it would translate into everyday life and activism. In their view, the black power movement was America's second civil war, a struggle not just for national liberation but also for the freedom of all of humanity.

A former member of the Socialist Workers Party and the Trotskyite cell, Correspondence, James Boggs in the 1960s forsook the organized Marxist movement in favor of revolutionary nationalism. Foremost, he disagreed with Marxist-Leninists' dominant focus on class and overlook of the impact of race on American society. He asserted that racial and economic inequality in the United States was not determined just by class, but by the entanglement of race and class. Boggs explained:

> When we talk about the *system*, we are talking about *capitalism . . . Black underdevelopment is a product of capitalism.* Black America is underdeveloped today because of capitalist semi-colonialism. We cannot look at the underdevelopment of racism separate from capitalism. The illusion that we could resolve racism without talking about the economic system came to an end when we arrived at the point of talking about power to control and develop our communities. Now we are forced to face the question squarely of *what system to reject and what system to adopt.* This has forced us to face squarely the relationship of racism to capitalism.[47]

He also criticized Marxist-Leninists for holding onto an undying commitment to "mechanical materialism"—that is, the economic determinist belief that the productive forces were the key determinant for man and society's evolution. Boggs explained that radicals who studied "the writings of Marx, Lenin, and Mao, in the mistaken belief that they can find in these documents—written at a completely different time and under completely different circumstances—the revolutionary ideology on which to build a vanguard party in the United States" eschewed the act of creating a new radical analysis and platform.[48]

Another factor that prompted Boggs's shift to revolutionary nationalism was his disenchantment with the civil rights movement's approach and agenda. He argued that despite its humanism and progressive assertion of civil disobedience, the civil rights movement was primarily aimed at instigating white acceptance of black participation in American public life. Boggs countered that if blacks simply had "access" to the system, then the oppressive logic and power behind the U.S. brand of racial capitalism would remain. The fight for rights did not challenge and question the system, but acknowledged that the system, devoid of racial discrimination, was acceptable. Boggs also added that the movement's strategy of nonviolence did not connect to the anger and fervor felt by Detroit's black workers, the black unemployed, and the city's black youth. Boggs countered that these groups instead related more to the African and Asian anticolonial movements that were using violence to fight for independence.

Boggs contended that the altering mood of and response by blacks against their oppression relayed a paradigm shift that went outside the bounds of Marxism-Leninism and the civil rights movement's platform and agenda. In 1964, Boggs called this shift "black political power."[49] Black political power, Boggs asserted, embodied a reimagining and reconstituting of human life, society, work, the economy, and politics. It challenged the U.S. prevention of black Americans' capacity and power to reach and fulfill their potential, capabilities, and talents as human beings. It also confronted the U.S. basis and standard of humanity and called for a new universal definition of what it meant to be human. Boggs explained, "Black political power . . . is the key not only to black liberation but to the introduction of a new society to emancipate economically the masses of the people."[50] In Boggs's view of black power, politics was the key site and space for black people to empower themselves and others. He rationalized that blacks, by obtaining political power, would be empowered to advocate and successfully mobilize campaigns that could advance a higher standard of humanity for all people. Boggs wrote, "Political power addresses itself to the ruling of all peoples . . . Any movement which is concerned with just ruling black people is not engaged in a true revolution . . . A revolution is involved in a world-wide moment."[51]

Boggs regarded the fight for black power as the historical extension and transcendence of the working-class and the civil rights movements. He argued, "Black Power is a scientific concept whose time has come . . . I consider myself taking the concept [Marx's theoretic] far beyond where Marx had taken it."[52] Black power conveyed an emerging black collective standpoint—one that suggested that the U.S. failure to value black Americans and the poor as human beings was producing grave possibilities for the future of the nation. Black power also represented the inevitable culmination of the U.S. development and its collision with the nation's black inhabitants. Boggs asserted, "What is at the heart of the concept of Black Power, is that a social force has grown up in this society that is in fundamental antagonism to this society, thus making conflict and violence inevitable."[53]

A guiding source for Boggs's analysis of black power was the philosophical writings of Mao Zedong. For one thing, Boggs deemed Mao's writings on dialectics and the relevance and importance of the masses as key to the movement's efforts to wage a successful revolution. In *Revolution and Evolution in the Twentieth Century*, James and Grace Boggs maintained that the CCP was able to seize and retain power because of its dialectical assessment of history and the political development of modern China.[54] The Boggses explained that the CCP's elevation of the Chinese peasantry and its efforts to involve peasants in the process of nation building separated the CCP from earlier Chinese revolutionary movements. By referring to itself as "the party of the peasants," the CCP took advantage of the fact that the peasants were numerically the largest population in China. The CCP recognized that time and time again, it was the peasants who were the first to challenge imperialist rule. The CCP linked itself with these anti-imperialist Chinese peasant movements and declared itself as their logical extension, thereby gaining a wide and expansive base of national support.[55]

The Boggses asserted that the CCP's focus on politicizing China's peasant class was unknowingly a vital contribution to Marxism-Leninism and the philosophy of dialectics. Conceived by nineteenth century German philosopher G. W. F. Hegel, dialectics pointed to the permanence of change and suggested that change was not just produced by external causes, such as nature, but also by human agency and the consciousness of human beings. This concept went against common ideas about history and development that posited that humans had already reached and were fulfilling their highest potential. Dialectics instead suggested that human beings did not just replicate the world, but also produced and determined it through thought and action. Hegel asserted that people and societies obtained knowledge by resolving conflicts between two opposing positions—by determining the synthesis between a thesis and its antithesis. However, in the dialectical process, the synthesis did not embody an ultimate conclusion and/or punctuation mark to the prior conflict but represented a new contradiction to be resolved. Dialectics, the Boggses maintained, demonstrated that "there is no 'final struggle,' no ultimate unity, no 'promised land' in which we just sit back and reap the benefits of past struggles."[56] Karl Marx's addition to dialectics was to conceive of it as dialectical materialism, a standpoint and ideology that argued that a person could comprehend the present and foretell the future by fleshing out the old and new contradictions produced by the altering processes of production and mankind's relationship to production. Lastly, Bolshevik Revolution leader V. I. Lenin cultivated Marx's idea into a political movement by thrusting dialectics onto "the stage of politics" where revolutionists created vanguard parties in order to "propagate their convictions to people and especially to the masses" in an "attempt to organize these people to struggle to make these convictions real." So, through these series of shifts, dialectics had been transformed from a revolutionary philosophy to a revolutionary ideology to a revolutionary politics.

Through dialectics, the Boggses explained, Mao grasped a key ingredient that was absent in all Chinese movements prior to the CCP: "the party— that is, living human beings, cadres who had dedicated their entire selves, not only their arms, legs, and hearts but also their minds to revolutionary change, who had consciously and responsibly accepted a theory and tried to implement a program based upon that theory, and who were now ready."[57] Mao believed that the party was the highest expression of the masses' ability to be critical and organized, and to learn from experience. It was therefore the party's duty to educate and politicize all Chinese citizens—most especially the most downtrodden, which in China's case was the peasants— to create and maintain revolutions. Only after being politicized could the Chinese masses remold China and its politics. Mao, according to Boggs, "demystified the fundamental laws of dialectics to the point where they can be consciously applied by hundreds of millions of peasants and workers to the most elementary as well as the most complex questions of production and politics."[58]

In addition, the Boggses stated that Mao's greatest strength was that he did not employ Marxism-Leninism as the lone strategy or guide for generating a revolution. China's history, politics, and cultural dynamics foreclosed it from following a strict European model of revolution. Mao thus bent Marxism-Leninism to the circumstances and climate of mid-twentieth-century China. Boggs observed of Mao:

> He began to acquire that intellectual freedom and boldness inseparable from great revolutionary leadership. . . . If the Chinese Communist Party was seriously struggling for power, it would have to quit trying to adapt the ideas of Marx and Lenin, and the scenario of the Russian Revolution for the Chinese scene . . . it had the awesome responsibility

for devising a new revolutionary scenario or strategy which would both break with and take advantage of the long Chinese past. It would have to create its own vision of the goal of a Chinese revolution, its own definition of revolutionary class struggle . . . if there was ever going to be a revolution in China, it would have to be a Chinese revolution.[59]

Mao did not perceive Marx's and Lenin's ideas as eternal truths. Consequently, he aimed to build upon their knowledge and organize a Chinese movement framed around the uniqueness of China's history and its culture. For instance, Mao recognized that Marx's conception of the working class could not be applied in China. According to Boggs, Mao discerned that China's "inexhaustible supply of youthful bandits and rebels roving the countryside" and its consequent "virtually nonexistent working class" eliminated the possibility of the nation being led by a party representing mainly the interests of the working class.[60]

Ultimately, Mao's model of revolution expanded on Lenin's act of shaping dialectics into a revolutionary politics. By focusing on the role that peasant participation could play in national struggles taking place in preindustrial societies, Mao and the CCP's view of revolutionary politics was more suited for a Third World and semicolonized context than Lenin's working-class model. Mao's position also advanced that of Soviet communists Lenin and Stalin because Lenin and Stalin did not theorize the postrevolutionary moment—the period after a communist government has been instituted but while the class struggle continues. While the Soviets claimed that communism had been triumphant when the Bolshevik Party overthrew the Russian Provisional Government to obtain power in 1917, Mao claimed that the communist revolution was not over.[61] Mao justified his position by asserting that revolutions were not just based on the transfer of power from one government to another, but rather entailed the development of the masses' ability to make political decisions. Mao declared that revolution was an ongoing process, a protracted struggle, that continuously worked to produce more involved and politicized citizens who questioned and participated in the construction of society.[62] The Soviets and Chinese, Mao asserted, had not yet accomplished this feat and were still in the stage of developing the minds and dialectical analysis of their constituents.[63]

Mao's prioritization, at least conceptually, of the masses' political maturation and direct engagement in the building of a modern China gave James and Grace Boggs (and other radicals) a meaningful and practical viewpoint of socialism, which they linked to the politics of the black power movement. In the Boggses' view, the challenge China presented to Western interests and its revolutionary and international influence among populations of color therefore made the PRC one of several pinnacle powers that could counter U.S. globalism.[64] The Boggses asserted that Mao and the CCP "opened up to the world a new vision of revolution as the continuing struggle to create a new more advanced humanity" and had "gone far beyond any other revolution in history."[65]

James Boggs believed that the Chinese Revolution's development and projection of a revolutionary line and its efforts to confront its own internal struggles made it a useful example for black American revolutionaries to study, comprehend, and appreciate. The CCP leadership, Boggs explained, had established a powerful ideological and practical unifying point—one that black revolutionaries needed to embody themselves. He insisted that black radicals and revolutionaries required "a line . . . a line as serious as the party line of the revolutionary communist parties of the type we have witnessed in Asia, a line which is adopted and implemented and/or violated only if one is ready to risk denunciation and expulsion from the movement." Boggs concluded, "As long as blacks are not ready for a line, they are also not ready for the long struggle ahead."[66] Like Mao and the CCP, black revolutionaries needed to dialectically grasp the particular contradictions and challenges they faced in the United States and connect them to the larger advancement of humanity. The Boggses asserted that by reviewing "the revolutions that have taken place around the world during our epoch as part of an historical whole, a continuous process of human liberation would advance one step at a time," in which black revolutionaries would be able to "draw some universal lessons from particular revolutions which will contribute to the next advancement."[67] They would learn that a revolution in the United States could only be implemented if they fleshed out the distinctiveness of U.S. history, U.S. historical contradictions, and the challenges the country faced. Black revolutionaries would consequently have to reject past strategies and develop a standpoint based on fresh analysis of U.S. history and the nation's current conditions and contradictions.[68] They would have to take responsibility for the transformation of U.S. society and the American power structure, and accept their duty as revolutionists. Revolutionaries, Boggs explained, "projected a concept of revolution . . . they evaluated the state of the world and their own society. They internalized the most advanced ideas about human development . . . They projected a vision of what a revolution would mean in their own country. They analyzed the different social forces within their country carefully to ascertain which forces could be mobilized to realize this vision. They carried on an ideological struggle."[69] For Boggs, black revolutionaries were thus in a similar position to that of the CCP. It was the former's duty and purpose to extend the concept of dialectics to respond to their historical challenge in the United States—the conditions created by racial capitalism and the rise of a postindustrial U.S. economy. Boggs believed that people, through political action and involvement, cultivated new viewpoints and structures of power, thought, work, and art—the different segments of human activity. Consequently, Boggs, like Mao, did not ignore the impact of structures on human consciousness but pointed to the role of human consciousness and human agency in transforming historical structures and institutions.

Both Boggs and Mao believed that institutions would not effectively change unless people first went through individual and collective experiences of transformation. Boggs explained, "Mao is not defining communism within the traditional distributive productive (economic) framework of 'To each according to his needs, from each according to his abilities.' His framework is rather the distinctively political one of 'Mankind consciously transforming itself and changing the world.'"[70] Mao drove the Chinese masses to *fanshen,* meaning to "overturn" or transform oneself. As the first step in any revolution, *fanshen* then represented not just an individual's self-transformation, but the transformation of society. Individual self-determination was a part of national self-determination. Boggs explained, "In Mao's new concept of transformation, goodness or responsibility to society requires *everybody,* intellectuals and masses, men and women, young and old alike, to *fanshen,* i.e., to struggle both against the internal limitations stemming from their position in the social structure and against those who try to maintain the structure which limits them . . . Thus the class struggle is the struggle to transcend the limitations of class society."[71]

Boggs determined that black revolutionary nationalists should import *fanshen* into their individual values and the values of their fight against racial capitalism. Boggs argued that the systematic oppression and disenfranchisement faced by blacks would not be transformed simply by a change in the power regime but also by a transformation of oneself. Black revolutionaries would therefore have to become the change that they demanded of the American system. They must project the humanistic implications of their struggles and "internalize a profoundly human vision of the goals toward which a revolution is moving."[72] It was important that they embody and project a revolutionary vision of the world and humankind's responsibility in shaping and transforming the world. He added that this revolutionary approach should be based on the principle of escalation.

With this type of approach, the movement could constantly transform itself to better challenge and respond to the various changes occurring in American society. As a movement of escalation, it would "develop a strategy that will build a movement around escalating demands and escalating struggles so that the movement of escalation assumes a momentum of its own."[73]

Boggs posited that cities offered the strongest opportunities to mobilize this kind of movement. In a 1966 article, "The City Is the Black Man's Land," he argued that U.S. cities vividly displayed the most prevalent contradictions of U.S. life.[74] As both "the dangerous society" and a "police state," U.S. cities were threatened by the violence and crime committed by those who lived in the city and by the policing and management of the city by police officers, social workers, educators, bankers, union leaders, landlords, and politicians—groups that were paid to protect private property and "rule the natives."[75] In addition, cities, once symbols of mass industry and development, were rapidly becoming ghost towns due to deindustrialization, white flight to the suburbs, and the closing of businesses.

Blacks and the poor, the two groups who suffered the most from these conditions, were drastically affected by all of this. However, they remained unable to improve these conditions because they did not hold power in the cities. American cities placed blacks at the depths and outskirts of the fruits and toils of their labor and of industrial development, and policed and colonized blacks in the ghettoes of the city's interior. Their neighborhoods were encircled by the wealth and progression of city life; however, their communities received only an iota of the benefits gained from the city's development. Prevented from taking full advantage of industrial and technological development, blacks in the cities would have to locate new purposes and activities to advance their communities and the nation at large. Boggs relayed, "In an advanced country like the United States . . . the black population, concentrated in the cities, has to be educated and mobilized to abandon outmoded methods of labor and prepare itself for the socially necessary activities of political and community organization, social services, education, and other forms of establishing human relations between man and man."[76] Stifled and oppressed by unemployment, crime, and policing, blacks and the poor would have to challenge the city power structure. It was vital that they perceive the city as a battleground for power. Boggs proclaimed, "The war is not *in* America's cities; it is *for* these cities."[77] Black control of cities would not be a reinvention of the wheel—maintenance of the state in a mirror image of how it was run before. Instead, cities would serve as models for a new humanism.

Boggs argued that it was black young adults and youth that would be affected most by this new humanism. It was they, he posited, who most especially needed new activities and visions to replace their searches for work, food, and the means to survive. Youth, Boggs argued, must be taught to feel a deep responsibility to their communities, neighborhoods, and cities. Rather than educate them to compete for industrial jobs that no longer existed, communities should educate youth to take control of the institutions that surrounded them in their everyday lives. Boggs described this as the cultivation of a "perspective of black self-government in the cities . . . as a profession and perspective toward which black youth should aspire and for which they should begin preparing themselves from childhood."[78] Black power would have to train young people to fight for control of the various institutions in their communities. Black power, Boggs asserted, had to transform into "something that is really meaningful in terms of our actual daily lives at work, in our communities and our neighborhoods, in our classrooms, our offices, on the streets, in our families."[79]

To conceive black power as a movement of escalation more importantly suggested an ultimate transformation of the U.S. government and its relationship to the U.S. public. "By establishing beachheads in one or more major cities, black revolutionary governments would be in the most strategic position to contend with and eventually defeat this national power structure," Boggs explained.[80] Cities would have to alter their relationship to the federal government and call on it, rather than the state government, to implement change. Boggs continued that this new relationship between the city and the federal government might necessitate the reconfiguration of the latter and thus produce a new federal constitution. A government produced by black power could rewrite the U.S. Constitution with a more humane projection of what it meant to be a human being.[81] With a new vision of America, people could then transform U.S. institutions and American values. Boggs stated: "The question of *whose* constitution, *whose* law and order, *whose* equality, *whose* justice, *whose* welfare, becomes a question of what kind of constitution, what kind of law and order, what kind of equality, what kind of justice, what kind of welfare; and the need arises to create a new constitution, a new law and order, a new equality, a new justice, a new welfare—in other words, a new political, economic, and social system."[82]

During the 1930s, Mao made a similar distinction. When Japan attacked Chinese cities, Mao argued that the CCP could defeat the Japanese by encircling the cities from the countryside. He explained that the Chinese countryside was the best site to wage a national revolution. This social context would force the Chinese peasants to fight against Japanese imperialism and against their oppression as a class. Peasants, Mao argued, therefore had the most at stake. They were fighting not only to defeat Japanese imperialism, but also against an economic and political system that allowed them no voice or participation in Chinese politics and society. They were waging a war against China's past and intended to establish a new Chinese society that valued their labor, creativity, and humanity.

Boggs concluded that blacks in U.S. cities, similar to Chinese peasants during the Chinese Revolution, could take control of cities if they projected an advanced concept of revolution. First and foremost, this would require that they stop conceiving the revolutionary process as ephemeral. Boggs asserted, "There is an urgent necessity to combat the widespread tendency, propagated by the mass media, to think of revolution in terms of a single tactical event or episode . . . Most people, including militants, think of a revolution in terms of "Instant Revolution" rather than in terms of a protracted struggle."[83] Various black militants and black nationalists who believed that rebellions, insurrections, revolts, and coups d'état constituted revolutions were wrong. Rebellions, insurrections, revolts, and coups d'état, Boggs explained, were "single events" that took place during revolutions. Revolutions were more significant because revolutions produced long-term transformation and the advancement of humankind. By understanding the task of revolution as long and enduring, blacks could better situate their goals and objectives. Once they grasped the purpose of their struggle, they could recognize themselves as the group most responsible for the projection of a new humanity. It would become clear to them, Boggs stated, that "blacks are pivotal to the advance-or decline of American society."[84] In this function they would not await change. They would actively fight for it.

Boggs determined that only this type of effort could challenge the basis of U.S. democracy and subsequently put forward a new, revolutionary, and humanist democratic order. He maintained that U.S. democracy justified the systematic oppression of certain groups by offering whites a strategic partnership with the state. U.S. democracy also did not equally distribute power and resources, but rather pushed citizens to compete for these things on an unequal terrain with no regard for ethics or morals. Boggs stated, "I believe in democracy, but I don't believe in being too damn democratic," because "it is only by looking at the whole world and seeing all the nations that have been dominated and exploited by all the democratic nations that you can begin to examine scientifically whether democracy has been a philosophy for liberating the world or for subjugating the world."[85]

Boggs's critique of democracy in the United States expanded on an evaluation of Western liberalism offered by Mao in his 1957 essay, "On the Correct Handling of Contradictions among the People." Mao wrote:

> This so-called two-party system is nothing but a device for maintaining the dictatorship of the bourgeoisie; it can never guarantee freedom to the working people. As a matter of fact, freedom and democracy do not exist in the abstract, only in the concrete. In a society rent by class struggle, if there is freedom for the exploiting classes to exploit working people, there is no freedom for the working people not to be exploited, and if there is democracy for the bourgeoisie, there is no democracy for the proletariat and other working people . . . Those who demand freedom and democracy in the abstract regard democracy as an end and not a means. Democracy sometimes seems to be an end, but it is in fact only a means.[86]

Boggs agreed with Mao's view. Americans were naïve to believe that democracy was an end that had already been accomplished and not a continuous process of political struggle, a protracted struggle. Boggs asserted, "Mao makes clear that democracy must not be regarded as an end in itself or as a symbol which moves some people . . . it is a political process, a procedure in which people engage in discussion, debate and controversy and thus arrive at political understanding and the capacity to make political conditions."[87] The Chinese Revolution therefore represented a decisive break with Western idealism and liberal democracy because it "provided the momentum for nationalist revolutions free of democratic illusions and therefore able to resist and define themselves against neo-colonialism."[88]

Ultimately, through Mao, Boggs discovered a complementary framework to evaluate and theorize the dilemma of projecting a higher concept of revolution. Mao devoted a great deal of time to the question, "what is a revolution?" Extremely daunting to Mao was his observation that after a change in power, societies often grew too comfortable with their new leadership. Mao was critical of societal complacency and reckoned that to think dialectically meant that a person had to conceive reality and revolution as both intrinsically contradictory. So, revolutions did not abruptly end, but brought along new contradictions and dilemmas to be resolved. Mao proposed that by constantly laboring to resolve old and new contradictions, groups could advance their struggles. He stated, "If you want to know a certain thing or certain class of things directly, you must personally participate in the practical struggle to change reality . . . only through personal participation in the practical struggle to change reality can you uncover the essence of that thing or class of things and comprehend them."[89]

Mao reasoned that revolutions were protracted struggles—that is, never-ending processes of transformation and struggle. Revolution was not simply "accomplished," and did not entail a definitive conclusion, but was a boundless and everlasting course of action that created new ideas, new values, and new ways of living. More important than a simple seizure of power and the indoctrination of a new group into the armchair of national leadership, revolutions captured political power for the purpose of advancing a higher morality and level of humanity. Revolutions were aimed at restructuring society and its values. The political struggle, therefore, was not a fight for an alternative state, but a redefining of the state and of society itself and the evolution of humanity. "Revolution is a specific way in which the evolution of man/woman is advanced . . . It initiates a new plateau, a new threshold on which human beings can continue to develop," the Boggses explained.[90]

Hence, the fight for black power represented the ongoing process of revolution and evolution. Black power and the new American Revolution represented a stage in the evolution of the United States and the humanity of all Americans. It had a tremendous task in front of it—to redefine U.S. society and the social relations between its members. It would have to answer difficult questions like, "How should people live today? What changes are necessary in our values, in our morality?"[91] It must recognize its process, revolution, as never-ending and dialectical. If so, then black power had all the potential to "enable the American people to renew and enlarge their sense of their own humanity."[92] Like the Chinese Revolution before it, the movement presented a unique challenge and opportunity for human possibility.

Boggs's vision has not yet come to fruition. During the mid-1970s, as the black power movement became weakened by inner turmoil among its constituents and attacks by the federal and local governments through police repression and COINTELPRO, the influence of Chinese communism and Maoist thought declined. President Richard Nixon's visit to China in 1972 and the signing of the Sino-American joint communique signaled that China was realigning itself. Its relationship with pro-Western Zairean leader Mobotu Sese Seko and alliance with racist and apartheid South Africa in supporting the National Front for the Liberation of Angola (FNLA) during the 1975 Angolan civil war relayed that China was working mainly toward its own interests, no matter who might be affected.[93] In the end, most pro-China black radicals comprehended these acts as China's "grand betrayal."

Be that as it may, black internationalists' engagement with Chinese communism and Maoist thought is one example of how the cultures and ideologies of non-Western locations have been and can be significant to black political activism and theoretical analysis. This expands our understanding of black internationalism and pushes us to consider the inclusion of many more sites and groups into the African Diaspora's historical and conceptual frame.[94] Additionally, black radical engagement of Chinese communism and Maoism during the Cold War reframes the postwar black freedom movement and U.S. race relations from an international perspective. This trajectory is one example of what cultural anthropologist Walter Mignolo refers to as "border thinking," or an "other thinking." Border thinking is not created and enacted by those in power but by those at the exteriors of power where, as Mignolo explains, "*local* histories inventing and implementing global designs meet *local* histories, the space in which global designs have to be adapted, adopted, rejected, integrated, or ignored."[95] So James Boggs is able to "invent and implement" Maoist thought—a global design—via his own local history and experience as a black man in the United States. In the process he is not simply accepting this global design on its own terms. He is, rather, adapting, adopting, rejecting, integrating, and ignoring some aspects of it, and not valuing it as the quintessential blueprint for revolution, but revaluing it via his own personal history and silenced epistemological standpoint.

NOTES

1. W.E.B. Du Bois, *The Autobiography of W. E. B. Du Bois: A Soliloquy on Viewing My Life from the Last Decade of Its First Century* (New York: International Publishers, 1968), 49.

2. Tracy B. Strong and Helene Keyssar, *Right in Her Soul: The Life of Anna Louise Strong* (New York: Random House, 1983), 322.

3. James Peck, *Washington's China: The National Security World, the Cold War, and the Origins of Globalism* (Amherst: University of Massachusetts Press, 2006).

4. Wu Cheng'en, *Monkey: Folk Novel of China,* trans. Arthur Waley (New York: Grove Press, 1994); Wu Cheng-en, *Journey to the West,* trans. W. J. F. Jenner (Beijing: Foreign Languages Press, 2003).

5. See Robin D. G. Kelley and Betsy Esch, "Black Like Mao," *Souls* 1, no. 4 (Fall 1999): 6–41; Vijay Prashad. *Everybody Was Kung Fu Fighting* (Boston: Beacon Press, 2001); Andrew Jones and Nikhil Pal Singh, eds., *The Afro-Asian Century, Positions: East Asia Cultures Critique* 11, no. 1 (Spring 2003); Bill Mullen, *Afro-Orientalism* (Minneapolis: University of Minnesota Press, 2004); Jeffrey Ogbar, *Black Power* (Baltimore: Johns Hopkins University Press, 2004); Heike Raphael-Hernandez and Shannon Steen, *AfroAsian Encounters: Culture, History, Politics* (New York: NYU Press, 2006); Fred Ho and Bill Mullen, eds., *Afro Asia: Revolutionary Political and Cultural Connections between African Americans and Asian Americans* (Durham, N.C.: Duke University Press, 2008).

6. Renmin Ribao, "Chairman Mao's Theory on the Differentiation of the Three Worlds Is a Major Contribution to Marxism-Leninism," *Peking Review* 45 (November 4, 1977): 24.

7. Besenia Rodriguez, "'De la Esculavitud Yanqui a la Libertad Cubana': U.S. Black Radicals, the Cuban Revolution, and the Formation of a Tricontinental Ideology," *Radical History Review* 92 (Spring 2005): 62–87.

8. Over the past thirty years, Mao and his reign have been demonized and lambasted, historically and culturally, by the non-Chinese and labeled by recent Chinese communist regimes as antiquated. Mao's policies for several of the key national initiatives during his period in office left many Chinese citizens mortified, starved, homeless, or dead, and produced a fearful public and citizenry that grew accustomed to government coercion and repression. The exposure of the atrocities of the Great Leap Forward, the Cultural Revolution, and Mao's individualized purges of party leaders, intellectuals, and any group that he saw as posing a challenge to his power have produced a robust anti-Mao discourse. In a recent ABC news report and several articles, Mao was matter-of-factly compared to Adolf Hitler ("Cameron Diaz Apologizes for Carrying Bag with Maoist Slogan in Peru," Associated Press, June 25, 2007; Jon Dougherty, "Mao More Lethal Than Hitler, Stalin," WorldNetDaily.com, November 29, 2005).

9. Nikhil Pal Singh, *Black Is a Country* (Cambridge, Mass.: Harvard University Press, 2005).

10. Grace Lee Boggs, *Living for Change* (Minneapolis: University of Minnesota Press, 1998), 152–54.

11. Richard Kagan, Introduction, in Ross Koen, *The China Lobby in American Politics* (New York: Harper & Row, 1974), xi.

12. The Cold War describes the conflict and competition over ideology, spheres of influence, power, and trade relations between the United States and Soviet Union from 1945 until 1990. The use of the term *Cold War* to describe this feud became prominent in 1947 after its use by writer Walter Lippman, who published a 1947 book entitled *Cold War*, as well as by presidential advisor Bernard Baruch and his speechwriter Herbert Bayard Swope. While the 1947 Truman Doctrine and 1948 Marshall Plan (European Recovery Plan) helped rebuild Western Europe and publicly advertised the United States as new "leader of the free world," these initiatives also endorsed a Euro-American development model that aimed to prevent the Soviet Union's access to and accumulation of foreign nations' natural resources. They signified the U.S. shift from a foreign policy based on collective security to one based on maintaining the balance of power. The Soviets response, the "Molotov Plan," an aid program to their own European satellites, was established also in 1947 and later developed into the Council of Mutual Economic Assistance (COMECON) in early 1949. Both plans, the Marshall and the Molotov, challenged the political ideology of the other's underwriter and secured trading partners and allies for the United States and the Soviet Union, respectively.

13. Walter LaFeber, *The Clash: The History of U.S.-Japan Relations* (New York: W. W. Norton, 1997), 231.

14. The CCP established a relationship with the Soviet Union after the CCP's founding in 1921. Yet at the 1945 Yalta Conference, the Soviets reneged on their support for their Chinese communist comrades. Soviet leader Joseph Stalin withdrew support for the

CCP when he obtained U.S. support for the restoration of Russian forces in Manchuria. The Soviets subsequently agreed to endorse the GMD, the CCP's opposition, and confirmed the deal by signing the Sino-Soviet Treaty of Friendship and Mutual Assistance with the GMD. The CCP countered by challenging and delegitimizing the GMD. The CCP placed troops in northeast China, near Siberia and in Soviet controlled territory, and proclaimed that despite the Sino-Soviet treaty, they knew that the Soviets supported the CCP's "cause for progressive democracy." Determining that the CCP would most likely win the war, the Soviet government responded by refuting its support of the GMD, and on October 4, 1945, the USSR announced its support for the CCP. The United States, in contrast, took a more lackadaisical approach in its support of the GMD. The United States did not invest the resources, finances, and weapons required for the GMD to defeat the CCP. The GMD constantly complained that it lacked the weaponry and finances to match the artillery and technical assistance that the CCP obtained from the Soviets (left over after the war with Japan). Much of this was caused by U.S. inexperience in Asia. While the United States understood the purpose of collective action in Europe in preserving a democratic and capitalist Europe, as shown in both world wars, it had limited, if any, real collectivist experience with Asia outside of missionary work and its alliance with Europe in maintaining the Chinese Open Door Policy established after the mid-nineteenth-century Opium Wars. So while a collectivist approach was emphasized in Europe after World War II, the United States took a strong unilateralist stance toward Asia.

15. Peck, *Washington's China.*

16. Chen Jian, *Mao's China and the Cold War* (Chapel Hill: University of North Carolina Press, 2000), 3.

17. Peck, *Washington's China,* 32.

18. James Peck best clarifies how the "freedom as anticommunism" discourse operates: "Freedom and the market cannot be separated . . . and the international market is the only force capable of promoting freedom's further development . . . it is "pure," so to speak . . . Freedom committed to cooperative ventures would restrict itself, and so such ventures are anathema to it . . . The question 'To what end freedom?' remains unasked . . . since they cannot speak easily of any values that limit such freedom. That is why balancing values, such as equality, fraternity, and community, so often appear as threateningly communistic. Communism . . . is a galaxy of liberally acclaimed values that have been twisted to attack freedom" (*Washington's China,* 32).

19. Koen, *China Lobby in American Politics.*

20. Ibid., 50.

21. Kagan, Introduction to Koen, *China Lobby in American Politics,* xi.

22. Edgar Snow, *Red Star over China* (New York: Random House, 1938); William Hinton, *Fanshen: A Documentary of Revolution in a Chinese Village* (New York: Monthly Review Press, 1966); Anna Louise Strong. *The Chinese Conquer China* (Garden City, N.Y.: Doubleday, 1949); Jack Belden, *China Shakes the World* (New York: Harpers, 1949); Agnes Smedley, *China's Red Army Marches* (New York: Vanguard Press, 1934); Graham Peck, *Through China's Wall* (Boston: Houghton Mifflin, 1940).

23. George Kennan, "A Fresh Look at Our China Policy," *New York Times Magazine,* November 22, 1964, 27.

24. U.S. Dept. of State, "Memorandum of Discussion of the 237th Meeting of the National

Security Council," February 17, 1955, in *Foreign Relations of the United States*, China, 1955–57, 2:285.

25. Dwight Eisenhower, *White House Years*, 2 vols. (Garden City, N.Y.: Doubleday, 1963–65), 2:369.

26. Koen, *China Lobby in American Politics*, 5.

27. Peck, *Washington's China*, 4.

28. Marc Gallicchio, *The African American Encounter with Japan and China: Black Internationalism in Asia, 1895–1945* (Chapel Hill: University of North Carolina Press, 2000), 158.

29. Ibid., 167–202.

30. Ibid., 164–65, 174–78. The 1943 repeal of the Chinese Exclusion Act increased the number of Chinese immigrants permitted to enter the United States.

31. "Telling Oriental Types Apart Great Mental Game on Coast," *Baltimore Afro-American*, January 3, 1942, 4.

32. Gallicchio, *African American Encounter with Japan and China,*159–202.

33. Ibid., 201.

34. Mao Zedong, "Statement Supporting American Negroes in Their Just Struggle against Racial Discrimination in the United States" (Beijing: Foreign Languages Press, 1963).

35. Du Bois, *Autobiography of W. E. B. Du Bois*, 47 and 51.

36. Ibid., 47.

37. Ibid., 51.

38. Gerald Horne, *Race Woman* (New York: NYU Press, 2000).

39. Ibid., 228.

40. Timothy Tyson, *Radio Free Dixie: Robert F. Williams and the Roots of Black Power* (Chapel Hill: University of North Carolina Press, 1999).

41. Peniel E. Joseph, *Waiting 'Til the Midnight Hour* (New York: Henry Holt, 2006).

42. Harry Haywood, *Black Bolshevik: The Autobiography of an Afro-American Communist* (Liberator Press: Chicago, 1978), 643.

43. James A. Geschwender, "Marxist-Leninist Organizations: Prognosis among Black Workers," *Journal of Black Studies* 8, no. 3 (March 1978): 279–98.

44. Heather Thompson, *Whose Detroit? Politics, Labor and Race in a Modern American City* (Ithaca, N.Y.: Cornell University Press, 2004).

45. James Boggs, "Monthly Review Correspondence: June 26, 1963," James and Grace Lee Boggs Collection, Walter P. Reuther Library of Labor and Urban Affairs, Wayne State University Archives, Detroit, Box 1, Folder 18.

46. James Boggs, *The American Revolution: Pages from a Negro Worker's Notebook* (New York: Monthly Review Press, 1963). Also see Grace Lee Boggs, *Living for Change*; Mullen, *Afro-Orientalism*; Stephen Michael Ward, "'Ours Too Was a Struggle for a Better World': Activist Intellectuals and the Radical Promise of the Black Power Movement, 1962–1972," Ph.D. diss., University of Texas at Austin, 2002.

47. FBI File on James Boggs, Freedom of Information and Privacy Act (FOIPA) #1039336, File HQ 100–405600, sec. 2, p. 103, "Meeting of All African Peoples Union to Commemorates the Birthday of Malcolm X, May 20, 1969" (the underlined sections are by Boggs's doing).

48. James Boggs, *Manifesto for a Black Party* (Philadelphia: Pacesetters Publishing, 1969), vii.

49. FBI-James Boggs, unnamed document, sec. 1, p. 120. Stephen Michael Ward argues that James Boggs was arguing for black power more than a year before the Meredith March of 1966.

50. James Boggs, *Racism and the Class Struggle* (New York: Monthly Review Press, 1970), 60.

51. FBI-James Boggs, "Meeting of All African Peoples Union to Commemorates the Birthday of Malcolm X, May 20, 1969," sec. 2, p. 101.

52. Ibid., sec. 2, p. 10.

53. Boggs, *Racism and the Class Struggle*, 102–3.

54. James Boggs and Grace Lee Boggs, *Revolution and Evolution in the Twentieth Century* (Monthly Review Press, 1975), 250–51.

55. Ibid., 49.

56. Ibid., 128.

57. Ibid., 55.

58. Ibid., 132.

59. Ibid., 58–59.

60. Ibid., 59.

61. Immanuel Wallerstein states, "One of the earliest signs of a major disagreement in the 1950s between the Communist Party of the Soviet Union and the Chinese Communist Party was a theoretical debate that revolved around the question of the 'gradual transition to Communism.' Basically the CPSU argued that different socialist states would proceed separately in effectuating such a transition whereas the CCP argued that all socialist states would proceed simultaneously . . . In effect the CCP was arguing that 'communism' was a characteristic not of nation-states but of the world-economy as a whole. This debate was transposed onto the internal Chinese science by the ideological debate, now known to have deep and long-standing roots, that give rise eventually to the Cultural Revolution" (*The Capitalist World-Economy* [Cambridge: Cambridge University Press, 1979], 11).

62. Boggs and Boggs, *Revolution and Evolution in the Twentieth Century*, 135.

63. The Boggses wrote, "What has been taking place in China for the last few decades is the result of Mao's reflections not only on the contradictions of Chinese society but also on the problems that the Russian Revolution raised and failed to resolve" (ibid., 138).

64. This was due to myriad factors and events, including the CCP's ousting of Japanese imperialism from Chinese borders, its defeat of the Western-supported Chinese Nationalist Party, and its protection of Korean sovereignty during the Korean War. However, the Boggses insisted that it was mainly due to Mao's leadership and intellectual insight.

65. Boggs and Boggs, *Revolution and Evolution in the Twentieth Century*, 48; Boggs, *Racism and the Class Struggle*, 82.

66. FBI File-James Boggs, "August 27, 1968 Letter to CORE," sec. 2, p. 64.

67. Boggs and Boggs, *Revolution and Evolution in the Twentieth Century*, 22.

68. Boggs, *Racism and the Class Struggle*, 82.

69. Ibid., 22.

70. Boggs and Boggs, *Revolution and Evolution in the Twentieth Century*, 64.

71. Ibid., 61.

72. Ibid., 67.

73. Boggs, *Racism and the Class Struggle*, 116.
74. Ibid., 39–50.
75. Boggs, *Manifesto for a Black Revolutionary Party*, 8.
76. Boggs, *Racism and the Class Struggle*, 43.
77. Ibid., 41.
78. Ibid., 42.
79. James Boggs, "Blacks in the Cities: Agenda for the 70s," *Black Scholar* 4, no. 3 (November-December 1972): 50–61.
80. Boggs, *Racism and the Class Struggle.*, 47.
81. Ibid., 76.
82. Ibid.
83. Boggs and Boggs, *Revolution and Evolution in the Twentieth Century*, 15.
84. Boggs, *Manifesto for Black Revolutionary Party*, viii.
85. Bogg, *American Revolution*, 11; Boggs, *Racism and the Class Struggle*, 34–35.
86. Mao Zedong, "On the Correct Handling of Contradictions among the People," in *Five Essays on Philosophy* (Beijing: Foreign Languages Press, 1977), 85.
87. Boggs and Boggs, *Revolution and Evolution in the Twentieth Century*, 73.
88. Boggs, *Racism and the Class Struggle*, 82.
89. Mao Zedong, "On Practice," in *Five Essays on Philosophy* (Beijing: Foreign Languages Press, 1977), 7–8.
90. Boggs and Boggs, *Revolution and Evolution in the Twentieth Century*, 19.
91. Ibid.
92. Ibid., 22.
93. *The Facts on Angola: News Reports from the Press from the U.S.A., France, Somalia, Tanzania, Algeria, the U.S.S.R., Guinea and Other Countries* (New York: Anti-Imperialist Movement in Solidarity with the African Liberation New York Committee, 1976).
94. For example, Kate Baldwin examines the relationships of Du Bois, Paul Robeson, Langston Hughes, and Claude McKay with Soviet communism and their travels to the Soviet Union. Baldwin argues that these experiences played a significant role in how these thinkers imagined and actively cultivated platforms that addressed their own individual, and black people's collective, place in the world. See her *Beyond the Color Line and the Iron Curtain* (Durham, N.C.: Duke University Press, 2002).
95. Walter Mignolo, *Local Histories/Global Designs: Coloniality, Subaltern Knowledges, and Border Thinking* (Princeton, N.J.: Princeton University Press, 2000), ix (emphasis in original).

REFERENCES

Baldwin, Kate. *Beyond the Color Line and the Iron Curtain*. Durham, N.C.: Duke University Press, 2002.

Belden, Jack. *China Shakes the World*. New York: Harpers, 1949.

Boggs, Grace Lee. *Living for Change*. Minneapolis: University of Minnesota Press, 1998.

Boggs, James. *The American Revolution: Pages from a Negro Worker's Notebook*. New York: Monthly Review Press, 1963.

————. "Blacks in the Cities: Agenda for the 70s." *The Black Scholar* 4, no. 3 (November-December 1972): 50–61.

————. *Manifesto for a Black Party*. Philadelphia: Pacesetters Publishing, 1976.

————. "Monthly Review Correspondence: June 26, 1963." James and Grace Lee Boggs Collection. Walter P. Reuther Library of Labor and Urban Affairs, Wayne State University Archives, Detroit, Michigan. Box 1, Folder 18.

————. *Racism and the Class Struggle*. New York: Monthly Review Press, 1970.

Boggs, James, and Grace Lee Boggs. *Revolution and Evolution in the Twentieth Century*. New York: Monthly Review Press, 1975.

"Cameron Diaz Apologizes for Carrying Bag with Maoist Slogan in Peru." Associated Press, June 25, 2007.

Chen Jian. *Mao's China and the Cold War*. Chapel Hill: University of North Carolina Press, 2000.

Dougherty, Jon. "Mao More Lethal Than Hitler, Stalin." WorldNetDaily.com, November 29, 2005.

Du Bois, W. E. B. *The Autobiography of W. E. B. Du Bois: A Soliloquy on Viewing My Life from the Last Decade of Its First Century*. New York: International Publishers, 1968.

Eisenhower, Dwight. *White House Years*. 2 vols. Garden City, N.Y.: Doubleday, 1963–65.

The Facts on Angola: News Reports from the Press from the U.S.A., France, Somalia, Tanzania, Algeria, the U.S.S.R., Guinea and Other Countries. New York: Anti-Imperialist Movement in Solidarity with the African Liberation New York Committee, 1976.

Fanshen, William Hinton. *A Documentary of Revolution in a Chinese Village*. New York: Monthly Review Press, 1966.

FBI File on James Boggs. Freedom of Information and Privacy Act (FOIPA) #1039336, File HQ 100–405600, sec. 2, p. 103. "August 27, 1968 Letter to CORE"; "Meeting of All African Peoples Union to Commemorates the Birthday of Malcolm X, May 20, 1969."

Gallicchio, Marc. *The African American Encounter with Japan and China: Black Internationalism in Asia, 1895–1945*. Chapel Hill: University of North Carolina Press, 2000.

Geschwender, James A. "Marxist-Leninist Organizations: Prognosis among Black Workers." *Journal of Black Studies* 8, no. 3 (March 1978): 279–98.

Haywood, Harry. *Black Bolshevik: The Autobiography of an Afro-American Communist*. Liberator Press: Chicago, 1978.

Ho, Fred, and Bill Mullen, eds. *Afro Asia: Revolutionary Political and Cultural Connections between African Americans and Asian Americans*. Durham, N.C.: Duke University Press, 2008.

Horne, Gerald. *Race Woman*. New York: New York University Press, 2000.

Jones, Andrew, and Nikhil Pal Singh, eds. *The Afro-Asian Century. Positions: East Asia Cultures Critique* 11, no. 1 (Spring 2003).

Joseph, Peniel E. *Waiting {{ap}}Til the Midnight Hour*. New York: Henry Holt, 2006.

Kagan, Richard. "Introduction." In Ross Koen, *The China Lobby in American Politics*. New York: Harper & Row, 1974.

Kelley, Robin D. G., and Betsy Esch. "Black Like Mao." *Souls* 1, no. 4 (Fall 1999): 6–41.

Kennan, George. "A Fresh Look at Our China Policy." *New York Times Magazine*, November 22, 1964, 27.

LaFeber, Walter. *The Clash: The History of U.S.-Japan Relations*. New York: W. W. Norton, 1997.

Mao Zedong. "On the Correct Handling of Contradictions among the People." In *Five Essays on Philosophy*. Beijing: Foreign Languages Press, 1977.

—— "On Practice." In *Five Essays on Philosophy*. Beijing: Foreign Languages Press, 1977.

—— "Statement Supporting American Negroes in Their Just Struggle against Racial Discrimination in the United States." Beijing: Foreign Languages Press, 1963.

Mignolo, Walter. *Local Histories/Global Designs: Coloniality, Subaltern Knowledges, and Border Thinking*. Princeton, N.J.: Princeton University Press, 2000.

Mullen, Bill. *Afro-Orientalism*. Minneapolis: University of Minnesota Press, 2004.

Ogbar, Jeffrey. *Black Power*. Baltimore: Johns Hopkins University Press, 2004.

Peck, Graham. *Through China's Wall*. Boston: Houghton Mifflin, 1949.

Peck, James. *Washington's China: The National Security World, the Cold War, and the Origins of Globalism*. Amherst: University of Massachusetts Press, 2006.

Prashad, Vijay. *Everybody Was Kung Fu Fighting*. Boston: Beacon Press, 2001.

Raphael-Hernandez, Heike, and Shannon Steen. *AfroAsian Encounters: Culture, History, Politics*. New York: NYU Press, 2006.

Ribao, Renmin. "Chairman Mao's Theory on the Differentiation of the Three Worlds Is a Major Contribution to Marxism-Leninism." *Peking Review* 45 (November 4, 1977).

Rodriguez, Besenia. "'De la Esculavitud Yanqui a la Libertad Cubana': U.S. Black Radicals, the Cuban Revolution, and the Formation of a Tricontinental Ideology." *Radical History Review* 92 (Spring 2005): 62–87.

Singh, Nikhil Pal. *Black Is a Country*. Cambridge, Mass.: Harvard University Press, 2005.

Smedley, Agnes. *China's Red Army Marches*. New York: Vanguard Press, 1934.

Snow, Edgar. *Red Star over China*. New York: Random House, 1938.

Strong, Anna Louise. *The Chinese Conquer China*. Garden City, N.Y.: Doubleday, 1949.

Strong, Tracy B., and Helene Keyssar. *Right in Her Soul: The Life of Anna Louise Strong*. New York: Random House, 1983.

"Telling Oriental Types Apart Great Mental Game on Coast." *Baltimore Afro-American*, January 3, 1942.

Thompson, Heather. *Whose Detroit? Politics, Labor and Race in a Modern American City*. Ithaca, N.Y.: Cornell University Press, 2004.

Tyson, Timothy. *Radio Free Dixie: Robert F. Williams and the Roots of Black Power*. Chapel Hill: University of North Carolina Press, 1999.

U.S. Dept. of State. "Memorandum of Discussion of the 237th Meeting of the National Security Council," February 17, 1955. Ed. John P. Glennon. In *Foreign Relations of the United States*, China, 2:285. Washington, D.C.: U.S. Government Printing Office, 1955–57.

Wallerstein, Immanuel. *The Capitalist World-Economy*. Cambridge: Cambridge University Press, 1979.

Ward, Stephen Michael. "'Ours Too Was a Struggle for a Better World': Activist Intellectuals and the Radical Promise of the Black Power Movement, 1962–1972." Ph.D. diss., University of Texas at Austin, 2002.

Wu Cheng-en. *Monkey: Folk Novel of China*. Trans. Arthur Waley. New York: Grove Press, 1994.

——. *Journey to the West*. Trans. W. J. F. Jenner. Beijing: Foreign Languages Press, 2003.

Toward Foreign Policy Justice in the Post-Bush Era

Michael L. Clemons

This volume has confronted a variety of contemporary issues dealing with the nature, quality, and consequences of African American participation in foreign policymaking and foreign affairs. At this critical juncture in U.S. and world history, the unanticipated election of Barack Obama to the office of president of the United States presents an opportunity for greater inclusiveness in the conduct of the nation's foreign relations. Among the recent important domestic and global developments likely to guide the response to the challenges facing the Obama administration is multiculturalism and the growing recognition of its potential material benefits.

The path-breaking post-civil rights era political strategy known as deracialization[1] facilitated the current transition to multiculturalism. In terms of language and symbolism, the complementary qualities of multiculturalism and deracialization, demonstrated in Obama's pursuit of the presidency and his overall approach to politics, continued into the early phase of governance by his administration. Characteristically, his campaign strategy was a classic deracialization approach, coupled with the tactical use of multiculturalist symbolism. If there is an irony behind his campaign and governance style, it may be his self-identification as African American. He has observed that it was because of race that others perceived and consequently treated him as they did during his formative years. However, today it seems that multiculturalism and deracialization operate in domestic society and at the global level in a manner minimizing the significance of race, ethnicity, and culture.

While it is premature to assess Obama's impact in foreign policymaking, it is useful to consider the implications of his presidency for the future foreign affairs influence of African Americans. Specifically, what do his political campaigns and the early days of his administration suggest about how he might pursue and prioritize U.S. foreign policy? In addition, how might his rise to power affect the formulation of a "just" foreign policy program?

The Meaning of Multiculturalism

Multiculturalism is a transnational ideological force that evolved because of struggles for power and influence between and among elites along racial and ethnic group lines. As ideology, multiculturalism stipulates the basic assumptions and goals for achieving egalitarianism in a diverse society. In contrast to its ideological role, multiculturalism functions too as a potentially guiding social force, at least in the United States, a predictable arrangement for a society that for the most part has had open borders in particular for those abroad seeking to escape political repression and persecution. Inherent to the idea of multiculturalism are the twin principled objectives of democratic proliferation and equal justice. It is on this basis that the American democratic experiment is situated and that the reification of the notion of foreign policy justice can occur.

However, uses of the concept multiculturalism offered in the scholarly and popular literature tend to sublimate race and ethnicity as contemporary societal factors influencing resource allocation. This tendency is dangerous in that it can preclude and/or undercut the practice of democracy. For example, although the empirical data show remarkable socioeconomic and political progress across racial lines in the United States since the 1950s, strong national evidence indicates that racial gaps persist in a variety of areas including income, educational achievement, homeownership, poverty, infant mortality, access to quality health care, and criminal incarceration. Regardless of the nation-state within which multiculturalism operates, race, ethnicity, and culture increasingly are filtered through the social lens of multiculturalism, frequently at the expense of genuine problem recognition and the opportunity for measurable material progress of non-dominant racial and ethnic groups. In other words, multiculturalism is often leveraged as a societal force (not necessarily geared toward the achievement of social equity and justice), while race and ethnicity are dismissed as serious vantage points for the analysis of social equity and the development of public policy.

Furthermore, multiculturalism is the context within which race, ethnicity, and culture evolve and consequently struggle to maintain relevance. Despite this, multiculturalism also is the framework within which Diaspora politics thrives. African American participation in foreign policy-making, therefore, can be enlightening for assessing the effects of race and ethnicity. Indeed, Diaspora politics provides the opportunity to operationalize multiculturalism. In the domestic arena, multiculturalism legitimates Diaspora politics by conditioning traditional governmental institutions for engagement with formerly marginalized or repressed racial and ethnic groups. In contrast, as a global transnational ideological force, multiculturalism, and therefore Diaspora politics, involves "the relationship between an ethnic group gaining effective voice in foreign policy and its adoption of American political ideals," as well as the "ethnic commitment to ancestral countries" (Shain, 1995, 70). In other words, multiculturalism is part of the binding force of the Diaspora.

Multiculturalism's Growing Significance

The growing national and international relevance of multiculturalism is inseparable from the history of democratic practice in the United States and perhaps even the world. Democratic practice deals fundamentally with whether the structure of society allows for inclusive participation in policy-making, including its actual practice and implementation. Tony Smith has pointed out that "democratic government . . . establish[es] political freedom by empowering the citizenry, allowing them to control their state by the free exercise of their rights of assembly, speech, and the election of public officials who will determine the law and enforce it subject to the consent of the governed" (Smith, 2000, 30). This notion springs from democratic theory, which focuses on "the connection between established—hidden and explicit—forms of social and political power, the intersection between systems of democratic representation and participation with systems of political administrative organization of public governance, and with political party systems" (Torres, 1998, 421). In this light, diversity, and by extension multiculturalism, is connected practically and conceptually to democratic practice.

Carlos A. Torres provides a notion of multiculturalism that incorporates addressing socioeconomic inequalities associated with racial or ethnic differences. He asserts that "we need a theory of multicultural democratic citizenship that will take seriously the need to develop a theory of democracy that will help to ameliorate, if not eliminate altogether, the social differences, inequality, and inequity pervasive in capitalist societies and a theory of democracy able to address the draconian tensions between democracy and capitalism, on the one hand, and among social, political, and economic democratic forms on the other" (Torres, 1998, 423). The concept of "multicultural democratic citizenship" carries special import in international politics. However, the dimensions of multiculturalism are more complex at the global level than in domestic society. It is conceivable that given Obama's multicultural background and his development as a national and international leader, the country is embarking upon an opportunity that may well lead to new directions and insights in U.S. foreign policymaking.

Rise to Presidential Power

Swept into office on the mantra of change, Barack Obama emerged on the scene of American presidential politics in a manner reminiscent of the tradition of African American dissent with regard to U.S. foreign policy.[2] Having stood in opposition to the war in Iraq from the beginning, his decision to vote against the war distinguished him among his colleagues in the Senate and the country's politicians in general. Although he was heralded for his unequivocal opposition to the Iraqi war and the manner in which the so-called "war against terror" was waged, his lack of foreign policy experience was an issue throughout the campaign. Still, his call for "change" was piercing and profound enough to stir the imaginations of millions who saw him as a symbol of hope and a new direction for the country. American citizens have a number of important rationalizations that substantiate their optimism for a new American foreign policy.

Below, we briefly examine Obama's articulation of deracialization and some of the explanations for why the American people, African Americans in particular, and the rest of the world are hopeful of coming changes in the nature and substance of U.S. foreign policy. While considering their benefits, we also explore the possible implications of multiculturalism and deracialization for the continuation of a foreign policy approach that falls short of addressing squarely the long-term consequences of colonialism and imperialism at the global level, and domestic policies that speak to the persistent effects of slavery and Jim Crow segregation in the contemporary era.

A graduate of Columbia University and Harvard Law School, and the first black editor of the *Harvard Law Review*, Barack Obama demonstrated the requisite elite academic credentials and political contacts needed to scale the wall of national politics. Before achieving success nationally, he worked as a community organizer on the Southside of Chicago, and eventually was elected to the Illinois state legislature, where he served from 1997 to 2004. After several terms as state senator, Obama turned his sights toward national office, initially running unsuccessfully for a seat in the U.S. House of Representatives. In 2005 he was elected junior U.S. senator from Illinois. After only two years in the Senate as a member of the 109th Congress, Obama decided to pursue the presidency.

Deracialization Campaign Strategy

Barack Obama's keynote address at the 2004 Democratic National Convention provided an effective entrée to the national and the world stages. In this speech, he masterfully applied the tactics of deracialization and effectively merged the deracialization approach with multiculturalism. Obama boldly declared: "There's not a liberal America and a conservative America—there's the United States of America. There's not a black America and white America and Latino America and Asian America; there's the United States of America" (Obama, 2004). These words were prescient of the tenor of Obama's vibrant and victorious presidential campaign, which concentrated on the similarities of Americans, rather than their differences. His speeches made clear that despite the candidate's racial identification with African Americans, his administration would avoid issues viewed as potentially racially polarizing and would focus on issues of broad interest to citizens, such as health care, education, the economy, and the Iraq War.

Joseph McCormick and Charles E. Jones characterize deracialization as: "Conducting a campaign in a stylistic fashion that defuses the polarizing effects of race by avoiding explicit reference to race-specific issues, while at the same time emphasizing those issues that are perceived as racially transcendent, thus mobilizing a broad segment of the electorate for purposes of capturing or maintaining public office" (1993, 76). Deracialization is therefore a political campaign strategy that subdues or disperses the potential polarizing effects of race by avoiding issues likely to be construed by whites as predominantly in the interest of African Americans (McCormick and Jones, 1993).

Based on the campaign of L. Douglas Wilder for the governorship of the Commonwealth of Virginia in 1989, Jones and Clemons (1993) developed a qualitative model of racial crossover voting. They identified several components of the model, including the deracialization strategy, political apprenticeship, party apparatus, the racial omsbudman function of mass media, and the "wild card factor," as germane to Wilder's election and the election of African American candidates seeking high-profile state and national elected office against majority candidates (usually white) in political jurisdictions where black citizens are a numerical minority. They concluded that singly and in combination, these variables were essential to Wilder's electoral success. Thus, deracialization causes voters to judge a candidate's worthiness for elected office based on whether they can effectively manage the murky nuance of race. It is interesting that while some white voters may be focused on finding evidence demonstrating the candidate's alignment with the black community and therefore his commitment to pursuing its goals (even at the expense of the white community), black voters seem more attuned to identifying candidate's actions that they believe run counter to their interests. The emergence of Rev. Jeremiah Wright as a wild-card issue in the 2008 presidential campaign is a case in point. While some white voters saw Wright as indicative of Obama's black radicalism and his veiled dislike of whites, many black voters viewed his association as indicative of a commitment to black people and their interests. So far in his administration, Obama, true to campaign strategy and approach, for the most part has been able to avoid the alienating effect of race on white support. It remains to be seen, however, whether his application of the deracialization strategy as illustrated by the Reverend Wright episode is foretelling of governance approach and style, and if white independent voters in particular will continue to provide vital political backing. It was only after considerable public criticism that Obama and his handlers assessed that the need to appear in Philadelphia to confront the issue of race had reached a critical stage. In this pivotal campaign speech, Obama spoke eloquently about his relationship with Reverend Wright to mollify the negative consequences of race that stemmed from his long-term association with Wright and his church. Obama's reluctant actions suggested that matters directly related to race should be dealt with only when political survival is threatened.

Theory of Third-Culture Children

Deracialization plays a role not only in domestic politics but also in the global arena. So, too, does multiculturalism, through symbolism and ideology. Notably, throughout Obama's campaign, and consistent with the deracialization strategy in reference to the treatment of domestic issues, little attention was paid to politics and prominent humanitarian concerns on the continent of Africa in such places as Darfur, Sudan, and Zimbabwe. The lack of attention to these matters reinforced the legitimacy of past U.S. response and behavior, and simultaneously, the campaign continuously hammered away at multicultural themes. For example, Obama was virtually branded as the African American son of a white woman from Kansas and a Harvard-educated African immigrant from Kenya. The campaign regularly reminded the public that Obama was born in Honolulu and raised in Kansas and abroad in Indonesia, suggesting that his diverse background was an asset since it would reach beyond the cultural parameters dictated typically by the personal backgrounds of American presidents. Throughout the primary and general elections, political opponents and mass media dogged Obama about his relative lack of foreign policy expertise. Hillary Clinton roundly criticized him for suggesting that the "four years he spent living in Indonesia as a child helped him develop a world view and gives him credence on the world stage" (Newton-Small, 2007, 1). However, the website of the U.S. Department of State (which, ironically, she currently heads) lends support to the theory of third-culture children by providing an entire webpage on the subject.[3] The State Department website points out that "third-culture kids are those who have spent some of their growing up years in a foreign country and experience a sense of not belonging to their passport country when they return to it. In adapting to life in a 'foreign' country they have also missed learning ways of their homeland and feel most at home in the 'third-culture' which they have created. Little understood by American schools, where they are often considered an oddity, what third-culture kids want most is to be accepted as the individuals they are" (http://www.state.gov/m/dghr/flo/c21995.htm, accessed December 22, 2008). Obama's multicultural background, according to the theory, should therefore be an advantage on the international stage, even though at various junctures throughout the campaign his background was problematic. On balance, however, his early popularity abroad meets or exceeds that of previous chief executives and some of the enthusiasm is likely associated with his multicultural background. It was reported, for example, that Obama's popularity in Southeast Asia is due to his having lived in Indonesia. Indonesian ambassador to the United States Parnohadiningrat Sudjadnan has pointed out that "back home people think of him as one of us, or at least one who understands us."[4]

Throughout the campaign, Obama demonstrated worldwide appeal on a number of different levels. A charismatic style, punctuated by an extraordinary oratorical ability, is fundamental to his capacity for worldwide appeal. However, his relatively limited international exposure led to the criticism from the campaign of John McCain that he had not yet traveled to Iraq and other places where the United States had some political, military, or economic interest. This campaign attack provided an unanticipated instrumental opportunity for Obama to demonstrate his ability to represent the United States abroad as the nation's chief executive. While in Berlin, Germany (on his way to Iraq), speaking before an estimated crowd of more than 200,000 at Victory Column in the Tiergarten, Obama "was treated with unusual deference. Local newspapers and television stations chased him around town, offering minute-by-minute updates of his whereabouts. Hundreds of people lined streets at several points around town as his motorcade passed by" (Zeleny and Kulish, 2008, 2). Demonstrating the breadth and style of his multicultural outreach, if not a genuine multicultural appeal, in his speech he stated: "Yes, there have been differences between America and Europe . . . In this new century, Americans and Europeans alike will be required to do more—not less. . . . The walls between old allies on either side of the Atlantic cannot stand. The walls between races and tribes; natives and immigrants; Christian and Muslim and Jew cannot stand. These now are the walls we must tear down" (Obama, 2008, 3). While in Europe Obama was careful to point out that George W. Bush was still commander-in-chief. Nonetheless, Republicans and pundits conveyed the view that his travels abroad were detrimental to Bush administration foreign policies, and that Obama's rock star appeal, while magnetic, in the end was devoid of a substantive foreign policy program. However, the speech was a call for the rekindling of cooperation with European allies, and in particular he pointed out the need for Europe to be more involved in Afghanistan by supporting NATO and increasing their troops (Zeleny and Kulish, 2008, 2; Erlanger, 2008, 1).

The complexity of multiculturalism beyond the domestic sphere, as illustrated by the affinity of Kenyans, demonstrates Obama's appeal as a native son and as a "Messiah" figure. For example, according to Edwin Okong'o, "Many poorly educated Kenyans have little or no understanding of the workings of the American government. They think that, if elected president, Obama would rule by decree, that if he tells Americans he wants to lift the land of his father out of poverty, he will be given a blank check to do so" (Okong'o, 2008). And yet, while Kenyans acknowledge Obama's heritage, some are incredulous that he will promote their country's interests. Okong'o points out further:

> After examining Obama's record, I would like to offer a modest dissent from the majority views of my countrymen and women. I won't go so far as to question his blackness, as many in the United States have, but I will say that he is not a Kenyan. He is in fact one of the very foreigners he urged us not to depend on. . . . I look and look but can't find one thing Obama has done, in his capacity as a senator, for Kenya's chil-

dren. Nor do I see President Obama doing a thing that would lift poor Kenyans out of the shanties of Kibera, one of Africa's largest slums with a destitute population of nearly a million people. He can, of course, continue to assail the Kenyan government for its corruption and tribalism, as he did on his visit last year, but—let me assure you—that won't change a thing. (Okong'o, 2008)

Thus, as in the United States, Obama's multicultural appeal to citizens abroad and his approach to other states has sometimes been met with a healthy dose of skepticism. Consequently, Obama's policy decisions will need to be a clear demonstration of his willingness not simply to "talk the talk" but to "walk the walk" in terms of using his multiple cultural capacities to shape a new lens through which to formulate the nation's foreign policy.

Opportunity for a New International Engagement?

In the post-Bush era, the fundamental question is whether the Obama administration can effectively embark upon a new international engagement. By definition, the new engagement will exploit the racial, cultural, and ethnic advantage in a manner that facilitates rather than detracts from the commitment to foreign policy justice. The new engagement will also repair America's relations abroad and recast its national image. In tackling this issue, it is useful to reflect on the future, noting that there are some latent problems associated with multiculturalism that surface in light of the persistence of race as a structural variable in American politics and society. One example is the rush by some citizens and policymakers to declare that the United States has achieved colorblindness without close examination of the racial and ethnic differences. Multiculturalism implies the erasure of racial and ethnic categories by redirecting the focus of policymakers and citizens in such a way as to obscure social reality. In essence, multiculturalism is evolving as a domestic and global force that competes with race and ethnicity in setting the parameters for social analysis that prescribes actions to bring about equality and justice and the desired consequences of social stability and peace.

As illustrated in several of the chapters in this book, African American participation in foreign policymaking has largely been noninstitutional due to structural, institutional, and cultural barriers. These barriers encouraged imaginative participation by black interest groups, which was demonstrably on the rise in the heyday of the civil rights era and only recently has entered a period of dormancy. The hard-won accomplishments of milestones such as the 1964 Civil Rights Act and the 1965 Voting Rights Act provided a window of opportunity for African Americans as individuals and through a variety of race-based nongovernmental agencies to direct their attention to U.S. foreign policy. Alexander DeConde astutely observes "by providing voter guarantees, this legislation [1964 Civil Rights and 1965 Voting Rights Acts] greatly increased the black electorate, thus assuring it meaningful political power." Consequently, "politicians quickly became more accountable than in the past to African-American pressures in foreign as well as domestic matters" (DeConde, 1992, 146). These and other achievements demonstrated to the world the consequential effectiveness of the civil rights movement in the United States, which ultimately provided a model for the transformation of apartheid South Africa into a racially inclusive society.

Today, however, there are some developments which potentially could set U.S. foreign policy on a path toward an unprecedented era of leadership and cooperation based on the vision of foreign policy justice presented by Ronald Walters (introduction, this volume). The meteoric rise of Barack Obama occurred when America's prestige abroad was severely tarnished. As a glimmer of "hope" in the midst of the decline of both the practical and perceived positive global image of the country and black influence in American foreign policymaking, Obama, the nation, and the world may have landed a historic opportunity. To be fair, it may have been the colossal failure of the Bush administration's foreign policy program and the deterioration of national and global economies that led people to believe such an opportunity is not beyond realization. Still, President Obama has been criticized by political opponents, including former vice president Dick Cheney, for portraying weakness in his interaction with world leaders by, for example, bowing before the Saudi king. Compounding matters are the excesses of domestic and global capitalism, augmented by unchecked unethical conduct, particularly in the financial industry. Combined, these developments have made more complex the reversal of conditions to an extent not seen nationally and worldwide since the Great Depression of the 1930s and 1940s. Hence, will the vision and leadership exercised by President Obama enable a surge in the foreign policymaking influence of African Americans and the consequent restoration of the U.S. image abroad, or will they yield the results of the past?

It is clear that democracy, the bedrock of foreign policymaking enabling participation beyond elites, will continue to affect interest group participation that can exert a foreign policy influence. At issue, however, is whether it is practical that African American foreign policy interests can and will receive equal time. Given multiculturalism and population diversity (societal features that propel Diaspora politics), interest group politics will likely persist as a means for influencing foreign policymaking. For the most part, Obama's foreign policy appointments have been consistent with expectations that they would be diverse and would constitute a virtual Democratic Party foreign policy "dream team." However, the holdovers from the Bush administration are striking, and the collective foreign policy records of Joe Biden (vice president), Hillary Clinton (secretary of state), Susan Rice (U.N. ambassador), Robert Gates (secretary of defense), and General James Jones (national security advisor) appear as echoes of the past. Whether Obama has the force of personality vital to exercising the full range of presidential power and managing the dream team will certainly be determined by the end of his first term in office.

Although Colin Powell and Condoleezza Rice provided a foundation and important segue to the present, it is indisputable that the Obama administration will be the main player in the unfolding chapter in U.S. foreign policymaking. By some assessments, Powell and Rice left legacies that were less than illustrious and largely overshadowed by the events of the day. Given the diminished international stature of the United States, attributable in part to the unilateralism of the Bush foreign policy program, and by many accounts the utter mismanagement of Middle East affairs, the United States under Obama's executive guidance has much work ahead to restore the nation's reputation and leadership stature. Students of U.S. foreign policy and African American politics need to closely monitor not only the appointments Obama makes to his foreign policy team, but also the quality and depth of leadership provided to the foreign policymaking process. The challenge facing Obama is whether he can lead and set the tone of the country in a manner consistent with that desired by the mass public, as demonstrated at the end of his predecessor's term in office. Of course, the alternative is to allow by inaction and lack of leadership the continued domination of foreign policymaking by traditional societal forces; it is doubtful thus far that President Obama can transcend this pattern. As president, he faces a number of challenges, some new and some longstanding. Among these are the ongoing division of nation-states along economic lines; the persistent association of nonwhite nation-states with poverty, deprivation, and governmental corruption; and the crystallization of radical Islam as a transnational force. Additionally, intrastate competition among Arab countries for dominance in Middle East politics and Iran's growing importance in this context are issues demanding attention.

True to the word of his campaign, President Obama ramped up the withdrawal from Iraq. At the end of February 2009 he announced plans to withdraw most U.S. troops from Iraq by the end of August 2010. At the same time, attention has turned toward Afghanistan, neutralizing a resurgent Taliban, and intensifying the search for Osama Bin Laden on Pakistan's mountainous border. In his December 1, 2009, address to West Point cadets, Obama said: "I have determined that it is in our vital national interest to send an additional 30,000 U.S. troops to Afghanistan. After 18 months, our troops will begin to come home. These are the resources that we need to seize the initiative, while building the Afghan capacity that can allow for a responsible transition of our forces out of Afghanistan." The goals of the policy are to reverse the momentum of the Taliban and to prevent Afghanistan from again becoming a safe haven for al Qaeda. Despite the president's desire to have U.S. troops out at the end of three years, the policy drew criticism from the left, which maintains that withdrawal will not take place quickly enough, and from the right, which argues that an arbitrary date of withdrawal, as Sen. John McCain has expressed, "emboldens our enemies and dispirits our friends" (Grant, 2009, 1). However, the success of the United States in these efforts will likely in part be a function of its capacity to lead and make the necessary shift toward multilateralism.

One reason to expect that Obama's Africa policy will be constructively different from that of previous presidents is his father's ancestral lineage and his personal connection to Africa, specifically Kenya, which is far more direct than that of any of his predecessors and indeed than of the vast majority of Americans of African descent. On Africa, however, thus far Obama's policies appear not to deviate significantly in substance from those of the previous administration. Early in his term, President Obama appointed retired general Scott Gration as special envoy to Sudan, and in his July 2009 speech before Ghana's Parliament, he referenced the genocide in Sudan (Middle East Online, 2009). At the beginning of his presidency, he also ordered a review of Sudan policy but was not present for the presentation of results in October 2009, which was made by Secretary Hillary Clinton, Ambassador Susan Rice, and General Gration, because of negative public relations associated with the policy. In an article in the *New Republic* Barron Young Smith laments, "That's a shame, because it signals to the world and the government of Sudan that Obama himself is not particularly engaged on the issue, it's a sad contrast to the deeply concerned speeches Obama gave in front of Save Darfur groups before he became president" (1). The policy itself lacks the teeth to stem violence in the region and is a far cry from the imposition of strong international sanctions on the country's oil industry or on the personal assets of its leaders. The new policy reflects the more conciliatory tone advocated by Gration. However, in addition to the administration's rejection of a proposal to ease existing sanctions, Sudan will remain on the state department's list of sponsors of state terrorism (MacAskill, 2009).

It will be fruitful to pursue in the future the following lines of research: (1) How might Obama's presence as head of state and commander-in-chief affect perceptions of the United States abroad? (2) To what extent might post-Bush era perceptions of American foreign policy be shaped by racial and cultural factors? (3) What are the long-term prospects for African American global participation? (4) How will race and multiculturalism be factored in light of the foreign policy leadership Obama provides? The answers to these questions may be useful for monitoring the global effects of race and ethnicity, and increasing our understanding of the advantages of multiculturalism and social diversity in an increasingly globalized world. However, if the Obama administration's treatment of the Durban Review Conference, held in April 2009 under the auspices of the United Nations, is an indication of the future, there will likely be little or no distinction from past administrations. The purpose of the Durban Review Conference was to assess the progress made by countries toward the goals set by the World Conference against Racism, Racial Discrimination, Xenophobia and Related Intolerance, held in Durban, South Africa, in 2001, in which the United States opted not to participate. At its website, TransAfrica Forum posted the following statement: "TransAfrica is extremely disappointed in the Obama Administration's decision to boycott the Durban Review despite the global efforts to pave the way for U.S. participation. While the Administration has stated this action does not signal apathy for the global fight against racism and xenophobia, it has sent a chilling effect throughout the developed and the developing world" (TransAfrica Forum, April 2009). At least eight countries withdrew their participation following the announcement of the U.S. decision not to participate. Imani Countess, TransAfrica Forum's senior director of public affairs, points out, "This decision is inconsistent with the values this Administration has touted. Engagement with the world must be based on mutual respect and partnership. Boycotting this conference sends a mixed message about the U.S.'s intentions when it comes to racism and intolerance" (TransAfrica Forum, April 2009).

In addition, as already shown, several issues related to Obama's rise to power are deserving of scrutiny because they potentially call into question his future contribution to the achievement of foreign policy justice. These include the deracialization strategy, his multicultural background and its application in governance, and the effectiveness of previous high-level African American foreign policy operatives. In regard to the last of these, such scrutiny seems fair, based on recent experiences. In the introduction to this book Ronald Walters points out that "the hope by many . . . was that they [Colin Powell and Condoleezza Rice] would exert the type of administration of foreign policy that elevates the African American interests to a reasonable balance with others. However, one finds that their loyalty to the regime that appointed them was a powerful limitation on their range of behavior" (Walters, 2009, 27). Hence, Walters raises serious questions concerning whether the post-civil rights era has accomplished the task of equalizing African American foreign policy interests with those of other groups. Although African American political appointees may have "expressed far greater fidelity to the institutional mores and processes than to their representative function of the community of which they were a part," Obama provides the first opportunity for case-study investigation of the policymaking behavior of an elected African American chief executive. It is unfortunate that experience has many observers wondering whether Obama can possibly affect the pendulum balance of African American interests in foreign policymaking. The critical distinction from the past, however, is that as president, he will potentially exercise institutional and informal powers and authority that were unavailable to Powell and Rice.

Furthermore, the pertinent effects of the domestic environment, which helped propel Obama's global reception, are quite salient. For many in the United States and worldwide, his achievement is the concretization of the American dream—it demonstrates how far the country has progressed domestically in race relations. By logical extension, therefore, many see this progress couched in terms of the notion that race is no longer a relevant factor in social relations in the United States. In other words, for them, Obama's historic win marks the achievement of racial equity and justice in American society, and hence, the same in the formulation and implementation of foreign policy. However, does the Obama victory truly mean that race at the domestic level is no longer a factor? If this is the case, then how does it translate globally? Is it reasonable that he would articulate the transference of values about racial and cultural justice in foreign policymaking to regions around the world long in conflict, such as the Middle East? Clearly, Obama's foreign policy rhetoric is distinct from that of the previous administration. In his address before the United Nations he asserted that America was not different from the rest of the world—it is subject to economic crises and military failures, and is capable of torture. He wants to restore the popularity of the United States but minimizes American exceptionalism, which might be seen as a challenge to the ideological basis of the foreign policy establishment. In her Senate confirmation hearings, Obama's secretary of state opined that "foreign policy must be based on a marriage of principles and pragmatism, not rigid ideology, on facts and evidence, not emotion or prejudice. Our security, our vitality, and our ability to lead in today's world oblige us to recognize the overwhelming facts of our interdependence" (Clinton, 2009).

Although Obama's multiculturalism has its advantages, it also has its complexities. Not everyone, for example, was thrilled by his victory. In a reported attempt to stem "the enthusiasm of Muslims worldwide about the American election, Osama Bin Laden's top deputy [Ayman al-Zawahri] condemned President-elect Barack Obama as a 'house Negro' who would continue a campaign against Islam that al Qaeda's leaders said was begun by President Bush" (Mazzetti and Shane, 2008, 1). That al Qaeda's leaders would characterize the president-elect as a "house Negro" or "Uncle Tom" is indicative of the complex dynamics of race, ethnicity, and multiculturalism in global politics. Al Qaeda sees Obama's victory as a challenge to its worldview and leadership in the Muslim world on at least two counts. First, Muslims around the world have expressed support for Obama. Second, and related, throughout the campaign Obama strongly emphasized that his administration would unrelentingly pursue those involved in the 9–11 attacks, especially Osama Bin Laden. Perhaps even more threatening to al Qaeda, Obama has demonstrated an extraordinary and early interest in connecting with the Muslim world. A January 26, 2009, television interview granted by the president to Hisham Melhem, an Arab-language-speaking Washington bureau chief for al-Arabiya, a Saudi-backed news channel headquartered in Dubai, illustrates this most saliently. *Time.com* reported the following: "Whether it was because of the chemistry between the men or Obama's scripted intention, Melhem came away with an interview that amounted to an unprecedented reach-out to the Muslim world by a U.S. President. Unprompted, Obama spoke about his own Islamic connections, noting that some of his family members are Muslim and that he had lived in the largest Muslim country, Indonesia. 'My job is to communicate the fact that the United States has a stake in the well-being of the Muslim world, that the language we use has to be a language of respect,' Obama said" (Macleod, 2009).

Moreover, by comparing Obama to Colin Powell and Condoleeza Rice, and simultaneously interjecting the views of Malcolm X (before his religious Hajj to Mecca), al Qaeda was seeking to tap into that segment of the African American community that most likely would be cynical of his victory. Suggesting that African American Muslims may be more tolerant of al Qaeda, a poll conducted by the Pew Center in 2008 revealed that "63 percent of foreign-born Muslims in this country had a 'very unfavorable' view of Al Qaeda, compared with 36 percent of African-American Muslims" (Mazetti and Shane, 2008, 2). Although these figures do not disaggregate African American Muslims into the various sects of Islam, it is perhaps reasonable to assume that al Qaeda leadership wanted to exploit and manipulate the historical circumstances of African Americans to its own advantage. Indeed, the Honorable Elijah Mohammad, who preached that whites were blue-eyed devils and the oppressors of black people, founded the Nation of Islam. He maintained that black people would be better off as a community separate from white society.

There are a number of important opportunities for the United States to benefit from the shift in the domestic climate, prompted in part by the willingness of increasing numbers of politicians on both sides of the political aisle to speak up in opposition to the Iraq war. However, in large measure, the degree to which Obama can be "successful" in the foreign policy realm is a function of the real and perceived qualities of his leadership at the domestic and global levels. Perhaps the efforts of the Free Movement of Iraqis that fielded eight candidates in Iraq's January 2009 provincial poll are indicative of Obama's inspiration and impact. The Free Movement is an indigenous movement of Iraq's more than 1 million citizens of African descent. Its secretary, Jalal Dhiyab, pointed out that "black people have been treated very poorly throughout history. The oppression has stopped us from joining the many levels of society . . . We are taking part in the new elections to give black Iraqis a new purpose in Iraq" (Chulov, 2009). Secretary Dhiyab observed that Obama's "victory was a milestone in the history of democracy throughout the world . . . [i]t's a victory for freedom" (Chulov, 2009). Hence, the world and the American public have strong confidence in the possibilities of foreign policy leadership under Obama. Despite the challenges outlined above, the election of Obama does indeed present a new and timely opportunity to position the nation as a preeminent global power and as the beacon of international justice.

Although Obama's rise to power may seem suspect because of the nature of his campaign, such cynicism may be due also to the political, institutional, and cultural constraints that apparently shaped the experiences of Powell and Rice. Only time will tell whether a national political campaign that was essentially devoid of overt, or even subtle or symbolic, racial and ethnic dimensions portends an American foreign policy justice that minimizes the operational utility and meaning of race and ethnicity. Without a doubt, the consequences of the deracialization strategy for foreign policymaking and domestic governance will be deserving of attention by scholars and students well into the future.

However, the problem of "free agency," which was faced by Powell and Rice, will need to be confronted head-on and immediately by President Obama. As the first African American commander-in-chief, he possesses unprecedented flexibility, especially in light of the foreign policy debacles of the Bush administration and the dilapidated state of American leadership around the world. In addition, having been elected by electoral and popular vote margins considered to give a governance mandate, Obama can potentially exercise considerable latitude in setting the tone and substance of American foreign policy. Clearly, the vantage point of the presidency is quite distinct from that of secretary of state and national security advisor, positions held by Powell and Rice. Noteworthy is that such latitude and independence has already been demonstrated by Obama's signing of executive orders "to close the detention center at Guantanamo Bay, Cuba, within a year, to ban the harshest interrogation methods, and to establish procedures for handling future detainees" (Latham, 2009). Despite criticism that aspects of his policies in this area are a continuation of the Bush-Cheney policies, the decision goes a long way toward restoring the U.S. position of moral leadership in the world. However, global support for the policy is apparently weak if the metric is based on support demonstrated by countries' willingness to accept detainees from Guantanamo Bay.

Despite the complexities outlined above, America's unfolding presidency offers an unprecedented opportunity to institutionalize the values of universal freedom and justice in U.S. foreign policymaking. However, whether or not Obama can actually live up to the tall order implied by the title "Leader of the Free World" and ignite momentum toward foreign policy justice is a conclusion that has yet to be written. Indisputably, his presidency is unfolding in a world that seems mesmerized by multiculturalism, despite its vagaries, and at the same time oblivious to persistent racial inequity and injustice. Still, it is plausible that the elevation of Sen. Barack Obama to the office of president of the United States will mark a crucial turning point in the quality of America's foreign policy engagement and connote a critical juncture in the institutionalization of the historic values of African American participation and influence in foreign affairs and foreign policymaking.

NOTES

1. For further information on the deracialization phenomenon, see also Byron D'Andre Orey, "Deracialization or Racialization: The Making of a Black Mayor in Jackson, Mississippi," *Politics and Policy* 34, no. 4 (2006): 814–36; and Georgia Persons, ed., *Dilemmas of Black Politics* (New York: HarperCollins College Publishers, 1993).

2. Dissent with regard to American foreign policy, according to Hanes Walton, Jr., is a long-standing pattern of behavior among people of African descent in the United States. Such dissent has frequently been tied to the conscientious pursuit of universal freedom and justice, historically an important interest of African Americans due to the systematic exclusion of the group from political, economic, and social participation.

3. The theory of "third-culture kids" (TCKs) was first promulgated in the late 1950s by a Michigan State University sociology professor, Ruth Hill Useem. According to Kay Branaman Eakin, Useem's research on North American children living in India "found that TCKs cope rather than adjust, becoming both 'a part of' and 'apart from' regardless of the situation within which they find themselves. Brought up in another culture or several cultures, they feel ownership in none. An American TCK may find more in common with an Italian or Indian TCK than she does with a monocultural U.S. teen" (Eakin, 1998, 18).

4. Ambassador Parnohadiningrat Sudjadnan's remarks are cited in Jay Newton-Smith, "Obama's Foreign-Policy Problem," *Time*, December 18, 2007. Located at http://www .time.com/time/printout/0,8816,1695803,00.html.

REFERENCES

Chulov, Martin. 2009. "Black Iraqis Make Their Political Debut in Provincial Polls." Guardian .co.uk, January 26. Located January 29, 2009, at http://www.guardian.co.uk/world/ 2009/jan/26/iraq-black-elections-obama.

Clinton, Hillary. 2009. Senate Confirmation Hearing of Senator Hillary Clinton as Nominee for Secretary of State. January 13. Located March 15, 2009, at http://www.cfr .org/publication/18225/transcript_of_hillary_clintons_confirmation_hearing.html.

DeConde, Alexander. 1992. *Ethnicity, Race, and American Foreign Policy: A History.* Boston: Northeastern University Press.

Eakin, Kay Branaman. 1998. *According to My Passport, I'm Coming Home.* Washington, D.C.: Family Liaison Office.

Erlanger, Steven. 2008. "Obama, Vague on Issues, Pleases Crowd in Europe." *New York Times*, July 25. Located on January 27, 2009, at http://www.nytimes.com/2008/07/25/ us/politics/25assess.html.

Fauntroy, Michael. "On Obama's Deracialization Strategy". Located January 28, 2008, at http://www.MichaelFauntroy.com.

Grant, J. C. 2009. "Obama Afghanistan War Speech Bombs: Withdrawal Timetable Mocked." *Associated Content News*, December 2. Located on December 6, 2009, at http://www .associatedcontent.com/article/2449126/obama_afghanistan_war_speech_bombs .html?cat=9.

Jones, Charles E., and Michael L. Clemons. 1993. "A Model of Racial Crossover Voting." In *Dilemmas of Black Politics*, ed. Georgia Persons. New York: HarperCollins College Publishers.

Latham, Judith. 2009. "World Welcomes President Obama's Executive Order to Close Guantanamo, Despite Concerns." January 30. Located February 1, 2009, at http://www.voanews.com/english/NewsAnalysis/2009–01–29-voa23.cfm.

Lothian, Dan, and Suzanne Malveaux. 2009. "Obama: U.S. to Withdraw Most Iraq Troops by August 2010." February 27. Located April 2, 2009, at http://www.cnn.com/2009/POLITICS/02/27/obama.troops/index.html.Macleod, Scott. 2009. "How al-Arabiya Got the Obama Interview." *Time.* January 28. Located January 30, 2008 at http://www.time.com/time/world/article/0,8599,1874379,00.html.

Mazzetti, Mark, and Scott Shane. 2008. "Al Qaeda Coldly Acknowledges Obama Victory." *The New York Times,* November 20. Located January 21, 2009, at www.nytimes.com/2008/11/20/world/middleeast/20qaeda.html.

McCormick, Joseph P., III, and Charles E. Jones. 1993. "The Conceptualization of Deracialization." In *Dilemmas of Black Politics,* ed. Georgia Persons. New York: HarperCollins College Publishers.

MacAskill, Ewen. 2009. "Barack Obama Opts for Softer Approach to Darfur Crisis in Sudan." *Guardian.co.uk.* October 18. Located October 23, 2009, at http://www.guardian.co.uk/world/2009/oct/18/us-barack-obama-sudan-darfur.

Middle East Online. 2009. "U.S. NGOs Unhappy with Obama's Darfur Policy." October 4. Located December 3, 2009, at http://www.middle-east-online.com/english/?id=34705.

Newton-Smith, Jay. 2007. "Obama's Foreign-Policy Problem." *Time,* December 18. Located at http://www.time.com/time/printout/0,8816,1695803,00.html.

Obama, Barack. 2004. Obama News and Speeches: Keynote Address at the 2004 Democratic National Convention. Obama for America. Located April 25, 2008, at http://www.barackobama.com/2004/07/27/keynote_address_at_the_2004_de.php.

Obama, Barack. 2008. "Obama's Speech in Berlin." Transcript. New York Times. July 24. Located March 15, 2009, at http://www.nytimes.com/2008/07/24/us/politics/24text-obama.html.

Okong'o, Edwin. 2007. "Obama-Mania Comes to Kenya." *San Francisco Chronicle.* March 25.

Shain, Yossi. 1995. "Multicultural Foreign Policy." *Foreign Policy* 100:69–87.

Smith, Tony. 2000. *Foreign Attachments.* Cambridge, Mass.: Harvard University Press.

Torres, Carlos Alberto. 1998. "Democracy, Education, and Multiculturalism: Dilemmas of Citizenship in a Global World." *Comparative Education Review* 42, no. 4:421–47.

TransAfrica Forum. 2009. "TransAfrica Forum Expresses Disappointment at Obama Administration's Failure to Attend World Conference Against Racism." April 20. Located December 6, 2009, at http://www.transafricaforum.org/media-center/news-releases/taf-disappointed-obama-admin-failure-attend-durban-review.

U.S. Department of State. 2008. *Transition Issues and the Foreign Service Child: Third Culture Kids.* Located December 22, 2008, at http://www.state.gove/m/dghr/flo/c21995.htm.

Young Smith, Barron. 2009. "Administration Finally Has an Official Darfur Policy. But Where's Obama?" *New Republic,* 1–3. October 18. Located October 19, 2009, at http://www.tnr.com/blog/the-plank/the-obama-administration-finally-has-official-darfur-policy-where%E2%80%99s-obama.Zeleny, Jeff, and Nicholas Kulish. 2008. "Obama, in Berlin, Calls for Renewal of Ties with Allies." *New York Times,* July 25. Located January 27, 2009, at http://www.nytimes.com/2008/07/25/us/politics/25obama.html.

ABOUT THE CONTRIBUTORS

Josephine A. V. Allen is professor of social policy and welfare, Binghamton University, and professor emerita of policy, analysis, and management, Cornell University. She helped create the Cornell Black Professional Women's Forum, which has lobbied for the recruitment, retention, and advancement of black women faculty and staff at Cornell. The Forum's collaboration with the National Science Foundation-funded CU-ADVANCE Center has helped to increase the number of women faculty in engineering and science. Allen holds the distinction of being the first African American woman to receive tenure at Cornell.

Michael L. Clemons is associate professor of political science at Old Dominion University in Norfolk, Virginia. He earned a Ph.D. in political science from Atlanta University, specializing in American politics and international affairs with an emphasis on the domestic and global political behavior of African Americans. In 2003, Clemons founded the *Journal of Race and Policy*, and became its first editor. He also served as the director of Old Dominion's Institute for the Study of Race and Ethnicity, and as founding director of its bachelor's degree program in African American and African Studies. He is currently completing his next book, which focuses on the purpose, nature, and logic of African American global participation.

Sekou Franklin is assistant professor in the Department of Political Science at Middle Tennessee State University (MTSU). He specializes in African American politics, civil rights policy, social movements, and municipal politics, and coordinates the Urban Studies Program at MTSU. He has published articles and book chapters on race and politics, juvenile justice, and social movements, and is currently working on a book analyzing intergenerational politics and social movement activism among the post-civil rights generation. He has also been an active member of several grassroots and antipoverty organizations, including the Ad Hoc Committee for Equity in Nashville-Davidson County, the National Poverty Engine, and the Tennessee Alliance for Progress.

Robeson Taj P. Frazier is assistant professor of communications at the Annenberg School of Communications, University of Southern California (USC). Before coming to USC, Frazier taught courses at New York University, Princeton University, University of California, Berkeley, and City University of New York. He obtained his doctorate in African Diaspora studies from the University of California, Berkeley. His research interests include exploring issues pertaining to race and ethnicity, comparative political economy, popular culture, sport, globalization, and transnationalism and internationalism. His work has been published in *Souls: A Critical Journal of Black Politics, Culture and Society,* the *San Francisco Chronicle,* and *Black Arts Quarterly.*

Supad Kumar Ghose is a doctoral student in the Department of History at Georgia State University, Atlanta. He previously taught at Bangladesh Public Administration Training Institute (BPATI), Virginia Commonwealth University, and Old Dominion University. While at Old Dominion, he served as a graduate research assistant in the Institute for the Study of Race and Ethnicity. As a scholar of the Swedish Institute, he studied at the University of Stockholm. He also studied at Old Dominion University and the University of Dhaka, Bangladesh. His current research explores visions of alternative world order, south-south relations, sociology of strategy and war, and cosmopolitanism.

Charles P. Henry is professor of African American studies at the University of California, Berkeley. In 1994 President Bill Clinton appointed him to the National Council on the Humanities for a six-year term. A former president of the National Council for Black Studies, Henry is the author/editor of seven books and more than eighty articles and reviews on black politics, public policy, and human rights. Before joining the University of California, Berkeley, in 1981, he taught at Denison University and Howard University. He was chair of the board of directors of Amnesty International U.S.A. from 1986 to 1988 and is a former NEH Postdoctoral Fellow and American Political Science Association Congressional Fellow. He was Distinguished Fulbright Chair in American History and Politics at the University of Bologna, Italy, for the spring semester of 2003. In the fall of 2006, he was one of the first two Fulbright-Tocqueville Distinguished Chairs in France teaching at the University of Tours. He received that university's Chancellor's Award for Advancing Institutional Excellence in April 2008. He holds a doctorate in Political Science from the University of Chicago. Henry's recent publications include *Ralph Bunche: Model Negro or American Other, Foreign Policy and the Black (Inter)national Interest* (an edited volume), and *Long Overdue: The Politics of Racial Reparations.*

William G. Jones holds a doctorate from Howard University in political science. He specializes in American politics with an emphasis on African politics and affairs and urban politics. He has worked as a researcher for national interest groups and has held several significant positions in local government and the nonprofit sector, including posts as director of planning for the cities of Portsmouth, Virginia, and Harvey, Illinois.

Minion Kenneth Chauncey "KC" Morrison is currently Frederick Middlebush Professor of Political Science at the University of Missouri-Columbia. He has held this post since June 1989, and from 1989 to 1997 he served as the University of Missouri's vice provost for minority affairs and faculty development. Earlier, he was associate professor of Afro-American studies and political science at Syracuse University, where he served as the chair of Afro-American studies for five years. Before joining Syracuse he was at Hobart & William Smith Colleges in Geneva, New York, and Tougaloo College in Mississippi. He has published in the two broad fields of African and Afro-American politics. His books include *Race and Democracy in the Americas: Brazil and the United States* (forthcoming, 2010), *African Americans and Political Participation* (2003); *Black Political Mobilization, Leadership and Power* (1987); *Housing and Urban Poor in Africa* (1982, edited with Peter Gutkind); and *Ethnicity and Political Integration* (1982). He has published many articles and reviews in such journals as *Polity, Comparative Political Studies, Comparative Studies in Society and History, Publius,* and *American Political Science Review.* Morrison is active in professional associations and numerous local community organizations. He is a past president of the National Conference of Black Political Scientists, the Columbia Commission on Cultural Affairs, and the Missouri Humanities Council. Currently he serves on the editorial board of the *American Political Science Review.*

Alvin Tillery is assistant professor of political science at the University of Notre Dame. He holds a Ph.D. in political science from Harvard University. His research interests are in the fields of American politics and comparative race and ethnicity. His dissertation, "The American Regime and Black Consciousness of Africa: From Martin Delany to Jesse Jackson, Jr.," examines the formation of a transnational (or Diaspora) identity among black Americans and how macro sociological forces, social movement dynamics, and partisan politics have shaped the way both blacks and whites have attempted to use this identity as a political resource. His essay "Black Americans and the Creation of America's African Policies: The De-racialization of Pan-African Politics" was published in Carol Boyce Davies, Ali A. Mazrui, and Isidore Okpewho, eds., *The African Diaspora: Old World Origins and New World Self-Fashioning* (Bloomington : Indiana University Press, 1999). His research has been supported by the National Science Foundation, the Institute for the Study of World Politics, the Leadership Alliance/Irene Diamond Fund, and the Mellon Foundation. As a teaching fellow at Harvard, he was awarded four Derek Bok Center Awards for Excellence in Teaching.

Ronald W. Walters is an internationally renowned expert on issues of African American leadership and politics. After attending Fisk University as an undergraduate, Walters earned his graduate degrees from American University. He has taught at Georgetown and Syracuse Universities; chaired the African and Afro-American Studies Department at Brandeis University and the Political Science Department at Howard University; and held the post of professor of government and politics at the University of Maryland. He serves as director of the African American Leadership Institute and Scholar Practitioner Program, and is a distinguished leadership scholar at the James MacGregor Burns Academy of Leadership. He served as a campaign manager and consultant for Rev. Jesse Jackson during his two presidential bids and was a policy adviser for congressional representatives Charles Diggs and William Gray. During the 2000 election season, he worked as a political analyst for Black Entertainment Television's *Lead Story*. He is a regular guest and commentator for several political talk shows on radio and television. As a scholar, Walters has penned eight books and published more than one hundred academic articles. His books have won several "best book" awards, and he has received numerous honors for his contributions as an "activist scholar." His book *The Price of Racial Reconciliation* (University of Michigan Press, 2008) has received accolades for its comprehensiveness and persuasiveness in the national debate on reparations.

Hanes Walton, Jr., is professor of political science and senior research scientist in the Center for Political Studies. His principal areas of interest include American politics, political parties, presidential elections, presidency, voting behavior, and African politics. At the Center for Political Studies he has received funding for several major studies, including the causes and consequences of civic engagement in America (Pew Foundation), the four-color mapping of all presidential elections from 1789 to 2004, and a panel study of the 2002 Georgia Confederate flag referendum. His current projects include a larger survey study of the Confederate flag as well as a geopolitical study of American presidential elections.

Ife Williams holds a doctorate in political science from Clark Atlanta University with specializations in black politics, African politics, international politics, and urban politics. In 1993 she was awarded a Minorities Postdoctoral Fellowship at the University of Illinois in African American Studies and Political Science. In 2001 she served as a Fulbright Professor in Political Science at the University of Dar es Salaam, Tanzania. An educator for over twenty-five years, she has worked to broaden the scope of the classroom as a multimedia producer of the documentaries "From Sea to Sea: Current Manifestations of Global Racism," "Payback: A Reparations Story," and "'Africa Is Not a Zoo.'" She has been involved in social activism around global reparations by serving as the nongovernmental representative for the United Methodist Church to the World Conference Against Racism (2001). She has also participated in groups such as the International Front of Africans for Reparations, Barbados (2002); Black Consciousness and Reparations Conference, Germany (2003); Movement Beyond Borders (2003); World Social Forum, Porto Allegre, Brazil (2004); Diaspora Afrique of France, National Coalition of Blacks for Reparations (N'COBRA); and the Global Afrikan Congress.

Ronald Williams II is a Ph.D. candidate in the Department of African American Studies at the University of California, Berkeley. He earned his undergraduate degree in Political Science from San Diego State University and a master's degree in Political Science from Howard University. His research and teaching interests include African American political organizations and U.S. foreign policy, Pan-Africanism, social movements, early twentieth-century black feminism, and African American political and social thought. He is currently working on his dissertation, which is a study of the organization TransAfrica Forum.

INDEX